23.11.07

GenXegesis

GenXegesis

Essays on "Alternative" Youth (Sub)Culture

John M. Ulrich

and

Andrea L. Harris

THE UNIVERSITY OF WISCONSIN PRESS/POPULAR PRESS

The University of Wisconsin Press
1930 Monroe Street
Madison, Wisconsin 53711

www.wisc.edu/wisconsinpress/

3 Henrietta Street
London WC2E 8LU, England

Library of Congress Cataloging-in-Publication Data

GenXegesis: essays on alternative youth (sub)culture
John M. Ulrich and Andrea L. Harris [editors].
        p. cm.
    "A Ray and Pat Browne book."
Includes bibliographical references and index.
ISBN 0-87972-861-2 (hardcover: alk. paper)—
    ISBN 0-87972-862-0 (pbk.: alk. paper)
1. Generation X. 2. Counterculture. I. Ulrich, John M. II. Harris, Andrea L., 1962–.
        HQ799.5 .G46 2004
        305.2—dc21

                                                2003007778

Table of Contents

Acknowledgments

For their careful reading and constructive suggestions we are grateful to Michael Barry and Dan Malachuk, both of whom helped to make this a better book. We thank Maria Bonn for her magnanimity and assistance in a time of need, and Lynn Pifer for her unflagging support and encouragement. For lending us their expertise with digital images, our thanks go to Mark Polonia and Marc McDowell. For helping us secure permission to reprint previously published material, we express our thanks to Bruce Carleton, Bob Gruen, John Holmstrom at *PUNK* Magazine, Shauna Lawrence at Johns Hopkins University Press, Robert Lecker at ECW Press, Virginia Lohle at Star File, Peter Marino at Sage Publications, Emma Murray at EMI, John Owens at *Travel Holiday* Magazine, Antony Shipani at mirrorpix.com, Michael Shulman at Magnum Photos, and Sandra Wake at Plexus Publishing, Ltd.

Portions of Neil Nehring's essay, "Jigsaw Youth vs. Generation X and Postmodernism," were previously published in Nehring's book *Popular Music, Gender, and Postmodernism: Anger is an Energy*, copyright © 1999 by Sage Publications. Reprinted by permission of Sage Publications. Jim Finnegan's essay, "Theoretical Tailspins: Reading 'Alternative' Performance in *Spin* Magazine," was previously published in *Postmodern Culture* 10:1 (1999), © The Johns Hopkins University Press. Reprinted by permission of the Johns Hopkins University Press. G. P. Lainsbury's article "Generation X and the End of History," previously appeared in *Essays in Canadian Writing*, vol. 58 (Spring 1996). Copyright ECW Press, Toronto and Montreal. Reprinted by permission of ECW Press.

We are grateful to Mara Naselli for her careful copyediting. Finally, we owe a great deal to Robert Mandel, Tricia Brock, Erin Holman, and the rest of the staff at the University of Wisconsin Press, and we thank them for their generosity and support.

GenXegesis

Introduction

Generation X

A (Sub)Cultural Genealogy

John M. Ulrich

Despite the tendency of many commentators to attribute its origin to Douglas Coupland's 1991 novel of the same name, the term "Generation X" first appeared in print nearly forty years earlier. Robert Capa first used the term in the early 1950s as the name for his project that would capture, through photographs and interviews, the lives of twenty-year-olds in the aftermath of World War II. Since then, "Generation X" has always signified a group of young people, seemingly without identity, who face an uncertain, ill-defined (and perhaps hostile) future. Subsequent appearances of the term in the mid-1960s and mid-1970s narrowed the referent for "Generation X" from Capa's "global" generation to specific sets of primarily white, male, working class British youth subcultures, from the spiffy mods and their rivals the rockers, to the more overtly negationist punk subculture. Since the 1960s, the term has continued to be closely associated with subcultural negationist practices and their often conflicted relationship to mainstream consumer culture. In his 1983 work *Class: A Guide through the American Status System,* Paul Fussell deployed the letter *X* as a kind of antistatus sign, designating as "Category X" those who negotiate the subcultural, mainstream divide with "insolence, intelligence, irony, and spirit"[1]—especially disaffected refugees from the American middle class. The popular success in 1991 of Coupland's novel *Generation X,* with its title and characters inspired by Fussell's Category X, soon brought the term to the attention of the mass media, and the intense, post-1991 media scrutiny of Generation X tended to disseminate the term quite literally, as a handy (if ambiguous)

3

moniker for the post–baby boom generation, rather than metaphorically, as a term that "defines not a chronological age, but a way of looking
at the world."[2] Since 1991 the explosion of media interest in Generation
X has accelerated this crossing of the divide between the subcultural
(or "alternative") and the mainstream. The popular success in the same
year of Coupland's novel, Richard Linklater's film *Slacker,* and Nirvana's
second album *Nevermind* (with its ironic antianthem, "Smells Like Teen
Spirit") left in its wake a plethora of mass-marketed Generation X books
and articles: cover stories in *Time, Newsweek, Atlantic Monthly, New
Republic, Business Week,* and *Fortune;*[3] demographic histories *(13th
Generation);* anthologies of fiction and personal essays by Xers *(Next
and Voices of the Xiled);* articles and books for advertisers on how to
capture the Generation X demographic *(Marketing to Generation X);*
political handbooks *(Revolution X);* satires *(Generation Ecch!);* personal
memoirs *(Prozac Nation);* religious studies *(GenX Religion);* sociological
studies *(Masks and Mirrors: Generation X and the Chameleon Personality),* film criticism *(The Cinema of Generation X: A Critical Study of
Films and Directors),* television criticism *(Gen X TV: The Brady Bunch
to Melrose Place),* the requisite anthology of excerpts from articles,
books, and interviews *(The GenX Reader);* and a whole host of additional
Gen X-related media phenomena, from ESPN's X Games and Pepsi's
Generation Next ad campaign to the college clothing line, SweatX.[4] As
this mainstreaming of the term in the early nineties clashed with its
subcultural pedigree, the public debates about the autonomy and authenticity of subcultural practices intensified, particularly in light of the
dual mainstreaming of "alternative" music and "independent" films,
both elements of popular culture closely identified with Generation X
(sub)culture.[5]

   This substitution of a demographic identity for a subcultural one,
coupled with the positing of Coupland's novel as its "origin," has effectively obscured the history of the term and its specific association with
particular historical subcultures. The term itself has thus taken on a
broader signification, representing an entire generation of Americans
across class, race, and gender boundaries. This introduction and the
essays in this collection seek to recover the term's "secret history," in
order to open Generation X to a truly critical interrogation, one that
resituates Generation X in its subcultural (even oppositional) context

and at the same time foregrounds the necessity of attending to its precarious, paradoxical position both inside and outside of the mainstream.

Still best known today for his photographic images of the Spanish Civil War and World War II, Robert Capa was a founding member of Magnum, a pioneering photojournalism agency. Capa and five other photographers owned and operated the agency, which was headquartered in Paris. In 1949, two years after the company's formation, Capa proposed an ambitious photo-essay project for Magnum, one that would focus on young people around the world who, in Capa's words, "were reaching their twentieth birthdays at the half-mark of the century, and who have a reasonable hope of living through the second half of it, and of celebrating the year 2000."[6] As Capa explains, "We named this unknown generation, The Generation X, and even in our first enthusiasm we realized that we had something far bigger than our talents and our pockets could cope with. Still, we were deciding to spread around the world and choose a young man and a young girl in each of twelve different countries, on five different continents, and try to find out their present way of life, their past history, and their hopes for the future."[7]

Originally slated to appear in *McCall's,* the project was withdrawn because of editorial differences. Versions of the piece eventually appeared in the United Kingdom in the 10 January 1953 issue of *Picture Post* under the title "The Queen's Generation: Young People in a Changing World," and in the United States as a three-part series titled "Youth and the World" in the January, February, and March 1953 issues of *Holiday.*[8] The complete project consisted of twenty-four individual portraits of young people in their early twenties from fourteen different countries (see figures 1 and 2). Despite its "global" perspective, the project exhibits a distinct emphasis on the experiences of western Europeans and Americans, who make up more than half of the individuals featured. The uncertainty of the future, particularly the possibility of war, provides the overall context for the photographs and the accompanying text. "We intended to present the problem of a generation," said Capa, "which has as its main problem 'going to war or not.'"[9]

Interestingly, many of those interviewed for the project responded to this problem of "going to war or not" by turning away from politics and world affairs altogether, and focusing on more local and personal

Figure 1.   "Generation X," 1953. Colette Laurent, of France, a part-time model and actress, featured in part 2 of *Holiday*'s "Youth of the World" series. Photo by Robert Capa. Reprinted by permission of Magnum Photos.

Figure 2.   "Generation X," 1953. Rudolf Kesslau, a coal miner from Essen, featured in part 2 of *Holiday*'s "Youth of the World" series. Photo by Robert Capa. Reprinted by permission of Magnum Photos.

concerns: Sylvia Andrews (England), we are told, "is not interested in politics, international affairs, or the United Nations";[10] Nancy Arnold (United States), a medical student, "has few interests outside" her career (20); Louis Pasquier (France) "knows little about the world in general" (12); Gerda Schwemmer (Germany) remains "without belief in anything very much beyond herself" (6); and Burhan Jabri (Syria) has simply "turn[ed] his back on politics" (6). While most likely a product of their recent experience (direct or indirect) of global warfare, this disillusionment with mainstream politics and detachment from the larger "adult" world is not linked, as one might expect, to an "alternative" vision of society, nor is it linked to a pessimistic view of the future. Instead, the majority of individuals interviewed offer a rather upbeat, if cautious, assessment of their prospects, with most defining their goals and hopes for the future in the conventional terms of family and/or work. Two exceptions to this cautious optimism are Robert Capa subjects: Colette Laurent of France and Rudolf Kesslau of Germany. Laurent is described in part 2 of the *Holiday* photo-essay as "desperately unhappy," with "no regular job, no real friends, no family."[11] A voracious reader and an admirer of Huxley, Caldwell, and Faulkner, Laurent espouses "no interest in politics," but unlike many of the others featured in the photo-essay, she sees little reason for optimism: "I think in the future the individual will lose more and more identity, so I do not think anything will improve. While I wish for progress, I am afraid of the civilization we have."[12] Kesslau, a teenage soldier during the war and now a miner in Essen, also declares himself to be apolitical ("No politics for me"), and asserts that "things are not good, but I don't think they will be any better, and I wouldn't be surprised if they got a lot worse."[13]

The bleakest assessment comes from Bertrand Russell, whose introductory essay, "Young People in a Changing Civilisation," accompanies the *Picture Post* piece. Its final paragraph begins, "If the generation which is now becoming adult is to play its part in saving the world, a number of difficult conditions will first have to be fulfilled. First and foremost its elders must allow it to remain alive" (7). Though Russell's call for "hope and intelligence" aided by "vigorous courage" as the only remedy for a world verging on disaster provides a sense of contextual urgency for the *Picture Post* photo-essay, the majority of the individuals interviewed do not share that sense of urgency or pessimism, and most appear, like the American Tad Lewis Kostrubula, to be "pretty typical of the present 'play safe' generation" (6). In this way, Capa's use of the term "Generation X" carries with it no particular connotation beyond the fact that this particular generation remains "unknown" at present and perhaps somewhat cautious and conservative. The letter *X* is meant here to function primarily as a placeholder, a variable or a blank to be filled in later, as these individuals (and millions of others) continue to shape their personal and collective histories.

Published eleven years after the Magnum piece appeared in *Picture Post* and *Holiday*, Charles Hamblett and Jane Deverson's 1964 book *Generation X* continues this sense of a generation with an as yet "un-

Figure 3. "Generation X," 1964. Originally published in the *Daily Mirror* in May 1964, this Ian Maitland photo appears on p. 87 of Richard Barnes's 1979 book *Mods!* (London: Plexus Publishing, 1991.) Reprinted by permission of mirrorpix.com and Plexus Publishing.

known" identity, but their focus—British youth subculture—is much narrower than Magnum's.[14] The book itself is a sociological document of sorts, an edited collection of interviews Hamblett and Deverson recorded with British youths, primarily those belonging to subcultural groups like the mods and rockers (see figure 3); supplementing the interviews are letters and other writings received in response to a request for contributions placed in the *Observer* newspaper. As Hamblett and Deverson assert in their foreword, it was their intent to produce "a book *by* the coming generation, rather than yet another one *about* them."[15]

Like Magnum's "Generation X" project, Hamblett and Deverson's intent is to capture the "voice" of this generation, with one important contextual difference: where Capa's Generation X faced the problem of "going to war or not," Hamblett and Deverson's Generation X is confronted by a new, equally threatening phenomenon—the increasing rapidity of "social and scientific acceleration." As the authors explain, "the problems of today's young are more acutely special than ever before. Thanks to postwar developments in mass communications alone these problems have become more concentrated, are more universally shared and more rapidly absorbed. Things, people, ideas get used up more quickly—yet are cast aside with same old primal ruthlessness. This is one of the problems the young must face and conquer: the problem of social and scientific acceleration at the expense of biological time. If they don't, they are in danger of becoming a generation of retreads, worn out before their natural time" (5). Hamblett and Deverson thus identify Generation X as the first to confront one of the hallmarks of late-capitalist, postmodern culture: the increasing rapidity with which "things, people, [and] ideas get used up" and discarded. The "social and scientific acceleration" that characterizes their milieu is clearly presented as a hostile environment, one that contrasts with (and threatens) the slower progress of "natural," "biological" time. The danger Hamblett and Deverson warn against, in fact, is nothing less than the full assimilation of Generation X into their accelerated cultural milieu. As a generation of "retreads," these young people would have no unique, well-defined identity; exhausted by the speed of cultural transformation, their identities die a premature death, "worn out before their natural time."[16]

What Hamblett and Deverson failed to anticipate, of course, is the extent to which cultural acceleration is fueled by those very things, people, and ideas it quickly discards. Cultural rubbish, in other words, is subject to being "picked" and recycled, put to use in another form or context—as hybrid, pastiche, collage, nostalgia (with or without irony), or plain old retread—a process now identified as coterminous with the formation of the postmodern cultural landscape. As we will see, this cultural reprocessing precisely describes the history of the term "Generation X." From 1964 on, it has been picked up and recycled in various contexts, most importantly with the publication of Coupland's 1991 novel *Generation X*, whose subtitle, "Tales for an Accelerated Culture," ironically echoes Hamblett and Deverson's warning about the dangers of "social and scientific acceleration" nearly thirty years earlier.

Given their positioning of Generation X in direct confrontation with the acceleration of society and technology, it is not surprising that Hamblett and Deverson choose to pay close attention to the voices of subcultural youth. This formative link between the term "Generation X" and youth subculture is an important one, for it is here that it might be read not only as an unknown blank to be filled in, but also as a negation or a denial, an X that crosses out a preexisting term or idea. Familiar negationist themes recur throughout the transcribed interviews and excerpted letters reproduced in Deverson and Hamblett's text, including the rejection of parental authority and the values of mainstream society; a repeated emphasis on the boredom of everyday life; a corresponding sense of the future as bleak or at best uncertain; and the cultivation of a subcultural milieu that revolves around various "signifying practices" involving sex, drugs, clothing, music, and/or violence. As Dick Hebdige observes in his now classic study *Subculture: The Meaning of Style*, subcultures are "expressive forms but what they express is, in the last instance, a fundamental tension between those in power and those condemned to subordinate positions and second-class lives."[17] This expression, says Hebdige, is a "response [that] embodies a Refusal" (132)—and by that he means a refusal of the basic cultural assumptions that structure social organizations. Because subcultures call into question the received, seemingly "natural" assumptions about the way society works, writes Hebdige, such a response functions as "the unwelcome revelation of difference which draws down upon the members of a subculture hostility, [and] derision" (132).

Hebdige's primary example of such a refusal is the punk subculture that emerged in London in the mid-seventies. Early punk style, Hebdige argues, is marked especially "by its refusal to cohere around a readily identifiable set of central values. It cohered, instead, *elliptically* through a chain of conspicuous absences. It was characterized by its unlocatedness—its blankness" (120). And, as others have argued, it's precisely this blankness that clears the way for new and creative signifying practices. As Greil Marcus puts it in his book *Lipstick Traces: A Secret History of the Twentieth Century*, the voice of punk "remains something new in rock 'n' roll, which is to say something new in postwar popular

Figure 4. "Generation X," 1976. This promotional poster collage appears in the liner notes for the Generation X *Perfect Hits* CD. Reprinted by permission of EMI.

culture: a voice that denied all social facts, and in that denial affirmed that everything was possible."[18]

Fittingly, it is precisely within the punk subculture in London in the mid-1970s that the term "Generation X" reappears, this time as the name of a punk band best remembered now as the one fronted by Billy Idol, before Idol went on to commercial notoriety with his solo career (see figure 4). In December 1976 the band took the name "Generation X" straight from the title of Deverson and Hamblett's 1964 publication, a copy of which sat on a bookshelf in the home of Billy Idol's mother, or so the story goes.[19] Their initial releases were blatantly anthem-like, focusing on generational difference in particular. Their first single, "Your Generation" (1977), for example, targeted the culture's dominant generation in its negationist chorus: "Your generation don't mean a thing to me." Subsequent singles, like "Wild Youth" and "Ready Steady Go" (probably their best-known single) offer similar refusals of the status quo in the name of a youth identity that differs significantly from the mainstream.

Such songs that assert generational identity or engage in intergenerational taunting are hardly unique in the rock music world. What is unique, however, is the way the punk subculture repeatedly defines its generational identity in terms of "blankness" or emptiness. By simply adopting the name "Generation X," this particular punk band transferred the term from the realm of pop sociology to popular culture; they appropriated and transformed it into a signifier of punk style, thus affirming the negationist "blankness" central to its identity, as Hebdige described.

The earliest (and best) example of an attempt to construct a generational identity in these terms within the punk milieu is a song written by a young musician in New York City named Richard Hell. The song was first recorded as a demo in 1975 and appeared the next year on the first EP by his band Richard Hell and the Voidoids. In the well-known chorus of his song, "Blank Generation," Hell literally inscribes *absence* as the signifier for the blank generation's identity: "I belong to the blank generation / and I can take it or leave it each time / I belong to the ———— generation / but I can take it or leave it each time." In the second verse of the chorus, no word is sung between "the" and "generation"; instead, we are given the aural equivalent of a blank space, to be filled in as one wishes, or not at all. Not surprisingly, the song was often interpreted negatively, as a failure (or worse, an unwillingness) to fill in the blank—a song that glorifies indifference, an anthem of a generation of losers. In an interview in 1978 with the rock critic Lester Bangs, however, Richard Hell claimed that "[p]eople misread what I meant by 'Blank Generation.' To me, 'blank' is a line where you can fill in anything. It's positive. It's the idea that you have the option of making yourself anything you want, filling in the blank. And that's something that provides a uniquely powerful sense to this generation. It's saying, 'I entirely reject your standards for judging my behavior.' And I support that entirely. It can be used politically as powerfully as it can be used artistically or emotionally, in the sense of saying, 'I have been classified null by the society that I live in,' and it can be accepted as a self-description in that way."[20] In the punk subculture, such an adoption of a "null classification" as a "self-description," as Hell puts it, necessarily entails a defiance marked by the deployment of an ironic self-consciousness. Hell himself, for example, was known to walk around in a T-shirt that read "Please Kill Me."[21]

This same ironic, punk self-consciousness pervades Coupland's 1991 novel *Generation X: Tales for an Accelerated Culture*. Although the subtitle alludes to Deverson and Hamblett's warning that youth must "face and conquer" the dangers of "social and scientific acceleration," Coupland's characters do not confront this acceleration, which they view as the inevitable and unchangeable condition of the late twentieth century. Instead, they seek to maintain an ironic distance from "accelerated culture" by embracing the "null classification" of marginal identity. Here, for example, is the narrator of Coupland's novel, explaining why he and his friends have exiled themselves to the desert of southern California: "We live small lives on the periphery; we are marginalized and there's a great deal in which we choose not to participate. We wanted silence and we have that silence now."[22] Throughout Coupland's novel, the desert functions as a metaphoric *X*, as both a negation of "social and scientific acceleration," and also as a blank space within which the main characters will now attempt to inscribe a coherent narrative of their lives, a new identity, if you will. As Coupland himself explained in an interview in the *New York Times*, "I'm interested in people my age and younger who have no narrative structure to their lives. The big structure used to be the job, the career arc, and that's no longer there. Neither is the family or religion. All these narrative templates have eroded."[23] Thus, in the novel *Generation X* we meet three characters who have dropped out, to a certain extent, of mainstream society and who seek to construct narratives out of their marginal, peripheral existence. As Andy, the narrator, says, "We know that this is why the three of us left our lives behind us and came to the desert—to tell stories and to make our own lives worthwhile tales in the process" (8).

The theorist Jean Baudrillard has described the desert in just this way, as a postmodern space *par excellence*, a space where "you are delivered from all depth," a space characterized by "a superficial neutrality, a challenge to meaning and profundity, a challenge to nature and culture

. . . with no origin, no reference-points."[24] For Baudrillard, the desert is simultaneously the embodiment of American culture and its critique: "the inhumanity of our ulterior, asocial, superficial world immediately finds its aesthetic form here, its ecstatic form. For the desert is simply that: an ecstatic critique of culture, an ecstatic form of disappearance" (5). The desert landscape, in other words, with its emptiness and its shifting surface, renders visible the superficiality of American culture and the triumph of the transparency of form over the depth of substance. At the same time the desert's vast void represents the end result of this triumph, what Baudrillard calls "the future catastrophe of the social," namely, its implosion and disappearance, its "desertification" (5). Baudrillard's desert is thus apocalyptic, a landscape at the end of history, at the end of the social, at the end of meaning, nature, and culture. The desert embodies both where we're going and where we are: "the whole of America," writes Baudrillard, "is a desert" (99).

While the desert in *Generation X* does function in ways that resemble Baudrillard's postmodern desert—at least on the surface—there are important ways in which the significance of the Gen X desert as a narrative and cultural space runs counter to Baudrillard's ecstatic, apocalyptic landscape. For example, Baudrillard posits the desert as the "aesthetic form" of our "asocial, superficial world" (5). In *Generation X*, however, the desert functions not as the aesthetic form of superficiality but as its *negation* and *erasure*. It is a fictional landscape opened up by the rejection of bourgeois entitlements and desires, and by the abandonment of the ironic surface of contemporary, postmodern culture. Dag, for instance, explains that he ended up in the desert after having reached a kind of midlife crisis in his mid-twenties that "wasn't just the failure of youth but also a failure of class and of sex and the future and I *still* don't know what" (30). "So the point of all this," Dag tells Andy, "was that I needed a clean slate with no one to read it. I needed to drop out even further. . . . So I split to where the weather is hot and dry and where the cigarettes are cheap. Like you and Claire. And now I'm here" (31).

Andy and Claire both reiterate Dag's desire for a "clean slate." Claire says she wanted "to go somewhere rocky . . . and just empty my brain, read books, and be with people who wanted to do the same thing" (36), and Andy tells us that he "needed *less* in life. Less past" (59). It is in this respect that the desert's emptiness functions as the "blank space at the end of a chapter," as a "marginal" space removed from the absurd clutter of the mainstream, and as a "blank" space in which an alternative story might be written. The desert is thus not an endpoint, the ground zero of social implosion, but a beginning point—it's on the margins, in the desert, where the narrative begins. Baudrillard's postmodern desert may very well be "a sublime form that banishes all sociality, all sentimentality, all sexuality. Words, even when they speak of the desert, are always unwelcome" (71). But the desert of *Generation X* is a desert born of the desire to recover the social and the sentimental, to reinscribe it in a new space that, rather than ecstatic and visible, remains subtle and private.

Given the novel's ironic take on postmodern pop culture, many commentators have dismissed *Generation X* as "self-absorbed"[25] or as a "campy postmodern self-parody."[26] Sophfronia Scott Gregory argues that the novel is "so peppered with trademarks, jargon and faux chic" that it fails as a work of literature.[27] Above all, says Mark Brett, writing in the *minnesota review*, the "book's plot, or rather its lack of one" is "not to be taken seriously."[28] Although the novel does seem to epitomize, in many ways (particularly in its form), the postmodern aesthetic of surface play and self-conscious irony, the narrative is surprisingly concerned with—even valorizes—the search for depth and meaning. And while reviewers may leave you with the sense that the narrative has little interest in pursuing this deeper meaning, the novel is actually downright sentimental about the sacredness of friendship, the spontaneous and selfless expression of love, and the value of narrative itself.[29] Ultimately, it is the pursuit of these sentiments that leads Andy, Dag, and Claire to abandon their urban lifestyles in Tokyo, Toronto, and Los Angeles for exile in the desert landscape of southern California.

In a brief essay in the June 1995 issue of *Details*, Coupland explained that his characters (and the title of his novel) were derived from the final chapter of Paul Fussell's *Class: A Guide through the American Status System* (1983), titled "The X Way Out."[30] In this chapter, Fussell describes a group of people who don't seem to fit within any of the typical class boundaries, and who, in fact, have discovered a "way out" from the entrapment of class-based presumptions and values. Fussell assigns these folks to category *X:* "X people constitute something like a classless class. They occupy the one social place in the U.S.A. where the ethic of buying and selling is not all-powerful. Impelled by insolence, intelligence, irony, and spirit, X people have escaped out the back doors of those theaters of class which enclose others."[31] Like a loosely confederated subculture, Fussell's "X people" reject bourgeois tastes and values, and express that rejection through parodic and satiric displays of middle class (and sometimes working class) status. Fussell's chapter maintains a mildly sardonic wit as he recounts various examples of X people's ironic behavior: their tendency "to eschew the obvious kinds of pets, leaning instead toward things like tame coyotes, skunks, peacocks, and anteaters" (181); their obsession with reruns from classic television series ("experiencing ecstasies watching for the fiftieth time Jackie Gleason's Chef of the Future" [183]); their pursuit of narrowly obscure subjects ("they may be fanatical about Serbo-Croatian prosody, geodes, or Northern French church vestments of the eleventh century" [184]); and their interest in multilingualism and global awareness, leading the "more self-conscious Xs" to "go so far in the international direction as to cross their sevens" (185).

This humorous tone, though, is not meant to undercut Fussell's main point about X category people: that they have managed, "through a strenuous effort of discovery in which curiosity and originality are indispensable" (179), to "disencumber themselves . . . from the constraints and anxieties of the whole class racket" (187). The result is a kind of playful, ironic freedom from the commodified, mediated experiences of consumer society, a freedom that forges an "alternative," deliberately marginal space for everyday life—a kind of fluid, (sub)cultural space with constantly shifting boundaries between the marginal and the mainstream.

Eight years later, Fussell's X people would be rechristened "slackers," a word closely associated with the term Generation X since the release of Richard Linklater's film *Slacker* in 1991, the same year Coupland's novel was published. Like Fussell's X people and Coupland's *Generation X* characters, the individuals depicted in *Slacker* also negotiate this shifting boundary between the margin and the mainstream through a combination of "irony, insolence, intelligence and spirit." While the film does not claim to represent an entire generation, Linklater has repeatedly made this association himself in various interviews and written statements. In the introduction to the book *Slacker* (which features a foreword by Douglas Coupland), Linklater says that prior to the making of the film, "I went from thinking (as I had been told over and over again) that my generation had nothing to say to thinking that it not only had everything to say but was saying it in a completely new way. It was a multitude of voices coexisting and combining and all adding up to something that certainly 'meant' something but couldn't easily be classified. Each individual had to find it in their own way and in the only place society had left for this discovery—the margins. I think that's where *Slacker* takes place."[32] Like the novel *Generation X*, the margin in *Slacker* functions as both a space born of the rejection of certain mainstream values, as well as a space within which new or "alternative" lives might be constructed. As Linklater has stated, "The dictionary defines slackers as people who evade duties and responsibilities. A more modern notion would be people who are ultimately being responsible to themselves and not wasting their time in a realm of activity that has nothing to do with who they are or what they might ultimately be striving for."[33]

The "realm of activity" Linklater refers to here is, of course, the everyday work world. From the slacker perspective, working is not the point of living; in fact, it impedes living. Work, from the slacker perspective, marginalizes who we are; thus, in the life of a slacker work must be decentered, relegated to the margins. As Linklater points out, this does not necessarily mean that slackers are unemployed; the difference is, says Linklater, that "if they have a job, the job doesn't have them."[34] And it is this choice, of course, that relegates the slackers themselves to the margins of society. When mainstream society looks at slackers, what it perceives is a lack of structure—the lack of that "career arc" that maps the trajectory of a normative lifestyle. Without that structure, mainstream society can find nothing to value; such lives seem worthless and wasted at best, and at worst, they seem to be an affront and an insult to everything "productive" society stands for. It is this realm of (in)activity—everyday life—that the work world has structured, colonized, and marginalized. *Slacker* seeks to reclaim that space, to occupy it as a realm of *creativity* rather than *waste*. This reclamation constitutes the politics of the film. As Linklater said in an interview in *Artforum*, "Politics are a lot more complex than just voting or aligning yourself on certain issues. Politics are also the politics of everyday life. To be dissatisfied and talk about it to even one other person is political."[35]

There is a tradition of sorts in the realm of political and social theory that concerns itself with the "politics of everyday life," and this tradition has, over the last twenty-five years, worked its way from the rather specialized realms of avant-garde art (Dada and Surrealism, for example) and revolutionary cultural politics (especially the activities of the Situationist International) into the realm of popular culture. I won't trace that history here,[36] but the key ideas—that everyday life is a cultural space worth struggling over, for example—are present in the punk subcultural style. Those ideas reappear in various ways in Fussell's X Category, in Coupland's book *Generation X*, and in Linklater's film *Slacker*.

Despite the subcultural, marginal position conferred by this "politicizing" of everyday life, Fussell makes a particular point of locating X people "firmly in the American grain" (186), *precisely because* their nonconformist individuality affords them the freedom to live lives unfettered by the "envy and ambition that pervert so many" (187). Fussell's assertion (meant to be reassuring) nevertheless reveals an unsettling irony about their social position. Bucking contemporary American bourgeois values in a "traditional" American individualist, nonconformist manner, the X people occupy a social realm that lies both within *and against* the "grain" of American culture. This ironic, ambiguous position is signified most clearly in Fussell's use of the letter *X* to designate their social category. *X* here marks an impossible spot, both inside and outside mainstream American culture, for which we have no preestablished terminology or identity—until now.

The term "Generation X" marks precisely this paradoxical borderline status (inside and outside, within and against the mainstream), with "X" capturing the dual sense of negation and freedom and "generation" signifying a kind of hyperbolic assertion of subcultural, rather than demographic, solidarity. At its root, the "insolence, intelligence, irony and spirit" common to the punk style, Fussell's X category, Coupland's characters, and Linklater's slackers, have their basis in a self-conscious awareness of this paradoxical situation. Here subcultural identity is dependent on its differential relation to the mainstream, and subcultural signifying practices are themselves routinely appropriated by the "accelerated," dominant culture, and thus "sold out" before their time. The ironic, detached stance toward consumer culture usually associated with Generation X in the 1990s is symptomatic of the self-conscious awareness of this paradoxical position. In a culture where "true" resistance and rebellion are said to be impossible because they are always already co-opted, where no "authentic" individual identity can be expressed, because it is always already mediated through commodities, self-conscious irony emerges as a kind of defensive subject position, a symbolic "resistance" painfully aware of its limited impact on the amorphous, all-pervasive consumer culture. As Ryan Moore has argued in his contribution to the anthology *Generations of Youth*, "After all, Coupland's novels could not produce their sense of torment without the coexistence of desire for the transcendent and the inclination that all accessible strategies are, in the end, exhausted and ineffectual."[37]

Although we have traced the extent to which the oppositional stance of Generation X draws on the negationist style of subcultures like punk, this particular paradoxical sensibility—a strong desire for authenticity and meaning, coupled with the sense that such desires are unlikely to be fulfilled—has its clearest antecedent among the Beats of the 1950s. In fact, this sensibility lies at the very core of John Clellon Holmes's essay "This is the Beat Generation," published in the November 1952 issue of the *New York Times Magazine*, just six weeks before *Picture Post* and *Holiday* published Robert Capa's photo series. While Capa attempted to encapsulate the hopes and fears of a global postwar generation, Holmes zeroed in on its American segment, describing it as the "beat generation," a term whose provenance he attributed to a 1948 conversation with Jack Kerouac. "More than mere weariness," writes Holmes, *beat* "implies the feeling of having been used, of being raw. It involves a sort of nakedness of mind, and ultimately, of soul; a feeling of being reduced to the bedrock of consciousness."[38]

Though the Beat Generation includes, at its extremes, both the "wildest hipster" and the "radical young Republican," Holmes tells us that "behind the excess on the one hand, and the conformity on the other, lies that wait-and-see detachment that results from having to fall back for support more on one's capacity for human endurance than on one's philosophy of life" (20). And yet, continues Holmes, "beneath the excess and conformity, there is something other than detachment. There are the stirrings of a quest. What the hipster is looking for in his 'coolness' (withdrawal) or 'flipness' (ecstasy) is, after all, a feeling of somewhereness, not just another diversion" (22). Given the collapse of social and moral values in postwar America, writes Holmes, "there have been few generations with as natural and profound a craving for convictions as this one, nor have there been many generations as ill-equipped to find them" (22). As a result, the quest for conviction and meaning is pursued at the individual and/or subcultural level; among the Beats there is no collective will to action, no articulation of a radical vision for the social and political transformation of postwar American society. As Holmes observes, for the hipster "there is no desire to shatter the 'square' society in which he lives, only to elude it" (22). The Beat Generation sensibility is therefore a largely introspective one, and as Holmes notes, such a sensibility feeds into the generation's "ever-increasing conviction that the problem of modern life is essentially a spiritual problem" (22).

Peeling back the layers of the Beat Generation's (sub)cultural style, Holmes finds at the core—beneath the excess and conformity, beneath the detachment—a generation on a spiritual quest for meaning and authenticity, but that self-consciously recognizes the likely futility of such a quest. Subsequent letters to the editor responding to Holmes's essay picked up on and confirmed this paradoxical position. Michael Theil, a student at Cornell, testified that "I and many of my friends show symptoms of belonging to this Beat Generation. We all want to believe in something, or possibly be defiant nihilists. But we do neither. We are caught in between, left merely with a longing to believe in something."[39] Going a step further, Al Ellenberg asserts in his letter that the continuing threat of war is responsible for both the desire for, and the destruction of, meaning: "Thus we are caught in a kind of purgatory," he concludes, "barren of faith and robbed of the consolation of even an affirmative unfaith."[40]

Holmes's delineation of the Beat Generation—particularly the notion of the generation's diagnosis of society's ills as a "spiritual problem"—found its clearest elaboration and popularization in the novels of Jack Kerouac. In Kerouac's tripartite vision, "beat" signifies the marginal (downtrodden, worn out), the spiritual (beatitude), as well as the creative and artistic (the rhythm of bebop and spontaneous prose). All three are linked to the individual pursuit of authenticity. It is largely a quietistic strategy, seeking fulfillment and meaning on the subcultural margins of society, rather than engaging in a collective political struggle for power with the dominant order. In a 1958 essay in *Esquire,* Kerouac insisted that the word *beat* "never meant juvenile delinquents; it meant characters of special spirituality who didn't gang up but were solitary Bartlebies staring out the dead wall window of our civilization."[41] The Beats are "subterranean heroes," Kerouac argued, "taking drugs, digging bop, having flashes of insight, experiencing the 'derangement of the senses,' talking strange, being poor and glad, prophesying a new style for American culture" (47). If the Beats could be understood as fomenting social change, it was only in the sense that they articulated "a certain new gesture, or attitude" that constituted "a revolution in manners in America" (62). Though Kerouac is often portrayed as descending into a reactionary, belligerent, alcoholic conservatism during the 1960s, the core of his ideas about the spirituality and apolitical cultural style of the Beats remained consistent from the early 1950s to the end of his life. Interviewed by William F. Buckley on *Firing Line* in 1968, less than a year before his death, a drunken Kerouac, by turns somber, playful, and absurd, insisted on the original "purity" of the life-embracing nature of his vision. He repudiated the idea that the Beat Generation was ever intent on pursuing political change: "the Beat Generation was a generation of beatitude and pleasure in life and tenderness. But they called it in the papers 'beat mutiny,' 'beat insurrection'—words I never used, being a Catholic. I believe in order, tenderness, and piety."[42]

Given the affinities between the Beat Generation and Generation X, certainly it's no surprise to find that the 1990s brought renewed attention to the Beats in general, and Kerouac in particular. In 1991—the same year in which Coupland's novel *Generation X,* Linklater's film *Slacker,* and Nirvana's second album *Nevermind* appeared—sales of Kerouac's *On the Road,* already steady at twenty-five thousand per year, quadrupled.[43] By 1994, *USA Today* heralded the return of the Beats and explicitly situated Kerouac as Generation X's spiritual mentor in an article titled "Kerouac's Back: A Restless Generation Finds a Muse."[44] Throughout the decade, in fact, the academic and mainstream press paid extraordinary attention to the Beats, as evidenced by the reissue of Kerouac's novels and poetry and the release of his previously unpublished creative work and letters; the appearance new critical works, biographies, anthologies, documentaries, and CD-ROMs about the Beats; an increasing number of university courses devoted to Beat literature; the 1993 "collaboration" between Kurt Cobain and William Burroughs; a high-profile NYU conference on the Beats on the 25th anniversary of Kerouac's death; and an even higher profile Beat Generation exhibition at the Whitney Museum the following year. The deaths of Ginsberg and Burroughs in 1997 also presented further occasions for revisiting and reassessing the Beats in the mainstream media.

Because it is largely symbolic, personal, and highly self-conscious, the particular kind of "cultural politics" associated with the Beats and Generation X doesn't sit well with those (especially on the left) who long for more direct, pragmatic, and collective political activity. Thus the personal politics of Generation X have been routinely and roundly denounced as narrow, self-absorbed, and above all complicit with the mainstream. Kevin Mattson, for example, has argued that such introspective, micropolitical strategies are irredeemably compromised because "personal liberation has become the status quo; it is the mantra of our consumer culture." "Hip detachment and cool irony," which Mattson describes as "the most important features of Generation X social criticism," merely reflect "an attitude that has become a fixture in contemporary popular culture."[45] Indeed, no one can doubt the pervasiveness of such appeals to individual rebellion and nonconformity in the advertising and entertainment worlds. As Thomas Frank has conclusively demonstrated in his book *The Conquest of Cool*, the marketing of "hip" consumerism has been a particularly effective form of advertising for at least four decades, and was especially dominant in the mid- to late-1960s.[46] Even so, the very presence and pervasiveness of such marketing does not necessarily render individual positions of resistance untenable or inauthentic. Frank freely acknowledges this point, explaining that he's intent on scrutinizing hipness exclusively from the perspective of the marketing world.[47] Mattson, however, dismisses any subjective, subcultural efforts at "personal liberation" as always already co-opted and thus futile. This dismissiveness—more and more in vogue, particularly in academia—is reminiscent of an old-fashioned leftist elitism that disdains any form of "politics" that engages with (and is thus tainted by) mass culture. Such a stance tends to perpetuate the distinction between "authentic" and "inauthentic" political strategies. Leftist elites insist that (sub)cultural practices remain ineffectual because they merely form a compromised "alternative" that must remain self-consciously ironic, precisely because it fails to challenge overtly the dominant political order. More importantly, this rigorous division of subversive activity into the mutually exclusive realms of "authentic" and "inauthentic" renders any possible relation between the two impermissible and unthinkable. And yet, as Ryan Moore reminds us, "such cultural practices [of the subcultural, do-it-yourself, postpunk kind] not only provide a self-sustained medium for experimentation with 'alternative' identities but also allow for the *process* of active collaboration in the creation of underground networks and lines of communication. If the creative content remains largely nihilistic and cynical, we must remember that the participatory form of collective self-empowerment can be appropriated for more explicitly oppositional ends."[48]

For Moore, the "nihilistic and cynical" content of (sub)cultural expression associated with the term Generation X is itself symptomatic of the postmodern "crisis of affectivity" (as theorized by Fredric Jameson and Lawrence Grossberg), a crisis exacerbated in the 1990s by "the downward mobility of the middle class."[49] Indeed, corporate downsizing, the expansion of low-pay service sector jobs, the increased reliance on temporary workers, the increase in dual-income households, the skyrocketing cost of health insurance and housing, the erosion of the buying power of the minimum wage, and the enormous disparity between the wealthy and everyone else have increasingly channeled the nihilism and cynicism associated with Generation X in an anticorporate direction. In fact, it is precisely this anticorporate sentiment (combined with the emergence of globalization in the late 1990s as the bête noire of labor unions, environmentalists, and student activists) that makes possible a strategic alliance between the detached, hip, cynical (sub)cultural sensibility of Generation X and a more overt, organized political struggle against the dominant corporate order.

Indeed, the necessary participatory structures for such an alliance appear to be emerging. Recent examples include the continuing (and remarkably successful) campaigns waged on college campuses against the sweatshop production of clothing bearing university logos, and the coordinated efforts of labor unions, greens, and anarchists against the WTO, the IMF, and the World Bank (as put into practice in mass protests in Seattle in late 1999, and in subsequent protests in Philadelphia, Washington, Los Angeles, Prague, Genoa, and elsewhere). In the realm of electoral politics, the decidedly anticorporate Green Party (complete with its roster of "alternative" rock star supporters, including Patti Smith, Ani DiFranco, Eddie Vedder, and Adam Yauch) has enjoyed growing visibility.

While it would be easy to argue that such oppositional, "alternative" movements represent legitimate, "authentic" structures for resistance (as distinct from the hopelessly compromised, merely subcultural stylings associated with Generation X), in my view the authenticity versus inauthenticity dichotomy simply doesn't hold here. *Any* oppositional activity in this accelerated, hypercapitialist age is always forced to define its identity and significance in relation to the mainstream. And indeed, any collective activity that seeks to alter the status quo must also understand that its effectiveness is largely dependent on the extent to which it can forge alliances across a wide range of boundaries (generational, racial, class, gender, and ideological), and capture a critical mass of what might otherwise be understood as "mainstream" support.[50] Resistance to the status quo, whether on an individual or a collective level, thus always necessitates a process of negotiation and renegotiation across the border between "alternative" and "mainstream" culture.

As an historical term, "Generation X" marks precisely this self-conscious process of negotiation and renegotiation. It foregrounds and problematizes the dichotomy between alternative and mainstream cultural formations, between authentic and inauthentic identities, between cynical and idealistic attitudes. The ten essays presented here offer a critical interrogation of this Generation X borderland in three different contexts (music and performance, print media, and electronic media) in an effort to assess the significance and efficacy of various (sub)cultural efforts to fashion "alternative" generational and/or individual identities within and against the seemingly pervasive consumer culture of our time. Although the contributors' conclusions are not uniform (some find more to be optimistic about than others), their shared approach is to reexamine the term "Generation X" in its (sub)cultural context, with a self-conscious eye toward the precariousness of its position as an "alternative" to the mainstream.

Music and Performance

Leslie Haynsworth's "'Alternative' Music and the Oppositional Potential of Generation X Culture" focuses on the way "alternative" music itself—initially subcultural but now marketed and promoted by the corporate music industry—has become a lightning rod for debate about "authentic" versus "co-opted" expressions of oppositional values. Arguing against the predominant view that any mass-marketed, widely popular, "alternative" band has ipso facto sold out, Haynsworth contends that subcultural ideologies can be articulated from within the dominant culture, despite the loss of their explicitly marginal status. Within the world of "alternative" music, she argues, the dissemination of subcultural values is itself ensured, ironically, by the pressure exerted on formerly subcultural music groups by the subcultures themselves, whose advocacy of authenticity and oppositionality is not only a hallmark of Gen X, but a force that continues to shape and reshape the dominant culture.

In his essay "Jigsaw Youth versus Generation X and Postmodernism," Neil Nehring seeks to reclaim the validity of rebellious, angry expressions in popular music that is usually denied by the "hip cynicism" of music journalists. Taking issue with contemporary postmodern academic theorists who disconnect emotion from reason and intellect and who disavow pop cultural expressions of anger and rebellion as "inauthentic" and "co-opted," Nehring turns to feminist philosophers to combat the devaluation of emotion in cultural criticism. Finding intense emotional commitment in the work of groups like Bikini Kill, for example, Nehring's argument counters the hip cynic's view of popular music, and offers an alternative to the identification of Gen Xers as "inarticulate wretches" unable to voice their experience, emotions, and desires.

Catherine J. Creswell's essay, " 'Touch Me I'm Sick': Contagion as Critique in Punk and Performance Art," locates pathology as the "characteristic performative gesture of the 1990s." Creswell notes that depression in particular is closely associated with Generation X identity, an association fueled by pervasive images of pathology in popular culture, especially in the performative depression of bands like Nirvana. Drawing on the work of Julia Kristeva, Creswell identifies the figure of the contagion as a key element in contemporary Gen X (sub)culture, reading the contagion as a body that crosses the boundary between health and illness, mainstream and degenerate, self and other. Death and loss are located at the very heart of an identity whose voice, like the depressive's, defers (even refuses) meaning. The voice of Generation X is thus a voice that "speaks" through fragments, ambiguities, and irony, and is therefore not easily reduced or interpreted.

Print Media

Daniel Lehman's essay "You Can See Nathan's from Here: Lobbing Culture at the Boomers" traces the Generation X tendency to embrace and recontextualize consumer culture to the 1970s magazine *Punk*, created by John Holmstrom and Legs McNeil, and published by Ged

Dunn. Lehman argues that *Punk* marks a decisive break with the hippie counterculture of the late 1960s and early 1970s, a break articulated via an oppositional, generational, do-it-yourself bricolage that prefigures the "cultural skirmishes" between Xers and baby boomers in the 1990s.

Jim Finnegan's article, "Theoretical Tailspins: Reading Alternative Performance in *Spin* Magazine," analyzes the way *Spin* theorizes itself as a mass cultural voice of Generation X by self-consciously reflecting on issues familiar to the academic practitioners of cultural studies: the meaning of subcultural style, for example, and the extent to which oppositional, "alternative" positions can be articulated within a mainstream, commodified context. In order to "read" *Spin,* Finnegan argues, we must acknowledge "the constitutive relationship between the media and subcultural identity," a relationship that is itself highly complex, and often contradictory. In this way, *Spin* may be read as more than "just a magazine"; it is a willing participant that both shapes (spins) and is shaped by youth culture.

In its analysis of the relationship between the media and the construction of Generation X identity, Kirk Curnutt's essay, "Generating Xs: Identity Politics, Consumer Culture, and the Making of a Generation," focuses on the way a number of Gen X-related titles—including *Generation Ecch!, Platforms, Prozac Nation,* and *Late Bloomers*—have sought to resist commodification by devaluing generational solidarity itself, in favor of individuality and autonomy. This "resistance," which Curnutt likens to Marcuse's "Great Refusal," is nevertheless itself commodified and marketed, caught in the bind of capitalizing on the very Gen X media industry that it simultaneously attempts to negate. In so doing, argues Curnutt, these works "dramatize the necessity of *not* abandoning the concept of generational belonging to the marketeers," for "to do so . . . is to exile ourselves from a site of cultural identity every bit as historically powerful and significant as class, gender, and sexuality."

In "Generation X and the End of History," G. P. Lainsbury reads Douglas Coupland's novel *Generation X* as an answer to Brian Fawcett's call for a "renewed" Canadian literature, one that addresses, in both form and content, the complex relationship between self, identity, and our late capitalist, "accelerated" culture. Drawing on the work of Fawcett, Jean-Francois Lyotard, and Arthur Kroker, Lainsbury argues that Coupland has produced a meditational bricolage on the end of history that advocates "a sensibility which can appreciate complexification,

rather than seeking escape in modernist fantasies of individual fulfillment and closure."

Electronic Media

Traci Carroll's essay, "Talking Out of School: Academia Meets Generation X," analyzes *Beavis and Butt-head* and *Mystery Science Theater*
as Gen X critical texts that both mimic and deconstruct academic
criticism. Beavis and Butt-head in particular figure as "paradigmatic
Gen X critics," whose combination of "violent humor, pathos, resistance to institutions and perverse creativity" constitute a kind of folk
criticism that imitates and mocks academic detachment by erasing the
critical distance traditionally valued by academic discourse. Carroll's
self-reflective essay then situates Gen X academics somewhere between
Beavis and Butt-head's couch critic position and the privileged, critically
distant position of the academic institution, creating a Gen X academic
identity akin to "institutional schizophrenia," occupying the border zone
between the marginal and the mainstream.

In Beat literature, as Katie Mills observes in her essay, "'Await
Lightning': How Generation X Remaps the Road Story," the road signifies the place of authentic and direct experience, as well as an escape
from society and consumerism. By contrast, television usually signifies
the opposite of the road—watching television is a mediated, passive,
inauthentic, cheap (but not thrilling) experience. For Generation X,
however, the desire for unmediated, authentic experience has the ring
of nostalgia and quaint anachronism. The road has become a TV chronotope, functioning as a sign of the real, but also as "a heuristic model for
alternative and activist ways to watch TV." Through a close look at tele-
visual representations of the road, such as Shauna Garr's documentary
The Ride and MTV's *Road Rules*, Mills reveals the way television and
the road mediate their messages, while simultaneously reshaping the
cultural significance of reality and rebellion.

Andrew Klobucar's "The Apocalypse Will Be Televised: Electronic
Media and the Last Generation" asserts that the indirect, private ap-
proach to social reform characteristic of Gen X "activist" groups like
Lead . . . or Leave parallels the recent rise in social consensus in U.S.
culture. Though the very title of their primary text, *Revolution X: A
Survival Guide for Our Generation*, suggests that Lead . . . or Leave

advocates a wholesale change of the social order, in fact, writes Klobucar, "those working with Lead . . . or Leave emphasize a pragmatic perspective in their agenda, expressing a will to negotiate with the state rather than transform it." Drawing on the work of James Livingston, Louis Althusser, George P. Landow, and others, Klobucar further argues that this conservative pragmatism is now increasingly enmeshed with the discontinuous, nonlinear structure of information technology—particularly the "logic" of the cyberspace environment, within which "the last traces of civic agency" are now disappearing.

Conclusion

Finally, Andrea Harris's conclusion, "Generation X X: The Identity Politics of Generation X," rethinks Generation X in terms of gender and sexuality in order to question the authenticity of an "alternative" youth culture that is predominantly male- and straight-identified. By examining several third wave feminist texts (Rose Glickman's *Daughters of Feminists,* Barbara Findlen's *Listen Up: Voices from the Next Feminist Generation,* and Robin Stevens's *Girlfriend Number One: Lesbian Life in the 90s*) as well as the music of Hole and Sleater-Kinney, Harris foregrounds "the ways in which these Generation X texts are explicitly marked by gender and sexuality, particularly through their use of strategies of feminist critique and resistance." The cultural productions of Generation X women, Harris argues, occupy a marginal position in relation to the "mainstream" Generation X texts produced by men, especially the canonical triumvirate of Coupland, Linklater, and Cobain. Indeed, the "alternative" status claimed by these mainstream Generation X texts, writes Harris, "is in fact a position appropriated from the truly alternative or marginalized of American culture—women, African Americans, queers, and the poor. And from this position—the culturally marked position of the marginal—a more authentic and radical questioning of dominant culture is already being made."

Postscript: After September 11

In the immediate weeks following the terrorist attacks of 11 September 2001, the editorial pages of the nation's newspapers were full of op-ed pieces proclaiming the end of Generation X's cynical, self-indulgent, quietistic attitude; Generation X, it was said, had finally experienced the defining historical moment that would shake it out of its cynicism and apathy, and confer upon it some sort of concrete identity and coherent, meaningful purpose.[51] Broadcast networks also picked up on September 11 as an allegedly defining moment for Generation X. National Public Radio, for example, devoted a portion of its Morning Edition program on 22 October 2001 to this very issue, with comments pro and con from such representative Gen Xers as Rob Seigel (editor-in-chief of the *Onion*), Elizabeth Wurtzel (author of *Prozac Nation*), and Rob Malda (editor and founder of the website *Slashdot: News for Nerds*). On 1 December 2001, CNN Headline News broadcast a segment called "Generation X Goes to War," featuring an interview with William Strauss (co-author of *13th Gen*), in which Generation X was portrayed as finally establishing a fixed, responsible, mainstream identity in the aftermath of the terrorist attacks on the World Trade Center and the Pentagon.

This interpretation of the impact of September 11 on Generation X, of course, occurred in a larger discursive context. In the weeks after September 11, various members of the media industry were declaring that the terrorist attacks marked "the end of the age of irony," a proclamation first offered (ironically, one feels compelled to say) by Graydon Carter, editor of *Vanity Fair* and founder of the satirical magazine *Spy*.[52] From his prominent post at *Time* magazine, Roger Rosenblatt further disseminated Carter's proclamation (though without reference to Carter) in his widely publicized article "The Age of Irony Comes to an End," published just two weeks after the September 11 attacks.[53] Though very much in vogue in the immediate wake of September 11, this "end of the age of irony" rhetoric began to lose its cachet over the next several months, and virtually disappeared as the initial shock of the attacks gave way to debate over what to do next. The various ensuing controversies— the proper actions and outcomes in Afghanistan, the legal status of Taliban prisoners held at Guantanamo Bay, the tactical failures of U.S. intelligence agencies, the assault on the civil liberties of the American citizenry, and the Bush Administration's abrupt shift in focus from Osama bin Laden to Saddam Hussein, to name only a few—quickly eroded the credibility of the "end of irony" proclamations. One need look no further than the contents of a new law dubbed "the U.S.A. Patriot Act" for evidence that irony (of one sort or another) is still alive and well.

For "Generation X," though, the early years of the twenty-first century have meant irony of another kind, as the history of the term has now come full circle. In the early 1950s, Robert Capa employed "Generation X" as the moniker for a global generation "which has as its main problem 'going to war or not'" (Whelan 278). Fifty years later, whether understood as a demographic category or a (sub)cultural sensibility, Generation X must once again grapple with this same problem, as the Bush administration expands its war on terrorism to include military action against nations it suspects of developing weapons of mass destruction and providing assistance to the al-Qaeda terrorist network. As of this writing, the war in Iraq continues. Before and throughout the course of the fighting in Iraq, protests against globalization, the World Bank, and the IMF have given way to massive antiwar demonstrations worldwide. In the United States, where prowar sentiment continues to run high, the antiwar/propeace movement clearly figures as the "alternative" (sub)cultural voice in relation to the mainstream, and various efforts are already underway to discredit or suppress that voice. The slogan "support our troops," for example, is widely disseminated throughout the United States either to weaken the antiwar position or to suppress dissent altogether. Antiwar protestors thus become eager to qualify their position by declaring that they "support the troops" but oppose the war, or even to retreat into a tacit acceptance of the war as a fait accompli because, they are told, the time is now past for debate; with the war underway, we must all "support our troops."

In this way, the prowar position both draws and polices the increasingly polarized border between the alternative and the mainstream. Now more than ever, it is up to the alternative voices to engage in a deliberate, self-conscious negotiation of that border. Only in this way will the "alternative" function as both negation and variable, an X that not only resists the status quo, but also crosses the border, marking a space for rearticulating the relationship between the alternative and the mainstream.

Notes

1. Paul Fussell, *Class: A Guide through the American Status System* (New York: Summit, 1983), 186.
2. Douglas Coupland, "Eulogy: Generation X'd," *Details,* June 1995, 72.

3. See Genia Bellafante, "Generation x-cellent," *Time*, 27 February 1995, 62; "Generalizations X," *Newsweek*, 6 June 1994, 62–70; Neil Howe and William Strauss, "The New Generation Gap," *Atlantic Monthly*, December 1992, 67–69; Suneel Ratan, "Generational Tension in the Office: Why Busters Hate Boomers," *Fortune*, 4 October 1993, 56–58; Alexander Star, "The Twenty-Something Myth," *New Republic*, 4–11 January 1993, 22–25; and Laura Zinn, "Move Over Boomers: A Portrait of Generation X," *Business Week*, 14 December 1992: 74–79.

4. See Neil Howe and William Strauss, *13th Generation* (New York: Vintage, 1993); Eric Liu, ed., *Next: Young American Writers on the New Generation* (New York: Norton, 1994); Michael Wexler and John Hulme, eds., *Voices of the Xiled: A Generation Speaks for Itself* (New York: Main Street, 1994); Karen Richie, *Marketing to Generation X* (New York: Lexington, 1995); Rob Nelson and Jon Cowan, *Revolution X: A Survival Guide for Our Generation* (New York: Penguin, 1994); Jason Cohen and Michael Krugman, *Generation Ecch!: The Backlash Starts Here* (New York: Simon and Schuster, 1994); Elizabeth Wurtzel, *Prozac Nation: Young and Depressed in America* (New York: Houghton Mifflin, 1994); Richard Flory and Donald Miller, eds., *GenX Religion* (New York: Routledge, 2000); Bernard Carl Rosen, *Masks and Mirrors: Generation X and the Chameleon Personality* (Westport, Conn.: Praeger, 2001); Peter Hanson, *The Cinema of Generation X: A Critical Study of Films and Directors* (Jefferson, N.C.: McFarland, 2002); Rob Owen, *Gen X TV: The Brady Bunch to Melrose Place* (Syracuse: Syracuse University Press, 1997); Douglas Rushkoff, ed., *The GenX Reader* (New York: Ballantine, 1994).

5. I use the term "(sub)culture" on occasion throughout these pages in order to make visible the conflicted, problematic relationship between "alternative" cultural formations and the "mainstream."

6. Anna Farova, ed., *Robert Capa* (New York: Paragraphic Books, 1969), 36.

7. Ibid., 36–37.

8. See "The Queen's Generation: Young People in a Changing World," *Picture Post*, 10 January 1953, 3–27; "Youth and the World: Part I," *Holiday*, January 1953, 90–105; "Youth and the World: Part II," *Holiday*, February 1953, 48–63; "Youth and the World: Part III," *Holiday*, March 1953, 42–59. Although the term "Generation X" did not appear in the published photo-essays in *Holiday* or *Picture Post*, the term does make an appearance in the December 1952 issue of *Holiday*, as the heading for a brief column announcing the impending publication of the "Youth and the World" series. (See "Generation X," *Holiday*, December 1952, 41.) In their column, the editors describe "Generation X" as the "projection name" for the photo-essay project, and explain that the term is "our tag for what we believe to be the most important group of people in the world today— the boys and girls who are just turning 21. These are the youngsters who have seen and felt the agonies of the past two decades, often firsthand, who are trying to keep the balance in the swirling pressures of today, and who will have the biggest say in the course of history for the next 50 years." December 1952 thus marks the first time the term "Generation X" appears in print, to the best of my knowledge.

9. Richard Whelan, *Robert Capa: A Biography* (New York: Knopf, 1985), 278.

10. "The Queen's Generation," *Picture Post*, 4. Subsequent references will be cited parenthetically within the text.

11. "Youth and the World: Part II," *Holiday*, 58. Text by Roger Angell.

12. Ibid.

13. Ibid., 62.

14. There is apparently no connection between Capa's use of the term "Generation

X" and Hamblett and Deverson's. Nor am I aware of any other appearance of the term in print between its brief mention in the December 1952 issue of *Holiday* and the publication of Hamblett and Deverson's *Generation X* more than a decade later.

15. Charles Hamblett and Jane Deverson, eds., *Generation X* (Greenwich, Conn.: Fawcett, 1964), 5. Subsequent references will be cited parenthetically within the text.

16. As if confronting cultural acceleration weren't enough of a challenge, Hamblett and Deverson conclude their foreword with an apocalyptic caveat: "the ultimate responsibility of Generation X is to guide the human race through the final and crucial decades of this explosive century into the enlightenment of the next one. Failure to achieve this enlightenment can only result in the total extinction of mankind" (6).

17. Dick Hebdige, *Subculture: The Meaning of Style* (London: Methuen,1979; reprint, New York: Routledge, 1990), 132. Subsequent references will be cited parenthetically within the text.

18. Greil Marcus, *Lipstick Traces: A Secret History of the Twentieth Century* (Cambridge: Harvard University Press, 1989), 2.

19. See the liner notes for *Generation X: Perfect Hits 1975–1981*, Chrysalis, D101950, 1991. Deverson and Hamblett's *Generation X* served as source material for punks in other ways as well; as Jon Savage points out in his book *England's Dreaming*, a quotation from *Generation X* concerning the mods and the 1964 "riot" at Margate appeared on a handbill promoting the Clash in October 1976 (Jon Savage, *England's Dreaming: Anarchy, Sex Pistols, Punk Rock, and Beyond* [New York: St. Martin's, 1992], 164).

20. Lester Bangs, *Psychotic Reactions and Carburetor Dung*, ed. Greil Marcus (New York: Knopf, 1987), 266. The use of the term "Generation X" in its polysemous sense of negating mainstream social identity, accepting the classification "null" as a self-description, and creating a space for the reinscription of a new identity parallels the letter *X* as used by the Nation of Islam. The *X* in a name like Malcolm X serves a similar negationist purpose (as the deletion or crossing out of a slave name, i.e., an imposed identity); it functions also as an appropriation of white society's classification of black identity as null or invisible, and of course, it serves as a blank space to be filled in, a space in which a new name will be inscribed. Punks in particular self-consciously asserted that their subcultural position was analogous to the subcultural position of minority populations. In the rest of his interview with Lester Bangs, Richard Hell, for example, suggests that the harassment and violence directed at punks by legal authorities and other white subcultures are similar to racially motivated abuse, because of the "significant difference" (as Hebdige would term it) signified by punk style. The lyrics for Richard Hell's "Blank Generation" appear on pages 14–15 of the insert accompanying the Richard Hell and the Voidoids CD *Blank Generation*, Sire 9261372, 1990.

21. Ibid.

22. Douglas Coupland, *Generation X: Tales for an Accelerated Culture* (New York: St. Martin's, 1991), 11. Subsequent references will be cited parenthetically within the text.

23. Steve Lohr, "No More McJobs for Mr. X.," *New York Times*, 29 May 1994, sec. 9, p. 2.

24. Jean Baudrillard, *America*, trans. Chris Turner (New York: Verso, 1988), 124. Subsequent references will be cited parenthetically within the text.

25. Victor Dwyer, "Puberty Blues: An Author Scans a New Generation," *Maclean's*, 24 August 1992, 60.

26. Mark Brett, review of *Generation X*, by Douglas Coupland, *minnesota review* 39 (Fall/Winter 1992–93): 184.

27. Sophfronia Scott Gregory, review of *Shampoo Planet,* by Douglas Coupland, *Time,* 19 October 1992, 78.

28. Brett, 184.

29. On this point see Ryan Moore, "'And Tomorrow Is Just Another Crazy Scam': Postmodernity, Youth, and the Downward Mobility of the Middle Class," in *Generations of Youth: Youth Cultures and History in Twentieth-Century America,* ed. Joe Austin and Michael Nevin Willard (New York: New York University Press, 1998), 256.

30. Coupland, "Eulogy: Generation X'd," *Details,* June 1995, 72.

31. Paul Fussell, *Class: A Guide through the American Status System* (New York: Summit, 1983), 186. Subsequent references will be cited parenthetically within the text.

32. Richard Linklater, *Slacker* (New York: St. Martin's, 1992), 4.

33. Andrew Kopkind, "Slacking Toward Bethlehem," *Grand Street* 11, 4 (1993): 179.

34 Linklater, 20.

35. Lane Relyea, "What, Me Work? Lane Relyea Talks with Richard Linklater," *Artforum* 31 (April 1993): 76.

36. For the best and most comprehensive account of this history, see Greil Marcus's *Lipstick Traces: A Secret History of the Twentieth Century.*

37. Moore, 256.

38. [John] Clellon Holmes, "This is the Beat Generation," *New York Times Magazine,* 16 November 1952, 10. Subsequent references will be cited parenthetically within the text.

39. Michael H Theil, Letter to the Editor, *New York Times Magazine,* 23 November 1952, 7.

40. Al Ellenberg, Letter to the Editor, *New York Times Magazine,* 23 November 1952, 7.

41. See Jack Kerouac, *Good Blonde & Others,* ed. Donald Allen, revised edition (San Francisco: Grey Fox Press, 1998), 47. Subsequent references will be cited parenthetically within the text. The *Esquire* essay, "Aftermath: The Philosophy of the Beat Generation," was published in March 1958. Two other Kerouac essays expound a similar view of the Beats, and both are included in the anthology *Good Blonde & Others:* "Lamb, No Lion," originally published in *Pageant* (February 1958); and "The Origins of the Beat Generation," originally published in *Playboy* (June 1959).

42. Substantial clips from this interview are included in the documentary *What Happened to Kerouac?* directed by Richard Lerner and Lewis MacAdams.

43. Doreen Caravajal, "A New Generation Chases the Spirit of the Beats," *New York Times,* 11 December 1997, sec. E, p. 2.

44. Ben Brown, "Kerouac's Back: A Restless Generation Finds a Muse," *USA Today,* 19 October 1994, sec. D, p. 1.

45. Kevin Mattson, "Talking about My Generation (and the Left)," *Dissent* 46, 4 (Fall 1999): 59, 61.

46. Thomas Frank, *The Conquest of Cool: Business Culture, Counterculture, and the Rise of Hip Consumerism* (Chicago: University of Chicago Press, 1997). Interestingly, in a notable case of co-optation, *Newsweek* described Frank as a "leading Gen-X cynic," an especially ironic moniker not only given Frank's dissection of "hip consumerism," but also given that this quotation appears as a blurb, along with twenty others, in the section "Praise for *The Conquest of Cool.*" The phrase "leading Gen-X cynic" thus becomes part of the text's marketing strategy, aimed squarely at hip consumers of cultural critique.

47. Frank, x.

48. Moore, 264.

49. Ibid., 253–54. Significantly, at the conclusion of his article in *Dissent*, Kevin Mattson also cites the downward mobility of the middle class as likely to mean that Generation X "might lend an open ear to a responsible left that focuses its attention on economic inequalities" (62).

50. Certainly the most successful of the organizations mentioned, the United Students Against Sweatshops, operates in precisely this fashion, combining tried-and-true protest methods (campus sit-ins) with strategic alliances (especially with labor and human rights organizations), while maintaining their headquarters in the bastion of mainstream politics (Washington, D.C.).

51. See, for example, Pati Poblete, "Disaster Steals the Innocence of Gen X," *San Francisco Chronicle*, 13 September 2001, sec. B, p. 10; Josh Zucker, "Once-dormant Generation Grows Up to Realities and Responsibilities: Untouched by War, Gen Xers Now See Way of World," *San Francisco Chronicle*, 16 September 2001, sec. A, p. 22; Eve Modzelewski, "Exhibiting Character: Founder of Generation X Group Views September 11 as Defining Point for His Peers," *Pittsburgh Post-Gazette*, 4 October 2001, sec. E, p. 3; Les Payne, "Now Gen X Has Its Own Unifying Moment," *Newsday*, 7 October 2001, sec. B, p. 6; Audra D. S. Burch, "Tragedy, War May Define Gen X the Way Vietnam Shaped Boomers," *Miami Herald*, 17 October 2001, sec. E, p.1; William Strauss and Neil Howe, "Sept. 11 Tragedy Marks Another Turning Point," *USA Today*, 29 October 2001, sec. A, p. 15.

52. Carter was quoted in a piece by Seth Mnookin for the website Inside.com entitled "In Disaster's Aftermath, Once-Cocky Media Culture Disses the Age of Irony," posted 18 September 2001. See also David D. Kirkpatrick, "Pronouncements on Irony Draw a Line in the Sand," *New York Times*, 24 September 2001, sec. C, p. 9.

53. Roger Rosenblatt, "The Age of Irony Comes to an End," *Time*, 24 September 2001, 79.

Bibliography

Bangs, Lester. *Psychotic Reactions and Carburetor Dung.* Edited by Greil Marcus. New York: Knopf, 1987.

Barnes, Richard. *Mods!* London: Plexus, 1991.

Baudrillard, Jean. *America.* Translated by Chris Turner. New York: Verso, 1988.

Bellafante, Genia. "Generation x-cellent." *Time*, 27 February 1995, 62.

Brett, Mark. Review of *Generation X*, by Douglas Coupland. *minnesota review* 39 (Fall/Winter 1992–93): 183–185.

Brown, Ben. "Kerouac's Back: A Restless Generation Finds a Muse." *USA Today*, 19 October 1994, sec. D, p. 1.

Burch, Audra D. S. "Tragedy, War May Define Gen X the Way Vietnam Shaped Boomers." *Miami Herald*, 17 October 2001, sec. E, p. 1.

Caravajal, Doreen. "A New Generation Chases the Spirit of the Beats." *New York Times*, 11 December 1997, sec. E, p. 2.

Cohen, Jason, and Michael Krugman. *Generation Ecch!: The Backlash Starts Here.* New York: Simon and Schuster, 1994.

Coupland, Douglas. "Eulogy: Generation X'd." *Details* (June 1995): 72.

———. *Generation X: Tales for an Accelerated Culture.* New York: St. Martin's, 1991.

Dwyer, Victor. "Puberty Blues: An Author Scans a New Generation." *Maclean's*, 24 August 1992, 60.

Ellenberg, Al. Letter to the Editor. *New York Times Magazine*, 23 November 1952, 7.

Farova, Anna, ed. *Robert Capa*. New York: Paragraphic Books, 1969.

Flory, Richard, and Donald Miller, eds. *GenX Religion*. New York: Routledge, 2000.

Frank, Thomas. *The Conquest of Cool: Business Culture, Counterculture, and the Rise of Hip Consumerism*. Chicago: University of Chicago Press, 1997.

Fussell, Paul. *Class: A Guide through the American Status System*. New York: Summit, 1983.

Generation X. *Generation X: Perfect Hits 1975–1981*. Chrysalis D101950, 1991.

———. "Your Generation." Chrysalis 2165, 1977; reissued in Chrysalis D101950, 1991.

"Generation X." *Holiday*, December 1952, 41.

"Generalizations X." *Newsweek*, 6 June 1994, 62–70.

Gregory, Sophfronia Scott. Review of *Shampoo Planet*, by Douglas Coupland. *Time*, 19 October 1992, 78–79.

Hamblett, Charles, and Jane Deverson, eds. *Generation X*. Greenwich, Conn.: Fawcett, 1964.

Hanson, Peter. *The Cinema of Generation X: A Critical Study of Films and Directors*. Jefferson, N.C.: McFarland, 2002.

Hebdige, Dick. *Subculture: The Meaning of Style*. 1979. Reprint, New York: Routledge, 1987.

Hell, Richard, and the Voidoids. *Blank Generation*. Sire 9261372, 1977; reissued 1990.

Holmes, [John] Clellon. "This is the Beat Generation." *New York Times Magazine*, 16 November 1952, 10, 19–20, 22.

Howe, Neil, and William Strauss. *13th Generation*. New York: Vintage, 1993.

———. "The New Generation Gap." *Atlantic Monthly* 270 (December 1992): 67–69.

Kerouac, Jack. *Good Blonde & Others*, edited by Donald Allen. Revised edition. San Francisco: Grey Fox Press, 1998.

Kirkpatrick, David D. "Pronouncements on Irony Draw a Line in the Sand." *New York Times*, 24 September 2001, sec. C, p. 9.

Kopkind, Andrew. "Slacking Toward Bethlehem." *Grand Street* 11, 4 (1993): 177–188.

Linklater, Richard. *Slacker*. Detour Film Productions, 1991.

———. *Slacker*. New York: St. Martin's, 1992.

Liu, Eric, ed. *Next: Young American Writers on the New Generation*. New York: Norton, 1994.

Lohr, Steve. "No More McJobs for Mr. X." *New York Times*, 29 May 1994, sec. 9, p. 2.

Marcus, Greil. *Lipstick Traces: A Secret History of the Twentieth Century*. Cambridge: Harvard University Press, 1990.

Mattson, Kevin. "Talking About My Generation (and the Left)." *Dissent* 46, 4 (Fall 1999): 58–63.

Mnookin, Seth. "In Disaster's Aftermath, Once-Cocky Media Culture Disses the Age of Irony." *Inside.com*, 18 September 2001.

Modzelewski, Eve. "Exhibiting Character: Founder of Generation X Group Views September 11 as Defining Point for His Peers." *Pittsburgh Post-Gazette*, 4 October 2001, sec. E, p. 3.

Moore, Ryan. "'. . . And Tomorrow Is Just Another Crazy Scam': Postmodernity, Youth, and the Downward Mobility of the Middle Class." In *Generations of Youth: Youth Cultures and History in Twentieth-Century America*, edited by Joe Austin and Michael Nevin Willard. New York: New York University Press, 1998.

Morrison, David Ashley. "Beyond the GenX Label." *Brandweek*, 17 March 1997, 23.

Nelson, Rob, and Jon Cowan. *Revolution X: A Survival Guide for Our Generation*. New York: Penguin, 1994.

Owen, Rob. *Gen X TV: The Brady Bunch to Melrose Place*. Syracuse: Syracuse University Press, 1997.

Payne, Les. "Now Gen X Has Its Own Unifying Moment." *Newsday*, 7 October 2001, sec. B, p. 6.

Poblete, Pati. "Disaster Steals the Innocence of Gen X." *San Francisco Chronicle*, 13 September 2001, sec. B, p. 10.

"The Queen's Generation: Young People in a Changing World." *Picture Post*, 10 January 1953, 3–27.

Ratan, Suneel. "Generational Tension in the Office: Why Busters Hate Boomers." *Fortune*, 4 October 1993, 56–58.

Relyea, Lane. "What, Me Work? Lane Relyea Talks with Richard Linklater." *Artforum* 31 (April 1993): 74–77.

Richie, Karen. *Marketing to Generation X*. New York: Lexington, 1995.

Rosen, Bernard Carl. *Masks and Mirrors: Generation X and the Chameleon Personality*. Westport, Conn.: Praeger, 2001.

Rosenblatt, Roger. "The Age of Irony Comes to an End." *Time*, 24 September 2001, 79.

Rushkoff, Douglas, ed. *The Gen X Reader*. New York: Ballantine, 1994.

Savage, Jon. *England's Dreaming: Anarchy, Sex Pistols, Punk Rock, and Beyond*. New York: St. Martin's, 1992.

Star, Alexander. "The Twenty-Something Myth." *New Republic*, 4–11 January 1993, 22–25.

Strauss, William, and Neil Howe. "Sept. 11 Tragedy Marks Another Turning Point." *USA Today*, 29 October 2001, sec. A, p. 15.

Theil, Michael H. Letter to the Editor. *New York Times Magazine*, 23 November 1952, 7.

Wexler, Michael, and John Hulme, eds. *Voices of the Xiled: A Generation Speaks for Itself*. New York: Main Street, 1994.

What Happened to Kerouac? Directed by Richard Lerner and Lewis MacAdams. Fox Lorber, 1998. Videocassette.

Whelan, Richard. *Robert Capa: A Biography*. New York: Knopf, 1985.

Wurtzel, Elizabeth. *Prozac Nation: Young and Depressed in America*. New York: Houghton Mifflin, 1994.

"Youth and the World: Part I." *Holiday*, January 1953, 90–105. Text by Roger Angell.

"Youth and the World: Part II." *Holiday*, February 1953, 48–63. Text by Roger Angell.

"Youth and the World: Part III." *Holiday*, March 1953, 42–59. Text by Roger Angell.

Zinn, Laura. "Move Over Boomers: A Portrait of Generation X." *Business Week*, 14 December 1992, 74–79.

Zucker, Josh. "Once-dormant Generation Grows Up to Realities and Responsibilities: Untouched by War, Gen Xers Now See Way of World." *San Francisco Chronicle*, 16 September 2001, sec. A, p. 22.

Part 1
Music and Performance

"Alternative" Music and the Oppositional Potential of Generation X Culture

Leslie Haynsworth

> Do you have the time to listen to me whine about nothing and everything all at once?
>
> Green Day, "Basket Case," 1994

Claiming alienation and anomie as its defining characteristics, Generation X culture explicitly locates itself outside the mainstream of American culture. Gen Xers define themselves largely through their rejection of dominant American values, and typically fashion their identities through the practices and iconographies of various "oppositional" subcultures, describing themselves as deadheads, slackers, stoners, punks. But as Generation X has itself become a major cultural phenomenon, the distinctions between these subcultures and the mainstream culture against which they define themselves have to a large extent collapsed, or at least become subject to interrogation. For example, the song lyrics quoted in the epigraph to this essay offer a quintessential expression of Gen X angst through their portrait of an individual who has ironic distance on the pettiness of his woes but can't stop whining about them anyway. The lines come from a multiplatinum album, Green Day's *Dookie*, which reached the number one position on the *Rolling Stone* charts. The commercial success of previously obscure punk bands like Green Day and the Offspring is only one indication that increasingly large numbers of young Americans have come to feel that antiestablishment

Gen X philosophies speak to their own lives. Because the Generation X audience has grown so large, the culture products such as music, art, and novels that voice its philosophies have become hot commodities, and are increasingly distributed through corporate rather than subcultural channels—major record labels, for example, instead of indies. Gen X culture has, in other words, become part of the dominant culture, despite its roots in alternative subcultures that claim an oppositional relationship to the mainstream.

This shift in positioning raises potentially troubling questions about the authenticity and integrity of contemporary Gen X culture. What happens to the subversive capacity of a counterculture youth movement when its music is played on Top 40 radio and its fashion statements are reproduced for mass consumption by chain stores in suburban malls? Do the oppositional voices of punk rockers and deadheads now simply speak to a wider audience, or does the commodification of punk instead signify its co-optation by corporate America? At what point along the road to commercial success does a countercultural statement—a Green Day song, say, or a Douglas Coupland novel—lose its integrity, its ability to generate real resistance to dominant culture? Is it possible to be subversive from within the system? Such questions are invariably raised and endlessly debated by those who claim membership in various countercultural movements whenever one of "their" artists or cultural practices crosses over into the mainstream. In the alternative music scene this argument is rehashed every time an "alternative" band or artist—one whose career began in relative obscurity and whose music is, at least initially, clearly different from mainstream, Top 40 fare—achieves commercial success. This obsession with their own "authenticity," their ability to remain oppositional or countercultural even as their texts and iconographies are absorbed into the mainstream, has in fact become one of the defining characteristics of contemporary Gen Xers.

And with good reason: a culture product from the margins can stake a claim to uncompromised integrity, but it is more difficult to assess the subversive potential of statements disseminated through corporate channels. The circumstances of production can no longer suggest oppositionality in themselves, and any subversive potential in a text must originate from the author's intentions. But authors, too, become less oppositional when their position with respect to dominant culture changes: if punk is, for example, the musical expression of the disenfranchised, how authentic and credible are the rantings of punk bands like Green Day, whose music has been embraced and promoted by corporate America? Do commercially successful artists who claim countercultural status continue to express subversive values in an attempt to preserve the *appearance* of artistic integrity, to camouflage their complicity with the mandates of the corporate entertainment industry? Or is the joke finally on corporate America itself? Can bands like Green Day actually use their celebrity status to invite interrogation of the very system of which they, as major-label rock stars, are a part?

Overrehearsed as they may be, such questions are important. Given that Gen X subcultures have traditionally voiced a collective protest against mainstream American values and practices, and given that these subcultures are increasingly becoming part of the very mainstream they have always eschewed, participants in counterculture youth movements rightly worry about the credibility of their claims to oppositionality and about their ability to maintain an oppositional stance when the culture products that voice countercultural values are produced under the auspices of the corporate entertainment industry. But the various artists— like the members of R.E.M., Nirvana, and Green Day—who have emerged from subcultural enclaves into the national spotlight generally insist that this shift in status and positioning has not altered their identities or their artistic vision in any significant way.

Focusing on the alternative music scene in particular, this essay will engage the various arguments advanced in this debate, as participants in this perhaps most definitive of Generation X subcultures, recognizing and troubled by their shifting cultural positioning, attempt to maintain control over the meaning of their own culture products. Does commercial success invariably signal capitulation to mainstream tastes and ideologies, making the culture product a controlled, co-opted product of industry norms? Or can a truly "pure" oppositional stance actually be promoted from within dominant culture? This question has become fraught with particular anxiety when the culture product under consideration is alternative music, because this music initially *was* the textual representation of a small subculture that was clearly disenfranchised from the mainstream. Throughout the 1980s, alternative bands almost always recorded for small independent record labels, never had "hit" songs or albums, and received little mention in the mainstream music press. In the 1990s, however, the very term "alternative music" became

ironic if not virtually oxymoronic: with the tremendous commercial success of bands like R.E.M., U2, and Nirvana, "alternative" became another category of mainstream music product, like classic rock, rap, or
soul. In other words, alternative music is no longer inherently alternative, and determining the ramifications of its incorporation into dominant culture is crucial to an understanding of just how oppositional, or
at least non–co-opted, contemporary Gen X culture really can be. Do
commercialized representations of an "alternative" ethic (like the commercially successful "slacker punk" records of Green Day and the Offspring), have any kind of authentic relationship to the practices and beliefs of the subcultures in which they claim their roots?

I suggest that they do. Subcultural ideologies can in fact emanate
from within dominant culture despite the fact that incorporation into
the mainstream entails a loss of explicitly oppositional *positioning*. However, any subversive potential that commercialized "alternative" rock
does have derives, ironically, from the subculture's insistence that it *cannot* have such potential. In other words, it is the very argument that any
initially alternative artist who achieves commercial success has sold out
to corporate America that in fact gives such artists leverage to attain such
success without compromising their subcultural ideals. Using Marxist
cultural theory as intertext, I argue that the alternative music subculture
demands that the authenticity of any oppositional culture product be
judged by its ability to reproduce the ideologies and iconographies of
the subculture from which it claims to originate. Through repeated invo-
cations of the dreaded term "selling out," the alternative music subculture has held its more commercially successful artists accountable for
the terms on which they achieve their success. These artists and the
culture industry itself have responded to this pressure by virtually bend-
ing over backwards to demonstrate that a counterculture stance *can* be
advanced from within dominant culture. Alternative bands whose music
has entered the mainstream are invariably represented in the mainstream press in terms of their ability to continue to reproduce subcultural ideologies, despite the fact that they have lost their marginal position. The subculture has, in other words, forced the culture industry
itself to promote, and even play up, the oppositional beliefs and practices of "alternative" bands in order to prove that these bands have not
lost their integrity. Consequently, beliefs and practices that initially ad-

hered only to small subcultural enclaves can and often do enter and reshape the nexus of mainstream American youth culture.

Examining the history of "alternative" music and the ways it has been assessed both by its original fans and by the mainstream media over the last decade or so, is thus a useful way into a discussion of the fate of Generation X itself as a youth movement that can continue to offer genuine alternatives to mainstream ideologies and values. Through readings of the different arguments made by various participants in the endless media discussion about the "integrity" of the music produced by commercially successful "alternative" artists like R.E.M., Nirvana, and Green Day, I propose that while Gen X culture may have lost the appearance of authenticity that stems from occupying an explicitly marginal position, Gen X ideologies retain their capacity to enter the mainstream relatively intact. But it is this very anxiety about the loss of its subcultural status, this angst-filled flurry of discussion about co-optation and selling out, that has given Gen X culture what leverage it has to infiltrate dominant culture without losing its oppositional identity.

> Pretty much if you don't have the video with the beautiful people in it and the dramatic story line, and if you don't have the single—that one kind of Dianne Warren song to put it through the big machine in the big studios that makes it sound like everything else—and if you're not cute, and we're not very cute, it is hard to make it in America.
>
> Kim Deal of the Pixies, 1990

> If we get mass exposure, it'll be because radio bent to us, not the other way around.
>
> Michael Stipe of R.E.M., 1983

> "Alternative" finally lands on the far side of the mainstream when Nine Inch Nails plays at halftime of the Super Bowl. The grand finale: As a pack of 1,000 wild dogs are unleashed on the crowd, Trent Reznor, Bobby McFerrin, Billy Ray Cyrus, Janet Jackson, Hammer, and 500 Special Olympians scream, "I want to fuck you like an animal."
>
> *Magnet* magazine "prediction" for the future of alternative rock, 1995

The year 1994 was, depending on which music magazine you read, either "The Year Punk Broke" (*Spin,* November 1994) or "The Year Punk

Got Broken" (*Magnet,* January 1995). It was, in other words, either the year mainstream youth culture got a little more hip when it discovered the punk sounds and punk ethos of bands like Green Day and the Offspring, or the year these bands "sold out," betraying the antiestablishment spirit of the subculture from which they claim to originate by deliberately pandering to mainstream tastes. Punk is not supposed to be popular. Loud and angry, it is, in fact, supposed to alienate most listeners. A profile of the North Carolina band Blue Green Gods in the indie-rock magazine *Puncture* approvingly notes, for example, that "in true punk rock fashion, Blue Green Gods have an endearing legacy of room ventilation. 'We've run them out the door all up and down the coast,' says Todd. Anne adds, 'People have said we're the worst band they've ever seen. Even shows where we've played really well, they just don't get the music.'"[1] Blue Green Gods have earned punk rock credibility, *Puncture* suggests, precisely through the inaccessibility of their music, which can make even an initially receptive audience flee in confusion.

But in 1994, punk became popular. Green Day's *Dookie* and the Offspring's *Smash* both went multiplatinum, spawning videos that went into heavy rotation on MTV and songs that topped the charts at commercial radio stations. Other punk bands like Rancid and Bad Religion suddenly found themselves being heavily courted by major record labels. Rancid's Tim Armstrong reports that Madonna even went so far as to send his band a nude photo of her as part of her effort to sign them to her Maverick label.[2] Like grunge a few years earlier, punk was suddenly the next big thing.

But far from being cause for celebration, this newfound popularity of their music put punk musicians in an uncomfortable position: true punks should, like Blue Green Gods, be running audiences out of the room, not attracting them in ever increasing numbers. A July 1995 write-up on Rancid in *Details* presents the band's situation as a sort of catch-22: "If Rancid don't sign autographs, they're assholes. If they get too successful, they're sellouts. Punk-rock fans demand that their heroes walk this fine line" (113). Signing autographs feels to Rancid like a betrayal of the punk ethos because "punk rock is about being equal with the audience and with everybody else, being a regular guy singing about regular things" (113). But, however unwillingly, the members of Rancid have become celebrities, and this status in itself threatens to negate their punk rock credibility.

Details revels in the ironies caused by the band's changing status, enthusing, "Rancid make punk the old-fashioned way. They live it. Three years ago they were Berkeley street kids. Now they're taking meetings with Madonna and turning down million-dollar record deals" (110). Punk would seem to be moving up in the world. But interviewer Seven McDonald is at pains to demonstrate that Rancid's increasing popularity has not compromised their punk rock integrity. "If [Green Day's] Billie Joe Armstrong has become the punk next door," she asserts, "Tim Armstrong (no relation) is the genuine article. His band plays fervent, populist, idealistic punk rock. . . . At twenty-nine, he has formed an identity rooted in the traditions of rebel music. . . . He turned down a $1.5 million record deal with a major label to stay with the indie punk label Epitaph. Green Day and the Offspring may have made punk rock clean and slick, but Rancid has brought back the street credibility" (112).

McDonald here establishes Rancid's "credibility" largely by defining them as more "authentically" punk than their more commercially successful punk rock brethren. But, significantly, more than their music itself, which is described only in passing in the *Details* article, what gives Rancid this punk credibility is their *behavior* in the face of incipient stardom: their refusal to sign with a major label and their reluctance to abandon the low-rent lifestyle out of which punk is supposed to be born. "'Punk rock is working-class music,'" notes Rancid guitarist Lars Frederiksen, and McDonald maintains that, "unlike some punk bands from the 1980s, Rancid were never middle class poseurs" (112). All the band's members, she points out, come from true working-class roots. Moreover, they remain attached to these roots even now that the volume of their record sales would allow them to adopt more luxurious lifestyles. For example, "even though Rancid was the focus of a highly publicized bidding war, Tim's lifestyle has changed little since then. He still lives in the same place he's lived for four years, a large Berkeley apartment with nine other punk rock kids. . . . Crack dealers hang out around the corner" (113). Although Rancid's second album, *Let's Go,* nearly went gold (meaning it sold almost five hundred thousand copies), "The only thing [Armstrong's] bought for himself is a walkman. 'I never had money my whole life,' he says. 'I honestly don't know what to do with it'" (113). Rancid have earned their "street credibility" by clinging hard and fast to a disenfranchised, working-class identity. "'I grew up knowing I was a freak,'" says Armstrong, who also asserts that, "'I am different. I'm not like you. I'm fucked up. I do what I want. I ain't gonna rip nobody off, but at the same time I ain't gonna follow any rule book'" (112). Such statements suggest a quintessentially punk ethos, yet Rancid's increasing popularity still makes their integrity an issue, to the extent that McDonald concludes her piece by allowing Armstrong this parting shot: "'I keep waiting for someone to call me a sell-out to my face,' says Tim, 'so I can say, "Did *you* ever turn down a million and a half dollars? I have'" (113).

Bands like Rancid that emerge from subcultural enclaves into the mainstream have to work hard to prove their growing fan bases don't make them sellouts, because alternative music subcultures have traditionally viewed popular music as a highly controlled culture product, shaped less by artistic vision than by industry norms. Jeff Calder of the Swimming Pool Q's—who calls his own rock 'n' roll career a "journey along the margins of America's Pop Republic"—puts it this way, "America's radio stations may once have been laboratories of experiment, but at the squalid dawn of the Reagan/Bush era they were ruled by formula."[3] Consequently, Calder asserts, while "visionary artists are still out there . . . the stream of rampant invention has lost access to the 'mainstream': the powerful radio systems of America" (272). The alternative music subculture began to cohere in the 1980s as, in response to the very crisis Calder identifies, college radio stations and a small cadre of listeners banded together to promote artists whose music was excluded from increasingly unadventurous commercial radio playlists. Representing just what its name suggests—an alternative to the mainstream—the genre had no distinctive sound; rather, it encompassed a tremendous range of musical styles: the hardcore of Hüsker Dü and the Minutemen; the garage rock of the Replacements and the Lyres; the guitar jangle of R.E.M. and Let's Active; the gothic rock of Bauhaus and Sisters of Mercy; and the synthesizer pop of Depeche Mode and Orchestral Manoeuvres in the Dark. The one thing all of these highly diverse bands had in common was that their music was deemed inaccessible to mainstream audiences who, as Calder puts it, had come "to expect and accept popular music of little vitality or depth" (273). Despite their many differences, in other words, these bands all shared alternative status. Alternative music was thus by definition not a particular musical style or practice but simply music that was too innovative, avant-garde, or political for mainstream tastes.

Given that a highly diverse range of artists historically share a common classification as "alternative" only because they all also share marginal status in the music world, it is easy to see why alternative artists and alternative music fans have been so quick to label any band that does cross over into the mainstream a "sellout." Anthony DeCurtis asserts that in the 1980s—when the lines between "alternative" and "commercial" rock were still clearly defined—artists virtually had to sell out to succeed: "Being a rock & roll star became a job" in the 1980s, DeCurtis maintains, "and true to the 1980s ethic, you'd better be willing to put in the hours and produce—to smile and make nice with the powers that be—or you might as well go back to the bars."[4] Kim Deal's reference in the epigraph above to a production process that makes a song "sound like everything else" and her suggestion that bands have to be cute "to make it in America" thus reflects a common belief among indie rock fans and musicians alike that commercial success in the music business stems less from an artist's talent or vision and more from his or her ability to replicate a preexisting commercial style and to play the corporate game, to be willing, for example, to make "the video with the beautiful people in it."[5] Deal offers these remarks as an explanation for her own band's failure to produce hit records despite the fact that they had always been critical darlings. The Pixies, she suggests, have languished in relative obscurity not despite but precisely because of their innovations and iconoclasm.

When Deal gave this assessment of the music industry in 1990, it was more or less accurate to the extent that alternative bands like the Pixies (such as Hüsker Dü, the Replacements, or Sonic Youth), whose music was lauded by critics and played heavily on college radio stations, were nevertheless ignored by commercial radio and the general public. But things changed in 1991, when indie darlings R.E.M., whose popularity had been growing slowly but steadily for nearly a decade, finally put out the breakthrough record *Out of Time* that catapulted to the top of the charts and received substantial Top 40 airplay, making R.E.M. one of the most commercially successful acts of the year. Months later, the boundaries between "alternative" and "mainstream" music were irrevocably blurred when Seattle grunge rockers Nirvana who, unlike R.E.M., were virtual newcomers even on the alternative scene, released their second album, *Nevermind,* which became one of the biggest selling records of 1992. Despite their commercial success, it was difficult to accuse either R.E.M. or Nirvana of willfully "selling out"; no one, from Nirvana's small group of original fans to the corporate moguls at the major label to which they'd just signed, expected *Nevermind* to achieve such phenomenal sales, because it sounded nothing like any of the other hit records out there at the time. R.E.M. "gradually built an audience through relentless touring and an inspiring refusal to compromise with the more absurd edicts of the music industry," according to DeCurtis, and the group remains "to this day . . . a model of how a young band can remain true to its own idiosyncratic vision and still reach large numbers of listeners."[6] The members of R.E.M. themselves had always insisted that fame and fortune were never their main objectives. When asked about the band's raison d'être in a 1985 interview, bassist Mike Mills replied, "We do it because around the corner is another thrill, not another thousand bucks."[7] Nor was the band interested in courting a commercial audience; in the words of guitarist Peter Buck, "The greatest music has always been made by individuals from unique standpoints without commercial considerations."[8]

R.E.M., Nirvana, and numerous other bands that got their start in the alternative music enclave have now gotten "mass exposure." So who bent toward whom? These bands' success would seem to belie Deal's assertion that popularity is achieved only through capitulation to industry norms. But given that so many indie rock "greats" like the Pixies and Hüsker Dü never got the kind of mass recognition achieved by R.E.M. and Nirvana, the cynicism of die-hard alternative fans is understandable. Did alternative rock create its own ever-increasing audience primarily through its own merits, finally attracting a large enough fan base that the mainstream music industry could no longer afford to ignore them? Or did bands like R.E.M. and Nirvana (and after them, Smashing Pumpkins, Soundgarden, Green Day, and the Offspring) sell out after all by making their music increasingly accessible to mainstream tastes?

Defenders of these bands and of the music industry itself insist that the recent success of "alternative" musicians represents a revitalization of contemporary music, and maintain that these artists have achieved commercial success largely on their own terms. "It must truly be morning in America," rhapsodizes *Spin*'s review of a December 1994 Green Day concert.[9] Marveling at the sight of "a phalanx of station wagons disgorging what one usher proudly called 'the cream of Long Island'" outside the concert hall, Michael Azerrad asserts, "Call 'em corporate punks, but face it: It's amazing how little Green Day's huge popularity has diluted its undeniable subversiveness. A few years ago, these same suburban concertgoers would have been seeing Poison or Warrant instead of hearing Billie Joe whine about jerkin' off, gettin' high, and growing up" (101). Green Day's popularity among suburbanites, as Azerrad sees it, represents a sort of revolution of American youth culture: rather than meekly accepting the slickly packaged music product fed to them by the music industry (Poison, Warrant), kids today are eagerly embracing bands whose oppositional stance remains undiminished by their popularity.

But the belief that artistic integrity and commercial success are mutually exclusive has died hard. Alternative music fans continue to assert that any commercially successful music is necessarily a controlled, co-opted product of industry norms, and that only bands that remain willfully obscure can have the kind of artistic integrity R.E.M wants to claim for itself. In her 1992 *Sassy* interview with Nirvana frontman Kurt Cobain, Christina Kelly remarks that "alternative rock fans have a way of slagging their favorite fans once they get famous," and Cobain agrees, recalling that he recently heard a college radio DJ go on "this half-hour rant about how Nirvana is so obviously business oriented and just because we have colored hair does not mean we are alternative. And I felt really terrible. Because there is nothing in the world I like more than underground music."[10] Cobain goes on to assert, as Azerrad does about Green Day, that his band's popularity is actually a positive sign for the future of the alternative rock ethos: "To be shunned by the claim that just because you are playing the corporate game you are not honest? You use [corporate America] to your advantage. You fight them by joining them" (83). But indie rock fans by and large continue to be suspicious of and reject this logic; reader mail in response to a favorable cover story on the Offspring in the March 1995 issue of *Spin* is typical: "[Offspring singer] Dexter Holland's comments only prove how much of a schmuck he really is. . . . I hope the Offspring do sign to a major label because Epitaph does not need them and punk rock does not want them." Another reader writes, "Chuck Eddy's testimonial on the Offspring has got to be the most moronic pile of horse-nonsense I've ever read. . . . Don't sell yourself short, Chuck. I know you can be not only the most mindless writer for *Spin* but also the most mindless writer for all of America's corporate (gasp!) magazines."[11] Because the Offspring

have embraced their mainstream audience and because they are glow-
ingly written up in publications like *Spin,* these readers suggest, they
have lost their punk rock credibility.

To a certain extent, this bickering about the implications of alternative music's newfound capacity to infiltrate the mainstream seems irrelevant given that the incorporation of alternative bands into the dominant
music culture now seems to be an irrevocable process. But the central
question being debated here is one that has occupied Marxist cultural
theorists for years: can subcultural groups actually infiltrate and change
the dominant culture in significant and meaningful ways, or is any culture product that is disseminated though mainstream channels itself altered and sanitized as it gets incorporated into the dominant culture?
The answer to this question actually derives from the way participants
on each side of the debate attempt to control the meaning of the text
in question—in this case, the music of bands like R.E.M., Nirvana, and
Green Day. As in the assessment of Rancid in *Details,* discussion of the
work of bands who have moved from subcultures into the dominant
culture is typically focused less on the music itself than on where it
comes from. We are, in other words, encouraged to determine the
"meaning" of this music through our knowledge of who is producing it
and how they are positioned with respect to dominant culture. Thus,
while bands like R.E.M. and the mainstream media that supports them
seek to draw our attention to portraits of the musicians themselves as
creative and iconoclastic individuals whose artistic vision remains unal-
tered by the circumstances surrounding the production of their music,
the alternative music subculture instead insists that these very circumstances of production *are* the determining factor by which the music
should be judged. The former position thus paints a picture of a static
artistic vision that, through its own merits and integrity, gets incorporated into a fluid and accommodating dominant culture, while the latter
suggests dominant culture is static and inflexible and that any band that
finds itself a part of this dominant culture has itself changed, allowing
its once unique perspective to be compromised by its accommodation
of mainstream norms.

The subculture, then, denies that its ideas, perspective, and cultural
output have any influence whatsoever on what dominant American culture looks like. I'll explore both why this claim carries such force and
how it actually functions to prove its proponents wrong. The argument

that any voice or cultural product disseminated through mainstream channels is necessarily compromised echoes the assessments of the modern culture industry advanced by Frankfurt School Marxists. In *Dialectic of Enlightenment,* for example, Max Horkheimer and Theodor Adorno contend that in capitalist society the task of the artist is "always to fit into business life as an aesthetic expert. Formerly, like Kant and Hume, they signed their letters 'your most humble and obedient servant,' and undermined the foundations of throne and altar. Today they address heads of government by their first names, yet in every artistic activity they are subject to their illiterate masters."[12] The change Horkheimer and Adorno identify and find so troubling is one of positioning: in precapitalist times all artists were explicitly "outsiders" who could therefore speak the truth as they saw it, unencumbered by their own investments in preserving the status quo. In modern society, however, many artists enjoy prestige, which is conferred from within "the system," and the imperatives of capitalist economies determine which artists will be granted such prestige. Any artistic voice that is disseminated through mainstream channels is thus necessarily compromised by its adherence to the rules of what Horkheimer and Adorno dub "the iron system" (120). Only voices from the margins have any artistic integrity, but these voices have no impact on dominant culture because "not to conform is to be rendered powerless" (133), in other words, to be shut out from communally-sanctioned artistic discourse. This assessment of modern culture sets up an either/or dialectic whereby artists and their work are either outside and oppositional or inside and co-opted by the system. The value of a text is thus determined by the way in which it is disseminated.

In contemporary cultural studies, the Frankfurt School model has largely been revised by the work of more recent theorists like Raymond Williams, who notes the existence of "emergent" cultural practices that develop in subcultural enclaves but can make their way into the dominant culture. As such practices create a rumbling around the margins, Williams explains, "the dominant culture [may reach] out to transform, or seek to transform, them. In this process, of course, the dominant culture itself changes, not in its central formation, but in many of its articulated features. But then in a modern society it must always change in this way, if it is to remain dominant, if it is still to be felt in real ways central in all our many activities and interests."[13] In other words, if a particular subculture's artistic output does begin to stir up more general interest, mainstream culture is virtually compelled to respond by embracing and replicating the subculture's texts and iconographies, or it will readily be perceived as inflexible and incapable of adapting to shifts in public tastes. This model does not deny that subcultural artistic practices will in all probability be impacted upon by the mandates of the culture industry in the process of incorporation, but in proposing that accommodation is a two-way street, Williams does interrogate Horkheimer and Adorno's claim that incorporation necessarily signifies simple co-optation. More importantly, Williams's account of the relationship between subcultures and the dominant culture allows for the possibility that subcultures can, albeit in perhaps limited ways, reshape the dominant culture in their own image.

But precisely because subcultures, by definition, reject or protest against mainstream values and tastes, their members remain invested in the belief that their own cultural output has value only insofar as it remains marginal with respect to the dominant culture. Thus the alternative music scene fetishizes iconoclasm. Consequently, so too does the music industry. Michael Jarrett notes that in music culture, "descriptions of conventionalization typically, perhaps always, employ a rhetoric of degeneration. They chart it as a downward course, a semiotic diaspora, and rely on readers decoding such a journey Platonically, as a deviation from the Good. Hence, popularization receives a plot—tragedy—and thereby the very notion of the authentic (pure code) is erected as something opposed to the conventional (popularized code)."[14] Because music consumers value "authenticity" and understand the authentic as the opposite of the popular, the corporate music industry is anxious to attach alternative rather than popular status to the "good" bands it promotes. As Jarrett observes, "We must remember that the music industry organizes itself around certain naturalized oppositions. It has a discourse. It speaks. Industrialization, through institutions such as radio, music publishing and licensing, and recording, sanctioned the antithesis that holds that 'authentic' music is something distinct from 'commercial' music. We consumers, in turn, inherit—organize our thinking by means of—this and other antitheses. . . . The assumption that bad (commercial) things happen to "authentic" music is sufficient to generate the real/fake distinction that has become musical common sense" (172). In other words, because subcultural output appears untainted by commercial considerations, authenticity is widely perceived in rock culture as a product of outsider status. The "integrity" and prestige this perception bestows upon "alternative" bands thus becomes a kind of cultural capital that the music industry itself exploits when it promotes bands with subcultural roots. Our tendency to value iconoclasm, Jarrett notes, "creates a consumer who understands the history of rock as a series of authentic moments that deteriorated into conventionalized moments, transforming the music into a field of 'commercial' imitations of some real thing, and it prompts histories organized around the proper names of acknowledged innovators" (172).

"Authenticity" sells records. Paradoxically, the music industry "literally banks on—makes money off" (172) of the belief that "corporate" rock is a bastardized and inferior version of the "real thing." But in order to preserve the appearance of authenticity, the industry and the "corporate" magazines *(Rolling Stone, Spin, Details)* that support it need to embrace the figure of the iconoclastic artist as a producer of music on his or her own terms. Thus, a 1992 *Rolling Stone* cover story on R.E.M. opens with the statement that "for R.E.M. the past twelve months have been the Year of the Big Music Biz Awards, and there's a small mountain of them piled in a corner of the band's office in Athens, Georgia. They're all still wrapped in their cardboard packing gathering dust, and they're all addressed to R.E.M. vocalist Michael Stipe, who couldn't care less."[15] In the semiotics of rock criticism, Stipe's artistic integrity stems as much, if not more, from this disinterestedness in corporate accolades as from the innovations of his band's music itself.

Alternative music fans are perhaps rightly suspicious of such claims of indifference on the part of crossover artists—if Stipe is so truly unconcerned with popular opinion or corporate promotion of his work, why did he agree to be interviewed in *Rolling Stone*? (Likewise, if Rancid's Tim Armstrong is so proud of having turned down major label record deals, what prompted him to pose for the cover of a "corporate" magazine like *Details*?) Such contradictions in self-presentation are likely only to increase the cynicism of readers who already view the culture industry, and the artists it embraces, with a jaded eye.

Nevertheless, by promoting these artists' countercultural stances, the corporate music industry and the mainstream music press *are* disseminating—and more importantly, endorsing—subcultural values, practices, and iconographies. Although, as Jarrett points out, the music industry co-opts and cashes in on our desire for the kind of "authenticity" that derives from an alternative musical practice, the fact remains that it is the various alternative music subcultures themselves that determine how "alternative" is defined. When *Details* makes so much of Rancid's "street credibility," they are directly replicating an ethos developed within the punk counterculture. And they are furthermore selling that ethos to the masses as a marker of artistic integrity and of countercultural hipness, encouraging fans both to admire and to emulate it. Thus, even as alternative music subcultures witness the transformation of their artistic output into mainstream fare, their practices and iconographies are, at least to a certain extent, also transforming mainstream youth culture. Green Day's Billie Joe Armstrong may be, as McDonald puts it, "the punk next door"—a more wholesome, cleaned-up version of the "real thing"—but Azerrad has a point when he asserts that, from a countercultural perspective, Armstrong as rock icon is a definite improvement over the members of Poison or Warrant. Green Day is clearly not the most radical or subversive band in punk rock history. But their emergence into the mainstream does make core punk values more palatable to a wider audience. And yet, paradoxically, it is precisely because die-hard punk rockers and the alternative music media continue to decry commercially successful "alternative" bands like Green Day that the music industry works so hard to promote these bands' most subversive qualities.

Magnet's mock "prediction" that Nine Inch Nails frontman Trent Reznor will soon be screaming his abrasive lyrics at the Super Bowl along with the likes of Billy Ray Cyrus, Janet Jackson, and Hammer (all of whom are widely perceived as sellouts) registers legitimate distress over the way "alternative" artists in increasing numbers are coming to seem like corporate tools. But this very concern over a kind of "authenticity" puts a tremendous amount of pressure on the corporate music industry to "prove" that it has not co-opted the alternative bands it incorporates. The discursive portraits of bands like R.E.M. and Rancid in mainstream magazines like *Rolling Stone* and *Details* suggest that dominant culture is in this respect very much subject to pressure from the margins. When the alternative music subculture reproduces the Frankfurt School's logic by insisting that "good" means "outside the system," they create a persuasive rhetoric that compels the culture industry to respond by demonstrating its capacity to allow for difference and subversion from within. This means that the culture industry is less tyranni-cal and monolithic than either the Frankfurt School or the alternative music scene would have us believe. It also suggests that, accurate or not, the "inside equals co-opted" argument is precisely what gives sub-cultures leverage to challenge and influence mainstream culture. To the extent that commercially successful "alternative" bands have achieved success on their own terms, they have done so largely because of their original fans' insistence that such an accomplishment is impossible.

Generation X itself, as a countercultural youth movement that em-braces a variety of alternative subcultures, faced the same kind of iden-tity crisis experienced by the alternative music scene when the corporate culture industry became interested in its output. The increasing absorp-tion of Gen X values and practices into mainstream youth culture signi-fies a perhaps irrevocable loss of pure countercultural status, which is troubling for a movement that is self-defined through its oppositional stance. But the history of alternative rock's incorporation into the music mainstream suggests that this kind of shift in a subculture's relationship with the dominant culture in fact gives the subculture leverage to infil-trate and reshape the dominant culture largely on its own terms. While I don't deny that a lot of the meaning a subculture attaches to its own culture products may get lost in the process of packaging these products for a mass audience, it is nevertheless the subcultures themselves that by and large retain the power to determine what constitutes "authentic," and hence valuable, cultural output. In this respect, Gen Xers have the capacity to assert control over the values attached to the culture prod-ucts that bear the "Generation X" label even as the corporate culture industry gains increasing control over the circumstances of their produc-tion.

Notes

1. Fred Mills, "Gods in Their Own Time," *Puncture* 27 (Summer 1993): 6.
2. Seven McDonald, "The Next Big Stink," *Details* (July 1995): 112.
3. Jeff Calder, "Living by Night in the Land of Opportunity: Observations on Life in a Rock & Roll Band," *Present Tense: Rock & Roll Culture,"* ed. Anthony DeCurtis (Durham: Duke University Press, 1992), 271, 274.
4. Anthony DeCurtis, "The Eighties," *Present Tense: Rock & Roll Culture,* ed. An-thony DeCurtis (Durham: Duke University Press, 1992), 5.
5. Quoted in Joseph Woodard, "Palatialized Rock-onteurs," 40.
6. DeCurtis, "The Eighties," 9.

7. David Fricke, "R.E.M.'s Southern-Fried Art," *Rolling Stone*, 5 March 1992, 50.

8. Jon Young, "R.E.M.: From the Earth to the Moon," *Trouser Press* 10, no. 6 (August 1983): 31.

9. Michael Azerrad, "Green Day," *Spin* 10, no. 12 (March 1995): 101.

10. Christina Kelly, "Kurt and Courtney Sitting in a Tree," *Sassy*, April 1992, 83.

11. "Point Blank: Letters," *Spin* 11 no. 3 (June 1995): 24.

12. Max Horkheimer and Theodor Adorno, *Dialectic of Enlightenment* (New York: Continuum, 1987), 133.

13. Raymond Williams, *Problems in Materialism and Culture* (London: Verso, 1980), 45.

14. Michael Jarrett, "Concerning the Progress of Rock & Roll," *Present Tense: Rock & Roll Culture*," ed. Anthony DeCurtis (Durham: Duke University Press, 1992), 168.

15. Michael Fricke, "R.E.M.: Artist of the Year," *Rolling Stone*, 5 March 1992, 45.

Bibliography

Azerrad, Michael. "Green Day." *Spin* 10, no.12 (March 1995): 101.

Calder, Jeff. "Living by Night in the Land of Opportunity: Observations on Life in a Rock & Roll Band." In *Present Tense: Rock & Roll Culture*, edited by Anthony DeCurtis, 271–301. Durham: Duke University Press, 1992.

DeCurtis, Anthony. "The Eighties." *Present Tense: Rock & Roll Culture*, edited by Anthony DeCurtis, 1–12. Durham: Duke University Press, 1992.

Fricke, David. "R.E.M.: Artist of the Year." *Rolling Stone*, 5 March 1992, 45.

———. "R.E.M.'s Southern-Fried Art." *Rolling Stone*, 7 November 1985, 49–50.

Green Day. *Dookie*. Reprise Records, 1994.

Jarrett, Michael. "Concerning the Progress of Rock & Roll." *Present Tense: Rock & Roll Culture*, edited by Anthony DeCurtis, 167–82. Durham: Duke University Press, 1992.

Kelly, Christina. "Kurt and Courtney Sitting in a Tree." *Sassy*, April 1992, 50.

Horkheimer, Max and Theodor Adorno. *Dialectic of Enlightenment*. New York: Continuum, 1987.

McDonald, Seven. "The Next Big Stink." *Details*, July 1995, 110.

Mills, Fred. "Gods in Their Own Time." *Puncture* 27 (Summer 1993): 6.

"Point Blank: Letters." *Spin* 11, no. 3 (June 1995): 24.

Sheridan, Phil. "Looking Back at 1995." *Magnet* 3, no. 1 (January 1995): 58.

Williams, Raymond. *Problems in Materialism and Culture*. London: Verso, 1980.

Woodard, Joseph. "Palatialized Rock-onteurs." *Santa Barbara Independent* 5, no. 213 (December 1990): 40.

Young, Jon. "R.E.M.: From the Earth to the Moon." *Trouser Press* 10, no. 6 (August 1983): 28–31.

Jigsaw Youth versus Generation X and Postmodernism

Neil Nehring

In 1991, the same year that Douglas Coupland's novel *Generation X* was published, academics who follow popular music (myself included) began to notice a peculiar phenomenon. As Andrew Goodwin described it at the time, "One of the most bizarre developments in the brief history of media and cultural studies is the way in which abstruse French theory has 'trickled down' into the popular consciousness, . . . so that the word 'postmodern' reached record stores, magazines and television programs just a few years after it entered the academy."[1] I was tracking at the same time a more specific postmodern notion that had begun to spread from purportedly radical academic work into music journalism: an insistence that any expression of rebellion in contemporary culture is inauthentic, merely a pose. According to this notion it is impossible for any emotional appeal in a commercial medium like popular music to be anything but a prostituted imposture, whether Kurt Cobain's vitriol or Michael Bolton's treacle.

There are actually two closely related ideas here: 1) all expression, even the most rebellious forms, is in one way or another tamed and made completely inauthentic by its "incorporation" into multinational corporate capitalism; 2) the transparent phoniness of a performer's emotional commitment makes it impossible for anyone to take the performance seriously and to make any commitment in return. An excuse for ridicule in the establishment press, the incorporation thesis has been a source of usually well-intentioned concern as well as hip cynicism in the music press. This particular postmodern argument has had a great deal of influence on contemporary literature about youth, as well, including Coupland's *Generation X*. In that novel, as in music journalism, an antagonism with roots in late 1970s punk rock—itself entirely vitiated by incorporation, according to the most prominent academic diagnostician of postmodernism, Fredric Jameson—is infused with a cynicism clearly derived from theories such as his. Bret Easton Ellis's hyper-jaded 1985 novel *Less Than Zero*, often cited with Coupland's, took its title from a 1977 Elvis Costello song; punk plus postmodern enervation, we will see, in essence equals Generation X.

That the mass media have exploited academic accounts of postmodernism indicates the usefulness of postmodernism in denying the authenticity of expressions of anger and discontent. The sad thing about the situation is this complicity, whether on the part of the academic originals or their (somewhat) younger epigones. (*Spin* was still quoting Jameson in the year 2000, while ridiculing people who find anything authentic in Harry Smith's *Anthology of American Folk Music.*) Since the 1950s and the coinage of the term "teenager," the dominant media in the age of consumerism have continually parlayed a general moral anxiety into "moral panics" over youthful "folk devils" (as sociologist Stanley Cohen put it when writing on mods and rockers in Britain in the 1960s)—at the same time hypocritically employing celebratory images of youth to denote the quasi revolutionary newness and the rejuvenating power of commodities. In the 1990s, however, smug ridicule, rather than fear and hysteria, was the stock-in-trade of the establishment thanks to the postmoderns. The 1990s variant of Generation X, unsurprisingly, appears in retrospect to have been dead on arrival. But the cynical postmodern ideas and attitudes that Gen X shared with the culture-at-large remain commonplaces that must be resisted.

In that respect, the first point that must be made, contrary to the impression created by the fairly recent discovery of the incorporation thesis, is that the ideas contained in it aren't really "post-modern" at all. Since the eighteenth century and the birth of modern aesthetics (or the philosophy of art), academics and other intellectuals have held that meaningless emotional appeals—"barbaric" appeals, according to Immanuel Kant's influential *Critique of Judgment* (1790)—are characteristic of the low or popular arts produced by the marketplace. This loathing of emotion follows the general philosophical view (until very recently) that emotion belongs to the body, and thus is no guide whatsoever to understanding. Emotion is inferior to reason, from this view, which is not to say that the passions are without power since they presumably always threaten to overcome the mind. This fear of the disruptive power of emotion is as much political as philosophical, always bearing at some level a concern over subordinate groups getting out of control. The fields of aesthetics and philosophy, as a result, have traditionally been self-contradictory, seeking to control the danger posed by insubordinate emotions by deriding them for their supposed weakness. The more specific argument that has come down to us as "postmodern" is that the mindlessness of emotions means that their causes can never adequately be articulated, whether in art or in life. By applying the traditional negative view of emotion to youth culture, "postmodern" academics and their journalist epigones find the expression of anger and resentment crippled by commercialization.

The best antidote to postmodernism can be found in feminist philosophical work on emotion, which strongly defends anger even in its "half-formed" stages. Feminist philosophy provides an entirely different perspective on angry music like that of the riot grrrls, whose punk rock is founded on much the same confidence in the educative power of emotion, and includes an explicit repudiation of postmodern cynicism. Feminist philosophy has developed over the last decade a compelling case for the inherent rationality of emotions by using "cognitivism" (in philosophy) and "social constructionism" (in psychology) to make the case for the interdependence of emotion and reason. Proponents argue persuasively that emotion always results from appraising or judging a social situation, and thus contributes significantly to reason. Feminist philosophers argue further that emotions are indivisibly a matter of the body and the mind, of physical responses and articulated judgment. The causes of emotion do need to be articulated, or rationalized. Otherwise emotions like anger can wind up directed at the wrong objects, as is the case when the perfectly reasonable resentment of less privileged white males, after the ravages of the class war being waged by the wealthy, takes the form of racism and sexism.

Perhaps the most influential of academic postmodernists with regard to denigrating emotion is Fredric Jameson. One of his central theses in the oft-cited 1984 essay "Postmodernism, or the Cultural Logic of Late Capitalism," proposes that a general "waning of affect" has occurred in postmodern life, most evident in a diminished emotional engagement with the arts. In the case of mass culture, Jameson does not mean that emotions are not available, but that their impact lacks any "depth." On the face of it, he seems to argue that through sheer inundation by mass entertainment, we've become jaded as our visceral responses have waned. We don't shock easily if at all anymore, though we may go through the charade of claiming we are still roused from time to time. What the loss of depth actually implies, however, is an absence of intellectual reflection, in keeping with the traditional view of intellectual passivity in the mass audience.

The disappearance of depth has resulted in a distinctly political loss, Jameson claims at the outset of "Postmodernism": "Overt expressions of social and political defiance no longer scandalize anyone, and are not only received with the greatest complacency but have themselves become institutionalized."[2] Accustomed to "the frantic economic urgency of producing fresh waves of ever more novel-seeming goods,"[3] everyone knows, presumably, that nothing really matters amid the ceaseless, furious circulation of commodities. Defiant music is just another consumer choice out of that chaotic whirlwind, meeting just another submarket taste like OK Cola provides a phony alternative to Coca-Cola. By 1995, Jameson's thesis on the commercialization of defiance had spread to the editorial page of my hometown newspaper: "Almost any kind of defiance, . . . every outrage, seems to quickly become a trend—from body piercing to grunge."[4]

In the shorter original version of Jameson's essay on postmodernism (in Hal Foster's 1983 collection *The Anti-Aesthetic*), Jameson actually includes punk rock itself in his thesis on complacency. Punk, he believes, is a primary example of the way offensive expression can be "commercially successful" and merely "taken in stride by society."[5] In the 1984 essay, Jameson detaches punk rock from his thesis in order to save it for his conclusion on the same dismal point: "We all, in one way or another, dimly feel that not only . . . local countercultural forms of cultural resistance and guerilla warfare, but also even overtly political interventions like those of the Clash, are all somehow secretly disarmed and reabsorbed by a system of which they themselves might well be considered a part, since they can achieve no distance from it."[6] As Howard Hampton notes in a review of Jameson's book *Postmodernism*, this "peculiar depopulation" of the world arbitrarily ignores "those stubbornly uneuphoric citizens of the multinational, multimedia economy [who find] in images of free-market abundance and democratized apathy a stunning poverty of the imagination."[7] There is no good reason, therefore, to accept that the possibility of refusal is precluded by the integration of aesthetic and commodity production. For one thing, this lament has been around for at least two centuries: the desire for "distance" or autonomy from commercial culture is precisely where postmodern theory only reproduces romantic and modernist aesthetics.

The incorporation thesis on art and commerce is nonetheless almost universally endorsed by present-day quasi leftist academics. Incorporation in this sense refers to the ability of capitalism to co-opt and sell any expression of dissent, no matter how unpalatable at first, and thereby eviscerate it. Pessimism over the presumably disastrous influence of commerce has become commonplace among hip journalists and alternative music fans, too, and in no small part thanks to postmodern academics. Leslie Savan, for example, repeatedly despaired in the *Village Voice* at "how easily any idea, deed, or image can become part of the corporate sponsored world, . . . a culture that sponsors rebellion, that provides the conflict that our society . . . would grow bored without." (This is undiluted Jameson: defiance meets with complacency as a result.) Thanks to the "corporate powers bark[ing] instructions at you to be rebellious," rebellion is reduced to the symbolic—"what you buy and parade as your identity."[8]

But if critics and scholars would relent on their anticommercial absolutism, says Angela McRobbie, they would find young people in every subculture, from grunge to hip-hop to riot grrrls, "learning and sharing skills, practicing them [while] making a small amount of money," and creating alternative job opportunities that can also be quite empowering. In the process of making music, clothes, and fanzines, attempting to earn a living "directly expresses the character of its producers in a way that is frequently in opposition to those available, received, or encouraged images or identities" offered by the dominant culture. What is too often seen as the "commercial, low ebb of [a] subculture" and the hastened process of its incorporation, ought to be considered central to it, instead, and a potential vehicle of change and social transformation.[9]

Lawrence Grossberg, an academic more extensively concerned with popular music, may have played a significant role in Jameson's thesis on the futility of anger migrating into music journalism. Grossberg's work obeys the academic's professional impulse to stake out ever more extreme ground: where Jameson claimed that the affective depth of defiance was merely diminished, Grossberg bluntly announced in 1988 that "meaning [or political ideology] and affect have *broken apart.*"[10] As a result, neither emotion nor ideology on its own offers any political hope. The disconnection of emotions like anger from any political significance has supposedly resulted from the triumph of neoconservatism, which Grossberg holds in unhealthy awe.

Mesmerized by power, he piles up postmodernist abstractions. The thesis on the split between emotion and intellect (or affect and ideology), in particular, has been a mantra in his publications since the late 1980s. The basis of this thesis is his conception of "authentic inauthenticity" (or "ironic nihilism"), typified for him by the meaningless, transparently calculated emotional intensity of a Bruce Springsteen. He argues that because we have all been trained to take nothing seriously, emotion and meaning have becomed detached: "The relationship between affect and ideology . . . has become increasingly problematic. . . . It has become increasingly difficult, if not impossible, in other words, to make sense of our affective experience and to put any faith in our ideological constructions. . . . Postmodernity, then, points to a crisis in our ability to locate any meaning as a possible and appropriate source for an impassioned commitment."[11] This last sentence on the disconnection of passion from meaning was reproduced ad nauseam in music journalism. As a result of that disconnection, presumably, we crave emotion alone, without consequences. When Grossberg says we are all "anesthetized," echoing Theodor Adorno and the Frankfurt School, it becomes apparent how much of this is merely recycled modernist pessimism.

Grossberg's thesis that affect and meaning have broken apart helped influence the condescending elements in the critical reception of Nirvana, the group whose success in the early 1990s resurrected punk in the popular press. Grossberg's pessimism was closely linked to a dismissal of the punk legacy in the first place. That's not to say his disposal of punk is very compelling, however, since he relies in large part on a ludicrous source, the novelist Bret Easton Ellis. Ellis's well-known first novel, *Less Than Zero* (1985), was a formative text in the picture of Generation X, in its nihilistic, "numbing invocation of designer names, eateries, [and] personal care products." As one young reviewer, Pagan Kennedy, aptly summed up the positive critical responses to Ellis's book, "The less one thought of kids, it would seem, the more one thought of Ellis."[12]

Grossberg's own low opinion of contemporary youth culture led him to esteem Ellis, or at least, to treat Ellis's contrived cynicism as authoritative. Grossberg uses Ellis for a very specific purpose: to describe the supposed bankruptcy of the "punk method" in the 1980s that resulted from the incorporation of punk's original antagonistic nihilism into the banal nihilism of consumer society.[13] In an essay cited by Grossberg, "Twentysomethings: Adrift in a Pop Landscape" (1990), Ellis claims "if some visceral rebellion remains" in forms like punk rock, "contemporary subversiveness is all on the surface. . . . Passion and affect are simply not worth the trouble."[14] This appears to be a direct paraphrase of Jameson's view that expressions of defiance are fabrications feeding complacency. Thus we find yet another instance of that supposedly general postmodern phenomenon, the closed circuit of expressive possibilities, that is really only characteristic of postmodern analyses and their endless repetition of one another. Ellis's essay was published in the *New York Times,* furthermore, indicating once again the close fit between establishment media and the ideas of quasi Marxist postmodernists like Jameson and Grossberg.

But Ellis's formulation is revealing in a more specific way as well, given his role in helping define the 1990s version of Generation X. Thanks to others like Douglas Coupland and Richard Linklater, too, Generation X, slackers, and the like have become identified with precisely the combination of attitudes described by Ellis: a punk-rock taste for deviance trivialized by postmodern cynicism over the commercialization of rebellion and cheapening of emotion. Jason Cohen and Michael Krugman's *Generation Ecch!* (1994)—which came to attention after endorsement by Courtney Love—exemplifies this particular postpunk mode, simultaneously satirizing and endorsing cynicism among "a bunch of rebellious losers. It's no accident that the phrase 'rebel without a clue' has become a bigger cliché than 'rebel without a cause.' It's sad to say, but looking at GenEcch through the pop culture that formed them [*sic*], as well as the books, movies and music the generation has produced itself, seems to validate conservative old fart Allan Bloom's bellyaching about the accelerating vapidity of post-TV youth [which Grossberg also endorses] and their complete lack of depth, smarts, feeling or history."[15] Cohen does successfully collapse the whole concept of Gen X, but his own scarcely differentiated invocation of *ressentiment,* or the unenacted resentment felt by the weak described by Friedrich Nietzsche, indicates that cynical (if hip) postmodernism derives directly from the fetid imagination of modernist elitism.

In citing Ellis on the irrelevance of affect, Grossberg winds up in a contradictory position because he knows there is still a desire for passionate music. His own argument is not that no one troubles with emotion but that strong affect and any meaningfulness (or ideology) are disconnected. The failure of popular politically conscious groups like U2, R.E.M., and Midnight Oil, as Grossberg rightly describes it, results from "a radical disassociation of the music's political content and the band's political position from the emotionally and affectively powerful appeals" of the music—which Ellis would deny even exist in the first place.[16]

Another example of Jameson's influence in academia also leads to the Generation X phenomenon, namely the Douglas Coupland novel that revived the label from Billy Idol's punk group, itself named after a British sociological treatise from the early 1960s. The path to Coupland starts with the compulsive, misleading citation of Jameson in Barry Shank's *Dissonant Identities: The Rock 'n' Roll Scene in Austin, Texas* (1994). Jameson, says Shank, "recognizes that commercial culture is an important site for political struggle,"[17] though as pointed out earlier, Jameson clearly believes just the opposite. By the time Shank wrote, academics had held so often that Jameson has given us progressive insights into postmodern culture that I'm sure Shank must simply be repeating scholarly common wisdom, rather than misreading Jameson.

Shank relies more heavily on another founding father of postmodernism (more specifically poststructuralism), the psychoanalyst Jacques Lacan, who was a prominent influence on Jameson's "Postmodernism" essay as well. Lacan has us driven forever by a "lack" of fulfillment of desire in our relations with other people, a futility beginning with our initiation into language. He recast Freud's Oedipal drama as the acquisition of language, in the sense that an infant becomes conscious of its difference from Others (with a capital O) through both family dynamics and the use of language. Differentiating persons and things, in other words, requires differentiating words themselves in order to name those objects. A passage occurs from the Imaginary Order, where the world is whole (or an extension of oneself, in the transitional "mirror phase") and all desires are met, to the Symbolic Order, where the empty world of language in which "real" experience outside language becomes inaccessible. Since words (or signs) have no direct or natural correspondence with objects, language only operates in the absence of things, and thus communication, desire, and wholeness can never be realized.

Shank uses Lacan to argue that postmodern young people do not make a very full transition from the Imaginary to the Symbolic Order. From the counterculture to the stereotypical Generation X, postmodern youth has supposedly remained infantile in its demands for instant, constant gratification. Where neoconservatives lament young people's refusal to accept "deferred gratification" and decry our culture's hedonism, Shank finds adolescents to be perfect postmoderns; advanced capitalism, obviously, depends on consumer hedonism. He's no happier than the neocons: postmodernity, he says, is like adolescence in "a heightened awareness of the pure possibilities of representation combined with an *absence* of social power and the inability to enforce discursively the qualities of those representations."[18] Our affect lacks depth, in other words; defiance can meet only with complacency.

According to another Lacanian analysis, by Fred Pfeil, postmodern young people are the products of "de-Oedipalization," or an excessive nurturing that leads to self-indulgence.[19] In Lacanian terms, the transition from the Imaginary to the Symbolic Order is incomplete. Pfeil puts a positive spin on the matter by taking the feminist view that emotional relations remain more vital, whereas Marxists would see advanced capitalism creating even more hedonistic consumers. The resulting diagnosis, however, sounds uncomfortably like that of neoconservatives who blame society's ills on Dr. Spock and permissive parenting.

Pfeil's de-Oedipalized young people are found "to swing from one pole of internality to another, from a rage at all that surrounds and threatens it to a deliriously dispersed self-exaltation."[20] In the latter case, the fulfillment of desire seems possible since young people are not fully absorbed into the Symbolic Order. Caught up in the quest for pleasure, they only sense "power" always threatening to intervene as an abstract, invisible force—the classic academic postmodern sensibility here attributed to Generation X—hence the impotent rage.[21] If postmodern self-indulgence is highly volatile, it is not terribly well controlled or focused. As Jameson and Grossberg have it, rage is disconnected from political articulation. The psychoanalytic view would add that the self-absorption of de-Oedipalized young people is what keeps the anger internalized and unenacted, except through more pursuit of consumer goods and entertainment calculatedly directed at the enraged. There is a schizoid split between actual affective experience and the prepackaged or rationalized outlets it finds (like angry music).

Douglas Coupland's 1991 novel *Generation X* is essentially a précis of all of the above ideas, as well as a gloss on the Jamesonian view of the world. The "world has gotten way too big—way beyond our capacities to tell stories about it"[22]—echoes Jameson's description of an "impossible totality." So the characters tell stories incessantly in an effort to grasp their situation. In keeping with the postmodernist stress on the fragmentation of identity and experience, however, those stories are never more than "a fragment of your own horror," the most vital form of storytelling possible.[23] Coupland predictably treats the consumer society as the cause of that fragmentation, though he spews out brand names as eagerly as Bret Easton Ellis.

The futile effort to grasp the postmodern age leads to something like the end-of-history thesis, the paradox of "historical underdosing" and "overdosing," where "nothing seems to happen" and "too much seems to happen" at the same time. The resulting paralysis is typified by "addiction to newspapers, magazines, and TV news broadcasts," a substitute for making history.[24] While Coupland scarcely celebrates the postmodern world, calling it "hell" more than once, his closeness to the likes of Jameson is evident in his favorable, nostalgic citation of a modernist, Rainer Maria Rilke. Rilke's typically elitist extolment of the "solitary man"[25]—implicitly the poet or intellectual aristocrat—seems jarring in a novel presumably about young people trying to create a sense of community. The reference indicates how thoroughly Coupland's outlook resembles that of his academic sources.

In contrast with Coupland's cynicism about history, Pfeil insists that youthful rage at authority might still release "historically new and progressive social forces."[26] But postmodern culture continually works to diminish that possibility, he adds, by diverting new energies into consumption—the conventional postmodern thesis on incorporation. Pfeil argues against the position of Jameson, Grossberg, and others that rebelliousness results from a psychology of arrested development that precludes any political significance. The pleasure of resistance is not to be discounted, though Pfeil doesn't seem convinced it takes on strong forms, given his citation of musicians like Laurie Anderson, Philip Glass, and the Talking Heads as exemplars in handling the postmodern condition.[27]

Pfeil's description of the combustible relation between self-gratification and rage is useful, but I would add that many young people make a fairly conscious *choice* between them, and that when they do so they choose the latter. Rage or anger, as feminist philosophy tells us, is *always* based in a judgment on a situation. In contemporary music, anger is quite intentionally focused on a culture offering what Pfeil rightly calls the "intrusive and monotonous" pleasures of instant gratification, "a menace to be resisted."[28] What sounds like irredeemable noise to the uninitiated is in fact a deliberate commentary on the cacophony of the *rest* of our culture—what passes for normal, like the media screeching about O. J. Simpson or Elián González. The noise of angry music is the same avant-garde force described by Richard Huelsenbeck in *En Avant Dada* (1920): "Every movement naturally produces noise." Furthermore, he believed that "noise is a direct call to action," not a sign of anger without political significance.[29]

However it came about, the importation of postmodernism into music journalism became apparent in 1991, when the postmodernist thesis on the meaninglessness of emotion was reproduced in a spate of articles precipitated by the first Lollapalooza tour, Nirvana's breakthrough with the *Nevermind* album, the rise of the riot grrrls, and the proliferation of gangsta and radical rap music. Echoing one another, journalists suggested a dysfunctional disconnection between "rage" and meaning in the new music. The visceral emotional impact of the music, from this view, is undercut by either inarticulate or indecipherable lyrical content. However, this argument betrays the classic self-contradiction by ridiculing supposedly weak-minded emotions, a view clearly motivated by a fear of the danger anger poses for authority.

The first mainstream article I noticed featuring full-blown postmodernism was published in August of 1991 in the *New York Times.* "Now is the Summer of Our Discontent," by Jon Pareles (popular-music editor for the *Times*), concerns the first Lollapalooza tour, a surprising success organized by Jane's Addiction. The tour featured a diverse group of performers including the industrial group Nine Inch Nails and the rapper Ice-T, a deliberate statement about their common outrage. Pareles's article does not actually concern Lollapalooza, however; the tour serves as the occasion for an editorial on the condition of youth music in 1991.

Pareles's reading of postmodernism is evident in his gloom over the ability of consumer society to make even the strongest emotion just another commodity. As in academic postmodernism, commercial incorporation splits emotion from meaning, making the performers' anger inauthentic, and thus an ingenuine basis for commitment: "This is the summer of rage—or, more precisely, the summer when rage sells. . . . Advertising has helped convince people they can forge an identity through consumption, and they can fill in that sense that something's missing with the right brand of running shoes or jeans or beer. Or an album. So people consume rage as entertainment."[30] The idea that choices in musical taste are no more important than the choice of shoes stretches matters quite a bit, just like Pareles's academic precursors. It makes no sense whatsoever to claim that people make the same emotional commitment to their Nikes that they do in listening to music. The license for Pareles to make all anger identical, nonetheless, is the postmodernist thesis that emotion and meaning have become entirely detached. Rage, supposedly, is "as inarticulate as it is widespread." The adherents of angry music, Pareles claims, "don't care much who or what that rage is aimed at. All they want is to feel that someone else is as angry as they are."[31] In just about any other case, the desire to discover others with similar feelings would be deemed a sociable, healthy impulse, but the feelings involved here are, of course, antiauthoritarian and thus unacceptable to establishment outlets like the *Times*.

The broader postmodern thesis, moreover, that emotion has become disconnected from ideology (or reason), is undermined by the argument put forth by some feminist philosophers that emotions are rational and educable judgments formed out of social interaction, that their related physical sensations are a meaningful part of that process, and that anger is the essential political emotion. If we understand that anger can be in itself a significant *cognitive* discovery (particularly for young women), the divide drawn between visceral anger in music and its presumably feeble, or at least indecipherable lyrical expression (an inarticulateness Pareles extends to the audience) simply doesn't hold up. It is simply impossible for affect to have no depth, or for affect and meaning to split apart, as postmodernists like Jameson, Grossberg, Pareles, and many others claim about punk rock and other expressions of anger.

In her 1991 essay "Reason and Emotion," Miranda Fricker makes a point salient to the objection frequently raised against bands like Nirvana: one can't hear the lyrics, hence the evident anger is incoherent and unfocused. Fricker points out that it is precisely because initial "half-formed feelings" lack articulation—as rock journalists such as Pareles claimed about Nirvana and its audience—that those feelings are "a potentially subversive force." The asset of such feelings is that they have not yet been fully subjected to "the accepted form of . . . rational judgment as expressed in language." Irreducible to language, half-formed feelings thus have a freer field of operation, "a looser and more flexible relation to the dominant ideology, than does our reason."[32] Indecipherable lyrics in the midst of angry cacophonous music might very well be a *virtue*, therefore, and we can certainly understand why the mainstream press continually worries over, ridicules, and condemns such artistic forms.

Peter Lyman even argues in "The Politics of Anger" that less articulate angry speech (or music) nonetheless participates immediately in public discourse by inherently questioning "the fairness of the rules of participation in rational discourse."[33] Anger without an articulated ideology, that is, has a peculiar advantage: it highlights not only the exclusion of deviant voices, but also, more significantly, the way "reason" itself often represents only "a rhetorical claim by the dominant about their legitimacy," as in the condemnation of angry music by the *Times*.[34] Contrary to the arguments of postmodern critics, therefore, such music accomplishes a great deal, conveying dissatisfaction with both the limited choices available in public discourse *and* the pretense of that discourse to have a rational view of a rational social order (the status quo).

Another feminist philosopher, Morwenna Griffiths, also considers "only partly conscious" or "inarticulate expression" perfectly legitimate and crucial, but adds that the interdependence of body and mind, of feeling and understanding, is found in the "intonation" or physical, material qualities of *all* language. The body, mind, and language cannot be separated into discrete phases of feeling, judgment, and articulation, respectively, but are always interacting with one another, and always in the context of appraising social situations: "understanding depends on shared language which depends on shared feeling; the understanding then contributes to both language and feeling."[35] The authors of *Emotion and Gender* likewise conclude that we find in emotion the foremost link between biological and social experience.[36]

This view of the political significance of emotion is precisely that of youth subcultures in the 1990s such as the riot grrrls, who have gone beyond feminist philosophers in turning the point against postmodernism. The new wave of young women making rock music in the 1990s, whether on independent or corporate labels, had no truck with postmodernist notions like Pfeil's that popular music can only be subversive by being "deadpan, indifferent, depersonalized, effaced, . . . effectively cancel[ing] the possibility of traditional audience identification."[37] The new female rockers tried instead to open up a new way of living for hordes of young women. They refused to be a victim of gender categorizing as feminists have long sought, while breaking with their elders' intellectual-literary bent by making self-creation a more exciting and attractive matter than studiously absorbing feminist tracts.

Groups like Bikini Kill defied "traditional roles and images open to women while simultaneously slashing through doctrinaire notions of feminism."[38] Bikini Kill's "florid, pen-pal rhetoric is such an essential emotional and intellectual process primarily because it's so much *fun:* Revolution as everyday play; girls getting off on rock gestures and nonsense without ever considering boy consent."[39] Musicians and audiences, together, have overcome a problem the authors of *Emotion and Gender* recollect in their girlhoods: "There are very few examples where we as girls played to an audience of peers. . . . There was a collectivity of action in many of the young men's [activities] that was almost completely absent from the women's."[40]

Advocating just such a collective effort in *Jigsaw* in 1991, Kathleen Hanna of Bikini Kill at first sounds postmodern, contrasting the real "world of constant flux" with the artificiality of "some forever identity."[41] But what she actually means is that "Jigsaw Youth" first have to break with learned identities, or "boxes and labels," and then they can put together the puzzle pieces of a more authentic identity out of the "fucked up culture" of parents and "TV people," the real chaos. "It seems like it will never come together," she says, "but it can and it does and it will," a distinctly antipostmodern sentiment. Thus it seems fitting that one commentator on Bikini Kill described them as "spit[ting] in the pale, male face of the Generation X cliché."[42] Hanna sums up the project in terms of elemental feelings: "I am not afraid to say things matter to me." She chides cliques who try "to dictate . . . what is and what isn't cool or revolutionary or resistance," and insists that "just because someone is not resisting in the same way you are . . . does not mean they are not resisting"—a perspective sorely lacking in academic and journalistic postmodernism. "Resistance is everywhere," Hanna believes; "it always has been and always will be [among] Jigsaw Youth, listening, strategizing, tolerating, screaming, confronting, fearless."

This impassioned advocacy is summed up in one of my favorite songs of the 1990s, Bikini Kill's "Carnival." The song's sheer gusto and speed of performance is a complete reversal of the dire, depressive effect of the opening subject matter—"16-year-old girls give head to carnies for free rides and hits of pot." The song is a declaration of young women liberating themselves from sexual abuse, while also celebrating the whole breakthrough of the riot grrrls and angry girl bands through the "carnival" metaphor. Most of the original riot grrrls were college students, moreover, and I suspect that the carnival metaphor indicates someone in Bikini Kill knows about Mikhail Bakhtin, whose work popularized the term among academics. A number of thinkers, such as Natalie Davis, Teresa Ebert, Nancy Fraser, Mary Russo, and Robert Stam, find his concept of carnival promising for feminism, along with the general materialism (or dialogism) of his argument (like Griffiths and Hanna) that a social contest is always occurring in the emotional inflection of language. As Stam sums it up, carnival "is more than a party or a festival; it is . . . a countermodel of cultural production and desire" like the feminist public sphere created by the riot grrrls, Lollapalooza, and others in which "all that is marginalized and excluded . . . takes over the center."[43] Especially by advancing the unruly or disorderly woman, says Davis, the function of carnival in early modern Europe was "first, to widen behavioral options for women"—just as making feminine anger acceptable is a central project of riot grrrl—"and second, to sanction riot and political disobedience for both men and women in a society that allowed lower orders [or in the present, subordinate groups like the young] few formal means of protest."[44]

Bakhtin most extensively develops his concept of carnival in *Rabelais and His World,* which was written in the 1930s, but remained unpublished until 1965 in part because its celebration of antiauthoritarianism was unacceptable under Stalinism. And indeed, rather than the high Middle Ages, Bakhtin clearly has something more contemporary in mind in his general description of carnival as a "dynamic expression" or "experience, opposed to all that was ready-made and completed." Essentially, Bakhtin describes an alternative to the specious identities proffered by consumer society, as Hanna describes it; it is an experience or expression opposed "to all pretense at immutability."[45]

The forms of speech that empower people in carnival, Bakhtin specifies, are comic compositions, specifically parodies, combined with "various genres of billingsgate," or "curses, oaths,"[46] and other "abusive language"[47] directed at people with power. This is a matter of collective activity, of individuals celebrating unification with a regenerated social identity and purpose. Marketplace speech (note the emphasis on commerce and the popular) permits "no distance between those who come in contact with each other," liberating them "from norms of etiquette and decency," a formulation clearly pertinent to women. People are thereby "reborn for new, purely [and truly] human relations"[48] for a new life, even, much as Bikini Kill once wrote in a fanzine that "this world doesn't teach us how to be truly cool to each other, and so we have to teach each other."[49]

Bakhtin's work on parody is most extensive in essays written at the same time as *Rabelais and His World* and collected in *The Dialogic Imagination*. The clown and the fool in carnival "struggle against conventions, and against the inadequacy of all available life-slots to fit an authentic human being"[50]—against the cardboard cut-outs of static identity attacked by Kathleen Hanna. When an artist like Hanna dons the "mask" of the clown as she does in the song "Carnival," she is tempting us to think that she exults abuse, sluts, vulgarity, and so on, when in fact she acquires the ability "to rip off [other] masks, . . . to rage at others," and "to betray to the public a personal life."[51] Bakhtin, in other words, contains very nearly the whole riot grrrl catalog: the exposé (or parody) of the whole process of feminine representation, the cultivation of the energy of anger (or billingsgate), and the revelation of personal experience according to the feminist commonplace that the personal is the political. In ensuring that "no language could claim to be an authentic, incontestable face," the clown's parody is "aimed sharply and polemically against the official language of its given time."[52] This antiauthoritarian emphasis in parody in *Rabelais and His World* leads to billingsgate, the outright curses and oaths against authority.

As one might expect, academic postmodernists have a reflexive, universalizing response to any optimistic reference to carnival: it's all "authorized transgression," or part of the closed circuit organized by power. Umberto Eco, for example, echoes well-known French postmodern theorists such as Jacques Derrida, Michel Foucault, Jean-François Lyotard in declaring that "the law" is always "overwhelmingly present at the moment of its violation" in carnival.[53] Carnivalesque attacks on authority through popular forms like rock music presumably serve only to drain away rebellious energies through permitted forms of release (yet another postmodern observation dating to the eighteenth century). Bakhtin took pains to resist such a view, distinguishing carnival with officially sanctioned feasts that (not unlike contemporary spectacles) "did not lead people out of the existing world order, [but] asserted all that was stable, unchanging, perennial."[54]

As a renewal simply of belief and hope (however angrily expressed), carnival is "not actually directed against institutions," Renate Lachmann points out, "but rather against the loss of utopian potential brought about by dogma and authority."[55] Dogma such as the counseling of futility and resignation in the form of Generation X is assailed and "dispersed through ridicule and laughter,"[56] in a dialectic in which negation, the critique of conformist common sense, becomes a source of the regeneration of hope. The postmodern accusation that carnival is only authorized transgression, in other words, is moot; the point isn't to escape from or overthrow the organization of power immediately. Even the best of contemporary carnival "ultimately leaves everything as it was before" as far as social institutions go.[57] But its energy nonetheless "offers a permanent alternative to official culture," a lasting, "irrepressible, unsilenceable" example of the possibility of refusing to express oneself in permitted ways.[58] The many young people I knew in the 1990s who felt and understood this in different ways did share one common trait: they all rightfully detested the rubric of Generation X as a fraud on their experience.

Notes

1. Andrew Goodwin, "Popular Music and Postmodern Theory," *Cultural Studies* 5 (1991): 186.

2. Frederic Jameson, "Postmodernism, or The Cultural Logic of Late Capitalism," *New Left Review* 146 (July/August 1984): 56.

3. Ibid.

4. David Lowery, "Shock Steps between Klein and His Ads," *Austin American-Statesman,* 31 August 1995, sec. A, p. 21.

5. Frederic Jameson, "Postmodernism and Consumer Society," in *The Anti-Aesthetic: Essays on Postmodern Culture,* ed. Hal Foster (Port Townsend, Wash.: Bay Press, 1983), 124.

6. Jameson, "Postmodernism, or The Cultural Logic of Late Capitalism," 87.

7. Howard Hampton, "Dueling Cadavers: Fredric Jameson Buries Modernism, the Mekons Dig Up the Bones," review of *Postmodernism, or The Cultural Logic of Late Capitalism,* by Frederic Jameson, *LA Weekly,* 9–15 August 1991, 44.

8. Leslie Savan, "Niked Lunch: Ads from the Underground," *Village Voice,* 6 September 1994, 51.

9. Angela McRobbie, "Shut Up and Dance: Youth Culture and Changing Modes of Femininity," *Cultural Studies* 7 (1993): 412.

10. Lawrence Grossberg, *It's a Sin: Essays on Postmodernism, Politics, and Culture* (Sydney: Power, 1988), 40, emphasis added.

11. Ibid., 39–43.

12. Pagan Kennedy, "Generation Gaffe," review of *American Psycho* by Bret Easton Ellis, *Nation,* 1 April 1991, 427.

13. Lawrence Grossberg, *We Gotta Get Out of This Place: Popular Conservatism and Postmodern Culture* (New York: Routledge, 1992), 186.

14. Quoted in ibid.

15. Jason Cohen and Michael Krugman, *Generation Ecch!* (New York: Fireside, 1994), 11.

16. Grossberg, *We Gotta Get Out of This Place,* 168.

17. Barry Shank, *Dissonant Identities: The Rock 'n' Roll Scene in Austin, Texas* (Hanover: Wesleyan University Press, 1994), 69.

18. Ibid., 133, emphasis added.

19. Fred Pfeil, "Postmodernism as a 'Structure of Feeling,'" in *Marxism and the Interpretation of Culture,* ed. Lawrence Grossberg and Cary Nelson (Urbana: University of Illinois Press, 1988), 383, 391–97.

20. Ibid., 396.

21. Ibid., 392–93.

22. Douglas Coupland, *Generation X: Tales for an Accelerated Culture* (New York: St. Martin's, 1991), 5.

23. Ibid., 13.

24. Ibid., 7–8.

25. Ibid., 59.

26. Pfeil, 396.

27. Ibid., 381–86. It is debatable whether there is actually a "postmodern" rock music; see Andrew Goodwin, "Popular Music," and *Dancing in the Distraction Factory: Music Television and Popular Culture* (Minneapolis: University of Minnesota Press, 1992).

28. Ibid., 399.

29. Robert Motherwell, ed., *The Dada Painters and Poets: An Anthology* (Cambridge: Harvard University Press, 1989), 28.

30. Jon Pareles, "Now is the Summer of Our Discontent," *New York Times,* 25 August 1991, sec. H, p. 20, 22.

31. Ibid.

32. Miranda Fricker, "Reason and Emotion," *Radical Philosophy* 57 (1991): 17–18.

33. Peter Lyman, "The Politics of Anger: On Silence, Ressentiment, and Political Speech," *Socialist Review* 11, 3 (May/June 1981): 66–67.

34. Ibid., 69–71.

35. Morwenna Griffiths, "Feminism, Feelings and Philosophy," in *Feminist Perspectives in Philosophy,* ed. Morwenna Griffiths and Margaret Whitford (Bloomington: Indiana University Press, 1988), 146.

36. June Crawford, et al., *Emotion and Gender: Constructing Meaning from Memory* (Newbury Park, Calif.: Sage, 1992), 181.

37. Pfeil, 384.

38. Sandy Carter, "Courtney Love & Liz Phair," *Z Magazine,* November 1994, 68.

39. Charles Aaron, "A Riot of the Mind," *Village Voice,* 2 February 1993, 63.

40. Crawford, et al., 189.

41. Kathleen Hanna, "Jigsaw Youth," *Jigsaw* (Spring 1991); also published in the liner notes for Bikini Kill, *The C.D. Version of the First Two Records,* Kill Rock Stars KRS204. All subsequent quotations from Hanna are from this source unless indicated otherwise.

42. Charles Aaron, "A Riot of the Mind," *Village Voice,* 2 February 1993, 66.

43. Robert Stam, *Subversive Pleasures: Bakhtin, Cultural Criticism, and Film* (Baltimore: Johns Hopkins University Press, 1989), 86, 95.

44. Quoted in Mary Russo, "Female Grotesques," in *Feminist Studies/Critical Studies,* ed. Teresa de Lauretis (Bloomington: Indiana University Press, 1986), 215.

45. Mikhail Bakhtin, *Rabelais and His World,* trans. Helene Iswolsky (Bloomington: Indiana University Press, 1984), 10 11.

46. Ibid., 5.

47. Ibid., 27.

48. Ibid., 10.

49. Quoted in Ann Japenga, "Punk's Girl Groups Are Putting the Self Back in Self-Esteem," *New York Times,* 15 November 1992, sec. H, p. 30.

50. Mikhail Bakhtin, *The Dialogic Imagination: Four Essays,* ed. Michael Holquist, trans. Caryl Emerson and Michael Holquist (Austin: University of Texas Press, 1981), 163.

51. Ibid.

52. Ibid., 273.

53. Quoted in Stam, 91.

54. Bakhtin, *Rabelais,* 9.

55. Renate Lachmann, "Bakhtin and Carnival: Culture as Counter-Culture," *Cultural Critique* 11 (Winter 1988/89): 130.

56. Ibid.

57. Ibid., 125.

58. Ibid.

Bibliography

Aaron, Charles. "A Riot of the Mind." *Village Voice,* 2 February 1993, 63, 66.

Bakhtin, Mikhail. *Rabelais and His World.* Translated by Helene Iswolsky. Bloomington: Indiana University Press, 1984.

———. *The Dialogic Imagination: Four Essays.* Edited and translated by Caryl Emerson and Michael Holquist. Austin: University of Texas Press, 1981.

Carter, Sandy. "Courtney Love & Liz Phair." *Z Magazine,* November 1994, 68–69.

Cohen, Jason, and Michael Krugman. *Generation Ecch! The Backlash Starts Here.* New York: Fireside, 1994.

Coupland, Douglas. *Generation X: Tales for an Accelerated Culture.* New York: St. Martin's, 1991.

Crawford, June, et al. *Emotion and Gender: Constructing Meaning from Memory.* Newbury Park, Calif.: Sage, 1992.

Fricker, Miranda. "Reason and Emotion." *Radical Philosophy* 57 (1991): 14–19.

Goodwin, Andrew. *Dancing in the Distraction Factory: Music Television and Popular Culture.* Minneapolis: University of Minnesota Press, 1992.

———. "Popular Music and Postmodern Theory." *Cultural Studies* 5 (1991): 174–90.

Griffiths, Morwenna. "Feminism, Feelings and Philosophy." In *Feminist Perspectives in Philosophy,* edited by Morwenna Griffiths and Margaret Whitford. Bloomington: Indiana University Press, 1988.

Grossberg, Lawrence. *It's a Sin: Essays on Postmodernism, Politics, and Culture.* Sydney: Power, 1988.

———. *We Gotta Get Out of This Place: Popular Conservatism and Postmodern Culture.* New York: Routledge, 1992.

Hampton, Howard. "Dueling Cadavers: Fredric Jameson Buries Modernism, The Mekons Dig Up the Bones." Review of *Postmodernism, or The Cultural Logic of Late Capitalism,* by Frederic Jameson. *LA Weekly,* 9–15 August 1991, 44.

Hanna, Kathleen. "Jigsaw Youth." *Jigsaw,* Spring 1991. Liner Notes for Bikini Kill, *The C.D. Version of the First Two Records,* Kill Rock Stars KRS 204.

Jameson, Fredric. "Postmodernism and Consumer Society." In *The Anti-Aesthetic: Essays on Postmodern Culture,* edited by Hal Foster. Port Townsend, Wash.: Bay Press, 1983.

———. "Postmodernism, or The Cultural Logic of Late Capitalism." *New Left Review* 146 (1984): 53–92.

Japenga, Ann. "Punk's Girl Groups Are Putting the Self Back in Self-Esteem." *New York Times,* 15 November 1992, sec. H, p. 30.

Kennedy, Pagan. "Generation Gaffe." Review of *American Psycho,* by Bret Easton Ellis. *Nation,* 1 April 1991, 426–28.

Lachmann, Renate. "Bakhtin and Carnival: Culture as Counter-Culture." *Cultural Critique* 11 (Winter 1988/89): 115–52.

Lowery, David. "Shock Steps between Klein and His Ads." *Austin American-Statesman,* 31 August 1995, sec. A, p. 21.

Lyman, Peter. "The Politics of Anger: On Silence, Ressentiment, and Political Speech." *Socialist Review* 11.3 (May/June 1981): 55–74.

McRobbie, Angela. "Shut Up and Dance: Youth Culture and Changing Modes of Femininity." *Cultural Studies* 7 (1993): 406–26.

Motherwell, Robert, ed. *The Dada Painters and Poets: An Anthology.* Cambridge: Harvard University Press, 1989.

Pareles, Jon. "Now is the Summer of Our Discontent." *New York Times,* 25 August 1991, sec. H, p. 20, 22.

Pfeil, Fred. "Postmodernism as a 'Structure of Feeling.'" In *Marxism and the Interpretation of Culture,* edited by Lawrence Grossberg and Cary Nelson. Urbana: University of Illinois Press, 1988.

Russo, Mary. "Female Grotesques." In *Feminist Studies/Critical Studies,* edited by Teresa de Lauretis. Bloomington: Indiana University Press, 1986.

Savan, Leslie. "Niked Lunch: Ads from the Underground." *Village Voice,* 6 September 1994, 50–51.

Shank, Barry. *Dissonant Identities: The Rock 'n' Roll Scene in Austin, Texas.* Hanover: Wesleyan University Press, 1994.

Stam, Robert. *Subversive Pleasures: Bakhtin, Cultural Criticism, and Film.* Baltimore: Johns Hopkins University Press, 1989.

"Touch Me I'm Sick"

Contagion as Critique in Punk and Performance Art

Catherine J. Creswell

Perhaps only within a generation shadowed by the threat of AIDS and trashed as the fallout of broken homes, inept schools, and economic collapse could Mudhoney's refrain, "Touch Me I'm Sick," serve as a defiant rallying cry, the only version of confrontationalism remaining in an era of political exhaustion. In fact, pathology emerged as a characteristic gesture of the 1990s. The dramatic rise in depression since 1955 came to coincide with an identification with the disease, what Elizabeth Wurtzel characterizes as the "mainstreaming of . . . depression"[1] or what Hal Foster notes, particularly within grunge music, as a stance of aggressive aphasia, "as if the subject of history, after the Worker, the Woman and the Person of Color was now the Corpse."[2] Arlene Croce, in her oft-quoted review of Bill T. Jones's dance "Still/Here," finds pathology to have become performance art: "Disease and death . . . are taking over the show."[3] Even more striking, by the mid-1990s images of death and disease had moved from the arts to consumer culture: the shaved head of the neopunk; the fatigued youth etched on the side of an OK Cola can; the pallid, shiny face of the "tubercular" model or the blank stare of her counterpart, the gaunt, greasy-haired waif.

The sudden pervasiveness of these depressed and diseased figures inspired commentators to read them synecdochically as the face of a generation or the mood of an era. The critical attention and controversy attending Jones's performances placed him in dozens of magazine photo spreads and made him, in Henry Louis Gates's words, "something of a poster boy for the Zeitgeist."[4] Within contemporary music, this performance of pathology has come to be associated with Kurt Cobain, singer-songwriter of Nirvana. In Wurtzel's view, the exploding sales for the band's second album, *Nevermind,* mark a "defining moment in depression culture."[5] Defined by the band's video image and the overwhelming popularity of its first hit single, "Smells Like Teen Spirit," Cobain became the figure for the peculiar tone of Nirvana's music, oddly both intense and resigned, satiric and self-deprecating, melodic and harsh. Despite his vehement resistance to the label or, perhaps ironically because of his resistance, Cobain became the "voice of a generation." His suicide in April 1994 was seen to reflect a "despair both individual and generational."[6]

The tendency to translate such performances into apparent signs or, more specifically, into personifications, however, obscures the interpretive difficulties they present. In Jones's work, AIDS is not troped but presented. In dances like "Last Night on Earth" where Jones concludes lying curled on a shroud-like garment, rasping the lyrics of an old spiritual, Jones presents the figure of a dying man and, since his announcement of his own HIV-positive status, is literally that dying man. His words address the final desired crossing over—"The River Jordan is deep and cold / chills the body but warms the soul"—but he remains a figure in suspension. His death is a performance, but a performance that presents a death-bearing body. He is a dancer who speaks, who is lent a voice, and yet is, perhaps more than any other dancer, a mute body. Jones's performance collapses the boundaries between the figural and literal, voice and body, the animate and inanimate. In the process, its elegiac address—an address that lends life to the absent in order, in turn, to enliven the speaker—is rendered unstable, even threatening.

Composed as a meditation on mortality in the aftermath of his partner Arnie Zane's death, "Still/Here" even more pointedly foregrounds such questions. Jones developed the dance from the gestures, words, and video images of participants in Jones's Survival Workshops, those who had identified themselves as terminally or seriously ill. As a result, the presence of these participants in the dance often served to mark their absence. As Jones writes, "The question remains with each viewing of their video portraits, each hearing of their recorded voices, where is 'here'?"[7]

As I shall argue, what Jones's dances set out so starkly—performances that are neither expression nor symptom—is at work as well in the music of Nirvana. Though, particularly since Cobain's suicide, Nirvana's music has been described as "songs of despair,"[8] the music resists any such clear translation. Despite song titles like "Lithium," depression is not reflected in Nirvana's work as much as it is, in fact, performed. In the lyrics' shifting of words from their meaning, reworking them into repetitions or sheer sound, Cobain's lyrics share characteristics with depressive speech. Words trail into repetitions ("I don't mind / that I don't have a mind"; "got to find a way to find a way") and inverse constructions ("I found it hard, it was hard to find"). Sentences meander, fail to find objects, or lose track of their subjects before collapsing: "our little band has always been and always will until the end." Phrases clump into strings of empty clichés whose own ostensible meaning is forced into contradictions or simple rhyme sound: "Take your time hurry up the choice is yours don't be late," "Give an inch take a smile," "Look on the bright side is suicide." Words slip into nonsense rhyme or vocables ("Hello, hello, hello, how low"; "go away, get away, get a way") or are linked on the basis of alliteration or assonance, often in pairs of oppositions that drive them from their assigned meanings (e.g., "bright side/ suicide," "obituary/birthday"). Most famously in "Smells Like Teen Spirit," the chorus "a mulatto, an albino, a mosquito, my libido" is bound together principally by repeated vowel sounds and an anapest beat. As the clinician might note, this speech is "interrupted, exhausted."[9] So seemingly weighted with affect, words become "ambiguous, repetitive or simply alliterative, musical . . . meaning appears to be arbitrary, or else . . . seems secondary, frozen."[10]

Nevertheless, if a depressive tone emerges in the music, this performance exists not as a symptom but a gesture, an aesthetic strategy. Composed of cut-up verse or fragments of cut-up verse, the lyrics cannot strictly be called expressive.[11] Moreover, the terms of psychoanalysis aren't so much descriptive of the songs as they are put on display within them. If the repeated refrain from the song "Lithium" functions as a revealing disavowal of pain, that very confession ("I'm not gonna cry"), like those in many of Nirvana's songs, makes disavowals and confessions its theme. Similarly, "Smells Like Teen Spirit" might be said to both suggest depressive rage and invoke it, concluding with the insistent cry "a denial." The bleak symbiotic relationship of "Drain You" suggests a desire to simultaneously incorporate and reject the other. Yet, this analysis isn't a buried truth but literally the song's own narrative, and the bright Beatlesque melody only further distances the song from its expression. The emergence of terms and narratives of psychoanalysis within these performances only serves to bracket off their images and words as appropriable gestures. In her study of melancholia and depression, Julia Kristeva finds that depressive speech can present a poetics. In wrenching signs from their apparent meaning, mourning opens onto a realm of language. Mourning "revives the memory of signs by drawing them out of their signifying neutrality . . . [Translation] seeks to become alien to itself in order to discover, in the mother tongue, a *total word, new, foreign to the language*' (Mallarmé), for the purpose of capturing the unnameable."[12] If depressive speech, or the language that resides at the border of symptom and expression, can be called a poetics, it shares similarities with what Dick Hebdige has called the "signifying practice embodied in punk."[13] For Kristeva, depressive speech is chiefly characterized by its deferral or refusal of meaning, and in this respect, it shares similarities with punk's "refusal to cohere around a readily identifiable set of central values," a practice that "gestured toward 'nowhere' and actively *sought* to remain silent, illegible."[14] For Greil Marcus, the sheer assaultive ugliness of the punks of the 1970s presented a "reversal of perspective, of values," a grim Saturnalia where "what had been bad—hate, mendacity and disease—was now good."[15] Whereas for Hebdige, the punk statement cohered "precisely through its lack of fit (. . . spitting: applause, anarchy: order). . . . It cohered, instead, *elliptically*, through a chain of conspicuous absences. It was characterized by its unlocatedness—its blankness."[16]

In assessing the harshness of the punks of the 1970s, Marcus finds them to be beyond style or statement, perhaps even beyond performance: "They were ugly. There were no mediations. A ten-inch safety pin cutting through a lower lip into a swastika tattooed onto a cheek was not a fashion statement; a fan forcing a finger down his throat, vomiting into his hands, then hurling the spew at the people on stage was spreading disease. An inch-thick nimbus of black mascara suggested death before it suggested anything else. . . . They were fat, anorexic, pockmarked, acned, stuttering, crippled, scarred, and damaged, and what their new decorations underlined was the failure already engraved in their faces."[17] The inchoate, primitive aggression of the punk gestures Marcus describes—spewing puke, pissing or spitting on fans or performers—marks not a revulsion as much as a desire to be both polluted and polluting. These punks do not merely identify with death and disease (as does the melancholic who conceives himself to be possessing some "congenital flaw"). They seek to be contagion.

In terms posed by anthropologist Mary Douglas, polluting persons enact a "symbolic breaking of that which should be joined or joining of that which should be separate"[18] and thus threaten coherent identity or order by disturbing the margins of the body or the well-regulated state. As Julia Kristeva formulates pollution or abjection, "It is thus not lack of cleanliness or health that causes abjection but what disturbs identity, system, order. What does not respect borders, positions, rules."[19]

But by the early 1990s, punk itself had grown familiar, and the disjunctions the style presented seemed to express merely irony rather than rage. If the curious tone of Nirvana's first hit, "Smells Like Teen Spirit," caused confusion—it was understood as an expression of youthful anger and as a "call to apathy," as an astute commentary on the times and as just big dumb fun, a defining moment in rock history that traded in shopworn musical riffs—this confusion was soon explained as the band's irony. Nevertheless, for several critics, irony couldn't suffice as critique. Understanding the song's video as commenting on a rock scene devolved into tableaus of "money, fame, and domination," Marcus, nevertheless, finds that "the irony in 'Smells Like Teen Spirit' can't really filter the corruption in rock."[20] In a 1992 *Village Voice* article, Ann Powers similarly observes that, although "the sound is as big and mad as punk ever was," it's ultimately impotent: "*Nevermind* and the whole bare-chested, long-haired, beer-guzzling Northwest trip is a desperate attempt to raise the phallus in a community that has reached a point of permanent flaccidity. The difference between Mick Jagger singing 'I can't get no satisfaction' and Kurt Cobain's sad moans is important: Mick had no trouble generating his desire, he just couldn't quite figure out where to stick it. *Nevermind* gets it up for a glorious moment. But after the tape runs out we can almost hear the quiet collapse of our wasted savior's manhood."[21]

Understood within Powers's and Marcus's terms, within a rock scene where "homosociality is the reigning paradigm"[22] and where music exists as a string of "clichés . . . pretested and presold,"[23] it might be easy to understand Nirvana's gestures as defeatist. What neither of these critics fully recognizes, however, is the degree to which *Nevermind* takes up their assessments as themes and displaces them into a peculiarly relentless form of parody, both upholding guitar-driven rock and berating its intensity as a certain masculine false consciousness.[24] As I shall argue, parody in Nirvana's music does not deride nor hopelessly repeat an original as much as it overrides concepts of origin and expression altogether. Although it removes the subject of intentional expression— or, perhaps, because it removes this subject, such parodic speech contains a subversive potential.

Just as parody's ultimate end may be uncertain or "blank," it remains unclear whether punk gestures, whether spewing puke or declaring oneself to be "stupid and contagious," can offer a sustained critique or poetics. Nevertheless, what these gestures put into question is the process by which we label the abject and that which is proper to the self. It is not that there is properly an "I," but rather, the act of naming the alien or the "polluting" establishes the boundaries of the self and the other.[25]

If, in Kristeva's psychoanalytic account, this exclusion or separation is marked also as the arrival of language,[26] the "polluting person" exposes this loss, the split upon which identity is founded. The "polluting person" reveals that body, state, or identity are not natural, inevitable orders but are asserted only through an act of expulsion or repression. These "performances of pathology" do not celebrate abjection but, rather, place death and loss at the very heart of identity.

Fatigue

The depletion experienced by Schumann is haunting the world of art in which we live today. We are all, artists and nonartists alike, survivors and curators, shoring up the art of the past, rummaging among its discards for new ideas.

Arlene Croce, "Discussing the Undiscussable"

It's a problem. Rock 'n' roll is getting older and older. For me, the '60s is the only real rock 'n' roll, and you only can try to copy it.

Jann, a rock fan interviewed by Thurston Moore
in *1991: The Year That Punk Broke*

Despite the predominance of guitar-driven, all-male bands in the Seattle scene, the Seattle sound as often parodied "testosterone" rock as celebrated it. It is within this context that we are best able to place Nirvana's own parodic gestures, or what I have called the performance of pathology.

By 1988 when Mudhoney—perhaps the definitive band of the Northwest—released its single "Touch Me I'm Sick,"[27] punk itself had grown old. In 1977, punk defiance chiefly found voice as a heretical graffiti strewn across the face of pop monoliths (a gesture captured in Johnny Rotten's Pink Floyd T-shirt, which he scrawled over with the words "I HATE").[28] By the late 1980s, the Pink Floyd and the Sex Pistols had their own recognizable and largely separate legacies. Punk disdain for mass-marketed rock 'n' roll and the musicianship and commercial production values that came to represent it was now confined to the growing yet isolated realm of independent or "indie/alternative" rock. If punk had come to overthrow rock 'n' roll, it was now merely a separate marketing niche. Its "reversal of perspective" had devolved into an appropriable oppositional stance, a suburban style.

Mudhoney's single with its distorted, amped, muddy-sounding guitars and its aggressively self-deprecating lyrics ("I'm full of rot . . . Well, I'm diseased and I don't mind") revives elements of punk, yet it does so with a sense of belatedness. Its refashioning of rock arrives as an odd parody, an over-the-top homage to garage rock. Rather than seek new themes or ignore pop song structures or technique, "Touch Me I'm Sick" spoofs rock 'n' roll seduction songs, which, like all seduction songs, celebrate the allure of the form itself. In rock music, this seduction arrives as a display of technical prowess or the raw power of thundering guitars. In an association that is already clichéd, this display becomes inseparable from sexual, specifically, phallic prowess. (In a sense, Jimi Hendrix both sets up and winks at this convention when he purrs, "aw, move over rover and let Jimi take over," before launching his guitar solo for "Fire.")[29]

In Mudhoney's song, this convention is not so much rebuffed as it is rendered crudely emphatic, absurdly overblown. Guitars not only thunder but threaten to blow out: in the seconds before the song's opening chords, we can hear the overcharged amps crackle and hiss. Striving for the blurred roar of garage rock, the guitarists in the opening measures still manage to overstate the case, piling power chords and bass notes on the drum's downbeat.

In the lyrics, self-derision slides into strutting come-ons and back again, but it is Mark Arm's vocals that send the self-accusing seduction over the top. If in his vocals Johnny Rotten seems choked with disgust, extending syllables and grinding consonants to distort words almost beyond recognition (turning "anarchy" into "AN — ARRRR — KAAA-YUH"), Mudhoney's Mark Arm manages to put on both punk rage and hard-rock swagger. He sings "I'm full of rot / Gonna give you—girrrl / Everything I got," shifting from a snarl to a woozy slur.

Arm's vocalizations alone suggest a pastiche of stock rock gestures: dropping a growling "uuuuh" on the opening downbeat and punctuating refrains with R & B styled wails and garage rock "yea-ahs." That he manages to cram several of these vocal gestures into the opening measures before spiking the first verse with a Jerry Lee Lewis shudder pushes the song into caricature. The campiness of the delivery blunts any tone of righteous disgust that the lyrics might otherwise inspire: "Well, I'm diseased—and I don't mind / I'll make you love me—till the day you die / Come Onnnn—Touch Me I'm Sick!" Combined with Arm's overboard vocals and the emphatic "grungy" guitars, the chorus foregrounds the song's seduction and renders it inept: "Come on baby now come with me / If you don't come, if you don't come, if you don't come . . . you'll DIE A-LOOOONE!"

Echoing generations of rock music, the opening phrase offers physical release, but the force of the repetition hollows out the seductive promise, playing it into a crude double entendre ("now come with me / If you don't come, if you don't come, if you don't come"). The singer stutters, repeating the plea as if flummoxed by the audience's unresponsiveness. If Mudhoney's single tips rock's seduction over flat on its face, the chorus's closing threat ("if you don't come / you'll DIE A-LONE!") anticipates the seduction's failure, recasting the appeal—carnal pleasure as a defiance of death, seduction's traditional appeal—with excruciating literal-mindedness.

In the era of AIDS, in which the pairing of death and Eros has been rendered painfully literal, the speaker's punk posturing takes on a new charge. In declaring, "Well, I'm diseased and I don't mind" and altering the final refrain to "Fuck Me I'm Sick!" the speaker declares himself to be the viral, "AIDS-bearing," "polluting" person of contemporary fantasy and renders rock's seduction contaminated and contaminating.[30] Rather than hold out its appeal, this seduction appears closer to a violent possession or forcing: "I'll make you love me till the day *you* die!"

The song's parody suggests how rock 'n' roll's seduction has become a problem. When rock's call to "come with me" no longer stands as an invitation to melt into sonic oblivion but only conjures a crude display of phallic power, it can only inspire rage and revulsion. Yet, when rage and revulsion have become part of rock's standard repertoire, punk rejection is no longer available. Listeners are left desiring and deflated in a "melancholy combination of rage and depression" (perhaps best expressed in another Mudhoney single, "You've got it, damn right you've got it. SO WHAT! Keep it out of my face").[31] Nevertheless, in finding a new threat in punk critique, "Touch Me I'm Sick" demonstrates the resources in self-deprecation.

When Nirvana released its first single off the *Nevermind* album in the fall of 1991,[32] "Smells Like Teen Spirit" struck something of the same curious tone as Mudhoney's "Touch Me I'm Sick." Its contradictory elements soon became read as a parody that held up and derided rock anthems.[33] Fragments of the song's lyrics and sound suggest a prototypical rock 'n' roll party. Bits of the lyric's wordplay conjure images of a gathering: "bring your friends," "our little group has always been and always will until the end," "hello, hello, hello. . . ." It is perhaps a party ("it's fun . . .") or a show with some of the latent threat of rock ("with the lights out it's less dangerous / Here we are now entertain us"). The song's structure, verse-chorus-verse with solo and twanging guitar notes accenting the opening bass line are readily recognizable rock 'n' roll formula. The power chords that announce the song are also familiar, recalling stadium rock of yore.

The video for the song reinforces this impression of a rock 'n' roll tableau. The video is set in a dimmed high school gym. A basketball standard and stage curtains appear in the background. The band stands on the gym floor, flanked by a teenage audience seated in the bleachers. Cheerleaders in pleated skirts, shaking pom-poms, address the crowd in the bleachers. At the beginning and end of the video, we see a janitor backstage with a bucket and mop, as if waiting to clean up the after-party clutter. Although the events unfold in slow motion and the gym is misty and dark, the setting would be appropriate for a Chuck Berry tune or a teen comedy, a nod to the pop cultural icons of "teen spirit."

Rock 'n' roll has traded in these images from the start, making, in turn, rock's own iconic images—Elvis's curled lip or Hendrix's kerosene-soaked burning guitar—serve as shorthand for the defiant exuberance of youth culture. In "Smells Like Teen Spirit," however, these images are turned slightly off-kilter. In the video, these almost iconic images of youth culture become strangely weighed down. Fans in the stands whip their heads back and forth to the beat, but their movement is drawn out, over-articulated, their hair flying forward in a perfect arc. The cheerleaders extend their pom-poms with slow deliberation as if their arms were weighted with dumbbells. Even the janitor's banal gestures—reaching into a bucket of water to retrieve a sponge, leaning heavily upon the mop—take on an impossible dolor. The band members themselves appear to be distracted, looking down at their instruments or struggling with broken guitar strings. The lead singer, Cobain, clutches the mike with both hands and hops briefly in emphasis with the ending chorus but soon leaves off. We see him smashing his guitar at the close of the video, but his effort seems fruitless. His guitar remains intact, and soon he is lost in the crowd that swirls around him.

In the final verse, Cobain speaks as a perfect stoner dude; perhaps he's one of the kids in the stands: "And I forget just what it is / And yet I guess it makes her smile / I found it hard it's hard to find / Oh, well, whatever, nevermind." The verse is hushed, and the words are drawn out thickly into a slurred lyricism. The singer lingers over the grinding "r" sound: "whut-eh-e-verr Ne-eh-verrmind." The chorus rocks, pushing the self-deprecation of the words into sarcasm by sheer force of its delivery ("I feel stupid and contagious! Here we are now, entertain us!"). And yet the verse suggests obscure obstacles, confusion, observations that slip away from articulation. Even the verses that suggest a rock 'n' roll gathering carry the suggestion of a speaker who's blocked in, thwarted by mysterious forces. Rather than a spontaneous uprising, this "group has always been and always will until the end," an observation that seems so stultifying and inevitable that the speaker loses interest in even completing the final verb. The hook, the greeting "hello hello hello," becomes wary, preceded by a slurred phrase, "oh no oh no oh no." The declaration "it's fun" turns ambiguous: "it's fun to lose and to pretend." Is this an ecstatic release or a humiliating slide into false consciousness?

In the video, the kids appear to be exuberant. They sing with the chorus, surf over the crowd, and at the end converge upon the band, and yet we see these events dimly, in drawn-out slow motion, frequently from camera angles slightly above the crowd. The video seems to place us in the midst of the event and yet creates a sensation of distance, as if we viewed it through a gas mask. In fact, there seems to be something unhealthy about this environment. The gym isn't merely dark but murky. A reddish mist suffuses the gym, wafting like clouds through the blurred glare of the stage lights. Even the figure of the cheerleader— that wholesome image of Americana, the buoyancy and high spirits of youth—appears corrupted. When she raises her arm to cheer, we see the dark stain of a tattoo extend across a triceps, an anarchy symbol stitched in place of the school insignia. Rock's teen spirit has grown rank.

For Marcus, this rankness, which can make the video's mist appear as "less the result of the usual video smoke machine than disease flaking off the listeners' skin, floating out of their mouths,"[34] is the "corruption" of rock in the 1990s, a subject that he believes the Nirvana video addresses. Contrasting the Nirvana video with one by the band Poison, also a concert scene played out in slow motion, Marcus understands "Smells Like Teen Spirit" to be a bleak parody. Whereas Poison's video presents a disdainful rock star striding in slow motion through a crowd of awestruck, quivering fans—what Marcus calls "a tableau of worship and hauteur, an advertisement carefully constructed out of clichés"[35]— Nirvana's "Smells Like Teen Spirit" recombines these clichés, marking them with "undifferentiated loathing and decay," a revulsion at the rock scene itself: "when you first glimpse Cobain, bassist Chris [Krist] Novoselic, and drummer David Grohl, they seem more than anything to be going through the motions for a crowd as sick of the ritual as they are."[36] Unlike the Poison video that, in Marcus's view, holds up the seduction of rock as a "pornography of money, fame, and domination,"[37] Nirvana's video seeks to end rock's siren call altogether: "The moods and talismans of five rock 'n' roll decades are in the little play, and as it finishes, implodes, scatters, it seems as good a death as the music could ask for."[38]

For Powers, the ferocious noise of "Smells Like Teen Spirit" only turns in upon itself and implodes. The violence or corruption that the song seems to reveal and attack collapses into "sad moans," and the song "ends up entangled, helpless, driving off a cliff."[39] What neither of these critics fully recognizes, however, is how thoroughly *Nevermind* takes up their critique. If Marcus characterizes much of contemporary rock as a "pornography of money, fame, and domination" and Powers understands this "corruption" or "pornography" as an impotent yet relentless machismo, Nirvana plays out this critique, presenting heavy metal drumming, the power chords of anthem rock, and even punk-styled shriekings under the heading of, to borrow the title of one *Nevermind* song, "Territorial Pissings." In fact, Nirvana's dismissal of heavy metal as an "exhausted" form that has devolved into a caricature of masculine threat and potency, "sexist innuendoes and pseudo-Satanism,"[40] suggests that the band doesn't as much lend itself to Powers's reading as play it out.

Whereas Powers attributes the popularity of "Smells Like Teen Spirit" to a certain overcompensation within a rock community on the verge of "permanent flaccidity," the song itself both sets up an anthem to rock and deflates it as a "denial." The only rock "savior" who appears in the video is disarmed. When the camera cuts to the lead singer for the star-turn guitar solo, we view Cobain hunched awkwardly over his instrument, struggling with a broken string. Rather than inevitably implying "testosterone," the "big and mad" sound of *Nevermind* churns up speakers who hold up their lack: "I feel stupid," "I'm neutered and spayed," "No, I don't have a gun."

In fact, Cobain seemed to revel in the deflating gesture. Accepting an invitation to appear on MTV's heavy metal show *Headbangers' Ball*, Cobain arrived wearing a yellow dress and announced, "I'm dressed for the ball."[41] In doing so, he managed to both poke fun at heavy metal's masculinist posturing and announce rock's "flaccidity": the new rock god is a girl.

Rather than being left to merely rummage through fragments of the past, Nirvana proceeds from fragments, borrowing elements of other songs or poems as a means of revisionary composition. Just as the lyrics are cut-up verse and often quote from pieces that are themselves cut-up poems, the music itself might be considered in somewhat the same manner. Although the musical elements can't be called quotations or, to use Cobain's expression, "rip-offs," since they do not exactly duplicate other songs, these elements often signal other genres or styles and yet are placed in new contexts. In "Smells Like Teen Spirit" Cobain may make use of the shifts in dynamics that the Pixies employed. He nevertheless sets them within a verse-chorus-verse song structure and with guitar elements that are more identified with traditional rock 'n' roll than experimental punk.[42] As Cobain explains, " 'Teen Spirit' was such a clichéd riff. It was so close to a Boston riff or 'Louie, Louie.' When I came up with the guitar part, Krist looked at me and said, 'That is so ridiculous.' I made the band play it for an hour and a half."[43]

Cobain examines the song's guitar part as a fragment of pop history, something borrowed and put to new use. It is perhaps this combination of elements that left many listeners of *Nevermind* with a disoriented sense of déjà vu.[44] It also produces the effect of dislodging or revising some of the song's more "clichéd" elements.

In this light, the fragments of pop history that emerge in the sound and lyrics of "Smells Like Teen Spirit," a song that Cobain describes as his attempt to write the "ultimate pop song,"[45] suggest a parody that would revise and read rather than hopelessly repeat. Like the cut-up method, such composition repeats recognizable elements and yet distances them from their sources, much in the same manner that irony distances speech from intended meaning.

The effect of Nirvana's parodic gestures can be tracked in their most overt parody, the video for "In Bloom." Conceived as a humorous response to public perceptions of the band members as "degenerates," the video stages a concert scene, setting the performance in the era of Ed Sullivan Show, the pop scene of the British invasion. To lend authenticity to the spoof, the video is filmed with the kinescope cameras used for TV shows of the 1950s and early 1960s. The concert scene is intercut with shots of the crowd: squealing girls who press their hands to their faces and shake their bouffants with embarrassed delight, boys who stand chewing gum, elbows pinned to their sides, snapping their fingers to the beat with a studied hipster cool. Perhaps these are scenes from the 1965 concert, the *T.A.M.I.* show. An emcee appears and announces the band.

Nirvana is dressed for its part, the band members appearing in identical striped suits, the guitarists wearing their instruments strapped high across their chests, the guitar necks protruding above their shoulders strolling-musician style. As he plays, the bassist Novoselic sways from side to side; he could be striking the opening chords for "Daydream Believer," emulating one of dozens of Beatle knock-off bands. Behind him, Grohl strikes the rhythm on a small drum kit, wearing a blonde wig that rides a little too high on his head. At the close up, Cobain steps before the mike. He appears wearing black plastic-framed glasses, his hair parted on the side and brushed close to the head. He extends a small clenched smile, jutting his chin slightly foreword. His eyebrows rise just above the center of his glasses' frame as if he were bracing himself, experiencing some difficulty in holding this expression on his face. He is, as announced, one of those "fine young men from Seattle," "thoroughly all right and decent."

The video, however, doesn't settle for a broadly sarcastic take on pop Nirvana. Intercut amidst the nostalgic dance party setting are scenes of daffy mayhem. In these scenes, we are made to see double, for on the same stage, through the same black and white haze of the kinescope camera, Nirvana emerges in dresses and Converse sneakers. The band appears in the style of little girls, in dresses with short bodices and puff sleeves, after the fashion of Dorothy in *The Wizard of Oz* or that favored by the punk band the Meat Puppets.

Whereas the pop Nirvana stood stiffly, this Nirvana alternately rampages like toddlers and moves with clumsily balletic gestures. Temporarily rid of his guitar, Cobain moves like an awkward enthusiast of eurhythmics, holding one arm aloft, the other extended behind him, as he steps forward and spins in slow arcs. Novoselic turns to his right and, extending one arm and leg behind him, cups one hand under his chin and smiles for the camera. In various scenes, they tear at the flimsy set, pitch hunks of plywood and other debris at the drum set, and shred their dresses.

Once they do pick up their guitars, they play with them lewdly. Striking the bass, Novoselic kneels on the stage and arches backward until he is almost flat on his back. Cobain, wearing his guitar at hip level, pulls its body between his legs, its neck extending before him. Approaching Novoselic, Cobain straddles him and extends his guitar, shaking it just over the bass. The gesture is reminiscent of the guitarists kissing each other on their first appearance on "Saturday Night Live," a spontaneous goof designed to confuse and offend. This "punk" Nirvana manages to be both foolish and vulgar at once.

Designed as a comic response to charges that they were "degenerates,"[46] the video appears to perform a simple "reversal of perspective." The video encourages us to take this "degenerate" image for the authentic Nirvana and dismiss the first, nostalgic pop Nirvana, those "decent" young men. It suggests of that pop Nirvana that "I may look clean cut but beneath the stiff repressed surface I'm a degenerate (I like to wear woman's clothes and emulate sex acts with my guitar)." It suggests as well that beneath its shiny, happy surface, pop music may not be so wholesome. In the video's opening moments, amidst the excited squeals of the teenage fans, the smiling, well-groomed singer of pop Nirvana steps forward to deliver the song's opening line: "Sell the kids for food." From the pleasant kinescope glow of this surface, we hear the grating edge of Cobain's voice as he draws out the line, and it is as if it now indicates, "You want clean-cut. All right, I'll give you your clean-cut, market-tested, demographically segmented, rock 'n' roll and expose it for what it is: a trading on youth culture for profit."

And yet while the "pop" and "punk" Nirvanas appear as almost symmetrical opposites, the stiffness of the first countered by the random behavior of the second, this symmetry casts both positions in doubt. The "In Bloom" video does not merely perform the simple "reversal of perspective" that Marcus attributes to the early punks. It is not that the "thoroughly all right and decent" pop image is revealed to be, in truth, degenerate and the punk image as authentic, but that both the pop and punk images are marked as performances. Punk Nirvana's gestures, when contrasted with pop Nirvana's, may appear more random and hence seem more spontaneous and "authentic," yet these gestures are as much quotations as are those of pop Nirvana. Pop Nirvana's manner of wearing guitars is as much a nod to British Invasion bands of the early 1960s as punk Nirvana's phallic guitar gestures refer to earlier rock bands. Moreover, these gestures are further distanced from any notion of authentic assertion by their presentation in drag, as it were.

The proliferation of parodic gestures in the "In Bloom" video makes it even more uncertain who's emulating whom. The boy in the audience, whose stiff, finger-snapping bobbing seems to mimic the lead singer's posture, might be just another fool for pop. Like the confused and thwarted speakers of *Nevermind*, he might be unwittingly possessed by a certain masculinist false consciousness. Or as the chorus says: "he's the one who likes all our pretty songs / And he likes to sing along / And he likes to shoot his gun / But he don't know what it means." And yet in a video in which all images are canny imitations, a specific source of emulation recedes in a hall of mirrors. The chorus could refer as well to the songwriter, the one who "didn't have any specific idea" behind his cut-up lyrics,[47] a punk with a penchant for pretty tunes, a "drag" performer who confesses a fondness for heavy metal and target practice.

In the "In Bloom" video, it is not about which image is the authentic Nirvana, the pop or the punk, nor is it whether rock bands can only repeat "tribute[s] to the tacky pop past."[48] Rather the video parodies both, simultaneously exposing the falsity of pop "happiness" and deflating punk rage. Each ironic image, in fact, serves as the inverse of the other, creating what might be called a doubly inverse image of Nirvana: the pop that is "degenerately" decent and the punk that is "decently" degenerate. In the process, this contradiction or double parody removes both positions from any claim of authenticity. As in what I have called the performance of pathology, this performance doesn't allow the viewer to draw simple distinctions between what is actual and what is performed, between the literal and the figural, but instead suggests that such binary divisions are themselves constructs. The performance reveals the performative nature of identity itself.

If Nirvana's performance collapses the distinction between the original and the imitation, it perhaps more accurately approximates what Judith Butler sees in gender parody, "a production which, in effect—that is, in its effect—postures as an imitation."[49] In this light, Nirvana's performances may be closer to pastiche than parody. Pastiche, in Fredric Jameson's terms, is the repetition that emerges when the concept of the "norm" disappears: "Pastiche is, like parody, the imitation of a peculiar or unique style, the wearing of a stylistic mask, speech in a dead language; but it is a neutral practice of mimicry, without parody's ulterior motive . . . without that still latent feeling that there exists something *normal* compared to which what is being imitated is rather comic. Pastiche is blank parody, parody that has lost its humor."[50]

Pastiche, what Jameson calls the experience of the postmodern, leads to an accelerated sense of fragmentation, "an experience of isolated, disconnected, discontinuous material signifiers which fail to link up into a coherent sequence."[51] The discontinuity that it represents and that he finds so disturbing is the removal of the ground of signification, "the transformation of reality into images."[52] We may also hear in Jameson's account a certain tone of depressive speech. Like depressive speech whose "meaning appears to be arbitrary or . . . secondary," pastiche fails to "link up into a coherent sequence."[53] Its words are drained of signification, rendered "blank," "speech in a dead language."

Depressive speech, in Julia Kristeva's terms, is a "denial of sequentiality, neutralization of the signifier."[54] The depressive's refusal of signification is the attempt to negate the loss of the essential other, the loss that language heralds. Such speech, nevertheless, may possess the power to "produce new languages—strange concatenations." If depressive speech seeks "to become alien to itself . . . for the purpose of capturing the unnameable,"[55] pastiche, in rendering itself painfully "blank," serves to expose the void upon which language is founded. It reveals identity to be not a ground but inhabited by this void, not an authentic but a posited figure.

In his essay, "Postmodernism and Consumer Capitalism," Jameson raises questions about pastiche's efficacy as political critique: "there is a way in which postmodernism replicates or reproduces—reinforces—the logic of consumer capitalism."[56] Marcus's description of a contemporary rock scene haunted by the 1960s and segregated into "efficiently predictable containable markets that can be sold identity, or anyway self-recognition, packaged as music"[57] echoes Jameson's discussion of postmodernist pop culture's "imprisonment in the past."[58] Marcus, like Jameson, also doubts the efficacy of parody.

In an article written after Cobain's death, Alex Ross expresses similar reservations, chiding the songwriter for his "naive" political gestures: "When he declared himself 'gay in spirit,' as he did in an interview with the gay magazine *The Advocate,* he made a political toy out of fragile identity. And his disavowals of masculine culture rang false alongside a stage show that dealt in sonic aggression and equipment-smashing mayhem. Who was he kidding?"[59]

This doubt about the uses of parody or pastiche is a doubt that there can be a politics without the subject of intentional speech. What these readings preclude, however, is the possibility of speaking "as," a certain performative power in language. Like Powers's first assessment of *Nevermind* as "testosterone" rock, Ross's reading reveals a tendency to render gestures into personifications of a performer's readable traits. Since the preponderance of rock guitarists have been and are men, one almost inevitably associates guitars and rock with men and comes to mark rock gestures, "sonic aggression and equipment-smashing mayhem," as masculine. In Powers's and Ross's terms, however, this association has hardened into an apparent sign as readily discernible as the "proper" either/or category into which one might place the sexed bodies of the performers. These writers, as do an overwhelming number of commentators on rock, transform what might more properly be called a figure (i.e., "rock as masculine" or "rock as phallic discourse") into a ground, and in turn, this "given" comes to organize a whole series of genres, sounds, or gestures into fixed binary categories. Thus, not only are aggressive guitars and guitar solos marked as male, but, "the narrative and the single voice" or the "ego"[60]—in short, identity—become inevitably masculine. Following Ross's conclusions in which guitar noise and "mayhem" are part of "masculine culture" and to be gay is to possess a "fragile identity," to be feminized in the pejorative sense of the word, rock's "sonic aggression" becomes, in his terms, not only male but fixed within a particularly hegemonic version of male heterosexuality.[61]

In that they suppose individuals refer synecdochically to the group in which they belong, such readings render all bodies or identities as apparent readable signs, fixing them within predictable binaries of male/female, insider/outsider, heterosexual/homosexual. Within such a model, the inversions of parody can only return to the established binaries of meaning; irony can only be defeatist. What the video performance of "In Bloom" suggests, however, is the extent to which these categories are constructs. In these performances, rock's traditional gestures of phallic mastery are not merely undercut but displaced altogether. By playing them out in drag, Nirvana separates these phallic gestures from male bodies and masculine expression, draining them of significance and exposing them as an empty and appropriable performance.[62] If in "Smells Like Teen Spirit" rock's lead guitarist is left unstrung and enervated, the "sonic aggression" of punk appears in the guise of a woman, in the wholesome feminine form of the cheerleaders who bear the punk regalia of tattoos and anarchist symbols or in the rampaging girl-children of "In Bloom." Placing rock's "phallic" gestures in drag does not merely reverse and helplessly maintain the established regime but reveals its gaps or contradictions. Such performances suggest how identity is not given but necessarily constructed and "fragile."

In reviewing Cobain's career, Powers comes to reverse her position, focusing on the uses of ambiguity and contradiction within Nirvana's music.[63] For Marcus, however, rock's complicity with a consumer culture that reifies and sells identity as image is a corruption that the irony of "Smells Like Teen Spirit" cannot reach. Irony, in fact, may never be overtly oppositional, and yet, in insisting upon clearly demarcated positions and statements, oppositional speech may never possess the power to disturb the established orders of meaning and identity. Like depressive speech or the affectless "blank" quality of pastiche, irony in its most radical form offers up words denuded of apparent or expressive meaning. It removes the subject of intentional speech. And yet radical irony preserves an absence within language and the subject. In its deferral of signification, such speech thwarts the subject's appropriation into meaning, its reduction to an apparent sign.

The peculiar ironic tone identified with grunge or Generation X, its particularly aggressive stance of self-deprecation, stems from this "resistance to interpretation," from an attempt to open a breach in identity marked as fixed and apparent. In this respect, it owes something to the aesthetic strategies of the avant-garde. Like Cobain, Jones composes from fragments of other works, gestures, and contradictory assertions, repeatedly constructing his dances as ironic or disorienting responses to public perceptions of him (famously naming one dance "Fever Swamps" after a line in an Arlene Croce review of his work). Confronted with these performances, Croce has blasted the work as mere displays of "pathology" and "victim art" (a remark strangely echoed in Hal Foster's take on the aesthetic of grunge as a desire to be "stuck in trauma").[64] Her response, however, doesn't so much read the work's resistance to criticism as render it the personification of its performer.

As I have attempted to suggest, these critics' readings reflect a desire to rewrite blank parody as apparent sign. Such readings reinscribe originary loss within a fixed register of meaning, return what is "blank" or illegible to the logic of gain. Their tendency to read gestures as personifications, in fact, only emulates the impulse to render mass culture into "predictable containable markets" or commodified identities. These performances, however, by triggering the collapse of distinctions central to interpretation, ultimately posit the subject as unreadable. Precisely by rendering speech blank, Nirvana's performances resist easy translation into the appropriable poses of postmodern capitalism.

Notes

1. Elizabeth Wurtzel, *Prozac Nation: Young and Depressed in America* (Boston: Houghton Mifflin, 1994), 297.

2. Hal Foster, "U.S. Fascinated by Romance of Wretchedness," *Buffalo News,* 18 January 1995, sec. F, p. 9.

3. Arlene Croce, "Discussing the Undiscussable," review of "Still/Here," choreographed by Bill T. Jones, *New Yorker,* 26 December 1994/2 January 1995, 59–60.

4. Henry Louis Gates Jr., "The Body Politic," *New Yorker,* 28 November 1994, 114.

5. Wurtzel, 308.

6. "Table of Contents," *Time,* 18 April 1994, 1.

7. Bill T. Jones, with Peggy Gillespie, *Last Night on Earth* (New York: Pantheon Books, 1995), 267.

8. Foster, sec. F, p. 9.

9. Julia Kristeva, *Black Sun: Depression and Melancholia,* trans. Leon S. Roudiez (New York: Columbia University Press, 1989), 33.

10. Ibid., 43.

11. As Cobain says of his lyrics, "I try to have some relation to some of the lines . . . but it's always changing. When I say 'I' in a song, it's not me, 90 percent of the time" (Jon Pareles, "Nirvana, The Band That Hates to Be Loved," *New York Times,* 14 November 1993, late edition, 32). "Mr. Cobain doesn't like explaining his lyrics, which he says he assembles from spiral-bound notebooks of bedtime jottings. 'It's just thumbing through my poetry books and going "Oh, there's a line," and writing it down. That's all I do'" (Pareles, 32). In an interview for *Melody Maker,* Cobain echoes this point: "Almost all of my lyrics have been cut-ups . . ." (Stud Brothers, "Dark Side of the Womb, Part I," *Melody Maker,* 21 August 1993, 28).

12. Kristeva, *Black Sun,* 42.

13. Dick Hebdige, *Subculture: The Meaning of Style* (1979; reprint, New York: Routledge, 1987), 120.

14. Ibid.

15. Greil Marcus, *Lipstick Traces: A Secret History of the Twentieth Century* (Cambridge: Harvard University Press, 1990), 67.

16. Hebdige, 120.

17. Marcus, *Lipstick Traces,* 74.

18. Mary Douglas, *Purity and Danger* (London: Routledge, 1969), 113.

19. Julia Kristeva, *Powers of Horror: An Essay on Abjection,* trans. Leon S. Roudiez (New York: Columbia University Press, 1982), 4.

20. Greil Marcus, "Notes on the Life and Death and Incandescent Banality of Rock 'n' Roll," *Esquire,* August 1992, 71.

21. Ann Powers, "A Shot of Testosterone," *Village Voice,* 3 March 1992, 8.

22. Ibid.

23. Marcus, "Notes on the Life and Death and Incandescent Banality of Rock 'n' Roll," 68.

24. Several songs of *Nevermind* seem to both celebrate guitar rock and mock its intensity as empty posturing. Over the heavy metal drums and distorted punkish guitars, the speaker of "Breed" seems to comment defensively: "I don't care, don't care if its old / I don't mind, I don't mind that I don't have a mind."

25. "Nausea makes me balk at that milk cream, separates me from the mother and father who proffer it. 'I' want none of that element, sign of their desire . . . 'I' expel it. But since the food is not an 'other' for 'me,' who am only in their desire, I expel myself, I spit myself out, I abject myself" (Kristeva, *Powers of Horror,* 3).

26. "Rather than seek the meaning of despair (it is either obvious or metaphysical), let us acknowledge that there is meaning only in despair. The child king becomes irredeemably sad before uttering his first words; this is because he has been irrevocably, desperately separated from the mother, a loss that causes him to try to find her again, along with other objects of love, first in the imagination, then in words . . . if there is no writing other than the amorous, there is no imagination that is not, overtly or secretly, melancholy" (Kristeva, *Black Sun,* 5–6).

27. Mudhoney, "Touch Me I'm Sick," Sub Pop, summer 1988. Rereleased on *Superfuzz Bigmuff plus Early Singles,* Sub Pop, SP21b, 1990.

28. Jon Savage, *England's Dreaming: Anarchy, Sex Pistols, Punk Rock and Beyond* (New York: St. Martin's Press, 1991), 114. See also Marcus, *Lipstick Traces,* 27.

29. The Jimi Hendrix Experience, "Fire," on *Are You Experienced?* MCA, RS 6261, 1967.

30. This trail of associations has been sketched in detail by Susan Sontag, who argues that AIDS has become the reigning metaphor for "contagion and mutation" (Susan Sontag, *Illness as Metaphor and AIDS and Its Metaphors* [New York: Doubleday, 1989], 155). The AIDS bearer or even the homosexual—connected in the homophobic imagination both with violation of taboo bodily boundaries and the disease that is the very figure of contagion—has been made to stand in as the "polluting person" of contemporary Western culture. Judith Butler also poses this argument in Simon Watney's *Policing Desire: AIDS, Pornography and the Media* (Minneapolis: University of Minnesota Press, 1988). See also Judith Butler, *Gender Trouble: Feminism and the Subversion of Identity* (New York: Routledge, 1990), 132.

31. Mudhoney, "You Got It (Keep It Out Of My Face)," Sub Pop, spring 1989. Rereleased on *Superfuzz Bigmuff plus Early Singles,* Sub Pop, SP21b, 1990.

32. Nirvana, *Nevermind,* DGC, DGCC-24425, 1991.

33. See the comments of Elizabeth Wurtzel in the epilogue to *Prozac Nation,* 295–311; Ann Powers, "A Shot of Testosterone," 8; Greg Tate, "Music: Love Chile," *Village Voice,* 28 September 1993, 71–72; Greil Marcus, "Notes on the Life and Death and Incandescent Banality of Rock 'n' Roll," 67–75; and Anthony DeCurtis, "Kurt Cobain 1967–1994," *Rolling Stone,* 2 June 1994, 30.

34. Marcus, "Notes on the Life and Death and Incandescent Banality of Rock 'n' Roll," 70.

35. Ibid., 68.

36. Ibid., 70.

37. Ibid., 68.

38. Ibid., 71.

39. Powers, "A Shot of Testosterone," 8.

40. Chris Mundy, "The Rolling Stone Interview," *Rolling Stone,* 23 January 1992, 40.

41. Ibid.

42. See David Fricke, "The Rolling Stone Interview," *Rolling Stone* 27 January 1994, 36–37.

43. Ibid.

44. See, in particular, the letters to the editor in the 1992 Village Voice readers poll, which ranked Nirvana's *Nevermind* album of the year ("We're Number One," *Village Voice,* 3 March 1992, 6).

45. Fricke, 36.

46. See Cobain's remarks in the "MTV Nirvana Special," aired May 15, 1994.

47. Stud Brothers, "Dark Side of the Womb, Part I," *Melody Maker,* 21 August 1993, 28.

48. Kurt Loder, "MTV Nirvana Special," May 15, 1994.

49. Butler, 138. As Butler says of drag and gender, "In imitating gender, drag implicitly reveals the imitative structure of gender itself" (137). Butler arrives at this argument via a reading of Esther Newton's discussion of drag in *Mother Camp: Female Impersonators in America.* In Newton's terms, drag performs a "double inversion": Drag says "'my "outside" appearance is feminine, but my essence "inside" is masculine.' At the same time it symbolizes the opposite inversion; 'my appearance "outside" is masculine but my essence "inside" is feminine'" (quoted in Butler, 137). It at once indicates that

"appearance is illusion" and yet translates what is commonly understood to be a ground of identity or truth—the body or what lies below the surface—into mere appearance ("my body may be masculine, but I am feminine"). According to Butler, the contradictory claims that Newton finds in drag cancel themselves out and remove identity from claims of authenticity or falsity and into the realm of performance.

50. Frederic Jameson, "Postmodernism and Consumer Society," in *The Anti-Aesthetic: Essays on Postmodern Culture*, ed. Hal Foster (Port Townsend, Wash.: Bay Press, 1983), 114.

51. Ibid., 119.

52. Ibid., 125.

53. Ibid., 119.

54. Kristeva, *Black Sun*, 20.

55. Ibid., 42.

56. Jameson, 125.

57. Marcus, "Notes on the Life and Death and Incandescent Banality of Rock 'n' Roll," 69.

58. Jameson, 116. Marcus's characterization of contemporary rock as "carefully constructed out of clichés that have been pretested and presold" ("Notes," 68) is consonant with Jameson's discussion of pastiche, particularly as it appears in what he characterizes as "nostalgia movies." If postmodernist pastiche suggests both the "death of the subject" and the desire to plug up this loss through an identification with cultural icons of the past, a "nostalgic desire . . . to live its strange old aesthetic artifacts" (Jameson, 116), recurrent references to 1960s rock reflect both "[contemporary pop music's] overwhelming sense of separation, isolation, segregation" and a vision of that decade as offering "a myth of wholeness—a wholeness that people who never experienced 'the Sixties' as fact or illusion, sometimes still feel as an absence, like the itch of a limb amputated before they were born" ("Notes," 68–69).

59. Alex Ross, "Generation Exit," *New Yorker*, 25 April 1994, 105.

60. Powers, "A Shot of Testosterone," 8.

61. In a period that saw a dramatic increase in the number of women rock guitarists and the emergence of various "queercore" bands, it's particularly ironic that the association between guitar power and phallic prowess, or more crudely, male (hetero)sexual prowess, should become so persistent as to carry the force of fact. But to be precise, it is not that rock music is a text whose voice and "meaning" is both gendered and fixed, but rather it is reading that establishes rock as a text.

Like Ross's, Powers's article, "A Shot of Testosterone," suggests how reading both directs and limits the scope of analysis. Although in a discussion that takes particular interest in the fate of women in rock music, Powers's assumption of rock's inherent "testosterone" renders all guitar noise as phallic and the noise that a woman guitarist makes as unreadable. In a review of the indie scene and women performers, Powers criticizes the ruling "homosociality" that marks the Seattle independent labels and makes no mention of the all-women punk bands emerging at the same moment in nearby Olympia, Washington ("Shot," 8).

62. The "In Bloom" video, much like "Smells Like Teen Spirit," pointedly attacks the figure of the rock star and the "pornography of money, fame, and domination" he represents. If the solo in the video for "Smells Like Teen Spirit" foregrounds broken strings and a befuddled lead guitarist, the video for "In Bloom" also makes use of an embarrassing accident: amidst the punk goofing, the camera zooms in and the viewer sees Cobain, riding astride Novoselic's shoulders, suddenly grimace. He stumbles from

his perch. Doubled over and still grimacing, he clutches his crotch, shuffles knock-kneed to the microphone just in time for the chorus. Whereas the "Smells Like Teen Spirit" video employs a disabled guitar to undercut the rock star's phallic mastery, the "In Bloom" video seems to use the vulnerabilities of the male body to the same purpose, spoofing rock virtuosity and punk rage in one blow. Moreover, despite persuasive evidence, we can't exactly mark this moment as an "authentic" accident or a slipping of the mask, for we don't see it as an outtake in an MTV blooper tape but in the final edit. Both costumes and bodies, acting and accidents, are part of the same deflating performance.

63. Powers comes to see the ambiguity and contradiction within Nirvana's music as an effort "to discover, in rock's language, an expression of power free of the usual machismo . . . to find . . . the messages in incoherence" (Ann Powers, prefacing remarks to her reprinted article, "Loud Fast Rules: Nirvana Plays the Cow Palace," in *Cobain,* edited by the *Rolling Stone* editors [Boston: Little, Brown, 1994], 52).

64. Foster, sec. F, p. 9.

Bibliography

1991: The Year Punk Broke. Directed by Dave Markey. Geffen Home Video DGCV-39518, 1993.

Allman, Kevin. "The Dark Side of Kurt Cobain." *Advocate* 9 February 1993: 35–43.

Azerrad, Michael. "Inside the Heart and Mind of Kurt Cobain." *Rolling Stone* 4 April 1992: 36–41, 96–97.

Brothers, Stud. "Dark Side of the Womb, Part I." *Melody Maker,* 21 August 1993, 26–28.

———. "Dark Side of the Womb, Part II" *Melody Maker,* 28 August 1993, 46–47.

Butler, Judith. *Gender Trouble: Feminism and the Subversion of Identity.* New York: Routledge, 1990.

Croce, Arlene. "Discussing the Undiscussable." *New Yorker,* 26 December 1994/2 January 1995, 54–59.

DeCurtis, Anthony. "Kurt Cobain 1967–1994." *Rolling Stone,* 2 June 1994, 30.

Douglas, Mary. *Purity and Danger.* London: Routledge, 1969.

Foster, Hal. "U.S. Fascinated by Romance of Wretchedness." *Buffalo News,* 18 January 1995, sec. F, p. 9.

Fricke, David. "The Rolling Stone Interview." *Rolling Stone,* 27 January 1994, 34.

Gates, Henry Louis Jr.. "The Body Politic." *New Yorker,* 28 November 1994, 112–24.

Hebdige, Dick. *Subculture: The Meaning of Style.* 1979. Reprint, New York: Routledge, 1987.

Jameson, Fredric. "Postmodernism and Consumer Society." In *The Anti-Aesthetic: Essays on Postmodern Culture,* edited by Hal Foster. Port Townsend, Wash.: Bay Press, 1983.

Jimi Hendrix Experience, The. "Fire." *Are You Experienced?* MCA, RS 6261, 1967.

Jones, Bill T. with Peggy Gillespie. *Last Night on Earth.* New York: Pantheon Books, 1995.

Kristeva, Julia. *Black Sun: Depression and Melancholia.* Translated by Leon S. Roudiez. New York: Columbia University Press, 1989.

———. *Powers of Horror: An Essay on Abjection.* Translated by Leon S. Roudiez. New York: Columbia University Press, 1982.

Marcus, Greil. *Lipstick Traces: A Secret History of the Twentieth Century.* Cambridge: Harvard University Press, 1989.

——. "Notes on the Life and Death and Incandescent Banality of Rock 'n' Roll." *Esquire,* August 1992, 67–75.

Mudhoney. "Touch Me I'm Sick." Sub Pop, summer 1988. Reissued in *Superfuzz Bigmuff plus Early Singles.* Sub Pop, SP21b, 1990.

——. "You Got It (Keep It Out Of My Face)." Sub Pop, spring 1989. Reissued in *Superfuzz Bigmuff plus Early Singles.* Sub Pop, SP21b, 1990.

Mundy, Chris. "The Rolling Stone Interview." *Rolling Stone,* 23 January 1992, 38–41.

Nirvana. *Nevermind.* DGC, DGCC-24425, 1991.

"MTV Nirvana Special." New York, MTV, 15 May 1994.

Pareles, Jon. "Nirvana, the Band That Hates to Be Loved." *New York Times.* 14 Nov. 1993. Late edition, 32–33.

Powers, Ann. "A Shot of Testosterone." *Village Voice,* 3 March 1992, 8.

——. "No Future: Kurt Cobain's Final Denial." *Village Voice.* 19 April 1994, 31–35.

——. Prefacing remarks to reprinted article, "Loud Fast Rules: Nirvana Plays the Cow Palace." In *Cobain,* edited by Fred Woodward and the *Rolling Stone.* Boston: Little, Brown, 1994.

Ross, Alex. "Generation Exit." *New Yorker,* 25 April 1994, 102–6.

Savage, Jon. *England's Dreaming: Anarchy, Sex Pistols, Punk Rock and Beyond.* New York: St. Martin's Press, 1991.

Sontag, Susan. *Illness as Metaphor and AIDS and Its Metaphors.* New York: Doubleday, 1989.

Table of Contents. *Time,* 18 April 1994, 1.

Tate, Greg. "Music: Love Chile." *Village Voice,* 28 September 1993, 71–72.

Watney, Simon. *Policing Desire: AIDS, Pornography, and the Media.* Minneapolis: University of Minnesota Press, 1988.

"We're Number One." *Village Voice,* 3 March 1992, 6–8.

Wurtzel, Elizabeth. *Prozac Nation: Young and Depressed in America.* Boston: Houghton Mifflin, 1994.

Part 2
Print Media

You Can See Nathan's from Here

Lobbing Culture at the Boomers

Daniel W. Lehman

Woodstock was a hip capitalist pajama party. Every time I look in the mirror, it's like watching a home movie.

Legs McNeil, resident punk of *PUNK* magazine, 1976

The official history of Generation X has overlooked its roots. The Generation X phenomenon originated in the political and generational struggle underlying marginal Anglo-American pop culture in the late 1970s, which then festered in the Reagan-era, and broke out into mass culture consumption in the 1990s. Mass media reporters of the Generation X phenomenon, upon rooting through copy morgues for the moniker's pedigree, uniformly end up granting credit to Douglas Coupland's 1991 novel. For example, a 1994 cover story on twenty-something *angst* was typical: "Generation X," reporter Jeff Giles informs *Newsweek* readers, was "named after an arch pop-arty Douglas Coupland novel that also gave us 'McJobs.'"[1]

Asserting the signification of Generation X as nothing more than an "arch, pop-arty" novel, or the excellent adventures of *Reality Bites* wanna-bes, plays into the baby boomer fantasy that a core challenge to boomer values can be managed easily. In turn, that fantasy rests on a seemingly willful misreading of the punks and their progeny, who embraced the dross of American contemporary culture, recontextualized it, set it on its ear, and exposed the emptiness within it by celebrating its very emptiness in black (and blank) humor. That move is fundamentally different from the archetypal hippie-boomer agenda. Whereas their older brothers and sisters (or parents) embraced a politics of engagement and a drive toward standards (on the left or right) of social engineering and moral correctness, the newer agenda played on the margins of culture, waged guerilla war on the values of its elders, and understood that while media construction may be inevitable, it can begin to be defanged by a subtle dialogic of style.

Newsweek's crediting Generation X to Coupland betrays the manner by which official myth making can overtake the memory of more challenging alternatives. Whatever Coupland's inspiration, many postboomer slam dancers will remember Generation X as one of a welter of British punk bands that, along with the Sex Pistols and such U.S. groups as the Ramones and Dead Boys, stormed the music industry from 1976 to 1979. "Your generation don't mean a thing to me," lead singer Billy Idol snarled in the Generation X band's signature anthem, "Your Generation," released in August 1977, well before Idol achieved fame in the 1980s as a "new wave" solo artist. Idol's lyrics were a self-conscious response to Pete Townsend of the Who, whose "My Generation" ("People try to put me down / talking about my generation") more than a decade earlier had helped define terms for emerging postwar boomer culture in both the United Kingdom and the United States.[2] Meanwhile, the Generation X band's defiance of the aging rockers who had dominated the pop charts with evermore produced and promoted corporate anthems was matched in New York's own burgeoning punk culture by "Blank Generation," a single cut in 1976 by Richard Hell and the Voidoids, a virtual house band of the downtown CBGBs scene. "I belong to the blank generation / I can take it or leave it each time," Richard Hell yelled over Robert Quine guitar licks that were more of a deconstruction than homage to Townsend's trademark guitar heroics.[3]

That generational challenge, which continued to influence the way the margin of the Generation X phenomenon constructed itself in the mid-1990s, is rooted in Lower Manhattan cultural fashion of the late 1970s. If the Bowery's CBGB OMFUG supplied the punk front its battle anthems and the Manic Panic or Trash and Vaudeville boutiques its razor-slashed uniforms, most of the insurgents took their marching theory from the fanzine- and comic book–styled *PUNK* magazine cranked out every couple of months or so from 1976–79 by publisher Ged Dunn, cartoonist and editor John Holmstrom, and Roderick Edwin "Legs" McNeil, self-styled "resident punk" and "counter intelligent" provoca-teur.[4] First dubbed *Teenage News,* the magazine's name was changed to *PUNK* in honor of lyrics penned by the protopunk band the Dictators: "Eddie is the local punk / throwing up and getting drunk / eating in McDonald's for lunch."[5]

Examined twenty years later, *PUNK* magazine clearly prefigures more recent and widely publicized cultural skirmishes between the busters and boomers: it was resolutely oppositional, resolutely genera-tional, and it marked the first time that avant-garde American culture managed to position those born in the ten years after World War II on the wrong side of the hip culture battlefront. In retrospect, it was easy pickings: *Rocky* had become everyone's idea of a good movie; the Eagles had mired themselves in record studios endlessly tuning and retuning their elaborate odes to the misery of wealth in the posthippie freeway-culture era; Bob Dylan had become enmeshed in investment scams; the sexual revolution had become entrusted to Erica Jong and *The Joy of Sex;* everyone looked like Judd Hirsch on *Taxi* with earth-toned polyes-ter and bushy 'burns; and the aging readers of the underground press were busy browsing *New York* for the ten best places to score brunch on the Upper West Side.

PUNK's editors, by contrast, were less interested in honoring or copy-ing dominant counterculture symbols than in obliterating them and re-casting their readers in a complicated new relationship to the very icons of dominant American culture, particularly the mass-mediated icons, that many baby boomers had resisted. *PUNK*'s "perfect reader," sketched in a May/June 1979 in-house advertisement for the fanzine, was a head-less teenager reading a copy of *PUNK*, whose front cover just happens to display a picture of the youth's own head (see figure 1). "Subscribe to the Magazine that makes Hamburgers out of Sacred Cows," advises the ad copy, which displays a queue of "liberals, music, pimples, children and dogs, Nazis, and Commies" being fed to the "monolithic punk meat grinder" (a commode with the "ring of truth" for its toilet seat and "the great melting pot" for its bowl) whose end product is shoveled to "John Q. Public . . . feeding the public's insatiable desire for media stimuli" (*PUNK* 17:3).

In an era before anyone had even thought to package "classic rock"

Figure 1.   Acephalous *PUNK* reader, from a May/June
1979 advert for *PUNK* magazine. Illustration © 1979 Bruce
Carleton. *PUNK* trademark used with permission of *PUNK*
magazine. Image reprinted by permission of Bruce Carleton and John Holmstrom.

as a radio programming strategy, Holmstrom was already complaining
in the *PUNK* issue cited above that the boomer-dominated U.S. culture
industry had become "boring dull fools who go to rock clubs, halls, and
coliseums too fucked up on drugs and booze to think and expecting a
television program. Today's rock fans debate, as if they are scholars, on
the points and facts of why Jimmy Page is a more virtuoso guitarist than
Ted Nugent. Their life's ambition is to become a professor at [a] college
on advanced rock history" (*PUNK* 17:36). And showing a remarkable pre-
science that would be fulfilled at the Woodstock 1994 credit card hoe-
down, Holmstrom scathingly envisions a ten-year Woodstock reunion
that anticipates the nineties-era youth complaint that the baby boomers
just don't know when it's time to get off the stage. Writing on March
27, 1979, Holmstrom begins a hand-lettered communiqué on Woodstock II, then scrawls "SHIT" atop it in block letters. He then draws a
two-headed arrow to another hand-lettered box and continues: "Old hippies never die—they hold reunions. Woodstock II is planned! The new
Who will make their U.S. debut there, Creedence Clearwater Revival

will revive, the Grateful Dead will play, also The Starship, Mountain, Crosby, Stills, Nash & Young etc. Ad nauseam. Two double live albums and a movie will come out of it. Aug. 21, 1979—10 years later we at *PUNK* are planning to manufacture lots of brown acid for sale at the event to make a bigger 'bummer' than ever! Yahoo!" (*PUNK* 17:7).

Elsewhere in *PUNK,* Legs McNeil debated the state of the modern world with Joey Ramone, conducted fictional "famous person" interviews with Boris and Natasha or the cast of Gilligan's Island (Jacobson, 20), and conceived and directed a photo comix, "Brat Patrol," featuring the punk band "Shrapnel" scouring the Connecticut countryside for its nemesis: "a bald aging fanatical flower child driven mad by excessive banana-peel smoking" (*PUNK* 16:19). Some of the magazine's moves, of course, were the sort of sophomoric ideas that one might expect from *Mad* magazine readers who, had they been in school, would have been about old enough to be, well, sophomores. But there was more to it.

Journalist and sometimes fiction writer Mark Jacobson, in his "Cool in an Uncool Time: Teenage Hipster in the Modern World" (1978), profiled Legs McNeil's hipster half-life for the *Village Voice.* It read like a storyboard for a 1990s-era *Reality Bites* spin-off, though it preceded the "Gen X" phenomenon by about fifteen years: "These days, Legs's professed only goal in life was to sing the theme song from Eva Gabor's TV show, *Green Acres,* before a packed house at Madison Square Garden. He had also been known to take an elevator to the top of the Empire State Building, look out on a perfectly clear night, and say, 'Wow, you can see Nathan's from here'" (Jacobson, 19). McNeil complained to Jacobson that he was tired of being told that he had missed such tasty tidbits of boomer lore as the Summer of Love or heading for the coast or battling the government. His resulting decision was to embrace, if certainly to recontextualize, the very same mainstream American culture that the counterculture had rejected. The trick, Legs decided, was to flip those cultural symbols with just enough ironic twist of the wrist that their power might be disarmed: "Legs decreed that in order to be cool one had to be hip to how to live in [the] contemporary landscape. It was a task an entire generation had called impossible, choosing instead to label the Modern World 'plastic' and cuddle themselves in the fantasies of 'going back to the land'" (20).

In his own way, Jacobson rejected the way the participatory ethic of New Journalism had been retooled for boomer consumer culture as much as *PUNK* did. In detailing the research for a *New York* magazine article that he never wrote, Jacobson reveals that *New York* editor Clay Felker—who a decade earlier had encouraged Tom Wolfe to write Ken Kesey's Merry Prankster story for the "New York" section of the old *New York Herald-Tribune*—wanted Jacobson to make Legs McNeil a punk "star" in the same way Wolfe had supplied the sixties generation with boarding passes to the Pranksters' magic bus. "The Felk," according to Jacobson, "frothing to finger still another trend, sent me to 'identify' punk, the crest of which was then beginning to media crash" (19). Jacobson's refusal to make Legs famous for *New York* (ironically the *Village Voice* article that tends to do just that) was to Jacobson the most "moral" act of his journalistic career: "I said, 'Legs, you asshole, I'm not taking the responsibility for making you famous'" (19). Jacobson's piece dramatizes the tension between author and subject ("He'd see me on The Bowery and shout, 'There goes the guy who didn't want to take the responsibility of making me famous'") and between performer and critic. This dynamic is perhaps best summed up by sociologist and culture critic Simon Frith in "The Cultural Study of Popular Music" as "an anxiety-driven search by radical intellectuals and rootless academics for a model of consumption—for the perfect consumer, the subcultural idol, the mod, the punk, the cool commodity fetishist, the organic intellectual of the high street who can stand in for them."[6]

This bob-and-weave approach to media construction and manipulation is one of the enduring legacies that Legs and his henchmen handed to baby busters. In England, sociologist Dick Hebdige (who credits the "minimalist aesthetic" of the 1976-era downtown New York scene as a founding source of British punk[7]) summed up these elusive dialogics in his landmark treatise on cultural studies, *Subculture: The Meaning of Style,* published in 1979. Hebdige describes an ethic that "plays back the alienation of youth onto itself" and discovers that "punk represents the most recent phase in this process. In punk, alienation assumed an almost tangible quality. It could almost be grasped. It gave itself up to the cameras in 'blankness,' the removal of expression, the refusal to speak and be positioned. This trajectory—the solipsism, the neurosis, the cosmetic rage—had its origins in rock" (28).

Further, Hebdige calls this "refusal to be positioned" *bricolage,* a term Claude Levi-Strauss used in his study of native iconography, *The*

Savage Mind, to signify the appropriation of the dominant images of colonialism and their retooling in the service of native opposition. Hebdige writes, "Like Duchamp's 'ready-mades'—manufactured objects which qualified as art because he chose to call them such, the most unremarkable and inappropriate items—a pin, a plastic clothes peg, a television component, a razor blade, a tampon—could be brought within the province of punk (un)fashion . . . so long as the rupture between 'natural' and constructed context was clearly visible" (106–7). Jacobson placed Legs and his punksters within a lineage of white hipsterdom that Norman Mailer explored in his landmark 1957 essay, "The White Negro."[8] The hipster stance, Mailer explained, grew out of the imminence of nuclear annihilation and fueled a response that adopted the bop rhythms of African-American style. But although he gave "big Norm" his due, Jacobson found something essentially different in the act that Legs was building, a difference built on the realization that mass culture had caught up with the apocalyptic angst and was, in fact, mass marketing it. Therefore, one way to respond was to take what they gave you and, like a veteran bricoleur, twist it in your own direction: "America has adjusted in profound ways to the specter of the apocalypse. Now we have throwaway television, throwaway burgers, throwaway housing. None of it has the permanence of the pants your mother bought an inch too long so they'd fit next year. The society has caught up to Hiroshima. We are living . . . in a fully fleshed out post-atomic world. Everything we touch, eat, and see has the singe of doom on it. So Legs doesn't need anyone to tell him secrets. He knows the scene as well as anyone. He needs no guide; he's on his own" (23).

PUNK magazine thus got wise to the goofy television culture and pulp narratives that ruled postwar pop marketing and made sure that its rupture remained visible front and center. The magazine's photo novel, "The Legend of Nick Detroit" (issue 6), starring Richard Hell and the members of Blondie, ripped B-movie gangster images from their context and recast them as legendary rock star outcasts who refuse to become rock legends. In "Mutant Monster Beach Party" (issue 15) Joey Ramone and Blondie's Debbie Harry were featured in the Frankie Avalon and Annette Funicello roles; its Dictators and John Cale cover (issue 11) unfurled a blank American flag. The editors sponsored "Draw the Punk" contests in the manner of the bogus art school come-ons and invited readers to draw graffiti on the face of Shaun Cassidy. They hosted a gala awards show November 13, 1978 (the band Generation X was nosed out for best album by Elvis Costello's *This Year's Model*) that they designed both to drive them into the media spotlight and into bankruptcy. Issue 16 reported, "Although PUNK magazine did lose enough money to go bankrupt . . . the one drunk who was so obnoxious that he had to be thrown out of this sordid affair became our new publisher—John Spacely" (PUNK 16:4).

It's not much of a stretch to see the clear lineage between this sort of self-conscious, media-savvy clowning and the scene in *Reality Bites* where Winona Ryder and her buddies pogo to the Knack's "My Sharona" in the cool neon of a convenience store to the somewhat bewitched, bothered, and bewildered stares of a store clerk.[9] It's a scene that, perhaps unwittingly, pantomimes *Easy Rider*'s shock-the-masses "Born to be Wild" alienation. Only this time, the rebellion is as ephemeral and cheap as a pack of Twinkies. And that's the point: real rebellion would cost more than the price of a Peter Fonda movie ticket, and the kids, unlike their elders, seem to know that few are willing to pay the price. That the Knack symbolized in 1979 the quick mass production (and certain death) of punk as palatable British power pop only completes a joke that Legs McNeil seemed to get a long time ago, as he showed in his "exclusive" interview with Alice Cooper in 1978 and published in PUNK's issue 17. "Shortly after our own Legs McNeil escaped the booby hatch after a prolonged heavy drinking binge," Holmstrom writes in his introduction to the piece, "he ran into Alice Cooper at a party. The two of them got together to compare notes" (PUNK 17:25).

Predictably, Legs chose for his own treatment a "discount mental place" that he had seen advertised on television (PUNK 17:26) while Cooper recalled that the only really scary moment during his hospitalization was when a patient flipped out and started to smash the ward's only television: "I had to stop her real fast," Cooper remembered, "because that was the only thing in the hospital that was keeping me real sane. If she broke the TV, I couldn't watch the 'Odd Couple' " (17:25). During the interview McNeil and Cooper imagine themselves watching the whole punk movement as a "Gong Show" act with a dead certain ending:

Legs: What's your favorite show?
Alice: I watch the "Gong Show" every day. That's my favorite. Chuck Barris is great. He is *great*.

Legs: Yeah, that song, "Palisades Park," he wrote.

Alice: Yeah, great song. Freddie Cannon.

Legs: I mean, he's done like everything, hit song, hit book.

Alice: Yeah, taught himself how to play guitar, self-taught. He's got a funny sense of humor, too. He's really . . . he ought to do . . . in fact, I was going to tell him he ought to do a whole punk show on the "Gong Show." Devote a whole show to punk rock.

Legs: You should go on there.

Alice: On his show? I did.

Legs: You did? I didn't know that. When did you go on?

Alice: I did the Anniversary Show. I did "On the Guillotine" and "I Think I'm Going Outta My Head." (Laughs)

Legs: Did you get gonged?

Alice: Yeah. (17:27)

Mark Jacobson saved his cheekiest honorifics for such hijinks in his "Cool in an Uncool Time" piece. Legs and his buddies, Jacobson says, were "reinventing cool before my eyes." They accepted the "crap of the Modern World, all that mind rot," and celebrated it instead of protesting it. "What a brilliantly existential decision! How modernistic a concept!" For Jacobson, Legs's self-mockery recalls Thelonious Monk on the piano or New York Knicks and Baltimore Bullets great Earl Monroe with a basketball: "With those two there has always been the tension between the dead seriousness of technique and the ironical understanding that in the scope of the universe all those hours developing a style like no one else might mean nothing. They could drop a bomb on you. You could get hit by a truck. The only sane way to deal with this looming spectre of random destruction was to have a sense of humor about yourself" (*PUNK* 17:21).

Of course there is also the chance that examined retrospectively, *PUNK* will remind twenty-first century readers of nothing so much as Beavis and Butt-head breaking bad at the mimeograph machine. In its worst gay disco-bashing and anti-British punk invasion moments, it can have that ring to it (as in a cartoon featuring gay clones embracing outside Studio 666 disco, or a "Try Punk Liker" cartoon with a recipe for scab cocktail from pus and monkey vomit).

Yet Holmstrom and McNeil's enduring charm is that every time you think you've had enough of them, you turn the page of *PUNK* and read something startlingly engaging that would strain the Beavis and

Butt-head attention span. Who else but Holmstrom and McNeil would think to question Clash bassist Paul Simenon on the hierarchy of the workplace that can fester even inside a punk band? "I always wanted to be a guitarist 'cause like they're always the ones . . ." Simenon confesses wistfully of the Clash's caste system in Holmstrom's exquisitely hand-lettered script: "I pretend I play a guitar, but it's too heavy, the bass. But guitar's really light. Like when Mick and Joe ain't lookin' I'll pick up their lead guitar and BAKAZKKRRS. It's really light. That's why I want to be a guitarist. But the bass is pretty easy. It's only got four strings—go out and bash it about" (*PUNK* 17:12). Played against Joe Strummer's musings about the Clash's working class and socialist af-fliliations, the interview attains arresting reverberations, some of which might have reached across the years to alienated students and youth everywhere and to the depressed white collar job market of the mid-1990s. "The universities are pumping out graduates," Strummer says, "in four and five year courses and there's nothin' for them to do. They can't get a job. They're all goin' on welfare. And the art schools are pumpin' out art students who become art teachers to teach more people to become art students to become art teachers to get more art students. It's just like one long insane—it's like pointless. All we're tryin' to go AHRRG! (Punches wall) BAM! BAM! BAM! It's just a feeble complainin' voice. . . . We're just a group—like BAM! BAM! BAM!" (*PUNK* 17:13).

Perhaps McNeil and Holmstrom's strongest and most enduring anticipation of alternative youth in the 1990s is their emphasis on what came to be termed DIY culture (also known as "do it yourself," though "disaffected independent youth" is an equally plausible translation). That move, more than incipient racism or homophobia, seems to explain their distrust of disco and the reinvention of British punk into the synthesizer-laced new wave. In a May/June 1979 review of the London Symphony Orchestra's "Classic Rock Volume One" cover album of Beatles, Stones, and Led Zeppelin tunes, Holmstrom predicts triumphantly that although Blondie's disco-driven "Heart of Glass" would be no stretch, "these twerps" in the LSO could never cover The Ramones' "Now I Wanna Sniff Some Glue" or The Kingsmen's "Louie Louie." He concludes, "For those who still know what rock 'n' roll is—that's enough" (*PUNK* 17:36).

The subtext of McNeil and Holmstrom's jeremiad against slick cor-

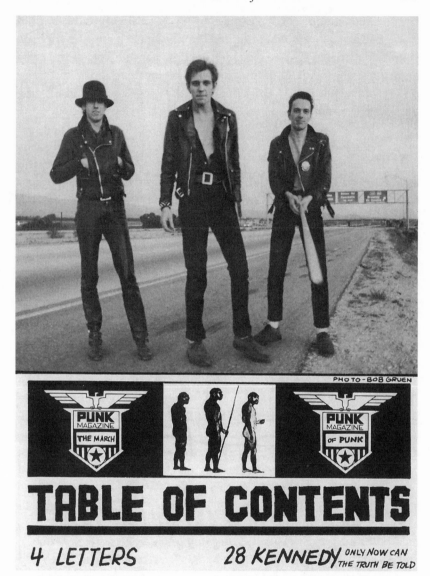

Figure 2.   From *PUNK* magazine no. 17 (May/June 1979). Table of Contents. Photo by Bob Gruen. Reprinted by permission of Bob Gruen and Star File.

porate production is their recognition that post-hippie youth had become but one more market commodity. So long as you wouldn't pin yourself down, they figured, you had a better chance to escape the ever-tightening web of mass production. Again, the link across the years seems well established. Considering all of the generational envy nagging the aging U.S. population, perhaps the baby boomers' most enduring complaint during the mid-1990s against what it called Generation X is that it hadn't yet found a way to market to the generation effectively. For example, of the 168 articles that mentioned "Generation X" (up from 20 the year earlier) in the 1994–95 UMI ProQuest general periodical database, five times as many articles (23) were published in *Advertising Age* than in any other single source. And the message of most of those articles was clear: "We can't figure out the buying patterns of these wonderkids and we're going to be dead if we can't get a reliable handle on all that disposable income."

Conceived in purely economic terms, that attitude fit perfectly with the "Generation X" construction mounted by generational pundits David Lipsky and Alexander Abrams (*Late Bloomers: The Declining Prospects of the Twentysomething Generation*). Lipsky and Abrams wrote in 1994 that Generation X is anxious to fulfill the marketing dreams of *Advertising Age* and *Fortune* and would do so gladly if only it had the funds to do the job. Their discussion of the "irony" of youth consumption patterns in the postboomer generation gains none of the sting of "bricolage," wherein certain segments of the generation have the ironic moxie to reinvent the conditions they are handed by the dominant generation. "Of all the terms this generation has had thrown at it," Lipsky and Abrams write, "the one perhaps most widely accepted is 'ironic.' It's no surprise: if you devote everything to getting ahead—if, in the argot of an earlier generation, you 'sell out'—and then discover that there is no market for the goods, what other response than irony is there?"[10] Lipsky and Abrams represented to commentators like Neil Howe (*13th Gen*) a segment of Busters that "seems to be very institutionally well connected, tends to be actually very cautious and conservative about their approaches to issues. They're anxious to please older people, anxious to have older people feel they're competent."[11]

But despite their *New York Times* Op Ed pieces, the *Good Morning, America,* and *Sonya Live* appearances, the book contract and lecture tours, Lipsky and Abrams didn't speak for everyone in their generation. Ironically, the other big growth term in publishing during the mid-

1990s was "punk," with ninety-nine hits on the UMI ProQuest charts for 1994–95. Both "Generation X" and "punk" became defining words for the mid-1990s generation then in its teens and twenties, although the latter term garnered little media attention. "Punk" pops up only in articles that cover the margins of culture, and nearly all of the articles cover music and fashion created afresh by kids who were still in diapers when Legs McNeil and John Holmstrom decided to name their magazine (and the movement that spawned it) "punk" after the Dictators' lyrics.

One surviving link between the two generations of "punk" is Thurston Moore, guitarist and cofounder of Sonic Youth, who, with his wife Kim Gordon, has been producing ear-jarring DIY music for most of the last twenty years. Like Legs McNeil, Moore migrated to Manhattan from the suburbs in the second half of the 1970s. One of the first concerts he took in was by the band Suicide, which Holmstrom had reviewed in *PUNK* as prompting riots in Europe when "angry 'rock' fans tried to kill them to stop their music" (17:7). As Moore recalls of his own experience, "Suicide [was] at their most terrorist vibe. Superloud, green lights, Alan Vega with this crazy hair and scar on his face, on his knees, shouting. He was so over the fucking top. He broke somebody's glass, then cut his chest open. He licked one guy's face. Halfway through the set all the tables were turned over, and people were defending themselves against Alan Vega. I remember driving home in our Volkswagen, going, 'What the hell was that?' But we knew we had to go back."[12]

After Moore's stretch with Glenn Branca's wall-of-noise guitar orchestra that was a staple of downtown Manhattan's avant-garde "no wave" in the late 1970s, Sonic Youth spent most of the 1980s playing music on bills with the Minutemen, Hüsker Dü, Black Flag, and the Meat Puppets—bands who honed their garage style on independent labels like Reflex and SST and made an art of "low fidelity" production. Although they were doing quite well enough on their own, Sonic Youth's most enduring bridge to kids in the 1990s was that they spent the first year of the decade introducing Kurt Cobain to the nation as the headline band on Nirvana's initial American tour. "These guys were like the Children of the Corn," Moore recalls of Nirvana. "They wore ripped flannel, had greasy long hair. Total backwoods freaks."[13]

In ways that specifically echo McNeil and Holmstrom, Moore recognizes the enduring resistance of marginal kids' culture to marketplace domination: all the money poured into Woodstock 1994 and its accompanying movies, videos, and compact discs (despite the Wood-stock promoters' desperate attempt to hop on the Green Day punk bandwagon by issuing the live "When You Come Around" video to MTV) couldn't guarantee a hit. Meanwhile, some lo-fi geeks like Weezer ("Say It Ain't So") made a big connection to the very youth that *Advertising Age* is trying to reach. If the *PUNK* magazine mimeograph was Legs McNeil's steel mill (Jacobson, 20), DIYers today have digitally generated and distributed fanzines and a welter of online web sites in their place. The instruments of cultural and political control may be far more pervasive now, but so are the instruments of resistance.

The bridge across the years is intriguing. Consider the following juxtaposition of quotes: the first from Jacobson's 1978 take on Legs McNeil's *PUNK* world and the other from Thurston Moore's 1994 interview with David Fricke.

How fabulous to have something new to dig after years of mealy-mouthed post-mortems in Berkeley. . . . I loved that the Ramones' first record was made in 18 hours and it cost only $6,000. Figures like that cut away the flab of indecision. So did the music. The Ramones song, "I Don't Wanna Walk Around with You," which has the lyrics, "I don't wanna walk around with you / I don't wanna walk around with you / I don't wanna walk around with you / So why you wanna walk around with me?" boiled away any other, superfluous ideas I had about high-school cool. It was all I needed to know about adolescence. It was as if the Ramones, none of whom were named Ramone, were saying to the dull '60s establishment: "See, we can express ourselves, fast, cheap, and good. We'll tell you about our own experience as teenagers, and it will be real." (Jacobson, 20–21)

Who knew what it was going to be like now in this weird post-Reagan America? That's one reason I like the music business. Because as horrible an empire as it is and as tacky as it is, it's always in transition. They try to control things as much as they can. But they can't—as much as they race around after it. And I like watching that. . . . [Former Minutemen bassist] Mike Watt has the best attitude. His bass is his broom. That's how he thinks of himself, as a worker. . . . I like the idea that it becomes more and more disparate. The harder it is to define a term like punk rock, the better it is to me. . . . Punk rock is a totally liberated genre. There's the kitchen sink—and you can throw anything you want in it.[14]

What Moore knows is that the soul of cultural bricolage is to change the terms of the definitions as quickly as you can be defined. The baby boomers and their postboomer allies during the 1990s attempted to co-opt that rebellion by marketing and declaring "Generation X" and "alternative" as the next big thing. Meanwhile, a truly alternative culture maintains its resistance through oppositional practice; music that defines culture around itself has always been the tension at its heart. As Simon Frith says, "young people use music to situate themselves historically, culturally, and politically in a much more complex system of symbolic meaning than is available locally."[15] The paradoxical aim of rock musicians, therefore, is to be "popular" in the sense of occupying a place in the community, rather than necessarily in sales. "The tensions emerge," Frith says, "when these two goals [community and commodity] are thought, for whatever reason, to be incompatible."[16]

Whatever legacy Legs McNeil, John Holmstrom, and the rest of the *PUNK* team left behind is built on that tension, that enduring incompatibility: it's a move that is resolutely postboomer. The challenge is to maintain that edge continually. The tension between community and commodity is alive, and the punning title of the Sonic Youth/Nirvana tour video, *1991: The Year That Punk Broke,* sums up the paradox lucidly. For once broken, punk is dangerous. It recalls Mark Jacobson on Legs McNeil: "I don't want to take the responsibility for making you famous."

McNeil and the editors of *PUNK* understood these contradictions as well as, and considerably earlier than, almost anyone else. This links them with the most threatening of today's Xers—now alive and busy downloading and remixing music on the Internet—in league against the least oppositional: "Legs advocated the elusive psychopathy of dealing with the fearsome swell of Modern America by celebrating it. This was a difficult and ultimately unhappy way to think. Especially for someone as bright as Legs. For him, saying Modern America is great is just more of the joke. But it's hard to keep laughing when you walk into a supermarket and hear the clerk singing 'You Deserve a Break Today' and you know that's the only song in the whole world he knows the lyrics to" (Jacobson, 25).

Notes

I wish to thank Robert Christgau and Andy Schwartz for assistance in the research of this chapter, as well as "R" and Mike at See Hear in New York City.

1. Jeff Giles, "Generation X," *Newsweek,* 6 June 1994, 63.

2. See Generation X, "Your Generation," Chrysalis 2165, 1977. See also the Who, "My Generation," Decca 31877, 1966.

3. Richard Hell and the Voidoids, "Blank Generation," Sire 6037, 1977.

4. John Holmstrom and Legs McNeil, eds., *PUNK*, nos. 1–17 (1976–79). All subsequent citations will be noted parenthetically by issue and page number.

5. Quoted in Mark Jacobson, "Cool in an Uncool Time: Teenage Hipster in the Modern World," *Village Voice*, 7 August 1978, 20. Subsequent references will be cited parenthetically within the text.

6. Simon Frith, "The Cultural Study of Popular Music," in *Cultural Studies*, ed. Lawrence Grossberg, Cary Nelson, and Paula Treichler (New York: Routledge, 1992), 180.

7. Dick Hebdige, *Subculture: The Meaning of Style* (London: Methuen, 1979), 25. Subsequent references will be cited parenthetically within the text.

8. Norman Mailer, "The White Negro," in *Advertisements for Myself* (New York: Signet, 1959), 302–22.

9. *Reality Bites*, directed by Ben Stiller, MCA/Universal, 1994.

10. David Lipsky and Alexander Abrams, "The Packaging (and Re-Packaging) of a Generation," *Harper's*, July 1994, 22.

11. Quoted in Martin Kihn, "The Gen X Hucksters," *New York*, 29 August 1994, 102.

12. David Fricke, "Better Living Through Feedback," *Rolling Stone*, 22 September 1994, 58.

13. Ibid., 56.

14. Ibid., 55–56.

15. Frith, 177.

16. Ibid., 176.

Bibliography

Fricke, David. "Better Living Through Feedback." *Rolling Stone*, 22 September 1994, 52–58, 115.

Frith, Simon. "The Cultural Study of Popular Music." In *Cultural Studies*, edited by Lawrence Grossberg, Cary Nelson, and Paula Treichler. New York: Routledge, 1992.

Generation X. "Your Generation." Chrysalis 2165, 1977.

Giles, Jeff. "Generation X." *Newsweek*, 6 June 1994, 62–70.

Hebdige, Dick. *Subculture: The Meaning of Style*. London: Methuen, 1979.

Jacobson, Mark. "Cool in an Uncool Time: Teenage Hipster in the Modern World." *Village Voice*, 7 August 1978, 1, 19–25.

Kihn, Martin. "The Gen X Hucksters." *New York*, 29 August 1994, 94–107.

Lipsky, David, and Alexander Abrams. "The Packaging (and Re-Packaging) of a Generation." *Harper's*, July 1994, 20–22.

Mailer, Norman. "The White Negro." In *Advertisements for Myself*. New York: Signet, 1959.

PUNK. Issues 1–17. Edited by John Holmstrom and Legs McNeil. New York: Punk Publications, 1976–79.

Reality Bites. Directed by Ben Stiller. MCA/Universal, 1994.

Richard Hell and the Voidoids. "Blank Generation." Sire 6037, 1977.

The Who. "My Generation." Decca 31877, 1966.

Theoretical Tailspins
Reading "Alternative" Performance in Spin *Magazine*

Jim Finnegan

> Media and commerce do not just cover but help construct music sub-cultures. . . . Subcultural capital is itself, in no small sense, a phenome-non of the media.
>
> Sarah Thornton, "Moral Panic, the Media
and British Rave"

> If you only talk to people who already agree with you, you are not a political organization. You're a support group.
>
> Elizabeth Gilbert, *Spin*, April 1995

In the June 1995 issue of *Details,* Generation X was declared dead on arrival by the very author who had himself risen to instant fame only a few years earlier with his first novel, *Generation X: Tales for an Acceler-ated Culture.* And indeed in the years since Douglas Coupland's *Details* pronouncement perhaps nothing has been assumed to be so thoroughly incorporated, so cliché, as the term Generation X. The common-sense consensus in both academic popular culture studies and subculture the-ory, as well as in the "alternative" youth culture industries themselves, is that Generation X is so passé, so universally unhip, that even by re-marking its passing one risks marking oneself as square beyond repair, like foolish white tourists who go to Harlem and speak nostalgically about the lost authenticity of the original 1920s Cotton Club. The word "Generation X" is deader than dead. Yet media images invoking the iconography of Generation X continue to proliferate in the youth culture industries, particularly in the pop music, television, fashion, and junk food markets. With the now familiar mix of manic-paced MTV jump-cuts, a multicultural brew of post-punk haircuts, piercings, and retro seventies grunge styles, neon-streak color bursts, rollerblade grrrl-power "attitude," and the requisite "cheese" of self-mocking irony, Pepsi's 1997 "Generation Next" campaign typifies the alternative youth marketing scene in the 1990s.

It is in this cultural climate of "alternative" simulacra that I want to take up theoretical issues surfaced by *Spin* magazine from the mid-1980s to the mid-1990s, as it sought to take avant-garde pop under-grounds and transform them into post–avant-garde, alternative "over-grounds." My theoretical goal is to make a first pass at "reading" *Spin* magazine in a cultural studies context, and in the process map the boundaries of Andreas Huyssen's construction of the "post–avant-garde" as the hope of a political postmodernism. "Some hope!" you may be thinking. For many people with personal investments in youth sub-culture scenes, *Spin* represents at best a laughable example of counter-feit alternative culture and at worst the very enemy of genuine subcul-tural resistance, the thing that threatens to rob a subculture scene of its essence of oppositionality.[1] While I agree with much of this line of argument, I am equally suspicious of the knee-jerk refusal of any-and-everything "commercial" expressed by so many subculture members and theorists. They have forgotten Stuart Hall's admonition that opposi-tion to the current state of capitalist society and culture does not neces-sarily mean a blanket refusal of the reproductive power of the commod-ity and commodification.[2] Opposition to postmodern capitalism, Hall points out, does not mean refusing *a priori* the productive and cultural forces of mass culture. Oppositional culture, or revolutionary ideology, means critiquing current hegemonic discourses of modernity and post-modernity; it also means rethinking and reconfiguring cultural-material forces at multiple local, national, and transnational levels.

Perhaps what is most offensive about *Spin* is its brashness, its haughty claim to cosmopolitan cultural hipness. *Spin* magazine, like Andy Warhol's Pop Art interventions a generation earlier, presumes to have already obliterated and transcended those traditional boundaries between mass-cult and high art, and between pop culture and progres-sive oppositional politics. It does so despite the fact that the contradictions of capitalist production and distribution, which fuel the worlds of pop and mass-cult, have only become more pronounced. In other words, *Spin* insists that one can have a genuine cultural revolution and maintain a brand-name consumer lifestyle too.

Realizing the unlikeliness of my own thesis, I nevertheless contend that *Spin* is a step in the right direction, and that *Spin* magazine may function as a popular progressive model—a structure of pop culture resistance. The *Spin* model offers a form that combines (sub)cultural opposition and mainstream fun, and it's a form that proved itself capable of keeping pace with the shifting forces of cultural Reaganism and the New Right in the late 1980s and early 1990s. The *Spin* model might, therefore, function as a counterbalance to the infinite adaptability presumed to be the defining characteristics of so-called late capitalism: its apparently endless capacity to appropriate all forms of subcultural resistance, oppositional meanings, or semiotic critique.

As such, *Spin* magazine also offers itself as an excellent case study to explore the practical implications of Michael Bérubé's claim that perhaps the single most important and difficult challenge for cultural studies critics is to think through the problems that arise when academics theorize popular audiences and subcultures that are already theorizing themselves.

This is an important challenge. As Bérubé argues, the very "existence and autonomy of the academic professions," which have been under relentless (and frequently successful) attack by misinformation and defunding campaigns from the cultural and political right, depends in no small part on mobilizing popular support from the very "ordinary people" that cultural studies frequently writes about and for, but not to. It depends, in other words, on our ability to popularize academic theory and criticism, which means "struggling for the various popular and populist grounds on which the cultural right has been trying to make criticism unpopular."[3] This is a difficult challenge, however, because academics must carry on this struggle in a world in which, as Bérubé notes, "there isn't a chance that academic criticism will ever be popular [and yet at the same time] the kind of criticism known as critical theory already is popular."[4] Academics must not only struggle for cultural ground that the Right explicitly targets; we must continue to build and strengthen coalitions with otherwise left-leaning mass media culture industries, where much of the fall-out from the PC wars ultimately lands.

That is, we must reach out to consumer subculture media like *Spin,* a magazine that in many ways is already popularizing academic criticism, but frequently does so by rhetorically positioning itself against academic discourses portrayed as being either too "serious," too "obscure," or too "PC."

Such academic work is of course already being done. Indeed, for many it's what cultural studies is all about in the first place. The most notable, sustained example of this kind of academic popular criticism can perhaps be found in the pages of *Social Text,* which regularly brings together people from a wide range of cultural positions (people who work in various culture industries, mass media, and academic disciplines) in an attempt to forge alliances and cross the great theory-practice divide. In the Fall 1995 issue of *Social Text,* for example, Andrew Ross hosts a symposium on "The Cult of the DJ" in which Ross, two mass media music critics, and two prominent dance music DJs discuss, among other things, the "changing role of DJs in the history of popular music" and reasons for the general neglect of dance music in the mainstream music press.[5] Though later on I will take issue with the way the term "mainstream music press" gets deployed in cultural studies' subculture criticism, the discussion in this *Social Text* symposium, as well as in the more fully developed book-length symposium on alternative youth culture edited by Andrew Ross and Tricia Rose (*Microphone Fiends: Youth Music and Youth Culture*), suggests that the relationship between academic discourses, "alternative" artistic practices, and commercial subculture magazines like *Spin* is more complex, more symbiotic and, as I hope to demonstrate here, not so problematic as many academics might assume. It demonstrates, for one, that one doesn't have to dig too deep to find so-called "academic" cultural criticism lurking just below the surface of nearly everything in the Gen X scene, despite the fact that antiacademic rhetoric (bordering sometimes on outright neoconservative anti-intellectualism) is standard Gen X fare.[6] It is within this more general symbiosis among critical theory, Madison Avenue, and oppositional subcultures that I want to apply a few subcultural models to one specific "mass-cult" medium, which explicitly markets itself as "oppositional." By working through the magazine's structure and then taking a close look at *Spin*'s coverage of riot grrrl in 1992 and a 1995 Diesel Jeans advertisement depicting two sailors kissing (an appropriation of an ACT UP's Gran Fury poster), I want to see what might happen if we try to take *Spin* magazine at face-value. What happens if I accept their unlikely marketing claims that, in the acts of reading *Spin*, I too can identify with, and participate in, an ongoing youth-music cultural "revolution"? What if I accept their claim that, with *Spin*'s help, I too can be a riot grrrl?

Though *Spin* is frequently scorned (by academics, its own readers, and various self-identified subculture members) as nothing more than a slick Gen X fashion magazine pimping corporate rock and Madison Avenue to the middle-class (mostly male) suburban youth, the writers and editors of *Spin* repeatedly defend themselves against such criticism, both directly in their writing and indirectly in their editing and design choices. They insist that *Spin* is a genuine organ of an ongoing youth revolution even if it is brought to you by the corporate world's latest-and-greatest, newest-and-coolest, mass marketing gimmicks. *Spin*'s tenth anniversary issue, "Ten Years That Rocked the World," for example, is framed by two essays that specifically position *Spin* at the fore-front of an ongoing Gen X youth "Revolution." The theme is under-scored in the title of this special issue, which echoes John Reed's *Ten Days That Shook the World* and thus locates *Spin* within a longer histori-cal tradition of radical journalism and a generational revolutionary tem-perament centered on images of "youth." Both publisher Guccione Jr., in his editorial column ("TopSpin"), and senior contributing writer Jim Greer, on the back page (what used to be called "SpinOut"), tell a retro-spective narrative that links the evolution of *Spin* magazine with the emergence of a "cultural and generational wave at the beginning of its ascension";[7] both define the mission of the magazine (Guccione refers to it as the magazine's "higher calling") as one that has evolved from an unselfconscious rock 'n' roll naiveté into a self- conscious mission to give voice to "Gen X or whatever we're calling it this week."[8] As Guccione states, "it was precisely our complete inappropriateness to the prevailing zeitgeist [of mid-1980s cynicism] that gave us our power and value and readership, all of which, eventually, became our conscious mission. We wrote about and for a then-disempowered generation, to which we belonged not (by now) by the citizenship of similar age, but by the uni-versal solidarity of purpose. Our readership's culture and causes and self-defining discoveries were ours too, and so were their enemies."[9] Responding to those readers who repeatedly attack the magazine in "Point Blank" (the letters page) for merely exploiting the Gen X scene

for commercial gain, Greer not only defends the mission of the magazine as a "rock magazine," he also defends the magazine's Madison Avenue commercialism as well, insisting that *Spin* is "more independent,
both in terms of corporate structure and mindset, than most so-called
independent record labels."[10]

These are no small claims—claims, I suspect, at which most academics and subculture members would raise a skeptical eyebrow.[11] Nevertheless, I contend that, sometimes by design and sometimes in spite of
itself, *Spin* does in fact manage to articulate what constitutes a popularized form of cultural studies criticism. It presents a kind of *Social Text*
for a particular mass youth audience as it were, in which the cultural-
political meanings of youth music (not always rock) and "alternative"
subculture scenes are explicitly addressed, and in which issues of representation are repeatedly brought to the surface, even if academic discourses are specifically avoided. More specifically, I take issue with the
kind of disgust that Dick Hebdige vents in *Hiding in the Light* toward
the *Face,* the 1980s British subculture consumer magazine that likely
inspired, or at least certainly influenced, the original conception and
design of *Spin.*[12] The first sections of this essay read *Spin*'s riot grrrl
coverage to address both Hebdige's critique of the kind of facile "flat-
earth" postmodernism produced by the *Face* and Sarah Thornton's critique of the tendency of subculture theory to ignore the role mass media
plays in the formation of youth subculture identities.[13] The final sections
engage the Diesel Jeans advertisement to question the larger tendency
within cultural studies to read subcultural practices as models for more
traditional forms of political organization.

Generation X: A Generation by No Other Name?

To say that cultural studies academics must get beyond their aver-
sion to Gen X posturing does not mean, however, that we must silence
our criticisms of those who speak in the name of Generation X (including *Spin*), particularly since, as Andrew Ross has noted, the Generation
X moment is one in which American youth are being scrutinized by a
glut of journalistic and sociological hacks in the most "frankly exploitative way" since the late fifties.[14] Ross's own take on Gen X seems to
be guardedly sympathetic at best. He suggests that the crucial questions
for academics writing about Gen X are (1) can Gen X discourses can

free themselves from the journalistic and sociological voices speaking on behalf of Generation X (even the more sympathetic ones such as Howe and Strauss's *13th Gen: Abort, Retry, Ignore, Fail?*); and (2) Can the "subject" of Gen X can be expanded beyond the narrow voice of white, middle-class heterosexual males—what Ross refers to as "those post-adolescents who were temporarily confused but [are] more likely to succeed in the long run, and thus fill the target consumer demographic with high-end disposable incomes."[15] Whether or not some construct of "alternative" culture (call it "Generation X" or whatever) can become a touchstone for a wider and more inclusive youth culture is by no means certain. And it will take more than academics analyzing grunge, rave, gangsta rap, or riot grrrls in papers with Gen X in the title and delivering those papers in conventional academic venues to forge any such multicultural alliances. If "Gen X" fails to become common coin to a broader range of youth subjects, then academics rushing to speak about or in the name of Gen X risk merely duplicating and sanctioning journalistic exploitative discourses.

It is perhaps fittingly ironic then that at the very moment a 1995 MLA Convention special session and a collection of academic essays was being prepared under the title "Generation X Culture," Douglas Coupland had declared "Gen X" dead on arrival in an article published in *Details*, the preferred "cross-over" magazine for many cultural studies academics. According to Coupland, Gen X has been eaten alive by the marketing "trendmeisters," who have taken what he believes was a genuine "way of looking at the world"—an implicitly "authentic" and "original" aesthetic perspective—and they've turned it into just so much more white noise.[16] That the term Gen X, along with the terms "slacker" and "grunge," became one of the "most abused buzz words of the early '90s" is hardly debatable, nor is the fact that Gen X has been appropriated by Madison Avenue style industries to a degree that exceeds all previous generational signifiers, such as those of the 1920s and 1960s, which have also been reductively associated with avant-garde and countercultural movements. What is debatable, however, is Coupland's specious attempt to maintain his status as "author" of the concept "Generation X" based on the fact that he has penned a decent, but hardly exceptional, first-novel by the same name. The novel is the epitome of the Gen X cliché: Coupland's aestheticized middle-class male suburban angst and self-indulgent narrative posturing cancels out whatever 1990s social realism may be at work. *Generation X* may arguably mark, not the beginning of the Gen X moment, but rather the beginning of the very corporate marketing appropriations he now only half-heartedly bemoans (Coupland's own characteristically camp, ironic phrasing is to say that it "was harsh").

By expressing my personal distaste for Coupland's novel, I do not mean to deny the important role that its mass popularity played in generating the cultural currency that Gen X signifiers now possess, however appropriated or narrow that currency may be. Nor do I mean to deny the very real economic, political, and cultural changes (everything that makes up the historical "reality" of the postmodern, late capitalist moment of our "accelerated culture") that inform and shape the generational angst of Coupland's novelistic world, however privileged and aestheticized that angst may be. Certainly I do not mean to align myself in any way with the openly hostile mass-media cranks, such as David Martin in his infamous *Newsweek* piece, who dismissively attack self-identified Gen X twentysomethings as whiners who should just shut up and live with it.[17] My objection to Coupland's representation of Gen X is less an aesthetic judgment than it is an ideological judgment about the kinds of narrow subject positions and the historical narratives that his novel articulates.

The way Coupland summarizes his novel and bemoans its mass-media appropriations in the *Details* article is itself enough to see the narrow focalization and ahistorical aestheticizing tendencies that make up Coupland's Gen X world. Though his three characters presumably live on "the fringe" and work at "dreary jobs at the bottom of the food chain," they do so because they, like Coupland, "decided to pull back from society and move there." Though they find themselves struggling to patch together individual identities in a dramatically reshaped environment, this environment is ultimately one that is, in Coupland's own words, a "psychic" reality more than a social or historically specific one. Coupland's claim that the worldview his characters manage to cultivate ("simultaneously ironic and sentimental") constituted "a new way of thinking I had never before seen documented" is another comment that seeks to affirm the originality of Gen X at the same time that it attests to the representational "authenticity" of his characters as part of some larger Gen X whole. Coupland asserts this authenticity again only as he claims authorship in his "Gen-X-cide," as if it were his to kill or to declare null and void because "boomer angst-transference" has reduced his characters and ideas to Madison Avenue stereotypes and media clichés. Coupland writes, "The problems started when trendmeisters everywhere began isolating small elements of my characters' lives . . . and blew them up to represent an entire generation. Part of this misrepresentation emanated from baby boomers, who, feeling pummeled by the recession and embarrassed by their own compromised '60s values, began transferring their collective darkness onto the group threatening to take their spotlight."[18] The problem with such reductive narratives, staked out in neatly packaged us versus them terms, is that they have in turn become the standard line of post-Coupland mass media Gen X historical clichés. (See, for example, the "valedictorian speech" delivered by Winona Ryder's character in the opening scene of *Reality Bites*, as well as Douglas Rushkoff's self-aggrandizing, pseudointellectual, misinformed, and homophobic manifesto and introductory blurbs in *The GenX Reader*.)[19]

Whether or not one believes Coupland when he attempts to set the record straight and locate the "origins" of the title of his book in the final chapter of Paul Fussell's book *Class* rather than the name of Billy Idol's punk band is really beside the point. Historically, long before there was Douglas Coupland's *Generation X*, Generation X was there— as a signifier and a signified, an attitude, a pose, an aesthetic, a sensibility, a way of looking at the world, and a way of looking at the economic and cultural political realities of post-Fordist capitalism and cultural Reaganism. Whenever it can be said to have arrived, Gen X was certainly as much a punk sensibility as it was the kind of neo-Beat bohemianism Coupland now (re)locates in Fussell's X class. Fourteen years before Coupland's novel caught the wave of media interest in Richard Linklater's independent film *Slacker,* Billy Idol's Generation X opened at the Roxy Club, and a month prior to that the Voidoids released their single "Blank Generation."

If there is in fact an "X sensibility" that describes "a way of looking at the world" rather than "a chronological age," it is nonetheless a historically specific sensibility, one that is popular now because of the more general and ongoing cultural and political backlash against youth, one that is not so new after all and one that's much more complex than

Coupland's reductive boomer versus buster narrative suggests. One that should not therefore be limited to the privileged romanticisms of new bohemian aesthetes.

I invoke this sound bite from punk history here not to distinguish between "authentic" and co-opted strains of Gen X, but rather as a check to the tendency in many self-identified media and academic Gen X discourses that define Gen X as an uniquely late 1980's and early 1990s scene or aesthetic. David Laing argues that to talk about the history of "punk rock" is really to talk about a discourse—a loose, fluid (frequently contradictory) consensus of voices between 1976 and 1978 that circulated in punk artifacts (records, zines), punk events (concerts, interviews, staged media hoaxes, and interventions), and punk institutions (underground, scene-specific record labels, clubs, and shops, as well as established record companies, radio stations, and the music press).[20] If in the early 1990s a similar kind of new consensus or discourse formation emerged under the sign Generation X (even if there can be no such directly stated signifier), then one thing that seems to separate it from its punk predecessors is the lack of any clearly identifiable artifacts, events, and institutions. If there are only a handful of Generation X novels and films about the lack of generational artifacts now taken up as artifacts themselves, if there is an emerging consensus that Generation X positions itself as a subculture but lacks any clearly identifiable subaltern scene, then what happens when we apply academic questions about the mainstream's appropriation of subcultural oppositional politics only to transform them into trite morality clichés for middle-class fashion consumers? Does it make any sense to even ask whether or not Gen X-identified symbols of disaffection and dissent have been appropriated as fashion symbols? Or should we be asking instead what happens when fashion symbols of images of disaffection and dissent are taken up and disseminated by people (like Coupland) who may or may not be disaffected but who nonetheless identify themselves as part of a newly disaffected generation emerging on the scene of their imagined postboomer wasteland?

How then, in other words, do I deal with the fact that everything I have just described and critiqued as the narrow privileged range of Coupland's Gen X world frequently gets articulated in the pages of *Spin* as "the voice of a generation"? How do I explain the fact that, when I discussed *Spin* magazine and Generation X with my undergraduate rhetoric students in the spring of 1996, we ended up switching roles and I was the one defending *Spin* against the students' teacherly, ironic, and theoretically informed critiques? This essay has, in fact, largely grown out of that 1996 course, where I found myself in the unlikely position of defending *Spin* against my students, half of them senior English and Rhetoric majors ten years younger than I. As part of this ongoing debate, one of my students wrote an essay arguing that this whole Gen X thing is all just one big (M)TV media scam in the first place. He only half-ironically, and rather convincingly, argued that Gen X is something that was invented by the MTV-*Spin*-Geffen music industrial complex, that the whole thing is just more white noise—the projection of pop industry workers and academics in their lower thirties (he meant me) waxing nostalgic for a punk past that they never really lived in the first place: "The whole thing makes me want to barf," he wrote. "The fact is that there is/has been an ongoing and Real punk movement since the mid-seventies and it lives and thrives in the streets and in the underground—where it belongs—and this Gen X crap is just yet another attempt to appropriate and somehow control the anarchy of real punk culture." And of course I think he's partly right. The thing that interests me, however, is that *Spin* magazine frequently says basically the same thing, and I think my student was getting some of his arguments against *Spin* for exploiting and appropriating the punk scene in their cover story "Green Day: The Year Punk Broke" (November 1995) from that very article. And if that's the case, then what the heck does that mean? What it means is you end up trying to "read" *Spin* by reading someone else reading *Spin* reading itself. Then you get thrown into theoretical tailspins—brought to you by the "Tailspinners," which is *Spin*'s name for their list of this month's feature writers, editors, and contributors, who, not unlike the contributors in a typical issue of *Social Text*, are drawn from a wide range of cultural positions, including established music critics, new journalists, fiction writers, musicians, and artists, as well as pop culture academics and other public intellectuals.

There is in fact another, perhaps even more significant, reciprocal chain of signification going on here alongside my student's reading of *Spin* reading itself. Take this sound bite from Guccione's January 1994 "TopSpin" column specifically addressing the Gen X phenomenon, which is also where my student was getting some of his rhetorical ammunition against *Spin* and which predates Coupland's *Details* "eulogy" of

Gen X by six months: "This year belonged to something that doesn't exist: Generation X. Generation X is a phantom, an hysterical hallucination of baby boomers, suddenly realizing they are no longer the life of the party. . . . With a speed befitting long-honed instincts of self-interest, they created the mythology of a blank generation that has inadvertently wandered onto the stage, awkward and whining, clueless as to what to do."[21] Unlike Coupland, however, Guccione isn't just haggling over Gen X property rights under the guise of narratives about "corporate marketing appropriations" (though that may be a factor and a legitimate critique of *Spin*); rather, his complaint against boomer-sponsored Gen X narratives is aimed at the insidious side effects they produce: deflecting attention away from the social and economic devastation wrought by 1980s boomer-complicit Reaganism and, most importantly for Guccione, further deflating the politically energized atmosphere of youth cultures that had galvanized around the 1992 Rock the Vote campaign. Guccione concludes his year-end editorial on a hopeful note, predicting that 1994 would be "a watershed year. Because, like it did in 1968 and 1969, America is ready to burst again." The prediction itself turned out to be woefully off the mark. The year 1994 of course brought instead Newt Gingrich's other, all-too-familiar Republican revolution and ushered in the era of the Clinton compromise. Yet, Guccione's allusion to the barricades of 1968 ironically locates Gen X once again back in the discourses of punk rock—not punk rock as my student would construct it (and as Coupland would reconstruct Gen X), not as an aesthetic "way of looking at the world" forever living in the wishful imaginary space of some "authentic" media-free underground streets, but rather punk rock as the Clash attempted to define it in explicitly extragenerational political terms. On the back sleeve of their first single release "White Riot"/ "1977" they wrote, "there is, perhaps, some tension in society, when overwhelming pressure brings industry to a standstill or barricades to the streets years after the liberals had dismissed the notion as 'dated romanticism' . . . the journalist invents the theory that this constitutes a clash of generations. Youth, after all, is not a permanent condition, and a clash of generations is not so fundamentally dangerous to the art of government as would be a clash between rulers and ruled."[22]

That Guccione and *Spin* will repeatedly critique the concept of Generation X as a boomer, media, Madison Avenue phantom while at the same time marketing the magazine as the voice of a generation (X), and frequently do so in explicitly political terms, is, to say the least, a contradiction, and one that's not easy to work through. But it's a contradiction that we will have to get used to if academics are going to, in Huyssen's terms, "catch on" and work in the same postmodern, post–avant-garde world that has been "home" to *Spin* and the youth cultures and subcultures it has been reporting and disseminating since the mid-1980s.

"Bone-Crunching Contradictions" and Theoretical Tailspins: *Spin* Is Not Just a Magazine

To live in the postmodern moment of contemporary youth cultures, according to Andrew Ross, is to live in a world in which confronting "bone-crunching contradictions" is the norm, a "daily item."[23] The particular "contradiction" that Ross uses to frame the academic and pop-cult dialogue in *Microphone Fiends* is the fact that, in the opening feature page of *Vibe*'s preview issue, Greg Tate launched the first major commercial magazine devoted to hip hop by hosting a "swinging assault on hip hop commercialism consciously spoken from within the belly of the Madison Avenue beast."[24] This is precisely the kind of contradiction that is both found on the pages of *Spin* and that constitutes the underlying logic of the magazine's mission, design, and style—a logic that may or may not be merely another face of the logic of consumerism as we have no doubt been conditioned to assume.

As a way of framing *Spin*'s specific coverage of riot grrrl in 1992, let's skim the surface of a few brief, relatively random samples of *Spin*'s own spin on its relationship to the postmodern.

Spins

Everything in *Spin* spins off the metaphors of the word *spin*. There was a good deal of media flap back in April of 1985, the date of *Spin*'s first issue, as to just what it meant to have another mass-circulation rock magazine enter the market. Was *Spin* actually *Rolling Stone* revitalized for a new emergent youth culture formation (a rock re-formation)? Was it to be *Rolling Stone* for an accelerated culture? If so, how so—as in merely having "advanced" one generation or as in having "progressed" (as in accelerating the revolution)? Or is the title of *Spin* merely a self-reflexive wink at a consumer culture gone mad, spinning out of control—spinning directionless in a world where there is no more up or down? Is "spin" a self-conscious, self-implicating metaphor for postmodern vertigo? Or, does it refer to political spin: a particular political spin or more generally the politics of spin at work in a media society, a testimony to the power of media in shaping the spin of the world? Or, is it something even larger in its philosophical implications: an entrance sign into a poststructuralist world where all meaning is relational and contingent? A world where Guccione's editorial column is titled "TopSpin" because that's how he is both positioned and positions himself—how he is positioned within the management hierarchy of the magazine, but also how he is socially positioned in terms of class, race, and gender more generally? Or, is the answer the obvious one: all of the above?

"Spins" is also the title of the album review section in the magazine, which (until recently) came framed by the following "Handy Omniscient Rating System" and which is typical of *Spin's* logic of the "bone-crunching contradiction":

Green = Go directly to your local record store. Buy this album. Immediately. Kill if you must.

Yellow = Whoa! Slow down pal! This album is pretty good, but you can't buy everything in the store. Can you?

Red = Stop it. Put that down. Go buy something to eat instead. You have to eat, too, you know.

But what kinds of critical space does *Spin* open up with such a gesture when the reviewers then go on to make serious critical distinctions about specific albums up for review? And exactly what irony survives when those reviews are framed by columns of advertising for these same CD releases? What picture is being drawn here of the reciprocal relationship between music industry advertising goals and those of *Spin* (an alternative music media industry) as it implicates itself in this process by drawing attention to the fact that a good review means you should go out and buy the merchandise? What does it mean, however, when each and every month anywhere from six to ten albums get the green light and another half dozen or so get the yellow? What narratives of youth poverty and affluence are being invoked here by this ironic ratings guide?

How does it map out consumer categories? Here's one possible reading of the implied ironic critique.

Green = poverty/the poverty of desire. Urban kids (implicitly of color?) killing for a pair of sneakers or a CD, killing for the (false) "image" behind some mass-produced band or album.

Yellow = affluence/the boredom of getting what you want. You suburban white kids who can buy everything, plus the guilt of knowing that your satiated poverty of (false) desire is got by someone else's (real) poverty.

Red = junkie/consumerism itself as a cultural psychosis. The shopaholic and the alternative music aficionado collapsing into one with *Spin* magazine as simultaneously the ultimate aficionado and the compulsive consumerist ideologue.

In the movement from "green" to "yellow" to "red," *Spin* not only offers a critique of advanced capitalism's multiple forms of false consciousness (affecting both the haves and the have-nots), it also grounds these "individual" or internalized moments of false consciousness in a deeper, cultural logic of consumer society, which, like the shopaholic aficionado, is driven toward a commodification of desire to the exclusion of basic social needs ("you have to eat, too, you know"). Yet, there's still the question of gauging the end effect of *Spin*'s ironic posturing and whether such irony facilitates or nullifies the possibility of any "cultural critique" taking place at all. Has *Spin* so thoroughly implicated itself in the advertising function of album reviews that it frees a space for critical narratives to speak themselves and, in that way, paradoxically lays bare an otherwise hidden logic of consumer capitalism? Or is the irony here (and throughout *Spin* more generally) merely another superficial postmodern wink at the reader that reasserts a consensus ideological space for business-as-usual where "there is nowhere else to go but the shops"?[25]

Similar sets of ironic questions can be generated by just about everything in the pages of *Spin*.

AIDS: Words from the Front

This is serious spin by *Spin* dropping its standard line of parodic Thompsonesque outlaw journalism. The fact that from January 1988 *Spin* sustained a monthly discussion of AIDS under the subheading "Words from the Front" and gave it a central place in the magazine is itself somewhat remarkable and commendable. However, it may also, as does everything else in *Spin,* raise more questions than it answers—which, regarding AIDS discourses, sometimes is and sometimes isn't a good thing. How, for instance, should one read *Spin's* long-running series of stories on whether or not HIV is the cause of AIDS, particularly as they take a pro-sex stance and popularize certain cultural analyses of AIDS discourses (e.g., Crimps's *AIDS: Cultural Analysis/Cultural Activism*)? On the one hand, these articles appear to popularize the cultural studies assumption that "AIDS does not exist apart from the practices that conceptualize it, represent it, and respond to it."[26] As such they may successfully deploy the discourses of pop culture journalism to deconstruct medical or scientific discourses and their authoritative claims to objective knowledge, demonstrating that, when it comes to AIDS, "no clear line can be drawn between the facticity of scientific and nonscientific (mis)conceptions."[27] Celia Farber's "Words From the Front" articles in particular seem to give popular voice to what Crimp describes as "the genuine concern by informed people that a full acceptance of HIV as the cause of AIDS limits research options, especially regarding possible cofactors."[28] They "perform a political analysis of the ideology of science" and in doing so also take a pro-sex stance. On the other hand, Farber's articles present these analyses in a regressive tabloid fashion by celebrating Peter Deusberg as a "maverick hero" without critiquing his views on the causes of AIDS. Nor does Farber adequately report the controversy surrounding those views, as the *Village Voice* did when Ann Fettner characterized Deusberg's views as a "regression to 1982," when the medical community viewed AIDS as a collection of diseases related to "the gay life style."[29] Other AIDS articles written for *Spin* are even more suspect, suggesting that *Spin's* preoccupation with the HIV controversy may be motivated more by a need to confirm a political-medical "establishment" conspiracy against "sex" than by a genuine desire to engage in AIDS cultural analysis and activism. If this is the case (and I'm not concluding here that in fact it is), what then separates *Spin's* reporting from the kinds of exploitative reporting that Crimp finds in the pages of the *New York Native,* which, according to Crimp, merely trots out "the crackpot theory of the week" and exploits "the conflation of sex, fear, disease, and death in order to sell millions of newspapers"?[30] Certainly the fact that *Spin* would run an article re-

hashing the "poppers theory" (November 1994) in a totally unselfconscious article that makes no mention of the homophobic medical-politics
surrounding this theory is cause for some concern, if not outright alarm.
Since silence equals death, *Spin* is at least not silent. But the fact that
silence equals death does not, of course, mean that the inverse is always
true: sound does not always equal life. Sometimes sound isn't voice, it's
just more noise, and as ACT UP cultural studies analyses of AIDS discourses have all too frequently demonstrated, some kinds of noise can be
deadlier than viruses. By positioning itself on the "front lines" of the AIDS
war, has *Spin* succeeded in articulating and popularizing an ACT UP frame
of reference on AIDS? Has it also in the process popularized the cultural
studies notions of hegemony as a "war of position," as in *Spin*'s 1989 infamous ad-stunt/political intervention of including a free condom with one
of its special issues?[31] Or, has *Spin* merely appropriated ACT UP rhetoric
as a kind of cutting-edge neopunk style, exploiting the AIDS epidemic
and PWAs as a way of furthering its own image of *Spin* as frontline pop
(i.e., *Spin* as shades of Michael Stipe)?

In fact, *Spin*'s relationship with the tabloid-styled *New York Native*
may be even more complex and problematic, as is made clear in Celia
Farber's outrageously off-the-mark "TopSpin" editorial on ACT UP
published in May 1992. Most outrageous (it would be funny if it weren't
so dangerously misinformed) is Farber's completely unselfconscious
presumption to lecture ACT UP on the dangers of being too "entertaining" and "absorbed" by the mainstream media. ACT UP and other activists need to realize, she concludes, that the mainstream media always
gets the last word: *"We don't use the media: the media uses us.* And the
government uses the media. If AIDS activism did not exist, as a vent
system for AIDS fury, the government would have reason to worry. As
it is they're grinning from ear to ear."[32] Talk about a bone-crunching
contradiction! Who's the "we" here? If *Spin* ain't "the media" then who
is? Again, if it weren't so dangerously inane, it might be funny. It's hard
to imagine how Farber, who has led the charge of *Spin*'s own brand of
mass media appropriations of ACT UP activism, can blame successful
ACT UP media interventions for derailing some imaginary "AIDS fury"
that would otherwise unleash itself, when of course those ACT UP and
Gran Fury successes are themselves the only reason Farber can conjure
up the signifier of "AIDS fury" in the first place.[33]

Sex in the 1990s

After ACT UP AIDS activism had lost much of its radical, alternative cachet, *Spin* shifted gears in 1995 and ran a series of self-identified, third-generation, sex-positive "feminist" articles under the heading "Sex in the '90s"—which again raises questions about the commodification of oppositional culture. How, for example, should one read Elizabeth Gilbert's feature article on "feminist porn" titled "Pussy Galore"?[34] Here is an article that has clearly been informed by cultural studies positions on the antiporn/"pro-sex" debate within feminism—positions such as those articulated in Ross's chapter on "The Popularity of Pornography" in *No Respect,* or in the *Social Text* special issue "Sex Workers and Sex Work." Again, one might ask whether this article, or similar *Spin* discussions under the heading "Sex in the '90s," survives the seemingly masculinist framing devices that accompany it. Take, for instance, the way this article gets framed on the contents page: "Pussy Galore. Sick of the same old sleaze, feminist pornographers are getting off their backs and behind the cameras. Meet the revolutionaries in the flicks-for-chicks business. By Elizabeth Gilbert." This blurb, along with the rest of the contents page blurbs, is printed over a black-and-white still photo from an S/M film covered in the article depicting a topless woman gazing down at her outstretched feet which are being suckled by a blond submissive dressed in a teddy and collar. In small print off to the side is the following photo caption: "Toe-lickin' good: A scene from An Elegant Spanking. See Elizabeth Gilbert's article on feminist porn." Of course, the first academic question is likely to be (and with emphasis), *who* is being invited to gaze into such a "revolutionary" porn world? Or rather, whose gaze is invited? Do such phrases as "pussy galore," "toe-lickin' good," or "flicks-for-chicks" appropriate masculinist porn-speak and re-articulate it in a sex-positive feminist-porn voice? Or are we seeing instead the limits of such acts of appropriation that have become increasingly commonplace in Gen X underground scenes and discourses? Is such a world, framed as it is here, revolutionary or merely exoticized for the titillation of male readers looking to rationalize their heterosexist porn appetites? Or, are we freed from struggling with these questions because Elizabeth Gilbert raises most of them herself in the article, as when she puts down her pen and picks up the camera to shoot some footage for a director while on the set of an S/M film, remarking in retrospect that she felt more like a tourist than a pornographer?

"The A to Z of Alternative Culture"

Let's take as one final example the issues raised when one attempts to analyze Craig Marks's multi-ironic introduction to *Spin*'s April 1993 "A to Z of Alternative Culture," a highly eclectic, kitsch "dictionary" of what it means to be Gen X in 1993 that lists, in mock encyclopedic style, items ranging from consumer products like Snapple to "in" bands like Nirvana and TV shows like the *Simpsons,* as well as underground subculture scenes like rave and riot grrrl.[35] Marks's introduction offers itself up as a perfect example of *Spin*'s trademark ironic style (marked by MTVish Gen X posturing):

The outpouring of scribblings recently about the generation born in the '60s and '70s reads like a misguided conclusion to that psych experiment where twins are separated at birth to answer the nurture versus nature debate. Could it be that these profiles of you and yours are nothing but covert attempts to reduce a complex, confounded generation to its lowest common denominator, thereby making it easier to blame you for all that's wrong with the world, and easier to exploit you when there's a new soft drink on the market? Does the word "duh" mean anything to you?

What your birthdate does provide you is common ground, a shared vocabulary. The items we've selected, when added together, do not equal your thoughts, feelings, fears, and aspirations. That's for you and your confidants to sort out. There is, though, a lexicon that develops among the members of a generation, a secret language that's so pervasive it's taken for granted. Asking a 40-year-old to comprehend a conversation between two 24-year-olds is as fruitless an exercise in code-breaking as reading the Daily Racing Form. What you'll find on the following pages is more the result of sifting through the contents of your pants pockets than of unlocking the door to your soul. We'll save that for next year's anniversary issue.[36]

What does it mean when *Spin,* which already ironically sells itself as *the* monthly tour guide to "alternative" scenes, publishes an A to Z guide to alternative culture? What does it mean when the music editor then writes an introduction to this pastiche cultural dictionary by announcing that these profiles you are about to read are reductive and commercially exploitative and that such a list could never really be compiled except as a set of already appropriated mass media stereotypes of a self-identified generational youth culture that could never really exist? What does it mean when Craig Marks goes on to suggest, in a seeming reversal, that a generational lexicon is "so pervasive it's taken for granted," and cites as proof of its existence the fact that it lies in the shared consumer goods found in the contents of our pockets?

Two months later, the editors throw into the mix, as *Spin* always does, that one last twirl: a reader's response to the A–Z tour guide that further implicates *Spin* as it simultaneously represents, constructs, and exploits the scene that never quite yet was: "Just when I thought SPIN had a clue, we get 'The A to Z of Alternative Culture.' Why can't people realize that the basis of an alternative culture is that it can't be alphabetized? A better title for the piece would have been '26 Steps to Becoming Trendy'—or better yet 'What's out for '93.'" Insofar as the article at issue is a simulacra of *Spin*, each of these substitute titles may be read as already popularized metacommentaries on what it means to read *Spin* magazine itself. Staked out here between these two reader-suggested titles to *Spin*'s alternative tour guide, lies a wonderfully complex and illustrative debate about the relationship between popularized postmodernism and essentializing patterns in cultural studies subculture criticism.

"26 Steps to Becoming Trendy": *Spin* as Just a Magazine

Of course, *Spin* magazine is only one of a growing number of mass-circulation pop-cult magazines that have learned, in a sense, to talk the talk of academic theory and cultural criticism. And even though I've invested more time than I'd care to admit in this essay and I consider myself a "fan" of *Spin* (whatever that might actually be), I, too, am sometimes inclined to dismiss it wholesale as so many of *Spin*'s own readers do. I am tempted to read *Spin* as merely a tour guide to what's trendy—to interpret *Spin* according to the logic of Hebdige's reading of *the Face*—as a magazine that articulates nothing more than a facile, flat earth postmodernism in which everything is always already commercially appropriated, where the line between the ads and the articles isn't just blurred, it collapses altogether, and for Hebdige it always collapses into the ad.

Borrowing Jean-Luc Godard's famous maxim, "This is not a just image. This is just an image," Hebdige reads *the Face* as a way of marking the differences between what he sees as "a just magazine" (*Ten.8*) and "just a magazine" (*the Face*). Comparing these two British youth culture magazines on points of design, content, and style, Hebdige maps a cultural terrain between, on the one hand, the last remnants of an avant-garde world (a three-dimensional world of words capable of historical perspective and motion over time) and, on the other hand, the emergent dominance of a postmodern, post–avant-garde world (a flat depthless world of images happily fixated on its own eternally changing kaleidoscopic present). According to Hebdige, *Ten.8*, with its more traditional magazine style and three-column layout, is a magazine capable of offering up "knowledge of debates on the history, theory, politics and practice of photography," whereas *the Face*, with its oversized "continental format," its emphasis on photo images and a design that blurs the boundaries between article and ad, ends up offering nothing but flat surfaces: "'street credibility,' 'nous,' image and style tips for those operating within the highly competitive milieux of fashion, music and design."[37] *The Face* is a magazine," argues Hebdige, that "goes out of its way every month to blur the line between politics and parody and pastiche; the street, the stage, the screen; between purity and danger; the mainstream and the 'margins.' "[38] Indeed, writes Hebdige,

All statements made inside *the Face*, though necessarily brief are never straightforward. Irony and ambiguity predominate. They frame all reported utterances whether those utterances are reported photographically or in prose. A language is thus constructed without anybody in it (to question, converse or argue with). Where opinions are expressed they occur in hyperbole so that a question is raised about how seriously they're meant to be taken. Thus the impression you gain as you glance through the magazine is that this is less an "organ of opinion" than a wardrobe full of clothes (garments, ideas, values, arbitrary preferences: i.e., signifiers). . . . As the procession of subcultures, taste groups, fashions, anti-fashions, winds its way across the flat plateaus, new terms are coined to describe them. . . . The process is invariable: caption/capture/disappearance (i.e., naturalisation). . . . Once named, each group moves from the sublime (absolute now) to the ridiculous (the quaint, the obvious, the familiar). It becomes a special kind of joke. Every photograph an epitaph, every article an obituary. On both sides of the camera and the typewriter, irony and ambiguity act as an armour to protect the wearer (writer/photographer; person/people written about/photographed) against the corrosive effects of the will to nomination. Being named (identified; categorised) is naff; on Planet Two it is a form of living death.[39]

Hmmmmm. Smells like team *Spin*. What's in *Spin* is out because being in *Spin* marks one as having already been "sold out" long enough to be included in *Spin*. Regardless of how frequently *Spin* may implicate itself in the ironic world of its own making, such acts are themselves, however, only part of the language of simulacra . . . every month the world of youth cultures and pop is made anew in the pages of *Spin* only to be declared dead already, only in turn to be made new and declared already dead again next month. Or is it?

"What's Out for '93": *Spin* as Not Just a Magazine

The *Spin* reader who wants to dismiss the magazine as a consumerist tour guide to what's trendy also, unwittingly, acknowledges in his letter that one might read *Spin* as a way of gauging what's not authentic alternative culture—as a guide to "What's out." The logic underlying this critique reflects Sarah Thornton's argument (as well as perhaps *Spin*'s self-conscious realization) that mass subculture consumer magazines such as *the Face,* however ironically scorned by people who identify themselves with underground scenes, nevertheless play a crucial, constitutive mediating role in the formation of subculture scenes and identities. In "Moral Panic, the Media and British Rave Culture," Thornton challenges the way cultural studies subculture theories "tend to position the media and its associated processes in opposition to and after the fact of subculture":[40] "Their segregation of subcultures from the media derives, in part, from an intellectual project in which popular culture was excavated out from under mass culture (that is, authentic people's culture was sequestered from mediated, corporate culture). In this way, the popular was defended against the disparagement of "mass society" and other theorists; youth could be seen as unambiguously active rather than passive, creative rather than manipulated. In practice, however, music subcultures and the media—popular and mass culture—are inextricable. In consumer societies, where sundry media work simultaneously and global industries are local businesses, the analytical division eclipses as much as it explains."[41]

We see this kind of interpretive "eclipse" at work in Hebdige's account of the "invariable" process he maps out regarding the relationship between *the Face* and the subculture scenes it covers: "caption/capture/disappearance." In her reading of British rave scenes, however, Thornton finds that, in the mainstream as well as in niche and zine media (and everything in between), one can chart a relationship that looks more like caption/formation/caption/re-formation. In this reciprocal relationship subcultures are not "subversive until the very moment they are represented by the mass media," but rather "become politically relevant only when they are framed as such," frequently by disparaging mass media and tabloid coverage that becomes "not the verdict but the vehicle of their resistance."[42] Moreover, Thornton argues that subculture theorists need to acknowledge the existence of mass media that cater specifically to countercultural desires of young people, what she refers to as "subcultural consumer magazines."

(White) Riot Grrrl: Who Really Wants a Riot Right Now?

Joanne Gottlieb and Gayle Wald take up a similar post-Hebdige position in "Smells Like Teen Spirit: Riot Grrrls, Revolution and Women in Independent Rock," where they conclude that the limits of riot grrrl "revolutionary" rock are to be found in the movement's self-imposed media blackout, some of which has remained in effect since 1992.[43] Though they concede that riot grrrls have legitimate reasons to fear and loathe masculinist "mainstream" media and the gaze of academia, both of which threaten (in different ways) to exploit and trivialize the movement and incorporate it into various forms of cultural tourism, Gottlieb and Wald conclude that such a stance against academia and the "popular" is ultimately politically regressive and elitist: "In pinning its resistance to the undifferentiated 'mainstream,' riot grrrl risks setting itself up in opposition to the culturally 'popular,' as well as to the political status quo; in this they echo the collegiate erudition and elitism of independent music generally. Moreover, in rejecting the popular, riot grrrl may preclude the possibility of having a broad cultural or political impact. . . . If riot grrrl wants to raise feminist consciousness on a large scale, then it will have to negotiate a relation to the mainstream that does not merely reify the opposition between mainstream and subculture."[44] This criticism is perhaps especially poignant when one considers that many riot grrrls are themselves current or former graduate students and that much of riot grrrl's neopunk "revolution" resides in the translation of academic feminist critical theory into everyday subcultural practice. For the purposes of my argument here, however, what's most relevant about Gottlieb and Wald's essay is not just that their conclusions about the limits of riot grrrl counterhegemonic practices echo

Thornton's analysis of the symbiotic, constitutive relationship between media and subculture identity, but that their essay is written at all. In their essay Gottlieb and Wald enact a performative criticism that, in the acts of composition, presentation, and publication, violates riot grrrl resolve to resist incorporation and the gaze of both "mainstream" media and academia. This is made all the more clear when one considers the ways Gottlieb and Wald undermine their own analysis by constructing riot grrrl as an "original" underground that "emerges as a bona fide subculture" and then gets "discovered" by mainstream journalism and subsequently popularized.[45]

This is precisely the kind of violation for which *Spin* magazine is routinely vilified, again by academics, subculture members, and so-called "mainstream" readers alike. Moreover, Gottlieb and Wald's implicit rationale for committing such a violation is identical to that which is frequently asserted in the pages of *Spin* as it reports and disseminates "alternative" underground scenes to "mainstream" readers—namely, "politics," or in the words of Gottlieb and Wald, the "possibility of [riot grrrl] having a broad cultural or political impact." Compare this statement to *Spin*'s own coverage of riot grrrl in the magazine's "Flash" section just prior to the movement's semiofficial 1992 media blackout: "When asked about their inspiration, many of the women involved cite Kathleen Hanna, lead singer of Bikini Kill. Hanna, however, doesn't exactly have mass-media savvy—she declined to speak to *Spin* and, with that, gave up the opportunity to reach thousands with her motivating voice."[46] To punctuate their certainly self-serving critique further, and to give riot grrrl the benefit of the mass media advertising plug that Hanna expressly tried to refuse, Daisy Furth concludes her brief *Spin* article by listing riot grrrl Washington D.C. contact addresses for "girl bands" and "girls interested in riot grrrl" (a rhetorical gesture that echoes *Spin*'s monthly Amnesty International updates, which appeared on donated ad-space for twelve months in 1991–92, including an entire special issue guest-edited by Amnesty International executive director Jack Healey in November 1991).

The bottom line from both Gottlieb and Wald and *Spin*'s perspective seems to be the same: if you really want to have a progressive riot (or a cultural revolution), first you have to assemble a crowd. And you can only do that by reaching out to others, even to those (or perhaps especially to those), who threaten to incorporate your slogans, your "look," and your politics into their own agendas and their own practices and pleasures of everyday life; and you can only do that if you're willing to work in the mediums of the popular. *Spin* sound bite: "Sinéad O'Connor: I don't believe that rock 'n' roll is only about entertainment. *SPIN* [Bob Guccione Jr.]: I don't either, but it's certainly an entertainment medium."[47] Or, as Elizabeth Gilbert would write in her article on feminist porn after being snubbed by a NOW spokesperson: "If you only talk to people who already agree with you, you are not a political organization. You're a support group." *Spin* writers and editors frequently echo academic critiques of the traditional divisions between the margins and the mainstream. Consider, for example, an article on Stone Temple Pilots (August 1995): "As mainstream rock bands continue to emulate indie ways, they become lightning rods for ridicule. 'Poseurs!' cry the righteous arbiters of indie. But shouldn't we encourage the mainstreaming of indie values?"[48] This is the core of *Spin*'s theory of its own relationship to mass culture—this is at once its angle into the market of subculture consumer magazines and its moral mission, what Guccione Jr. calls its "higher calling."

The arguments against *Spin* successfully articulating or performing any such cultural criticism should by now be familiar. One might argue that *Spin* doesn't perform an act of criticism by publishing a "Flash" article on riot grrrl, and that it performs, instead, a double act of Madison Avenue mainstream incorporation. On the one hand, it appropriates riot grrrl interventions to serve a masculinist spectacle of rock ideology, the kind of thing that Ross defines as "some homosocial version of young, straight males out on the town, partying, and so on." On the other hand, it appropriates an academic critique of the relationship between popular culture and mass media to serve its own self-congratulatory, self-promoting, moralistic editorial voice. One might argue that riot grrrl revolution is, to return to Hebdige's phrasing, merely the latest commodity to appear in *Spin*'s endless parade of revolutionary youth cultures as fashion that it deploys to better market its own self-styled image of "street credibility." In this regard, one might note that the word "grrrl"—which in riot grrrl usage performs a multivalent intervention into, and recuperation of, the language of patriarchy, as well as a critique of the woman-centered discourses of mainstream feminism—appears on the pages of *Spin* as "girl." *Spin* articles do give a certain voice to riot grrrl concerns about masculine-media appropriations: "At a recent CBGB Bikini Kill show, many guys panted at the prospect of seeing Hanna topless (she had doffed her shirt at a previous gig), turning a

potential act of defiance into an oglefest." But those same *Spin* articles
also tend themselves to "ogle" at and invite male readers to be titillated
by riot grrrl displays of women's rage: "Some of the older females present saw the show as just a Poly Styrene/X-Ray Spex retread. But to the
younger, less jaded Goo-girls, Hanna is the Angriest Girl. They understand. They see this scary, sexy girl, who pogos while singing about sexual abuse, as the future of punk rock—where girls can have fun for a
change." With the final sentence of the article collapsing riot grrrl anger
into Cindy Lauper's "girls just wanna have fun," one might conclude
that, indeed, "violation" is the appropriate word to describe *Spin*'s riot
grrrl reporting and its diluted critical performances; *Spin*'s refusal to
respect riot grrrl's "no" in response to its media advances mimics sexual
violence.

Though there is no doubt some validity to each of these claims, the
problem with such arguments is that (1) they all depend upon a return
to an interpretive paradigm that constructs riot grrrl subculture as existing apart from and outside of the multiple levels of media (mass media, tabloid media, niche or zine media, as well as subculture consumer
media, and academic media), which are in fact the materials out of
which subcultures and undergrounds are made; and (2) they presuppose
that a valid, qualitative (if not quantitative) distinction can be drawn
between *Spin*'s violation of riot grrrl media blackouts and the violation
performed by Gottlieb and Wald's academic essay, which is of course
only the tip of a whole wave of riot grrrl papers that began hitting the
beaches of traditional academic venues. Gottlieb and Wald turn to riot
grrrl performances to validate academic gender-as-performance criticism while at the same time holding those performances up as a model
for future feminist political strategies: "Using performance as a political
forum to interrogate issues of gender, sexuality and patriarchal violence,
riot grrrl performance creates a feminist praxis based on the transformation of the private into the public, consumption into production—or,
rather than privileging the traditionally male side of these binaries, they
create a new synthesis of both."[49] But Gottlieb and Wald themselves
tend to reify the opposition between mainstream and subculture, and
in the process exaggerate the antihegmonic resistance of the subculture.
Making such an intellectual and political investment in a "popular" scene
that refuses to engage the popular almost as a matter of policy, however,
makes me wonder exactly what kind of praxis we're really talking about
here, bringing to mind Steven Tyler's joke about rock critics: "Why do

rock critics like Elvis Costello? Because they all look like him."[50] But even assuming that riot grrrl has indeed managed (in spite of itself) to mobilize a popularized form of feminist cultural criticism centered on a Hebdigian postmodernist "problematics of affect" (the subsequent mass popularity of Courtney Love and other popularized "angry womyn" grrrl-styled "alternative" rock bands indicates that is has), it could only do so, as Gottlieb and Wald themselves hesitantly acknowledge, in its popularized forms in the mass media:

Possibly, the riot grrrl movement would have been significantly diminished had it not been for its careful coverage [in *Sassy*], which gave a mass audience of teenage girls access to a largely inaccessible phenomenon in the rock underground. This suggests a variation on Dick Hebdige's model of ideological incorporation in that—in this case—the media, beyond its function to control and contain this phenomenon, may also have helped to perpetuate it. *Sassy*'s role in publicizing and perpetuating the riot grrrl phenomenon may arise from a gendered division in the experience of youth culture, with girls' participation gravitating towards the forms, often mass-market visual materials, that lend themselves towards consumption in the home. While it appropriates riot grrrl subculture as a marketing strategy, the magazine also enables riot grrrl culture to infiltrate the domestic space to which grrrls—particularly young teenagers—are typically confined.[51]

All of which tends to circle without directly facing the more fundamental questions of exactly where riot grrrl performances might be said to perform and who in fact might be said to perform them, which ultimately leads to a question of who qualifies to identify themselves as part of the riot grrrl revolution: underground rock bands and underground zines, certainly; readers, writers, and editors of *Sassy,* maybe; but presumably not readers (let alone writers and editors) of the likes of the *Village Voice, Rolling Stone,* and *Spin.*

Of course, there are important differences to note between underground scenes and mass media disseminations of underground messages and styles, between the reading spaces and reading practices of contemporary teenage girls and boys (though Hanna herself allows that boys too, like Bikini Kill's guitarist, can be "girly boys"); however, Gottlieb and Wald's compulsion to police the boundaries between *Sassy*'s "careful," "respectful," and ideologically "committed" mass media disseminations on the one hand, and an otherwise undifferentiated mass of "mainstream" media dilutions on the other, seems to me to overplay all of these differences, especially given the collegiate nature of "alternative" youth cultures more generally. The overall effect of this is to exaggerate riot grrrl underground agency in "infiltrating" the mainstream with presumably more "authentic" riot grrrl articulations and to discount any empowering potential in the readerly consumption of mass media marketing appropriations of those articulations.

Thornton claims that because mass media is the stuff out of which subcultural identity is formed, we must concede that subcultures are themselves likely to be more passive than we have been led to believe. The converse of this may be, however, that subculture consumer magazines (their articles and ads) are more actively subversive than we have been led to assume. From this perspective, one could argue that riot grrrl as Gottlieb and Wald construct it not only risks "echoing the collegiate erudition and elitism of independent music generally" by positioning itself against the "mainstream," but rather it was from the start already collegiate, erudite and elitist. It remained so in part because riot grrrl subculture identity grounded itself in limiting rather than expanding the stage upon which it would perform popularized articulations of academic feminism, which, as Gottlieb and Wald acknowledge, remains itself a largely collegiate white middle class woman's (as opposed to "girl's") tradition, culture, and movement. *Spin* writer Charles Aaron was perhaps (ironically) correct, then, when he prematurely concluded in his *Village Voice* article on the movement that riot grrrl circa 1992 would turn out to be only a white college women's riot after all (though he might have emphasized that's significant in and of itself!). Aaron missed the mark, however, when he failed to see riot grrrl media coverage itself as a constitutive part of that subcultural resistance movement—a movement of cultural critique that (even more ironically) may have only appeared to evaporate in news photographer's "flash" to later reemerge (in spite of everyone) in other, more popular popularized forms.

Conclusion: Post-Scripts (Again): Cultural Work in the "Always Forever Now"

Part of our point is that nobody owns these images. They belong to a movement that is constantly growing—in numbers, in militancy, in political awareness.

Douglas Crimp, *AIDS demo graphics*

I want to conclude by way of a brief turn back to Hebdige's "Post-Scripts," which make up the conclusion of *Hiding in the Light*. Hebdige grudgingly accepts that, like it or not (and he clearly doesn't), postmodernism is "here" to stay, so we might as well "get used to it." Meaning, it's time to stop complaining about the postmodern (or waxing nostalgic for those more knowable "modernist" times that never quite were anyway) and figure out how to work within it—how to "work it."

Diesel Jeans and (ACT UP) Cultural Work

So let's begin again by taking Hebdige at face value. Let's allow that *Spin,* like *the Face* and *Vibe* and other consumer subculture magazines, not only blurs the line between article and ad, it collapses it all together. And let's allow that it all collapses into the ad. Following Thornton's line of thinking, ads like Diesel Jeans' "Victory," which was published as a full two-page spread in the opening pages of *Spin* in 1995, can be read as a post–avant-garde countercultural intervention (commercial to be sure) that does not merely appropriate "original" ACT UP signs of subcultural opposition, but in fact resemanticizes and disseminates (popularizes) those oppositional values on a scale that no subcultural articulation ever could. There are indeed multiple moments of commercial appropriation taking place here, appropriations of what traditional subcultural theories would either explicitly or implicitly define as "original" or "authentic" ACT UP oppositional signs. The slogan and logo for the ad series, which appears at the bottom corner of all the Diesel Jeans shock ads, borrows directly from ACT UP subcultural styles and rhetoric. The logo features a profile face of a punk, new wave rebel whose image calls to mind ACT UP's initial appropriation of earlier punk-rock looks; surrounding that profile, arranged like the print surrounding an activist logo, is the series slogan printed in the fashion of ACT UP protest slogans: "Number 80 in a Series of Diesel 'How to . . .' Guides to SUCCESSFUL LIVING for PEOPLE interested in general HEALTH and mental POWER." The central image of the two sailors kissing on the dock at a World War II homecoming victory celebration is specifically an appropriation of a 1988 ACT UP poster titled "Read My Lips" featuring two World War II era sailors in a similar pose of loving embrace and full-mouthed kiss, an in-your-(heterosexist)-face assertion of gay pride and resistance, the visual equivalent of "we're here, we're queer, get used to it." However, this "original" ACT UP poster, which was produced by

Gran Fury to promote a "kiss in" protest rally, itself borrows from similar tactics of appropriation deployed by 1960s antiwar protests. In fact, this Diesel ad bears an even more direct resemblance to Eisenstaedt's famously staged World War II V-J Day photograph, which was itself incorporated into a 1968 Vietnam War Protest poster promoting the parodic celebration of "VD Day: The End of the War!"

The Diesel Jeans "Victory" ad therefore ends up being not merely a commercial appropriation of ACT UP signs of subcultural resistance, but rather an appropriation of what was itself an ACT UP appropriation. The questions facing us, in light of Thornton's critique of cultural studies' tendency to romanticize and essentialize subcultural resistance are, what, if any, kinds of oppositional cultural work (including queer cultural critique) may survive the commodification process? What other kinds of oppositional images might be for sale? Does this image of commodified queerness mark or elide the cultural-historical systems of power and social struggle that lie behind the multiple appropriations taking place? The expected "disclaimer" is clearly present in the lower left corner where a man is wearing a placard in which a sampling of the song "God Bless America" ("America, God shed his grace") reads as a moral and religious invective against homosexuality. But it's difficult to imagine that virtually all of the activism of the "original" Gran Fury "Read My Lips" poster gets lost in the popular commercial appropriations here. In fact, when one considers that the timing of the ad proclaiming "victory" comes right on the heels of newly-elected President Clinton's soon-to-be doomed attempt to lift the ban on gays in the military, this appropriation might be interpreted as reflecting a fuller image of the important role World War II played in the historical development of gay and lesbian identity and community in America. The realpolitik optimism of this ad may have been misplaced; however, the larger political successes of ads such as this and of commodified queerness more generally is not to be located in any direct influence they may have on public policy, but rather in their ability to win popular consent for the free and open expression of "outlaw" sexuality. As one reader of an earlier version of this essay said in response to someone else's dismissal of this ad's politics as merely an appropriation of the latest image of suburban "alternative" hipness: "Yes, but that may be precisely the point. We want and need for young people to be able to look at images like this, or video images of Madonna kissing a woman, and see them as 'cool.'"

The potentially successful populist politics of this ad and similar consumer culture appropriations reveals the limitations of Crimps's claim that ACT UP subcultural pop art interventions succeed in breaking down the barriers of mass culture and high art, which earlier generations of Pop artists sought but failed to achieve. In *AIDS demo graphics*, Crimp credits ACT UP's Gran Fury with having successfully circumvented "the fate of most critical art" in the twentieth century, which is to be "co-opted and neutralized" by the overriding commodity constraints of the art world: "Postmodernist art advanced a political critique of art institutions—and art itself as an institution—for the ways they constructed social relations through specific modes of address, representations of history, and obfuscations of power. The limits of this aesthetic critique, however, have been apparent in its own institutionalization: critical postmodernism has become a sanctioned, if still highly contested, art world product, the subject of standard exhibitions, catalogues, and reviews. The implicit promise of breaking out of the museum and marketplace to take on new issues and find new audiences has gone largely unfulfilled."[52] Crimp claims that ACT UP's Gran Fury delivers on postmodernist art's failed promise to break out of the twin confines of "the museum and the marketplace" because they target their art-politics at the "streets" of AIDS activism. Though Crimp is justified in his critique of pop as museum-bound cultural critique, in his celebration of Gran Fury he tends to fall into the reverse trap of exaggerating and romanticizing the authenticity and independence of queer subculture, much in the same way as George Chauncey does in his analysis of gay subcultures in the 1920s and 1930s, as Hebdige does with punk in the late 1970s, and as Gottlieb and Wald do with riot grrrl in the late 1980s.

Cultural studies subcultural theories, as important as they are in mapping the complexities of power relationships operating according to the "spectacle" logics of consumer capitalism, frequently fail to take full account of the constitutive role that mass media technologies play in the long history of dissatisfied people locating ruptures in the hegemonies of cultural dominants and rearticulating resistant cultural practices within those ruptures. What *Spin* magazine offers us, then, is a demonstration of the limits of relying on subcultures as a paradigm for political action and activism against a global system of multinational consumer capitalism. That's the bad news. The good news is that rethinking the post–avant-garde politics of *Spin* may lead to new, more successful strategies

of Left coalition-building between intellectuals, countercultural celebrities, consumer-subcultural media industries and "the people" Stuart
Hall called for in the conclusion of *The Hard Road to Renewal*.[53]

When one more fully acknowledges the interdependent, symbiotic
relationship between the media and subculture identity formations, *the
Face* becomes more than "just a magazine." And so too does *Spin*, which
since the late 1980s increasingly positioned itself in more explicit political cultural terms and which had always been more explicitly "political"
than *the Face* from the very beginning. But *Spin* may arguably be "a
just magazine" as well, not because it offers up the kind of academic-
friendly, rational argument and criticism that Hebdige locates in *Ten.8*,
but rather precisely because it uses irony and hyperbole to mobilize an
effective form of "sound bite" criticism—because *Spin* manages to
reach, with its Gen X posturing and hyperbolic irony, the kinds of readers that neither Hebdige nor media-phobic undergrounds ever will:
those center-leaning, educated but decidedly not academic, generally
conservative but still reachable mass cult readers against whom both
subculture theorists and undergrounds scenes ritualistically define
themselves, but upon whom they must also depend if their alternative
cultural politics are going to be effective.

Jeans II: Celebrating Whose Specialness?

In arguing that contemporary Left pop culture academics need to
rethink their relationship to commodified media technologies through
which progressive cultural politics work, I do not mean to suggest that
Spin magazine has arrived at the promised land of post–avant-garde
political postmodernist practice. Rather, I'm suggesting that its appropriations of riot grrrl and ACT UP counterculture have functioned progressively and that the *Spin* model of commodified resistance represents
a viable strategy. In many ways, of course, *Spin's* appropriations do function conservatively, particularly regarding issues of race and race representations. Since the advent of *Vibe* (which now owns *Spin*), *Spin* appears to have abandoned its 1989 to 1993 political vision of an alliance
between alternative rock and hip-hop manifesting itself under the ban-
ner of some vaguely defined multicultural Gen X signifier. The magazine
continues to market itself as Gen X radical chic, but regarding race,
Spin in 1996 and 1997 resorted to merely paying lip service to hip-hop

as an imaginary postracist ally to the implicitly-coded white world of Gen X iconography.

In the post–Gen X, postpunk, post-*Vibe* world of the late 1990s, "Gen X" ironically remained a potent signified for both *Spin* and its fashion-music advertisers, even though any and all explicit signifiers of Gen X have long since gone past being passé. Moreover, the percentage of multiethnic imagery associated with Gen X iconography continues to grow in inverse proportion to the rise of de facto ethnic segregation and racial conflict over the last two decades. Similar to *Spin*'s riot grrrl coverage, the current proliferation of multiethnic Gen X signs again raises complex questions about commodified images of progressive political ideals and the resistant practices of subordinate peoples. In the construction of an explicitly multiracial Gen X hipness, are we seeing a progressive proliferation of racial integration imagery in a neoracist age that seems to have forgotten the brief respite of 1960s integration idealism, or are we seeing instead merely another set of "postracist," feel-good images that only fuel current, so-called voluntary segregationist trends by white consumers who deny the existence of racial difference and racism even as they run out to buy stylized images of urban, racially-coded hipness?

The narrative logic of *Spin*'s racial positioning can be seen in a Levi's SilverTab advertisement featured in the October 1997 issue of *Swing: A Magazine About Life in Your Twenties*, itself a spin-off (albeit short-lived) of the *Spin* phenomenon. In this ad, which is typical of the Silver Tab campaign, a kitsch late 1970s family portrait that screams white-bread suburbia gets intruded upon by a moment of interracial "contact." The 1970s suburban dress, the stiff poses and the sterile smiles of the family stand in stark juxtaposition to the relaxed posture, the gently mocking smile and the "alternative" street style of an urban female hipster whose punked-out afro touches the white housewife's do-it-yourself-perm cut. Of course, the "in joke" of the ad is that white people aren't hip. But the deeper irony, the implied commercial message of the ad, seems to be that white people, these twenty-something college students who read *Swing* and *Spin*, can in fact purchase a kind of second-degree hipness through Levi's SilverTab products. White people can't be hip, but they can achieve a level of hipness by ironically acknowledging the fact of their unhipness. This is the appeal of urban hip-hop styles for suburban whites more generally, made all the more ironic here since the product is not really hip-hop attire at all but instead pretty run-of-the-mill suburban casual wear, which is perhaps also designed to sell images of economic and social uplift to a secondary market of black middle-class twentysomethings. (In the advertisement, the black woman relaxing alone in the elegant chair has now lost much of her former punk and hip-hop signifiers in favor of a decidedly more assimilated, middle-class posture.) For the white twentysomething, the emotional appeal is partially located in the way that wearing an image of interracial integration offers the consumer a feel-good sentiment of racial harmony in the midst of racial segregation, racial tensions, and perhaps even their own race prejudices.

The images of multiracial, multicultural harmony are now common ad stock. But in our increasingly segregated society, it remains to be seen whether any of the progressive taboo-shattering meanings of ads like the popular Benetton's United Colors series will survive the neo-colonialist race or race essentialist meanings implied by these kinds of shock "idea" ads which are so crucial to *Spin* magazine's own streetwise and "alternative" hip currency. Benetton's United Colors ad series has become for many skeptics of political postmodernism the epitome of commercial appropriations masquerading as social protest imagery. Appignanesi and Garratt contend, for example, that Benetton's appropriation of photojournalism and the stylized imagery of social protest "art" merely appropriates the "hyperreality" cachet of those original forms, gleaning that reality onto the unreal construct of the magazine ad page and condensing it down to the image of the Benetton product name and logo—a purely commodified image (and for Appignanesi and Garratt it is only an image) of global identity and "social conscience."[54] One famous ad, featuring two copulating horses, one "black" and one "white," is obviously staged and, similar to the camped-up homosexual overtones in the Diesel Jeans ad, the visual racial marking is really over-the-top. The straight blond mane of the female horse and the kinked and curled mane of the "black" horse is as camped-up as the applauding, beef-cake sailors or the phallic shape of the submarine with "sea-men" descending from the tip in the Diesel ad. But there is still the vexing question of whether this image of interracial contact deconstructs race as a binary black-white discourse or whether it reconstructs race essentialist myths by reifying race as a set of natural attributes? Does this image force readers, particularly young white readers, to confront their internalization of deeply entrenched racial taboos? Does it make the breaking of taboos "cool" in the same way that the Diesel Jeans "Victory" ad makes the image of homosexuality a cool transgression, or does it merely allow consumers to trick themselves into feeling multicultural, "third-world hip," or radical-chic, through their fashion purchases? The questions are easy to form. The answers, of course, are the hard part. It should be clear, however, that it is too easy and counterproductive to dismiss as appropriation the constitutive role that commercialism and commodification play in the historical, material construction of progressive cultural studies ideals: internationalism, economic justice, racial harmony, gender parity, and sexual liberation.

Always Already the Spin Doctors

Subcultural capital is, as Thornton points out, "in no small sense" constructed out of and by media and commerce. It is equally important, however, to keep reminding ourselves that subcultural capital is at once a form of academic cultural capital as well. The cultural dollar signs may take different forms, but Gottlieb and Wald, Ross and Rose, and *Social Text* are all cashing in on the riot grrrl phenomenon, too. Though academics do so in the higher registers of subculture theoretical discourses, and only after first expressing the appropriate academic sensitivity about "who will speak for whom, and when, and under what conditions or circumstances,"[55] we all unavoidably traffic in the spectacle of "street credibility." As am I in this very essay. As are so many other graduate students who are trying to scramble for cultural studies vita credits to compete in a job market that, professors tell us with simultaneously sinister and apologetic jocularity, probably isn't going to materialize after all. As were the hundreds of graduate students who paid $95 to deliver papers at an open-invitation Cultural Studies conference at the University of Oklahoma in 1990, which, according to Cary Nelson, only "testifies to the sense that putting a 'Cultural Studies in the 1990s' label on your vita is worth an investment in exploitation and alienation."[56] But cultural studies capital circulates beyond the traditional academic systems of credentials and rewards as well. As Clint Burnham notes in the conclusion to *The Jamesonian Unconscious,* cultural studies theory and criticism is itself being consumed by graduate students and other "alternative," self-identified Gen X readers as mass culture:

I would argue that many intellectuals of my generation read the work of Jameson, and theory in general (Jameson means something else) as mass culture; by my generation I suppose I mean those born in the late fifties or in the sixties, Generation X as my fellow Canadian put it. . . . [I]n this milieu, Jameson and Butler and Spivak and Barthes are on the same plane as Shabba Ranks and PJ Harvey and Deep Space Nine and John Woo: cultural signifiers of which one is as much a "fan" as a "critic," driven as much by the need to own or see or read the "latest" (or the "classic" or the "original") as by the need to debate it on the Internet and in the seminar room. You think *Rid of Me* is good? Check out *4-Track Demos*. *True Romance* is more of a John Woo film than *Hard Target*. If you like *Gender Trouble*, check out *Bodies That Matter*. Jameson's piece on Chandler in *Shades of Noir* is a remix of his older essay and samples some of the comments on modernism at the end of *Signatures of the Visible*.[57]

And this comes to us in a Duke University trade paperback that is self-consciously designed to be a simulacra of Jameson's own *Postmodernism, or The Cultural Logic of Late Capitalism,* which is itself now (in)famous amongst critics and reviewers for its self-consciously styled presence as "a gorgeously produced 400-page document."[58] By the time I finished Burnham's text, I could no longer be certain why I had originally plunked down my VISA card and paid $17.95 for this aesthetically pleasing book (no longer merely a "text") whose marketing blurb, appearing both in the Duke University Press mail-order catalogue and on the back of the book, sounds a lot like a heady academic version of that subscription junk mail I keep getting from *Spin:*

Imagine Fredric Jameson—the world's foremost Marxist critic—kidnapped and taken on a joyride through the cultural ephemera, generational hype, and Cold War fallout of our post-post-contemporary landscape. In *The Jamesonian Unconscious,* a book as joyful as it is critical and insightful, Clint Burnham devises unexpected encounters between Jameson and alternative rock groups, new movies, and subcultures. . . . In an unusual biographical move, Burnham negotiates Jameson's major works . . . by way of his own working-class, queerish, Gen-X background and sensibility. Thus Burnham's study draws upon an immense range of references familiar to the MTV generation, including *Reservoir Dogs,* theorists Slavoj Žižek and Pierre Bourdieu, *The Satanic Verses,* Language poetry, the collapse of state communism in Eastern Europe, and the indie band Killdozer.

I don't know about you, but I definitely hear the sound of some bones crunching now—but can anyone tell me with any degree of certainty anymore who's doing the crunching and who's being crunched?

Notes

1. My position in relation to *Spin* and the contemporary music and subculture scenes it covers is primarily as a fan of so-called popular "alternative music," what Robert Christgau insists should more accurately be called "college rock," and even here I am more of a tourist and fan than a fellow traveler in any specific indie scene. I have, however, been reading *Spin* (or perhaps as Hebdige would have it, I've been "cruising" *Spin*) since 1986, when I was introduced to the magazine while attending a small Midwestern state college by a friend from Decatur, Illinois, who read *Spin* with, what seemed to me then, an odd intensity to determine his position in relation to the "mainstream" and some notion of a true punk "underground."

2. Stuart Hall, "The Meaning of New Times," in *Stuart Hall: Critical Dialogues in Cultural Studies*, ed. David Morely and Kuan-Hsing Chen (London: Routledge, 1996), 223–37.

3. Michael Bérubé, *Public Access: Literary Theory and American Cultural Politics*. London: Verso, 1994), 176.

4. Ibid., 161.

5. "The Cult of the DJ: A Symposium," *Social Text* 43 (Fall 1995): 67.

6. In a May 1994 *Spin* cover story on Courtney Love, for example, Dennis Cooper points out that Love grew up in a liberal intellectual environment and "remains an avid reader of feminist theorists like Susan Faludi, Judith Butler, Camille Paglia, and Naomi Woolf," but neither he nor she articulates anything that even remotely smacks of academic criticism—even though there is clearly a long, rich history of academic feminist cultural critique and avant-garde artistic intervention associated with the name of Love's band alone (Dennis Cooper, "Love Conquers All," *Spin*, May 1994, 42). It is perhaps true that one doesn't need to be an academic feminist to interpret the band's name, Hole, as a cultural critique of the hegemonic sexual ideologies of phallic domination, nor does one need to be a professor of pop culture to link the band Hole to its many punk predecessors, such as the Slits—the first all-woman punk band whose members, like so many other early punk rock musicians and contemporary "alternative" musicians, walked straight out of their university studies and into the punk "streets." There is, however, something troubling about the way contemporary popular artists deny their academic backgrounds and intellectual influences. Similarly, many academics, whose cultural writings may be influenced by the postmodernism they (we) encounter in pop culture, are equally reluctant to acknowledge the knowledge that they derive from their own practices as fans and consumers, though they are increasingly eager to acknowledge their pleasures. And this is true, despite the fact that both popular music artists and academics luxuriate in the art of surreptitious quotation of one another.

7. Bob Guccione Jr., "TopSpin," *Spin*, April 1995, 24.

8. Jim Greer, "Letter From Dayton, Ohio, Bureau," *Spin*, April 1995, 224.

9. Guccione, April 1995, 24.

10. Greer, "Letter From Dayton, Ohio, Bureau," 224. Though I don't take it up here, *Spin*'s relationship to the PC wars is particularly interesting and, as with everything else in *Spin*, contradictory. Both *Spin* and Guccione Jr. have been very vocal concerning the censorship of pop music. In fact, in the mid 1980s when Tipper Gore and the PMRC were waging their war against youth, Guccione Jr. propelled himself to the status of celebrity/public intellectual, regularly debating William F. Buckley and the usual cast of right-wing pundits on CNN's Crossfire and similar news talk shows. Yet, when it comes to academics and their battles with many of these same pundits, *Spin* has remained uninterested at best, too often picking up anti-PC catchphrases from the New Right along the way.

11. I say my "suspicion" because I don't personally know many academics who read *Spin*. If one can judge academic readership by the availability of library resources, then I would suspect that indeed very few do. Trying to research the early years of *Spin* proved to be a bit of an unexpected challenge. The Chicago Public Library was the only library in the state of Illinois that I could find holding *Spin* since its first issue in April 1985, including the University of Illinois, which is the only college or university out of the forty-two state and private schools on the state-wide library computer search system that carries the magazine at all (and the University of Illinois started carrying it only from 1994 on). Moreover, *Spin* is not indexed in the *Reader's Guide to Periodicals* or any bibliographic indexes or databases that I'm aware of (with the exception of the *Music Index*, which started indexing *Spin* in 1989, but only very selectively music-specific articles).

12. Dick Hebdige, *Hiding in the Light: On Images and Things* (London: Routledge, 1988).

13. Sarah Thornton, "Moral Panic, the Media and British Rave Culture," in *Microphone Fiends: Youth Music and Youth Culture*, ed. Tricia Rose and Andrew Ross (New York: Routledge, 1994), 176–192.

14. Andrew Ross, introduction to *Microphone Fiends: Youth Music and Youth Culture*, ed. Tricia Rose and Andrew Ross (New York: Routledge, 1994), 4.

15. Ibid., 3.

16. Douglas Coupland, "Eulogy: Death of Gen X," *Details,* June 1995, 72.

17. See David Martin, "The Whiny Generation," in *The GenX Reader*, ed. Douglas Rushkoff (New York: Ballantine, 1994), 235–37.

18. Coupland, "Eulogy," 72.

19. Rushkoff as self-aggrandizing: "Exposed to consumerism and public relations strategies since we could open our eyes, we GenXers see through the clunky attempts to manipulate our opinions and assets, however shrinking" (Douglas Rushkoff, introduction to *The GenX Reader* [New York: Ballantine, 1994], 5); pseudointellectual: "Our writers are our cultural playmakers and demonstrate an almost Beckettian ability to find humor in the darkest despair, a Brechtian objectivity to bracket painful drama with ironic distance, and a Chekhovian instinct to find the human soul still lurking beneath its outmoded cultural façade" (8); misinformed: "To most of us, concepts like racial equality, women's rights, sexual freedom, and respect for basic humanity are givens. We realize that we are the first generation to enter a society where, at least on paper and in the classroom, the ideas that Boomers fought for are recognized as indisputable facts" (6); homophobic: "We watched a sexual revolution evolve into forced celibacy as the many excesses of the 1970s and 1980s rotted into the sexually transmitted diseases of our 1990s" (5).

This is not to say, however, that academics and public intellectuals aren't guilty of similar kinds of lazy thinking. Take for example, this throw-away comment made by Frank Owen in "The Cult of the DJ" symposium concerning the mainstream music press and its refusal to cover dance music: "What I can't understand, though, is how the current rock scene is portrayed by some rock critics as radical. I listen to a band like Pearl Jam, and I guess they're critical favorites, but to me they sound like Bad Company. I mean, am I wrong or are they Bad Company? Why is grunge radical? What is so radical about it?" ("The Cult of the DJ: A Symposium," 78). Owen, who was a music editor at *Spin* for two years and who received an M.A. from the Center for Contemporary Cultural Studies at the University of Birmingham in England, ought to know better—making his sweeping dismissal of any and all politics of grunge in the context of this symposium on dance music DJs appear suspect, perhaps even patronizing. Certainly, he should realize that Pearl Jam isn't just a sound but also a look, an attitude, a stance; he should realize, as Ross has noted elsewhere, that, among other things, grunge asserts "a politics of dirt . . . as a scourge upon the impossibly sanitized, aerobicized world of 90210" (Introduction to *Microphone Fiends*, 5). However white and middle-class the grunge phenomenon is (Ross also characterizes it as white suburban kids "style slumming with a vengeance"), there is something "radical," or at least oppositional, about it, not least in the fact that at the very moment Owen was making these comments Pearl Jam was waging its legal battle and media campaign against the monopolistic price-fixing practices of Ticketmaster.

20. Dave Laing, *One Chord Wonders: Power and Meaning in Punk Rock* (Milton Keynes, England: Open University Press, 1985), viii.

21. Bob Guccione Jr., "TopSpin," *Spin,* January 1994, 12.

22. Quoted in Greil Marcus, *Lipstick Traces: A Secret History of the Twentieth Century* (Cambridge: Harvard University Press, 1989), 11–12.

23. Ross, Introduction, 1.

24. Ibid.

25. Hebdige, *Hiding in the Light,* 168.

26. Douglas Crimp, "AIDS: Cultural Analysis/Cultural Activism," in *AIDS: Cultural Analysis/Cultural Activism,* ed. Douglas Crimp (Cambridge: MIT Press, 1988), 3.

27. Paula A. Treichler, "AIDS, Homophobia, and Biomedical Discourse: An Epidemic of Signification," in *AIDS: Cultural Analysis/Cultural Activism,* 37.

28. Douglas Crimp, "How to Have Promiscuity in an Epidemic," in *AIDS: Cultural Analysis/Cultural Activism,* 238.

29. Ibid.

30. Ibid., 237–38.

31. Though even here, when one considers the practical uses of this condom, *Spin* might once again be accused of promoting its own radical image rather than any substantive subcultural resistance, in this case putting hype before health; for, as a reader of an earlier version of this paper pointed out to me, one would really have to question whether or not this condom, after going through the rigors of mass circulation magazine distribution, would even be safe. (My thanks to Elizabeth Majerus for this comment, as well as for her responses to the essay as a whole.)

32. Celia Farber, "TopSpin," *Spin,* May 1992, 12, emphasis added.

33. Most of this seems to be a case of journalistic sour grapes resulting from Farber having been publicly spanked by ACT UP and the *Advocate* which, I think correctly, denounced Farber's 1989 *Spin* article on AZT as dangerously overstating her case about evidence of the drug's risks and how that should impact the medical decisions made by people living with AIDS.

34. Elizabeth Gilbert, "Pussy Galore," *Spin,* April 1995, 150.

35. Craig Marks, "A to Z of Alternative Culture," *Spin,* April 1993, 38–52.

36. Ibid., 38.

37. Hebdige, *Hiding in the Light,* 158.

38. Ibid., 161.

39. Ibid., 170.

40. Sarah Thornton, "Moral Panic, the Media and British Rave Culture," in *Microphone Fiends,* 189.

41. Ibid., 188.

42. Ibid., 184.

43. Joanne Gottlieb and Gayle Wald, "Smells Like Teen Spirit: Riot Grrrls, Revolution and Women in Independent Rock," in *Microphone Fiends*, 250–74.

44. Ibid., 271.

45. Ibid., 262–63.

46. Daisy Furth, "For Girls About To Rock," *Spin*, April 1992, 26.

47. Bob Guccione Jr., "Special Child" (an interview with Sinéad O'Connor), *Spin*, November 1991, 48.

48. Michael Azerrad, "Peace, Love and Understanding," *Spin*, August 1995, 57.

49. Gottlieb and Wald, "Smells Like Teen Spirit," 268.

50. "Cult of the DJ," 75.

51. Gottlieb and Wald, "Smells Like Teen Spirit," 265–66.

52. Douglas Crimp, with Adam Rolston, *AIDS demo graphics* (Seattle: Bay Press, 1990), 19.

53. Stuart Hall, *The Hard Road to Renewal: Thatcherism and the Crisis of the Left* (New York: Verso, 1988).

54. Richard Appignanesi and Chris Garratt, *Introducing Postmodernism* (New York: Totem Books, 1995), 138–39.

55. Bérubé, *Public Access*, 271.

56. Cary Nelson, "Always Already Cultural Studies: Two Conferences and a Manifesto," *Journal of the Midwest Modern Language Association* 24, 1 (1991): 26.

57. Clint Burnham, *The Jamesonian Unconscious: The Aesthetics of Marxist Theory* (Durham: Duke University Press, 1995), 244.

58. Bérubé, *Public Access*, 127.

Bibliography

Appignanesi, Richard, and Chris Garratt. *Introducing Postmodernism*. New York: Totem Books, 1995.

Azerrad, Michael. "Peace, Love and Understanding." *Spin*, August 1995, 56–58.

Bérubé, Michael. *Public Access: Literary Theory and American Cultural Politics*. London: Verso, 1994.

Burnham, Clint. *The Jamesonian Unconscious: The Aesthetics of Marxist Theory*. Durham: Duke University Press, 1995.

Cooper, Dennis. "Love Conquers All." *Spin*, May 1994, 38.

Coupland, Douglas. *Generation X: Tales for an Accelerated Culture*. New York: St. Martin's Press, 1991.

———. "Eulogy: Gen X'd." *Details*, June 1995, 72.

Crimp, Douglas. "AIDS: Cultural Analysis/Cultural Activism." In *AIDS: Cultural Analysis/Cultural Activism*, edited by Douglas Crimp. Cambridge: MIT Press, 1988.

———. "How to Have Promiscuity in an Epidemic." In *AIDS: Cultural Analysis/Cultural Activism*, edited by Douglas Crimp. Cambridge: MIT Press, 1988.

Crimp, Douglas and Adam Rolston. *AIDS demo graphics*. Seattle: Bay Press, 1990.

"The Cult of the DJ: A Symposium." *Social Text* 43 (Fall 1995): 67–88.

Farber, Celia. "TopSpin." *Spin*, May 1992, 12.

Furth, Daisy. "For Girls About To Rock." *Spin*, April 1992, 26.

Gilbert, Elizabeth. "Pussy Galore." *Spin*, April 1995, 150.

Gottlieb, Joanne, and Gayle Wald. "Smells Like Teen Spirit: Riot Grrrls, Revolution and Women in Independent Rock." In *Microphone Fiends: Youth Music and Youth Culture,* edited by Tricia Rose and Andrew Ross. New York: Routledge, 1994.

Guccione, Bob, Jr. "Special Child" (interview with Sinéad O'Connor). *Spin,* November 1991, 42.

———. "TopSpin." *Spin,* April 1995, 24.

———. "TopSpin" *Spin,* January 1994, 12.

Greer, Jim. "Letter From Dayton, Ohio, Bureau." *Spin,* April 1995, 224.

Hall, Stuart. *The Hard Road to Renewal: Thatcherism and the Crisis of the Left.* New York: Verso, 1988.

———. "The Meaning of New Times." In *Stuart Hall: Critical Dialogues in Cultural Studies,* edited by David Morely and Kuan-Hsing Chen. London: Routledge, 1996.

Hebdige, Dick. *Hiding in the Light: On Images and Things.* London: Routledge, 1988.

Huyssen, Andreas. *After the Great Divide: Modernism, Mass Culture, Postmodernism.* Bloomington: Indiana University Press, 1986.

Laing, Dave. *One Chord Wonders: Power and Meaning in Punk Rock.* Milton Keynes, England: Open University Press, 1985.

Marcus, Greil. *Lipstick Traces: A Secret History of the Twentieth Century.* Cambridge: Harvard University Press, 1989.

Marks, Craig. "A to Z of Alternative Culture." *Spin,* April 1993, 38–52.

Nelson, Cary. "Always Already Cultural Studies: Two Conferences and a Manifesto." *Journal of the Midwest Modern Language Association* 24, 1 (1991): 24–38.

Ross, Andrew. Introduction to *Microphone Fiends: Youth Music and Youth Culture,* edited by Tricia Rose and Andrew Ross. New York: Routledge, 1994.

Rushkoff, Douglas. Introduction to *The GenX Reader.* New York: Ballantine Books, 1994.

Thornton, Sarah. "Moral Panic, the Media and British Rave Culture." In *Microphone Fiends: Youth Music and Youth Culture,* edited by Tricia Rose and Andrew Ross. New York: Routledge, 1994.

Treichler, Paula A. "AIDS, Homophobia, and Biomedical Discourse: An Epidemic of Signification." In *AIDS: Cultural Analysis/Cultural Activism,* edited by Douglas Crimp. Cambridge: MIT Press, 1988.

Generating Xs

Identity Politics, Consumer Culture, and the Making of a Generation

Kirk Curnutt

Prominently featured in *Newsweek*'s 1994 end-of-the-year special issue is an essay entitled "Talking 'Bout Our Generation" in which columnist Karen Schoemer asks why "nominating a spokesperson for a generation" has become a more contentious process than "nominating a President of the United States."[1] Each time the media turns its attention to potential figureheads for Generation X, "a chorus of naysayers immediately pipes up" to denounce them as contrived, insincere, and most strikingly, as irrelevant to its "real" identity. For Schoemer, the example par excellence is the response generated by Kurt Cobain's April 1994 suicide. As soon as memorialists from the nightly news and MTV to the *Nation* and the *New Republic* began to interpret the punk rock star's death as a synecdoche of generational despair, a symbol (as the story went) of the anxiety and rootlessness felt by an age group facing a future of downward mobility and diminished expectations, detractors vigorously resisted the association. "I never heard Kurt Cobain being called the voice of my generation until his death," claimed a typical letter to the editor in *Rolling Stone*'s commemorative issue, apparently from a reader unfamiliar with previous editions of the magazine in which Cobain was repeatedly dubbed just that. "What exactly is the problem here?" Schoemer asks. "Is Generation X really such a mess that no one wants to take responsibility for leading it?" Or does its "oft-ballyhooed lack of consensus" doom it to intragenerational squabbles over the relevance of its own cultural artifacts, whether punk rock, youth-culture films, or Woodstocks 1994 and 1999? In the midst of such debate, she acknowledges, "the temptation is to conclude that there is no Generation X, but we all know in our hearts that's not true. . . . Maybe the right hero hasn't come along yet; maybe the right hero never will. It's a hard job, and as far as this generation is concerned, nobody has to do it."

Schoemer's essay acknowledges an intriguing phenomenon within the voluminous discourse on Generation X that this essay will explore. How is it that generational solidarity is devalued while it is simultaneously invoked? The essay hints at an intriguing phenomenon within the voluminous discourse on Generation X that deserves analysis: while commentator after commentator has disputed if not derided the notion that a generational identity exists, spokespersons nevertheless emerged in the early to mid-1990s to enable its construction in the cultural marketplace. The strategies of articulation were by and large negative; because their overriding impulse was to dismiss the significance of generational characteristics, the assessments concluded on a note of determined indifference, with observers not only refusing the possibility that a cohort could be meaningfully defined, but that such a definition would have any significance to the lives of individual members. This stance marks a significant departure from past debates about generational identity. Once upon a time a youth-culture icon like F. Scott Fitzgerald would dress down hoarier adversaries who dismissed talk of flappers, petting parties, and bobbed hair as faddish and trendy. As Fitzgerald insisted, a writer's responsibility was first to "the youth of his own generation," and only then to "the critics of the next, and the schoolmasters of ever afterward." Now, however, no twenty- or early thirtysomething pundit can speak *about* his or her peers without first insisting that he or she wouldn't presume to speak *for* them. Indeed, claims like Fitzgerald's have given way to awkward disclaimers. If you are novelist David Leavitt, early in your career, you write two of the first proto–Generation X articles?—"The New Lost Generation" for *Esquire* and "New Voices and Old Values" for the *New York Times Book Review*, both published in May 1985—only to find yourself ridiculed in conservative mouthpieces like the *New Criterion* and *Ariel* as a "Brat Packer," a purveyor of narcissistic, juvenile fictions. You then spend the next decade attempting to be perceived as a mature artist by assuring interviewers that you are "more interested in writing about literature than . . . in being a spokesman for my generation. . . . That's not something I want to be. I was interested in it at that point, but that's not what I'm interested in anymore."[2] Or if you are Douglas Coupland, you write the 1991 novel that popularizes the term Generation X and immediately establish your authority as a spokesperson by serving as a consultant to *Twenty Twenty Insight* (a trade publication advising advertisers on how to reach young consumers, by narrating promotional pieces on MTV), and by writing Berlitz-styled decodings of Gen-X speak in the *New York Times* and the *New Republic*. Only then you find yourself condemned as a "poser who has profited by perpetuating a generation's self-loathing."[3] Thus, by the time your fourth novel is scheduled for publication, a scant four years after *Generation X* first appeared, you are admonishing your peers to "refuse to participate in all generational debates."[4]

Even if you are a relatively unknown author like Ian Williams, you describe yourself in the contributor's notes to an anthology subtitled *Young American Writers on the New Generation* as "the sarcastic spokesman for the twentysomething generation in the book *13th Gen: Abort, Retry, Entry, Fail*" before adding this qualification: "He hopes that if he were ever to *say* something like 'spokesman for the twenty-something generation' that the audience would take him out back and shoot him like an old horse."[5] Given the prevalence of such demurring among Generation X commentators, one thing is clear: a youth-culture hero, as John Lennon might have phrased it, is no longer something to be.

Typically, ambivalence toward this idea of a generational spokesperson is credited to the fabled refusenik mentality of Xers, our supposed resistance to the selling of our self-image in a consumer culture bent on commodifying our attitudes and entertainment interests. After a lifetime of exposure to advertising appeals, the argument goes, we have grown a hard shell of marketplace savvy and cynicism that protects us from any product seemingly contrived according to demographic generalizations. As Debra Goldman warned in a 1992 article in *Adweek*, "A target market all their lives . . . this generation of young malcontents is taking it personally,"[6] and never more so, it seems, than when the commodity appropriates our identity politics. Yet too much of this opposition stages itself as a facile contest between "us" and "them" as we, a generation whose only common denominator is our desire not to be stereotyped, resist the colonizing force of media hegemony. In fact, the essays and editorials that dismiss Generation X as a media concoction often sound as though they might have been lifted from the pages of Herbert

Marcuse's *One Dimensional Man* (1964), the tract widely credited with popularizing the Frankfurt School theory of the "culture industry" in the aftermath of World War II.[7] When, for example, Alexander Star dismisses Generation X as the product of a "middle-aged retailing of youth empowerment" that "assembles a generic youth culture . . . from above precisely because it doesn't exist from down below,"[8] he echoes the conspiratorial tone that runs throughout Frankfurt School criticism when it argues that corporations are in the business of manufacturing lifestyle accoutrements that dull the critical acumen of consumers craving their images. When Richard Blow advises his peers that our "one constructive option" is to "reject the media hype and disband altogether," he implies that generational solidarity is a false need, a desire imposed upon us by those with a vested interest in making us think as a target market.[9] And when Coupland complains that "trendmeisters" from the start misunderstood that Generation X is morally offended by "demographic pornography" because it is devoted to the "notion of individualism,"[10] he, like Marcuse, defines resistance wholly in the context of an "autonomous personality" whose higher powers of rationalism can only be achieved through a "Great Refusal" of the indoctrinating power of community. If Generation X and all that it signifies is just another marketing niche, the culture industry's device for homogenizing a pool of forty-six million consumers with an annual buying power of $125 billion, then anyone who identifies him or herself as a spokesperson for it willingly becomes what Marcuse calls "a cog in the culture-machine."[11]

What goes unasked when resistance is touted as the only strategy by which Generation X can prevent itself from being reduced to "Generalizations X"—a bit of wordplay that is itself now clichéd—is whether the individualism that "we" so desire might not be naturalizing a different ethos of consumer conformity, one that encourages us to buy, accrue, and indulge in a realm of introverted, purely personal pleasure. That is, in an environment in which generational solidarity is continually dismissed and devalued, we are encouraged to consume without forging what Lawrence Grossberg calls "affective alliances," those networks of identification by which we collectively demonstrate how cultural artifacts "organize [our] emotional and narrative life and identity."[12] As the "Great Refusal" becomes the rallying cry against the X image, that attitude is absorbed and reflected back in an array of consumer appeals;

thus, as a generation congratulates itself for taking to heart the Tho-
reauvian notion of letting one's life run counter to the machine, the
machine merely mimics that attitude to ensure its continued livelihood.
By attributing the question of generational identity to spurious profit
motives then, we hardly bring a halt to the Generation X industry, which
rattles and hums along with industrial fortitude. Instead, resistance
helps enculturate what Mark Crispin Miller describes as the superior
"knowingness" of individualism, which confers to each of us "the widespread illusion that we have all somehow recovered from a bout of vast
and paralyzing gullibility."[13] Congratulating ourselves for being too
smart to fall for appeals to solidarity and fraternity, we fail to question
whether we might be succumbing to an equally pernicious sensibility
in which we think of ourselves as existing without the formative ties of
generational experiences.

In what follows, I want to examine how generational solidarity is
devalued at the same time that it is invoked in a set of nonfiction books,
all published in 1994 and devoted to analyzing the identity politics of
Generation X. Obviously, one could trace the rise of the "Great Refusal"
in any number of more popular media, whether rock music, film, or
fashion. Yet I choose this genre because it dramatizes an intriguing paradox: although they critique the commodification of our generation, these
books are themselves commodities targeted at us and thus must negotiate a contradiction that *Publisher's Weekly* describes as "reap[ing] the
profits" of "generational slogans" while "call[ing] them into question."[14]
These books enact varying styles of resistance, whether irony (Jason Cohen and Michael Krugman's satirical *Generation Ecch!*), "guerrilla" nostalgia (Pagan Kennedy's *Platforms: A Microwaved Cultural Chronicle of
the 1970s*), ennui and disaffection (Elizabeth Wurtzel's *Prozac Nation:
Young and Depressed in America*), or socioeconomic analysis (David
Lipsky and Alexander Abrams's *Late Bloomers: Coming of Age in Today's America*).[15] Despite the range of approaches, these texts inevitably
employ what John Downtown Hazlett has argued is the core device of
generational discourse: they construct "an authorial stance that sup-
presses the individual self at the same time that it exalts . . . the collective
self to which the author belongs" while striving to "*create* the need [to
belong] for those to whom the need has not occurred."[16] Each work thus
in its own way claims the right to speak to its generation without seeming
to speak for it. As we shall see, the images of X that these books generate

may attempt to negate the clichés and redefine the buzzwords, but inevitably they succumb to their own commodification as they are caught within the combine that is contemporary media culture.

In *Generation Ecch! The Backlash Starts Here,* Cohen and Krugman distance themselves from fellow generational pundits by claiming that they will neither attack the media nor refute the "slacker" stereotype of a peer group willing to sacrifice any pretense of political interest for a moment of sheer fun: "This book will put to rest the allegations that this generation is dysfunctional and anti-intellectual. It most certainly is."[17] Instead, Generation X's responses to these images bear the brunt of their sarcasm. However comforting it may be to assume that the "fever" of generational definition was heightened by "old-fashioned capitalist greed" on the part of demographers and advertisers, "all the hubbub has prompted a self-absorbed and self-important generation to rationalize its own existence, ascribing significance to meaninglessness" (10). The question of "who we are" is a factitious one, for to enter the debate is to mire oneself in youth-culture clichés that have been applied to successive generations as far back as "a certain melancholy Prince of Denmark." "All young people eventually grow up to complain about 'kids today,'" they write in their concluding paragraphs. "It's both a rite of passage and a vicious . . . cycle" (215). To complain, oppose, and refute media images is a tacit act of "supporting the whole scam" (22) that encourages only lazy self-preoccupation. Given their insistence that pondering our collective identity only perpetuates the self-absorption of which we are continually accused, it is not surprising that *Generation Ecch!* offers one of the most straightforward assertions of consumer individualism: "A word of advice to all you yo-yos wasting precious TV time thinking about this nonsense: Get over it. Go live your life. . . . Just worry about yourself, one of the few things the generation is supposed to be good at. . . . It's not that big a deal" (23).

Of course, one could suggest that Cohen and Krugman are themselves supporting the "scam" (and being supported by it) by writing their book, yet the argumentative strategy by which they analyze the significance of MTV, Quentin Tarantino films, "graphic novels," and of course, grunge rock seeks to protect them from such a charge. As its onomatopoetic title suggests, *Generation Ecch!* not only skewers those who would presume to find sociological import (rather than pleasure) in pop-culture artifacts and experiences, but it consistently devalues the desire for generational solidarity as an adolescent craving for connection that the marketplace both encourages and perpetuates. Thus, the 1985 John Hughes film *The Breakfast Club* is deemed "clever for the way it manipulates little teenage minds by appearing to speak directly to and for them . . . [by] reflect[ing] their own petty problems and deepest shallow feelings of depression and ennui" (59). Novelists like Coupland, Bret Easton Ellis, and Donna Tartt are dismissed *en toto* for "portray[ing] a generation to itself without any special insight, aesthetic integrity or provocative narrative. . . . [Their] books do more than simply hold a mirror up to *Ecch*—they are *Ecch*, with all the generation's worst characteristics expressed as literary form, style, and content" (117). Finally, the popularity of rock bands like Nirvana and Pearl Jam is a monument to *"Ecch's* generation-wide feelings of victimhood. [They] voice the emotions of an audience *sooo* [tortured] by family and society that they cannot express themselves in any other way but their Tower Records purchases" (179). In this book's view then, Gen X culture signifies little more than a clever recycling of traditional teen angst and alienation; it may be fun to indulge in such feelings, the authors imply, but that doesn't mean we should take it all so seriously.

According to Miller, the derisive tone in such excerpts offers an appealing rhetorical strategy because its "easy jeering gaze" extends to readers "the cold thrill of feeling ourselves exalted above all concern, all earnestness, all principle, evolved beyond all innocence or credulity, liberated finally out of naive moralisms into pure modernity."[18] In Generation X satires, the thrill of ridiculing the idea that a Nirvana song might mirror the emotional world of its audience arises from a supposed repudiation of the value system that would deem rock a serious medium. We can negate the debate, the message seems to be, by refusing even to consider the idea that Cobain "spoke for" his generation and irreverently dramatize how little it does affect us. Thus, in a line that *Newsweek* deemed indicative of Xers' "kill-your-idols" attitude, Cohen and Krugman contrast the sensationalism of Cobain's suicide to the death of another Generation X icon, actor River Phoenix, who overdosed in a chic Hollywood nightspot in 1993: "Kurt decided that if he couldn't control his own myth he would put an end to it, and he did so with more showmanship than he ever demonstrated onstage. Blowing your head off sure beats accidentally OD'ing and doing the chicken in front of the Viper Room."[19]

Just how subversive is such ironic posturing? Not very. As David Foster Wallace judiciously suggests, satire, ridicule, and irony all strive to function as a "creative instantiation of deviance from bogus values," a rebellion frustrated when they become *the* language in which values are expressed—or, rather, the language in which we profess that we would never be tricked into valuing the "bogus" in the first place. Such a stance flatters us with a sense of "canny superiority" that arises from a sense of detached spectatorship that at once "shields the heaper of scorn from scorn" while it "congratulat[es] the patron of scorn for rising above the mass of people who still fall for outmoded pretensions."[20] The problem, however, is that as scorn is heaped upon commodities that themselves exploit a scornful attitude, the ridicule must perforce become more vigorous, which, in the case of *Generation Ecch!*, means more vituperative. How, for example, can we speak ironically of a song like "Smells Like Teen Spirit" that makes ironic its *own* status as a commodity in lines like "Here were are now, entertain us"? As self-anointed "Debunkers of the Realm," Cohen and Krugman attack the affective alliances the song inspired during the height of its popularity in the winter of 1991–92 by describing it as "the most significant breakthrough for punk rock since the Knack's 'My Sharona.'"[21] Of course, the ideal reader here is expected to know that "My Sharona" is not *really* a punk song, merely one that appropriated punkishness and briefly made it palatable to late-1970s suburbia. By the book's conclusion, the satiric impulse is so exaggerated that the authors can only articulate their disdain for the "over-intellectualized hand-wringing" of the debate with a cranky insult: "These people"—anyone who presumes that the identity of Generation X deserves discussion—"are idiots!"

Of course, some will say that *Generation Ecch!* is just a joke that shouldn't be taken too seriously—but that is precisely my point. Satire allows Cohen and Krugman to enter the Generation X marketplace claiming that their product exists outside of it, thus assuring would-be consumers that purchasing the book does not include them among the "idiots" who hunger for a sense of shared generational identity. This distance is vividly demonstrated by the product's placement, for the book is stocked in the humor section of retail chains, safely distanced from other generational titles. Settling itself alongside the likes of Letterman Top-10 list collections, Dave Barry anthologies, and *The Funniest Insult Joke Book, Generation Ecch!* can deemphasize the seriousness of its own message and assume what appears to be the neutrality of "innocent" good humor. A similar strategy can be seen in the book's marketing campaign. "Everybody says, 'I don't want to be a spokesman for my generation,'" Krugman is quoted in a *Rolling Stone* blurb. "We're happy to. We have nothing nice to say, but we have no problem with that." And lest anyone believe that "important" could not be substituted for "nice," he adds this piece of self-deprecation: "Nobody should think that much about some of the [pop-culture] things we wrote about."[22]

In a discourse in which nothing is serious, the authors can spend an entire chapter dismissing Lollapalooza, the annual concert festival that sold itself as an alternative-culture bazaar, as "*the* event for the generation that's dying to be led around by its nose ring"[23] and then, without fear of contradiction, appear at the following season's New York show to publicize their book. The satirical stance allows them to advertise their work to the very target audience they ridicule for being at Lollapalooza in the first place. Equally intriguing, Cohen and Krugman can manage a publicity coup when photographed for *Rolling Stone* with Cobain's widow Courtney Love—described as "a more [or] less spectacular, if overly lipsticked, blonde bombshell" (145)—who actually addressed the crowd from the stage as "Generation Ecch." Love even provided *Generation Ecch!* what may be the ultimate in ironic endorsements: "Kurt would have loved the mean stuff"[24]—including, presumably, the "mean stuff" that whimsically described his suicide as "an early morning breakfast of buckshot . . . the [same] breakfast Ernest Hemingway ate."[25]

By framing the debate as a pursuit fit only for "idiots," *Generation Ecch!* reveals why, as Wallace writes, irony and ridicule can at once be "entertaining and effective" and yet function as "agents of a great despair and stasis."[26] As it devalues the affectivity of generational ties, the book implies that to avoid ridicule one must suppress "expressions of value, emotion, or vulnerability," for in a world in which "other people become judges, the crime is naïveté." Fearing accusations of ingenuousness, we become "allergic to people" as "riskily human encounters seem even scarier," and, as a result, our capacity to connect meaningfully through popular culture diminishes (181). A more ameliorative attempt to employ irony can be traced in Pagan Kennedy's *Platforms*, a "history of the seventies for the pop-culture generation that came of age then," which explores why, if that decade's formative events (Kent State, Watergate,

Jonestown) were far from trivial, our generation has come to assume that "our concerns were."[27] For those who spent their juvenescence combing their "Scott Baio haircuts" while listening to Kiss albums under the gaze of a Farrah Fawcett poster, history has amounted to little more than the kitschy joke that satirists like Cohen and Krugman insist is the sole value of popular culture. Only by examining how fads and trends reflect the "rapid, bewildering upheaval in social values" of the 1970s can we begin to understand why we so defensively insist that they are unworthy of deep emotional investments and revel in their cheery banality. Thus, "we study the seventies not to escape into our fantasy version of that time but to become more aware of how the present got to be like it is. . . . We never forget that the seventies are our future" (121).

While Kennedy's persistent use of "we" implies that a generational mind set does exist, she nevertheless protects herself from accusations of "supporting the scam" by insisting on her own version of the "Great Refusal." Because the 1970s were the first decade in which nostalgia became a "full-fledged industry, a market segment, an imaginary past intended to help the bummed-out masses blot out the present," we must resist the commercially motivated "manufactured memory" that inspires *Brady Bunch* revivals and retro disco dance nights at the Ramada Inn (7). To do so, we must look back with "guerrilla nostalgia," a "more ironic, more self-aware" critical stance that resists the temptation to smirk at the detritus of *Charlie's Angels,* blaxploitation films, and CB radio. However amusing or embarrassing they might seem, such phenomena embody significant transformations in cultural perceptions of gender, race, and class that continue to affect us.

Despite the claim that it is an ironic strategy then, "guerrilla nostalgia" actually attempts to transcend the contempt and scorn that erodes *Generation Ecch!*'s satire into vituperation. The reason is that, for Kennedy, the nostalgia industry itself perpetuates that alienating sarcasm that extends to us a false individualistic sense of "canny superiority." By breaking history into discrete units of pop-culture styles, nostalgia exaggerates the discontinuity between periods, rendering even relatively contiguous moments remote, distanced, and disconnected. In the 1970s, as our past is compressed for the first time into an elementary set of ideograms, with the 1950s equaling a leather jacket and the 1960s equaling peace signs and love beads, time becomes little more than a succession "of cutesy, dopey fashion movements that . . . seemingly happened on some other planet" (7). As the gap between then and now expands, our ability to recognize and appreciate the desires motivating these styles is exhausted, and the instinct to identify across temporal boundaries evaporates. As we grew up looking backward then, we learned that "the people in those old photos weren't us," and "we sneered at their innocence" (7). To counter this enculturated cynicism and disdain, guerrilla nostalgia seeks to renarrativize our shared history, to lock it within a linear time scheme. "In looking back at the seventies—because we are products of the nostalgia-crazy seventies," she writes, "it is tempting to turn the decade into sound bytes: happy-face buttons, bell-bottoms, mood rings" (121). But existing in a world of sound bytes has the negative effect of teaching us to live life, as one of Coupland's *Generation X* characters complains, "as a succession of isolated little cool moments."[28] Only by acknowledging affective ties can we hope to build a sense of communal identity.

The approach, on the whole, is far more persuasive than *Generation Ecch!*'s insistence that the issue is not worth examining. In one intriguing passage, Kennedy explores how a "tyranny of grooviness" arose in the 1970s as shifting lifestyle norms were instantly "trivialized" and "exploited" when packaged as accouterments of hip: "Movements like women's lib and the sexual revolution became *products*. For instance, one ad for the Singer Collection of Ethnic Fabrics proclaimed 'Love Thy Neighbor' over a picture of a black model with her arm on the shoulder of a white one—achieving a racial harmony had become as easy as buying the right fabric."[29] As commodities became devices for articulating ideologies, "a stunning array of disposable, faddish products" emerged and disappeared, their sole purpose "to help the buyer feel hip." Growing up in a designer environment in which fashion expedited political billboarding, we could not help but associate personal consumption with relevance. "Is it any wonder that so many of us got caught without our mood rings on, wore the wrong kind of jeans, and generally felt like losers in the seventies?" she asks. "No wonder those of us who grew up [then] are so obsessed with pop culture. We spent our formative years chasing fads; our social status depended on whether our bell-bottoms dragged in the right way under the heels of our Olaf Daughters clogs" (22). In such moments, the difference between *Platforms* and *Generation Ecch!* is clear: whereas Cohen and Krugman would ridicule naive peers who let themselves fall for those fads, Kennedy's irony is self-directed and thus inclusive. By avoiding the derision that passes for superior insight, she makes a credible case for why we are persistently represented as glib, cynical, and ironic.

Yet if the intent of the book is to encourage Generation X to integrate its identity politics within a linear sense of history, it is an intriguing paradox that it effectively impedes this imperative by breaking its own narrative flow into a succession of "cool," alienated moments. Borrowing the format of nearly every Generation X book since Coupland's novel, *Platforms* presents itself as a collage, the body of its main narrative crowded by marginalia, including quotations, sidebars, illustrations, and even minitestimonials in which Kennedy and her peers recall how frightening it was to ride school buses in the dark during the fall of 1973 when Nixon suspended daylight savings time, or how exhilarating it felt to "crash" hard-rock concerts in the days of festival seating. The nonlinear format is an obvious attempt to evoke a multimedia experience that better accommodates thirty-and-under audiences for a whom an unbroken page of print poses a formidable and laborious reading task. As David Shields has noted, the juxtaposition of various design elements achieved by such layouts dramatizes a cultural sensibility in which "information [is] crowding out imagination," yet that thematic point can obscure the fact that the form is actually a "sophisticated appropriation and transformation of the 'infotainment' format," in which history is packaged as entertainment.[30] In an effort to attract younger readers, such books mimic the brevity of the mass-culture media, and by doing so, they function as agents that naturalize the discontinuity and disconnected feel of contemporary life. Kennedy herself describes the effect of the collage's "short spurts of language intercut with graphics" as "turn-[ing] history into sound bytes, little blips removed from the flow of time."[31] Given that her argument is that Generation X should integrate itself within this temporal flow, it is curious indeed that the form subjects its reader to the very process the book attacks.

At first glance, Elizabeth Wurtzel's *Prozac Nation* might not seem particularly relevant to debates over Generation X's identity politics. As a memoir of the author's long-running battle with depression, the book critiques several *au courant* psychological and pharmaceutical curatives. Frequently, however, Wurtzel drops the autobiographical veil to suggest that her condition bespeaks a broader generational malaise: "While depression is a problem for any age group, the sense of it as a normal state of mind, as an average part of getting through the day . . . does seem unique to people who are now in their twenties and thirties."[32] Generation X's "misery chic" and its adoption of the "Underachiever and Proud of It" ethos implies that ennui is a defense against the insecurities of contemporary social life: "Perhaps what has come to be placed in the catch-all category of depression is really a guardedness, a nervousness, a suspicion about intimacy, any of many perfectly rational reactions to a world that seems to be perilously lacking in the basic guarantees that our parents expected: a marriage that would last, employment that was secure, sex that wasn't deadly" (301–2). While the argument is hardly new, what is important here is the way that such assertions allow Wurtzel to present her life story as symbolic of her generation's, thus positioning herself to speak for her peers without claiming to do so. The jacket copy is less reserved about making the point: "Giv[ing] voice to the high incidence of depression . . . *Prozac Nation* is a collective cry for help, a generational status report on today's young people." Despite its confessional aura, the book belongs to a genre that includes Fitzgerald's *The Crack-Up*, Plath's *The Bell Jar*, and Susanna Kaysen's *Girl, Interrupted,* in which authors, by describing their breakdowns as symbolic of their respective times, deftly position their narrative *I*'s as constituent of *us*.

The strategy is initially persuasive because, unlike Cohen and Krugman, Wurtzel does not dismiss popular culture for pandering to "feelings of victimhood." Instead, she interrogates the emotional energy she invested in favorite rock songs, exploring how they exacerbated her mood as much as they consoled it, thus, ideally at least, inviting readers to reflect upon the power of such artifacts to affect us. She contemplates suicide while listening to the Velvet Underground, for example, then cuts herself to the accompaniment of Patti Smith's *Horses*. She finds herself mimicking the British nihilism of "the Clash, the Who, the Jam, the Sex Pistols," knowing full well that "talking about toppling the system in the U.K. . . . had nothing to do with being so lonesome you could die in the U.S.A." She listens to Bob Dylan's "You're a Big Girl Now" for hours hoping that "repeated listenings would deflate the song's meaning, make its disastrous lyrics more mundane," only to discover that repetition revealed "new elements of tragedy to focus on, new reasons to be empathic" (228). Appropriating music as a mirror of her anguish, Wurtzel dramatizes how the affective power of popular culture risks solipsism, for reading these songs exclusively within her own precarious emotional state distances her from her family, rendering her inconsolable: "It was always like this: I'd be lying helpless in my room," while her mother would "be lying helpless in hers, there was nothing we could do to make each other feel better" (48). In such moments, we recognize that popular culture's power to affect may dissuade affective alliances as much as encourage them.

This recognition leads Wurtzel to warn of the dangers of transforming disaffection into a cultural style. Misery chic is ultimately an alienating force, for, like satire and nostalgia, it confers to individuals a sense of superiority by assuring them that their pain is more intense, more tragic, and more worthy of attention than the pain of others. Patricia Mayer Spacks, in her cultural history of boredom, describes how "all-purpose declarations of alienation" such as Wurtzel's function: in conspicuous displays of apathy and ennui, "the privileged man or woman, separated by good fortune from the mass of humanity, transforms the sense of separation into psychic inability to find experience— the kind of experience others have—gratifying."[33] In this perspective, pleasure is conformity, but despair, discontent, angst—whatever "intense" descriptive we choose—assures us that we feel more intensely, observe things more sharply, than others—that we stand alone. ("Why should I care about happiness?" Bob Dylan once responded to an interviewer's question. "Any idiot can be happy.") While it is far too flippant to dismiss depression for encouraging this individuation, Wurtzel rightly protests the frequency with which that state of mind is celebrated as a creative force. "Madness is too glamorous a term to convey what happens to most people who are losing their minds," she writes.[34] "You associate madness with Zelda Fitzgerald in all her rich, gorgeous, cerebral disturbedness . . . it's Kurt Cobain . . . looking like a man . . . who needs help badly and wears his desperation like a badge of cool . . . it's Pete Townshend smashing his perfectly good guitar to bits and pieces; it's every great moment in rock and roll, and it's probably every great moment in popular culture" (259). Such images perpetuate the notion that depression is cathartic: "Madness draws crowds, sells tickets, keeps *The National Enquirer* in business. Yet so many depressives suffer in silence, without anyone knowing, their plight somehow invisible until they adopt the antics of madness which are impossible to ignore" (260).

At heart then, *Prozac Nation* cautions Generation X against defining itself through "antics of madness" as the author repeatedly expresses her own hopes for the communal pleasures of marriage and family. Yet, sadly, Wurtzel contradicts this message by doing the very thing she warns against—commodifying her depression. Nowhere is the temptation to turn anguish into a "badge of cool" more obvious than in the book's cover photograph, in which the author, slouching and listless, stares forth with the sort of withdrawn passivity that has become a stylistic cliché of Gen X imagery. Indeed, with a pose of glamorous fragility ("courtesy of Shirley Ip, Irina, and everyone at the Peter Coppola Salon," according to the acknowledgments), Wurtzel looks every bit like one of the "bonethin [fashion] models" whose "gloomy, miserable expressions" and "anorexic, clinically depressed" demeanor she complains makes depression trendy. Not surprisingly, several reviewers felt compelled to comment on the picture, reading it as symbolic of either vanity or self-promotion. As one reader lamented, Wurtzel seemed to allow "brazen self-revelation" to dissolve into "infotainment—harmonizing with myselves, as it were."[35] A book that could have inspired an invigorating colloquy on the dangerous relationship between therapy and publicity, one that would invite a generation to question its tendency to glamorize its sullenness, instead entered the marketplace ridiculed for its supposed self-aggrandizement and lack of empathy. Sadly, a number of major magazines, including *Esquire* and *Entertainment Weekly*, named *Prozac Nation* one of the worst books of 1994, an unfair reception that highlights the difficulty that Generation X faces as it articulates its identity in an environment that encourages the public ritual of personal confession, only to condemn it as narcissism.

Of all the generational books published in the 1990s, David Lipsky and Alexander Abrams's *Late Bloomers* speaks most emphatically for Generation X as it argues that adverse economic conditions prevent us from achieving adulthood. Too financially insecure to afford marriage, at times reduced to living with our parents, enrolling in the extended summer camp of graduate school to wait out massive downsizings in industry and business, we find ourselves trapped in a state of suspended adolescence, quickly becoming "old at being young." The lament is nothing new in Generation X discourse, but what makes *Late Bloomers* intriguing is the assurance with which Lipsky and Abrams invoke the communal "we": "We watch the idyllic commercials on television" in which couples "are free from grinding care, from personal accountancy. They have their own homes. They entertain there. They are stable and social. . . . This is what America wants us to want, and we do. That freedom from money worry; that ease. That life, the ease that comes from finding a space in it in which to live."[36] By insisting that "we" only want the upward mobility that was supposed to be both our inheritance and our legacy, Lipsky and Abrams can reject the stereotype of an entertainment-addled generation obsessed with "sensation and not [with] achievement": "We are not 'unprecedented' . . . We are not a strange new group with disturbing new attitudes." Initially, such assertions echo Cohen and Krugman's glib reminder that disaffected youth ever since Hamlet have suffered the slings and arrows of their elders' outrageous criticism. But whereas *Generation Ecch!* claims that there is no collective identity, *Late Bloomers* insists that historical happenstance has forged an undesired one for us: "Does anyone really think that if we had money . . . we would be any different from what young American adults have always been?" (46).

To prove that what we really want as a generation is to overcome the collective cash shortage that stunts our maturation, Lipsky and Abrams examine how we acquired the reputation for being veteran teenagers living a "happy life on the margins." The most astute observation in the book is the recognition that, during its short life span, Generation X has been subjected to two vastly different stereotypes: "In the 1980s, American journalists had projected their fears about what success would mean for the country onto young people. Were we becoming a nation of the soulless, driven only by economic and material passions?" (35–36). The tone of "fond vexation" of this Reagan-era commentary arose from the disappointment that baby-boomer journalists felt upon learning that the succeeding generation cared more for material than spiritual affluence. In the aftermath of the 1990 recession, however, many of these same journalists "began to project their fears about what failure might mean for the country onto young people," and the result was the now-clichéd slacker image that "suited the new economy very well. It was easiest to believe that if young adults weren't working, it was because they *no longer wanted to work*" (35–36). As Lipsky and Abrams demonstrate, much of the evidence for this supposed shift in generational attitudes was anecdotal and perpetuated itself as it was "reported, repeated, and finally returned to the country as truth" (20) when adopted into advertising and television campaigns. Their argument is more than a critique of the reportorial practices of lifestyle articles and essays, for the authors suggest a darker motive: what if this commentary was "performing an unconscious kindness" by "creat[ing] a new character for our generation," one that would "be less disappointed by the country we would inherit as we stepped into adulthood" (48)? With its vague hint of a media conspiracy theory, the suggestion is thoroughly Marcusian in tone, though certainly not in content. That is, if Marcuse accuses the media of defining the "Happy Consciousness" as the material gratification of one's desires, Lipsky and Abrams complain that it now persuades us that we care little for possessions. Their "Great Refusal" thus does not refute the ideology of individual gratification but actively seeks to reinstitute it in the horizon of our opportunities.

To explore how the media's slacker image masks the dispiriting economic realities that have reduced us to being "disappointed pragmatists . . . people who had decided they would give everything to getting ahead, [only to find] that goal very difficult to achieve," Lipsky and Abrams analyze Generation X attitudes toward the job market, the family, marriage, and sex (151). If their repeated discovery that our insecurities arise from a lack of disposable income grows predictable, their argument is nevertheless curious for its unmitigated faith in the value of rugged economic individualism. Amazingly, whereas other commentators attribute the Gen X mindset to the social upheavals of the sixties and seventies, Lipsky and Abrams claim that our exposure to divorce, absentee parents, and the sexual revolution whetted our appetite for adulthood as we assumed familial and domestic responsibilities early on: "As kids we were programmed to mature extremely quickly. And then we'd found—just at the age when we could have put those lessons into practice—that we couldn't get any older" (151). We were on the right track, the book claims, until the economy bottomed out. For Wurtzel, the disappearance of childhood contributed to the psychological instability of our generation; but for Lipsky and Abrams, while not an entirely positive effect, growing up quickly at least inculcated the values of autonomy and independence, two virtues that Generation X has no place to practice: "The pain for us, for children raised in the seventies and eighties, is that society's needs changed midstream. . . . We have to be wait to be adults until society has more places for adults—the society now has more adults than places" (105).

It may seem unfair to criticize Lipsky and Abrams for arguing what seem to be fairly obvious insights: Generation X's standard of living *does* compare unfavorably to previous generations; we *have* seen more divorce and family dissolution than our parents and grandparents. And yet *Late Bloomers* also dramatizes the paradox that our economic disenfranchisement has become a cottage industry, an entrepreneurial enterprise in which the role of generational spokesperson provides a gateway to high-profile media exposure, lucrative book deals, and even, in Lipsky and Abrams's case, a two-million dollar deal with Sony Entertainment to develop a documentary on—yes—Generation X's financial anxieties. What does it mean that a career can be made by assuring your generation that it is locked in a fiscal spiral? Something of an answer is suggested by a *New York* profile of Lipsky and Abrams, which questions whether these "Gen X hucksters" are "out to save an America in decline—or just to get on some cool talk shows." Like reviews of *Prozac Nation,* the unflattering article portrays the team as little more than Barnumesque publicity hounds. Although obviously slanted in its cynical view of the business of generating Xs, the *New York* article nonetheless raises the question of whether *Late Bloomers* might perpetuate those media images that the book sets out to demolish. We may be "the first demographic group in history to stage a rebellion against its own press clips,"[37] but because we also generate those press clippings, one is forced to wonder whether Lipsky and Abrams might also be doing their peers an "unconscious act of kindness" by acclimating us to a world of diminished expectations. That concern is highlighted by the closing quotation of the piece, in which Abrams dismisses Woodstock 1994: "This was supposedly the Generation X Woodstock . . . but it was really a babyboomer scam to sell products to young people. . . . On the positive side, I did get to write an op-ed column for the New York *Post* and appear on a local and national radio call-in show. Obviously, that's good publicity" (107). Few quotations acknowledge the unsettling opportunism that drives the Generation X industry, suggesting that what passes for punditry might instead mark what ideas are most compatible with the marketplace.

Postscript: From Ten Years On

Except for the addition of a few topical references, the above essay was written in 1994–95, a period in which, I now realize, my interest in the question of generational identity was inspired at least partly by my turning thirty. Recently, I reread a 1994 *Publisher's Weekly* interview with David Dutton, Cohen and Krugman's editor at Simon and Schuster, for the first time since composing the piece. I found myself struck by Dutton's stated doubt that the then-spate of generational titles emerging from major publishing houses would prove to have lasting significance: "I can't imagine anybody referring back to these [works] in 10 years, or that this trend will extend beyond another three or four seasons"[38] (quoted in Maughan and Bing 52). The prediction, of course, has proved accurate. In the half-decade since Generation X discourse raged most intensely, media interest (as opposed to academic interest) has all but died, confirming for many detractors what they had suspected all along that the debate was a fad. As a result, the post-Kennedy, pre-Reagan demographic has by and large reassumed the cloak of cultural inscrutability it wore before the early 1990s. Recently, cultural commentators have officially marked the demise of their interest by turning their diagnostic attentions to their heirs of X, whom in a fit of alphabetical determinism they dub "Generation Y." Unlike baby boomers, who well into their middle age remain the subject of countless analyses, Xers have failed to inspire studies of their postadolescent adulthood. More than a decade after first entering the cultural vernacular, terms such as *twentysomething* and *slacker* remain the only obvious touchstones for articulating our collective experience.

As such, I find it lamentable that the books I discuss here have been so quickly forgotten (only *Prozac Nation* remains in print). Over the intervening years I have distributed excerpts to students for discussion, and I continue to cite them in my own scholarly work on youth culture. I remain intrigued by them because they evince the struggle that Generation X waged and should still be waging to establish a proprietary sense of self outside the realm of incessant media images and cultural talk. Because they reveal the inevitable reinflection of various forms of the "Great Refusal" within a commodification process that encourages individualism over solidarity, these texts dramatize the necessity of *not* abandoning the concept of generational belonging to the marketeers. To do so, I contend now as I originally did, is to exile ourselves from a site of cultural identity every bit as historically powerful and significant as class, gender, and sexuality. The early 1990s were a time in which generational identity was a hot commodity precisely because resistance to it discouraged communal affective investments in popular culture. Now, slouching toward forty, many of us believe that our generation could have benefited better by not wholesale rejecting the question of "who we are." Instead of negating the debate, we should have approached it mindful of a simple consumer philosophy: *caveat emptor.*

Notes

1. Karen Schoemer, "Talking 'Bout Our Generation," *Newsweek,* 26 December 1994, 32.

2. Michael Schumacher, *Reasons to Believe: New Voices in American Fiction* (New York: St. Martin's Press, 1988), 178.

3. Quoted in Douglas Rushkoff, ed., *The Gen X Reader* (New York: Ballantine, 1994), 12.

4. See Douglas Coupland, "Eulogy: Generation X'd," *Details,* June 1995, 72.

5. Quoted in Eric Liu, ed., *Next: Young American Writers on the New Generation* (New York: Norton, 1994), 233.

6. Quoted in Rushkoff, ed., *The Gen X Reader,* 288.

7. Herbert Marcuse, *One Dimensional Man* (Boston: Beacon, 1964).

8. Alexander Star, "The Twentysomething Myth," *New Republic* 4–11 January 1993, 23, 25.

9. Richard Blow, "Twentynothing," *Washington Post,* 13 December 1992, A15.

10. Coupland, "Eulogy," 72.

11. Marcuse, *One Dimensional Man,* 65.

12. Lawrence Grossberg, *We Gotta Get Out of This Place: Popular Conservatism and Postmodern Culture* (New York: Routledge, 1992), 84.

13. Mark Crispin Miller, "Deride and Conquer," *Watching Television,* ed. Todd Gitlin (New York: Pantheon, 1986), 228.

14. Shannon Maughan and Jonathan Bing, "Tuning into Twentysomething," *Publisher's Weekly,* 29 August 1994, 49.

15. Jason Cohen and Michael Krugman, *Generation Ecch! The Backlash Starts Here* (New York: Simon and Schuster, 1994); Pagan Kennedy, *Platforms: A Microwaved Cultural Chronicle of the 1970s* (New York: St. Martin's, 1994); Elizabeth Wurtzel, *Prozac Nation: Young and Depressed in America* (New York: Houghton Mifflin, 1994); David Lipsky and Alexander Abrams, *Late Bloomers: Coming of Age in Today's America, the Right Place at the Wrong Time* (New York: Times Books, 1994).

16. John Downtown Hazlett, *My Generation: Collective Autobiography and Identity Politics* (Madison: University of Wisconsin Press, 1996), 9, 46.

17. Cohen and Krugman, *Generation Ecch!,* 10.

18. Miller, "Deride and Conquer," 225.

19. Cohen and Krugman, *Generation Ecch!,* 151.

20. David Foster Wallace, "E Unibus Pluram: Television and U.S. Fiction," *Review of Contemporary Fiction* (Fall 1993): 177.

21. Cohen and Krugman, *Generation Ecch!,* 142.

22. Quoted in Michael Runiber, "Days of Whine and Poses," *Rolling Stone,* 8 September, 1994, 21.

23. Cohen and Krugman, *Generation Ecch!,* 155.

24. Jancee Dunn, "Random Notes," *Rolling Stone,* 3 November 1994, 17.

182   KIRK CURNUTT

25. Cohen and Krugman, *Generation Ecch!*, 148.
26. Wallace, "E Unibus Pluram," 181.
27. Kennedy, *Platforms*, 121.
28. Douglas Coupland, *Generation X: Tales for an Accelerated Culture* (New York: St. Martin's, 1991), 8.
29. Kennedy, *Platforms*, 22.
30. David Shields, "Literary Pointillism," *ANQ* 5 (October 1992): 240.
31. Kennedy, *Platforms*, 7.
32. Wurtzel, *Prozac Nation*, 301–2.
33. Patricia Myers Spacks, *Boredom: The Literary History of a State of Mind* (Chicago: University of Chicago Press, 1995), 252.
34. Wurtzel, *Prozac Nation*, 259.
35. Julia Phillips, "Young, Depressed, and Self-Obsessed in America: Elizabeth Wurtzel's Premature Proazculations," *Vanity Fair*, September 1994, 118.
36. Lipsky and Abrams, *Late Bloomers*, 11.
37. Martin Kihn, "The Gen X Hucksters," *New York*, 29 August 1994, 98.
38. Maughn and Bing, "Tuning into Twentysomething," 52.

Bibliography

Blow, Richard. "Twentynothing." *Washington Post*, 13 December 1992, sec. A, p. 15.
Cohen, Jason, and Michael Krugman. *Generation Ecch!: The Backlash Starts Here.* New York: Simon and Schuster, 1994.
Coupland, Douglas. "Eulogy: Generation X'd." *Details*, June 1995, 72.
———. *Generation X: Tales for an Accelerated Culture.* New York: St. Martin's, 1991.
Dunn, Jancee. "Random Notes." *Rolling Stone*, 3 November 1994, 17.
Goldman, Debra. "The X Factor." In *The Gen X Reader*, edited by Douglas Rushkoff. New York: Ballantine, 1994. 279–86.
Grossberg, Lawrence. *We Gotta Get Out of This Place: Popular Conservatism and Postmodern Culture.* New York: Routledge, 1992.
Hazlett, John Downtown. *My Generation: Collective Autobiography and Identity Politics.* Madison: University of Wisconsin Press, 1996.
Kennedy, Pagan. *Platforms: A Microwaved Cultural Chronicle of the 1970s.* New York: St. Martin's, 1994.
Kihn, Martin. "The Gen X Hucksters." *New York*, 29 August 1994, 94–107.
Lipsky, David and Alexander Abrams. *Late Bloomers: Coming of Age in Today's America, the Right Place at the Wrong Time.* New York: Times Books, 1994.
Liu, Eric, ed. *Next: Young American Writers on the New Generation.* New York: Norton, 1994.
Marcuse, Herbert. *One Dimensional Man.* Boston: Beacon, 1964.
Maughan, Shannon and Jonathan Bing. "Tuning into Twentysomething." *Publisher's Weekly*, 29 August 1994, 48–52.
Miller, Mark Crispin. "Deride and Conquer." In *Watching Television*, edited by Todd Gitlin, 183–228. New York: Pantheon, 1986.
Phillips, Julia. "Young, Depressed, and Self-Obsessed in America: Elizabeth Wurtzel's Premature Prozaculations." *Vanity Fair*, September 1994, 118–20.
Rubiner, Michael. "Days of Whine and Poses." *Rolling Stone*, 8 September 1994, 21.
Rushkoff, Douglas, ed. *The Gen X Reader.* New York: Ballantine, 1994.

Schoemer, Karen. "Talking 'Bout Our Generation." *Newsweek*, 26 December 1994, 32.

Schumacher, Michael. *Reasons to Believe: New Voices in American Fiction*. New York: St. Martin's Press, 1988.

Shields, David. "Literary Pointillism." *ANQ* 5 (October 1992): 239–40.

Spacks, Patricia Meyer. *Boredom: The Literary History of a State of Mind*. Chicago: University of Chicago Press, 1995.

Star, Alexander. "The Twentysomething Myth." *New Republic*, 4–11 January 1993, 22–25.

Wallace, David Foster. "E Unibus Pluram: Television and U.S. Fiction." *Review of Contemporary Fiction*, Fall 1993, 151–94.

Wurtzel, Elizabeth. *Prozac Nation: Young and Depressed in America*. New York: Houghton Mifflin, 1994.

Generation X and the End of History

G. P. Lainsbury

Generation X, by Canadian writer Douglas Coupland, is a novel that has achieved widespread popular recognition. According to the perverse logic of the literary establishment, its popularity calls into question its validity as a literary text. And yet this is a novel worth looking at seriously, if only for the influence it has had on contemporary culture. *Generation X* achieves its effects by taking aim at concerns close to the heart of middle-class, North American life, an intention dismissed by contemporary critics obsessed with the appeal of the marginal and the oppressed—anything but the kind of relatively comfortable, suburban, middle-class existence that most book-reading North Americans live, no matter how much they might protest against it in the subversive space of their private lives. As Andrew Palmer, the novel's central character, explains, "You see, when you're middle class, you have to live with the fact that history will ignore you. You have to live with the fact that history can never champion your causes and that history will never feel sorry for you. It is the price that is paid for day-to-day comfort and silence. And because of this price, all happinesses are sterile; all sadnesses go unpitied."[1]

What connects most of the literary writing being done in Canada at this time is its inwardness, its emphasis on the liberation of individuals within the private sphere allowed them within late capitalist reality. As Brian Fawcett points out in an essay entitled "Something Is Wrong with Alice Munro," the kind of low-modernist approach that has become the unofficial CanLit orthodoxy takes too small a bite into "the enormously enlarged complexity of the human condition" as it manifests itself in the late twentieth century.[2] Fawcett's argument centers on the assertion that this kind of fiction is an ineffective medium for the promotion of social change, "that private liberation doesn't create a liberated world" (71). Fawcett proposes that literature can reclaim the kind of effectiveness it had in the pretelevision era by adopting some of the assemblage techniques used in other art forms—combining "historiography, reportage, philosophical analysis and a massive influx of data . . . along with a dose of murderous scepticism concerning the word 'fiction'" (73)—and by determining the contexts in which "printed literature remains more effective and efficient than any other medium" (73), describing "the full vertical density of human reality" (74). Fawcett is talking about a literature that is willing to confront that area where public and private interests meet, a literature in which writers acknowledge that there is more to being human in the late twentieth century than the gratification of obscure, elitist aesthetic impulses.

Fawcett outlines in his essay some possibilities for a Canadian literature that recognizes the postmodern as a moment in "the perpetual 'revolution' and innovation of high modernism . . . a cyclical moment that returns before the emergence of ever *new* modernisms,"[3] and which pursues with vigor the problem of the cosmopolitan self of the enlightenment metanarrative of emancipation, the subject of Eurocentric history. Coupland was intuitively responding to such a challenge when he set out to write *Generation X*.[4]

There can be little doubt that *Generation X* is intended to test a reader's preconceptions as to what a novel should be. On the most obvious level this is apparent in its embrace of technological innovation and its appropriation of techniques from other media. The infoblip sidebars are indicative of a joy taken in the sheer profusion of terminology— they are a mutant crossbreed of the continental aphoristic tradition and the pragmatic considerations of magazine journalism in an era of declining print literacy. The reader is aware at all times of being inside a constructed thing rather than inhabiting the capitalistic dreamspace of contemporary realism, where the experience of fictional others is offered up as yet another mode of consumption. Coupland's training in the visual arts influences his construction of the book. Even its size and shape serves to defamiliarize the reader. It just does not look like a novel. Then there is a bizarre juxtaposition of the bland homogeneity of the well-groomed, white, middle-class cartoon characters and the flip iconoclasm of their utterances, not to mention a hip reference to the American pop

art tradition of Lichtenstein et al. Finally, there are the omnipresent
paragraph symbols and the cloud-motif "openings" at the start of each
chapter—a stylistic tic that calls attention, through their absence, to the
conventions of the literary presentation of material.

Generation X addresses both public and private concerns of the cosmopolitan self trying to make its way through the confusion of a late
capitalist world. That the novel will address the economically emanci-
pated private self of bourgeois individualism is made clear in the opening scene, where the young Andrew Palmer travels into the heart of the
North American prairie to witness a total eclipse of the sun. He comes
not as a young scientist, but as a precocious philosopher concerned with
authenticity. There, at the moment of singularity, he experiences the
mood that will thereafter define his existence, "a mood of darkness and
inevitability and fascination—a mood that surely must have been held
by most young people since the dawn of time as they crooked their
necks, stared at the heavens, and watched their sky go out."[5] Of course,
what separates the experience of the generation of young people to
which Andrew Palmer belongs from that of all preceding generations
is the ontological status of the sun. The sun is still the life-source, but
it no longer occupies the unambiguous central and positive position it
has had in virtually all human symbologies; now it is also a potentially
lethal entity. The first chapter of *Generation X* is thus called "The Sun
is Your Enemy" (3).

The parts of the novel that concern the private experience of the
individual deal with phenomena such as transcendent moments, what
one character calls "takeaway," the one moment that "defines what it's
like to be alive on this planet" (91), and magical gestures such as the
Christmas morning candlefest scene (146–47), where all the witnesses
to Andy's pyrotechnics experience distortions in time and space, and
partake in something bordering on the mystical. The novel ends on another such note, when Andy is touched by the forces of randomness,
singled out by a "cocaine white egret" in a crowd of tourists who have
stopped to witness the "supergravitational blackness" (177) of a stubble
field. The egret grazes his head with its claws, cutting his scalp. This
gesture signals with infallible theologic to the dozen or so mentally re-
tarded teenagers who witness it that he is a holy man, one to be paid
obeisance to, and they bury him in a "crush of love" in an attempt to
express their sense of wonder. These parts of the novel are the most

lyrical, but can only achieve their full resonance within the context of the novel's public aspects.

Coupland has stated in various interviews that his novel was originally intended to be a nonfiction handbook of Gen X behaviors and attitudes. This original intention accounts for the inclusion of the statistical appendix (181–83) and the essayistic nature of the many acute observations about those who come before and after the *shin jin rui*:[6] the naïveté of the parents who "take shopping at face value" (68); the baby boomers, whose stranglehold on the social, economic, and psychic agenda of North American life provides the hegemony against which Gen X struggles in vain; and those perky, postliterate global teens who "embrace and believe the pseudoglobalism and ersatz racial harmony of ad campaigns engineered by the makers of soft drinks and computer-inventoried sweaters" (106). Coupland documents the lifestyle options open to postboomers, from basement suite subculture to conspicuous minimalism. In a world that "has gotten too big—way beyond our capacity to tell stories about it" (5), Coupland creates a number of interlocking narratives in an attempt to confront the largeness and complexity of the postmodern world, rather than creating either a high-modernist, self-referential monument, or a work based on a "realistic epistemology . . . which conceives of representation as the reproduction, for subjectivity, of an objectivity which lies outside it."[7]

Generation X is a meditation on the end of history. The year 1974 is assigned occult significance as "the year after the oil shock and the year starting from which real wages in the U.S. never grew ever again."[8] These are the events that mark the great divide between the historical and posthistorical eras—the profound, structural changes in the world economy that mark the emergence of late capitalism as a distinct stage in the evolution of how human beings organize their existence on the planet.[9] The optimistic spin on the prevailing reductive orthodoxy is that the world has been saved from history by the free market.

Coupland's decision to write a novel rather than a work of nonfiction is an interesting one. According to Jameson, Lyotard argues in *The Postmodern Condition* that the "revival of an essentially narrative view of 'truth,' and the vitality of small narrative units at work everywhere *locally* in the present social system, are accompanied by something like a more global or totalizing 'crisis' in the narrative function in general."[10] This crisis of legitimation in the various postmodern perspectives is the result of the lack of validity assigned to the teleological metanarratives of emancipation, those world-historical narratives that justify the sufferings and injustices of the present in terms of a better future.

This is the end of history that Francis Fukuyama talks about in his influential essay in "The National Interest," the end of an era of global ideological conflict that calls upon individuals to display romantic virtues such as "daring, courage, imagination and idealism" in the pursuit of competing visions of utopia.[11] Fukuyama proposes that the grand march of history "will be replaced by economic calculation, the endless solving of technical problems, environmental concerns, and the satisfaction of sophisticated consumer demands."[12] According to Fukuyama, western liberal ideology has won the world-historical game of dialectic, but at a cost. With the end of history, which is mediated by the metanarratives of European metaphysics, comes the feeling that it is no longer possible to commit meaningfully to something larger than the self or the economic extensions of the self. As Lyotard explains, capital "does not need legitimation."[13] Political and geographical distinctions are meaningless in the posthistorical global village; everywhere is the same because the same stores are found in malls anywhere.[14] Members of Gen X are addicted to "newspapers, magazines and TV news broadcasts," and yet "nothing [of any real consequence ever] seems to happen" (7). Crisis is everywhere, omnipresent and perpetual, but it all seems to fail to add up to anything more significant than the psychic state of panic itself. There is no middle ground between historical under- and overdosing. Spectacularism itself, "a fascination with extreme situations" (50), is the birthright to those suckled under the sign of the Cuban Missile Crisis.

The most extreme of all possible situations is nuclear conflagration itself, and it has always been taken as a given by members of Gen X that this is how their world will end. Thus it should come as no surprise that a good part of Gen X imagination is devoted to the idea of apocalypse.[15] Coupland shows how the imagination deals with the unimaginable when he coins concepts such as "Survivalousness: The tendency to visualize oneself enjoying being the last remaining person on the earth," or a "Mental Ground Zero: The location where one visualizes oneself during the dropping of the atomic bomb; frequently, a shopping mall."[16] The end of the cold war is an anticlimactic end of history for the characters in *Generation X*, because they had always taken for granted that the end of history and the end of the human species would be synchronous events. Now they have to try to reconcile themselves to living in an era where they will die alone and where their deaths will signify nothing.[17]

Vietnam, an ironic last-gasp attempt to reengage state action and the historical metanarrative of emancipation, was a staple in the television diet that helped to form the consciousness of Gen X. It was part of the "background odor" of a Gen X childhood. As Andrew Palmer says, "They *were* ugly times. But they were also the only times I'll ever get—genuine capital *H* history times, before *history* was turned into a press release, a marketing strategy, and a cynical campaign tool."[18] It ironic that the only history Gen X ever knew firsthand was also centered on the only war that America ever lost outright (the war of 1812 usually being considered a draw). There is a pervasive sense among members of Gen X that Henry Luce's "American Century" is already over, that the most ambitious political and social experiment in the history of the world peaked with the official optimism of the late fifties. Members of Gen X gird themselves for this new reality with philosophies like "Lessness: A philosophy whereby one reconciles oneself with diminishing expectations of material wealth" (54). The economic forecasts for Gen X reflect the bleak but demographically predictable outcome of their numbers: they are to be the first generation of young North Americans who will not surpass their parents' standard of living. Raised at a level of material comfort heretofore unknown to human beings on a mass scale, members of Gen X mask their sense of betrayal and hopelessness with cynicism.[19] Everything is a joke when the master narratives of European history no longer serve to legitimate the way things are. Party politics are "corny—no longer relevant or meaningful or useful to modern societal issues, and in many cases dangerous" (80). Distrust of politicians is nothing new, but widespread distrust of the whole democratic process, of the system itself, is.

The cynicism of Gen X might be usefully compared to what Arthur Kroker calls "a carnivalesque mood of bitter hysteria at already living on borrowed time after the catastrophe, with nothing to lose because one is cheated of life anyway."[20] The future only exists as commodity, onto which people project a putative sense of ownership. In the novel Andrew Palmer knows he has found a kindred spirit when Claire starts talking about "what it's like when everyone starts carving up the future into nasty little bits . . . talking seriously about hoarding cases of

Beef-a-Roni in the garage and gets all misty-eyed about the Last Days."[21]
The Last Days are now, and strange compensations are required to reconcile this knowledge with the blunt fact of natural process. Ergo
"Strangelove Reproduction: Having children to make up for the fact
that one no longer believes in the future" (135). The end of history and
the accompanying lack of belief in the future is the liquidation of the
project of modernity, which engraves in European consciousness an "ir-
reparable suspicion . . . that history does not necessarily have a universal
finality," a transcendental historical idea as its terminus.[22]

Throughout the novel, the characters engage in a kind of therapeu-
tic, oral storytelling regime. Most of the stories concern alienated individuals who feel a profound need for integration into either a social or
spiritual order; in other words, each of them feels a need for their existence to be legitimated by reference to a narrative that would make
sense of it. While discussing the relationship between legitimation and
narrative, Lyotard proposes an interesting paradox, that narrative is
about forgetting the past rather than remembering it: "a collectivity that
takes narrative as its key form of competence has no need to remember
its past. It finds the raw material for its social bond not only in the
meaning of the narratives it recounts, but also in the act of reciting them.
The narrative's reference may seem to belong to the past, but in reality
it is always contemporaneous with the act of recitation" (22). Jameson
characterizes this forgetting as "a way of *consuming* the past,"[23] and this
formulation helps us to understand the chapter of *Generation X* entitled
"Eat Your Parents." Dag advises Andy to forget the past, to "eat" his
parents: "Accept them as a part of getting you to here, and get on with
life."[24] Andy is advised to consume the narrative of his individuation,
which has as its origin the territorialization of the family, to make a
conscious effort to forget his microhistory in order that he might enable
himself to act in the present more effectively.

The focal point of Gen X consciousness, its producer and product,
its medium and message, is television. By default, television becomes
for Gen X a replacement for the discredited master narratives of western
civilization. While religious and political ideologies that attempt totalizing interpretations of human existence fall by the wayside, the fragmentary, anecdotal method of television is in ascendancy. Television becomes the medium in which members of Gen X see their situation
reflected most clearly, complete with regular breaks for consumerist

fantasy or attendance to the needs of the body. As master narrative, television becomes the reference tool for all moral questions. Thus the phenomenon of "Tele-Parablizing: Morals used in everyday life that derive from TV sitcom plots" (120). Knowledge of the names of characters from certain 1970s situation comedies is the password for inclusion in Gen X culture. As children, members of Gen X might watch *The Brady Bunch* after school, and then watch the fall of Saigon on the news with their parents over dinner. Each seemed equally real or unreal, each had the same truth-content.

This inability to draw distinctions between the real and unreal, the lack of a sense of the hierarchical, is one result of the effect of electronic culture on the psychic development of Gen X. It is the Kierkegaardian "leveling process" taken to new, unheard of extremes. People live in places like Palm Springs, where there is no weather—"just like TV" (10). Absurdist tourists go "Historical Slumming . . . visiting locations such as diners, smokestack industrial sites, rural villages—locations where time appears to have been frozen many years back—so as to experience relief when one returns to 'the present' " (11). History is now only a sanitized theme park[25] that members of Gen X enjoy vicariously, comfortable in the knowledge that they can just step back outside into the familiar flatlands of their existence at any time.

The ironic pilgrimage is all about the flattening of cultural distinctions. In the novel a character visits "the grave of Jim Morrison at the Père Lachaise cemetery in Paris."[26] It is "super easy to find [because] people [have] spray painted 'This way to Jimmy's' all over the tombstones of all these dead French poets" (88). The nihilistic delight that the speaker takes here in the ascendancy of the values of popular culture (free of historical context) over those of traditional, high culture (loaded down with history) is the triumph of form over content, of the consumerist self over the self as defined by the historical entity of the state.[27]

Coupland addresses the futility of the search for meaning in the posthistorical era with the concept of "Terminal Wanderlust: A condition common to people of transient, middle-class upbringings. Unable to feel rooted in any one environment, they move continually in the hopes of finding an idealized sense of community in the next location."[28] But these hopes will never be fulfilled for members of Gen X because there is no transcendence of place, only stops on the remote control of location. The mall is the television version of place—it represents the victory of commerce over utopian ideology. Everywhere is now a mall. According to Arthur Kroker, "Shopping malls are liquid TVs for the end of the twentieth century. A whole microcircuitry of desire, ideology and expenditure for processed bodies drifting through the cyberspace of ultracapitalism."[29] The mall is "the real postmodern site of happy consciousness. Not happy consciousness in the old Hegelian sense of a reconciled dialectic of reason, but happy consciousness, now, in the sense of the virtual self—a whole seductive movement, therefore, between a willed abandonment of life and a restless search for satisfaction in the seduction of holograms."[30] According to this line of thought, the mall is the natural habitat of posthistorical human beings, virtual beings looking for evidence (traces) of their virtual selves reflected in the objects of their desires.

Throughout this essay, I have been arguing that the novel *Generation X* is a challenging fictional text that, through the conflation of happy circumstance (timing, market penetration, and so forth) has become a pop-culture phenomenon. The novel is more than a codification of Gen X lifestyle choices—although many readers have interpreted the book as "prescriptions for healthy living in the post-historical era," this is obviously an insufficiently critical reading. I do not mean to suggest that Coupland consciously set out to construct a critique of posthistorical society, either. Intentionality is not the point here and now. As a good *bricoleur*, Coupland has assembled from the fragmentary experience offered Gen X human beings a fictional construct that works. One must not forget that this is a work created in the spirit of play—irony is the dominant mode. Surely the hotel on the Baja peninsula where the characters are heading to at novel's end is another ironic comment on lost utopianism (116); that guests who write a funny joke on the bathroom wall will be allowed to stay for free deflates the kind of hippie wisdom that was the currency of other, earlier utopian communities.[31] In the final scene Andrew Palmer comes over the crest of a hill to find the huge black mushroom cloud rising out of the supernatural lushness of California's Imperial Valley. Careful readers will recognize this scene as an ironic reworking of a scene from John Steinbeck's novel *The Grapes of Wrath*. There, the Joads, coming over a crest very much like the one that Andrew Palmer crosses, stop their truck to stand, "silent and awestruck, embarrassed before the great valley."[32] The richness that the valley suggests is the promise of America, the embodiment of the enlightenment dream of a history in which all will be free and all will prosper. But Coupland's Imperial Valley, although still rich, has now been transformed by agribusiness into a food factory; its abundance chemically stimulated by various technologies, it no longer holds out any promise for the collectivity, but instead serves the needs of corporations and their shareholders. Living in a postindustrial, posthistorical, late capitalist world erodes belief in the state as entity and organizing principle.

Finally, we can see just how well Coupland's novel fulfills the requirements for a practical, forward-looking literature that Brian Fawcett proposes. Although *Generation X* does take into account the private experience of its characters, this is seen to be subsumed by the larger, public issues that the novel evokes through its use of assemblage techniques and wide-ranging cultural allusions. *Generation X* challenges its readers to avoid the dangers of reduction, of trying to bring the many things that the novel does into agreement with a preexisting worldview. It is necessary to try to practice what Lyotard calls a "resistance to simplism and simplifying slogans, to calls for clearness and straightforwardness, and to desires for a return to solid values."[33] A return to simpler times is clearly impossible; instead people must learn to live in the complexity of a world that they have participated in creating. Complex works of art such as *Generation X* can help them to do this. The complexification entailed in avant-garde artistic praxis "bears on the sensibilities . . . not on expertise or knowledge."[34] The thoughtful confrontation of reader with avant-garde text helps to shape a sensibility that appreciates complexity, rather than seeking escape in modernist fantasies of individual fulfillment and closure.

Notes

1. Douglas Coupland, *Generation X* (New York: St. Martin's, 1991), 147.

2. In *Unusual Circumstances, Interesting Times and Other Impolite Interventions* (Vancouver: New Star Books, 1991), 69.

3. Fredric Jameson, foreword to *The Postmodern Condition: A Report on Knowledge,* by Jean-François Lyotard, trans. Geoffrey Bennington and Brain Massumi (Minneapolis: University of Minnesota Press, 1984), xvi. See also Lyotard: "Postmodernism . . . is not modernism at its end but in the nascent state, and this state is constant" (*The Postmodern Condition,* 79).

4. This is not to suggest that Coupland actually used Fawcett's essay, or even that he was aware of it. However, in a reader's report on an earlier version of this essay,

Brian Fawcett pointed out that he thought Coupland was influenced by the opening statement in *Cambodia: A Book for People Who Find Television too Slow*, where Fawcett talks about making subtexts visible in order to communicate ideas to a general public, a goal that "contemporary artistic theory and practice discourages" in favor of private communication between members "of a new kind of privileged class" (Toronto: Talonbooks, 1986, 4).

5. Coupland, *Generation X*, 4.

6. "New human beings," the Japanese name for Generation X (56).

7. Jameson, foreword to *The Postmodern Condition*, viii.

8. Coupland, *Generation X*, 40.

9. Lyotard begins *The Postmodern Condition* by stating that "the status of knowledge is altered as societies enter what is known as the postindustrial age and cultures enter what is known as the postmodern age. This transition has been under way since at least the end of the 1950s, which for Europe marks the completion of reconstruction" (3). Lyotard locates this rupture or moment of transition slightly before the first members of Gen X are born; whereas Coupland, whose methodologies are more intuitive and artistic than scientific and analytical, locates it during the childhood of the generation.

10. Jameson, foreword to *The Postmodern Condition*, xi.

11. Francis Fukuyama, "The End of History?" *National Interest* 8, 16 (Summer 1989): 18.

12. Lyotard states that capitalism "calls for the complete hegemony of the economic genre of discourse" (Jean-François Lyotard, *The Postmodern Explained*, ed. Julian Pefanis and Morgan Thomas [Minneapolis: University of Minnesota Press], 58).

13. Ibid., 59.

14. Coupland, *Generation X*, 4.

15. Coupland's fascination with nuclear apocalypse is again addressed in the second part ("The Dead Speak") of the story "The Wrong Sun" (*Life after God* [Toronto: Pocket Books, 1994], 113–27).

16. Coupland, *Generation X*, 62, 63.

17. *Life after God* takes this pervasive sense of meaninglessness as its starting point. The narrator in "Thinking of the Sun," the first part of "The Wrong Sun," says: "When you are young, you always expect that the world is going to end. And then you get older and the world still chugs along and you are forced to re-evaluate your stance on the apocalypse as well as your own relationship to time and death. You realize that the world will indeed continue, with or without you, and the pictures you see in your head. So you try to understand the pictures instead" (Coupland, *Life after God*, 108).

18. Coupland, *Generation X*, 151.

19. Lyotard calls the postmodern "a period of slackening" (*The Postmodern Condition*, 71).

20. Arthur Kroker et al., "Panic USA: Hypermodernism as America's Postmodernism," *Social Problems* 37, 4 (November 1990): 444.

21. Coupland, *Generation X*, 37.

22. Lyotard, *The Postmodern Condition*, 51.

23. Jameson, foreword to *The Postmodern Condition*, xii.

24. Coupland, *Generation X*, 85.

25. The main character of Coupland's second novel, *Shampoo Planet*, proposes this idea as a business scheme (*Shampoo Planet* [Toronto: Pocket Books, 1992], 199–201).

26. Coupland, *Generation X*, 88.

27. In an essay on constitutional narratives, Jerald Zaslove identifies the plight of

Carl Schmitt as "wanting to equate the legal state with 'the cultural edifices built by the European spirit' whose 'significance is no less than that of those great works of art and literature usually identified as the sole representatives of the European spirit'" ("Constituting Modernity: The Epic Horizons of Constitutional Narratives" *Public* [1994]: 70).

28. Coupland, *Generation X*, 171.
29. Kroker, "Panic USA," 449.
30. Ibid.
31. Coupland, *Generation X*, 116.
32. John Steinbeck, *The Grapes of Wrath* (New York: Viking Press, 1939), 236.
33. Jean-François Lyotard, *The Postmodern Explained*, 84.
34. Ibid.

Bibliography

Coupland, Douglas. *Generation X: Tales for an Accelerated Culture*. New York: St. Martin's Press, 1991.

———. *Life after God*. Toronto: Pocket Books, 1994.

———. *Shampoo Planet*. Toronto: Pocket Books, 1992.

Fawcett, Brian. *Cambodia: A Book for People Who Find Television too Slow*. Toronto: Talonbooks, 1986.

———. "Something Is Wrong with Alice Munro." In *Unusual Circumstances, Interesting Times and Other Impolite Interventions*. Vancouver: New Star Books, 1991, 68–74.

Fukuyama, Francis. "The End of History?" *National Interest* 8, 16 (Summer 1989): 3–18.

Jameson, Fredric. Foreword to *The Postmodern Condition: A Report on Knowledge*, by Jean-François Lyotard, vii–xxi. Translated by Geoff Bennington and Brian Massumi. Minneapolis: University of Minnesota Press, 1984.

Kroker, Arthur, et al. "Panic USA: Hypermodernism as America's Postmodernism." *Social Problems* 37, 4 (November 1990): 443–59.

Lyotard, Jean-François. *The Postmodern Condition: A Report on Knowledge*. Translated by Geoff Bennington and Brian Massumi. Minneapolis: University of Minnesota Press, 1984.

———. *The Postmodern Explained: Correspondence, 1982–1985*. Edited by Julian Pefanis and Morgan Thomas. Translated by Don Barry et al. Minneapolis: University of Minnesota Press, 1993.

Steinbeck, John. *The Grapes of Wrath*. New York: Viking Press, 1939.

Zaslove, Jerald. "Constituting Modernity: The Epic Horizons of Constitutional Narratives." *Public* (1994): 63–77.

Part 3
Electronic Media

Talking Out of School
Academia Meets Generation X

Traci Carroll

It was an educated class, turned loose with an idle brain and plenty of time to devise mischief.

> Sutton Griggs, *Imperium in Imperio*

Freud doesn't like schizophrenics. He doesn't like their resistance to being oedipalized, and tends to treat them more or less as animals. They mistake words for things, he says. They are apathetic, narcissistic, cut off from reality, incapable of achieving transference; they resemble philosophers—"an undesirable resemblance."

> Deleuze and Guattari, *Anti-Oedipus*

It is time to prepare ourselves and our institutions for a world that will be phasing out mass employment.

> Jeremy Rifkin, "After Work"

As a physics major at University of California San Diego, Mike Judge, the creator of *Beavis and Butt-head,* recalled a period when he questioned the value of his education in both economic and creative terms. In a 1993 *Rolling Stone* interview, Judge remembers thinking, "The counselors always said that if you got a degree in engineering and physics, you'd always be able to find a job, which is not true, but I was thinking, 'At least I can make some money while I'm trying to do what I want to do.'" Having experienced higher education's false promise of fulfilling employment, Judge describes his period of artistic gestation as a year of "'slow, mindless work' for a military contractor."[1] Not coincidentally, the same issue of *Rolling Stone* also features an article on the accelerating transformation of full-time, benefit-holding jobs into temporary, part-time jobs: "The Temporary Miracle," by William Greider.[2] This essay is, in part, an attempt to historicize myself and my un(der)employed peer-colleagues as Generation X academics who, like Judge, feel that in our changing economic climate, educational institutions are not only failing to perform their ostensible function of enabling graduates to find satisfying work, but that their reluctance to question their changing role in this economy attests to a contempt for the kinds of learning, thinking, and intellectual production that occur outside the institution. When I began working on this article, I considered myself fortunate to have a full-time, temporary teaching position, yet like Judge, I identified to some degree with Beavis and Butt-head as critical alter egos that reflected my institutional schizophrenia, the sense of internal division experienced by the Generation X academic.[3] Since abandoning the institution for the difficult but more satisfying work of parenting, practicing massage therapy, and teaching yoga (none of which requires even a bachelor's degree), my sense of split self has vanished, yet it still characterizes the experience of academia for many of my peers.

What does it mean to be a disaffected critic, uncomfortable in one's social and political climate, but alienated as well from the academic institution that supposedly allows one to perform a political critique? How is a postmodern aesthetics of disaffection different from a modernist poetics of alienation? Prior to answering these questions, we must also consider the problems of agency and generalization that immediately arise with the mere mention of the phrase "Generation X": What is Generation X, anyway? Who coined the term and why? Is it in any way a consistent, coherent social movement? How does one talk concretely about a generation that seems to define itself in negative terms—who we are not, what we don't have or can't do, what is disappearing from our future? Do people in this age group apply this phrase to themselves? Why or why not? Although a complete theorization of Gen X is beyond the scope of this essay, my readings of Douglas Coupland's novel *Generation X*, Mike Judge's *Beavis and Butt-head*, and Joel Hodgson's *Mystery Science Theater 3000* do take up the final question about group identification and its relation to cultural criticism.[4] The common emphasis on critical production in all these texts suggests that one of the reasons many of us do find the term appealing is that it offers coherence and confers some sense of integrity on an otherwise bleak social and economic reality by emphasizing the resilience of human creativity, the desire to express and to create beauty regardless of social position or institutional authority. The examples of Gen X culture treated here concern themselves primarily with a group production of critical texts that both mimic and deconstruct academic criticism. I will not only explore the ways in which academic critical theory can illuminate these examples of Generation X culture, but I will also consider what the foregrounding of critical discourse in immensely popular TV shows like *Beavis and Butt-head* and *MST3K* can tell us about academia. Both of these shows feature fictional characters commenting on media, in effect, talking back to the screen. Beavis and Butt-head critique music videos while the characters of *MST3K* mock B-movies.

Although both programs, as well as Coupland's novel, use group critical production as their main structuring principle, I am specifically interested in Beavis and Butt-head as paradigmatic Gen X critics. One of the hallmarks of Gen X criticism is its communal nature; this intensely communal method of producing texts is perhaps a reflection of Gen X's sense of being abandoned by its parent generation. Why are Beavis and Butt-head such powerful figures, such useful metaphors in this context? The particular combination of violent humor, pathos, resistance to institutions, and perverse creativity that characterizes *Beavis and Butt-head* highlights one of the main thematic concerns of Generation X criticism: a sense of making something out of nothing, of creating something out of an ever-shrinking economic security that is perceived as a nothing, an empty set, an "X." While Beavis and Butt-head embody this sense of political powerlessness, they seem to lack altogether the highbrow, postmodern self-consciousness that pervades the other critical texts I treat here. However, Judge frames Beavis and Butt-head's poetics of disaffection with a powerful critique of their social conditions, suggesting that their lack of self-awareness is a direct reaction to the force exerted by school and advertising. The implications of Judge's critique of education are expressed more directly by advocates of home schooling such as John Taylor Gotto. Gotto traces the American system of compulsory education back to Fichte's "Address to the German Nation," which responded to Prussia's defeat in 1806 by Napoleon's army of amateur soldiers and advocated forced schooling that taught the populace to take orders.[5] Gotto argues that "schooling after the Prussian fashion removes the ability of the mind to think for itself. It teaches people to wait for a teacher to tell them what to do and if what they have done is good or bad. Prussian teaching paralyses the moral will as well as the intellect. It's true that sometimes well-schooled students sound smart, because they memorize many opinions of great thinkers, but they actually are badly damaged because their own ability to think is left rudimentary and undeveloped." According to Gotto, Horace Mann and other American educational reformers were eager to adopt the Prussian system, primarily to help homogenize hordes of Catholic immigrants. Gen X texts reflect the operation of an educational system that encourages the development of obedient workers and consumers, but they also testify to a rebellious, indomitable spirit of individuality that resists being controlled or directed.

The main portion of my reading here deals with the way *Beavis and Butt-head* highlights the quality of self-consciousness that is common to both academic and non-academic Gen X critical discourse. My discussion begins, however, by turning some attention to the historical conditions that generate Gen X culture's concern with critical production, powerlessness, and self-consciousness. Of the three texts I've chosen, Coupland's novel makes the most significant commentary on the historical shift experienced by young adults entering the world of work. For this reason, his novel provides an important insight into the attitudes toward work, education, and institutional power represented in the TV shows. The very name "Generation X" suggests both an intensified sense of self-awareness and a lack of identity; it is the generation that is conscious of being a generation with no qualities. Coupland argues that members of Gen X have a peculiarly self-contradictory experience of history. He suggests that ours is a generation without history, or without economic precedent for our shifts in economic fortune and without a decisive historical moment, like the Vietnam War, that will retrospectively lend a sense of political or social integrity to our age group. At the same time, Coupland also implies that ours is a generation with too much history; it is fixated on the idea that it occupies a historical turning point and is intensely aware of making (or not making) history in some way.[6] Coupland thus revises Fredric Jameson's assertion that "history is what hurts" by suggesting that the future is going to hurt worse: "how sweet and sad all moments of life are rendered by the tripping of a camera's shutter, for at that point the future is still unknown and has yet to hurt us."[7] Or in Butt-head's words, we "got no future" from which we can imagine looking back to see our history in the making. The moments of emotional self-indulgence in Coupland's novel seem to leave us with a more pessimistic and politically informed brand of New Criticism in which the future matters more than history and the production of narrative almost redeems the pains of existence, but not quite.

Is there any validity to Coupland's claim that Gen X is a landmark generation? In Raymond Williams' s analysis, all generations share a sense of cultural specificity: the "concept of 'commonly experienced time' is crucial in the idea of a cultural generation, and this form of analysis has since [the mid-nineteenth century] been common in cultural history."[8] But Williams also shows how the meaning of "generation" has drifted away from its original, strictly biological sense. "Generation" took on its cultural associations in the eighteenth and nineteenth centuries and is increasingly used in the late twentieth century to refer to machines and computers. Williams remarks on the prevalence of "some strange but increasingly common uses of *generation* to describe successive types of manufactured objects" since the 1950s, which speaks to the way in which "manufactured objects" are increasingly doing away with the need for human employees.[9] As generations of computers replace generations of people, the reproduction or "generation" of humans becomes economically obsolete. From this perspective, it is tempting to see Gen X as the beginning of the end of the need for people. The insistence upon creative commentary in Coupland's work and in Gen X popular texts, however, continually reasserts human value. These moments of creative insurgency may look adolescent or self-indulgent, but they reflect the hope for a future in which we value each other more deeply, a future in which our children have the courage to find or create new institutions that truly address the need to learn and think independently.

If we are a generation of people being replaced in the labor force by new generations of computers and machines, why specifically is this generation named with an X? Algebraically, x is the unknown, a placeholder. Certainly the increasing prevalence of part-time, temporary work creates a feeling of anonymity and infinite replaceability in the labor market; employee x could just as easily be employee y or z. But Coupland's novel suggests another, more problematic and illuminating association of Generation X with the X used by black Muslims in the

1960s to signify the retrieval of a racial past that is in danger of being completely erased. The ease with which Coupland appropriates the black nationalist X reveals a largely unacknowledged racial specificity to Generation X discourse. A comparison of grunge and hip hop, for example, shows that lyrics by white grunge bands tend to embrace abjection while rap lyrics, as Robin Kelley argues, are characterized by a braggadocio that symbolically reclaims power.[10] Part of the Generation X sensibility seems to derive from the fact that a widespread lack of economic opportunity, which has been a longstanding experience for African American youth, is now impacting large numbers of white youth for the first time.

Are members of Gen X merely indulging in a nostalgia for lost economic power and privilege? If Gen X were a solidly middle-class social formation, this description might hold true, but many young people from differing class backgrounds share a justifiable sense of outrage about the widening gap between the poor and the wealthy in the United States. Despite this economic common ground, however, Coupland's appropriation of the black nationalist X to refer to a nameless generation spawned of economic decline still conveys a sense that all the good history has already been taken, in particular by African Americans. Malcolm X explains his adoption of X to represent a stolen or hidden cultural legacy, "the true African family name that he could never know," in place of the European surnames that had been "imposed upon (his) paternal forbears."[11] Coupland's use of the X as a metaphor for being stripped of significance also surfaces in the novel's reference to *Invisible Man*. Dag, one of Coupland's main characters, describes quitting his job as the kind of archetypal descent that is politicized by Ellison's nameless protagonist who dwells underground, waiting for a political opening from which to emerge: "Now: when you become a Basement Person, you drop out of the system."[12] Dag quits work and starts reading. His nonparticipation in his social world gives him precisely the critical distance he needs to become an obsessive reader: "All events became omens; I lost the ability to take anything literally" (31). This distance does not, like that of the academic, carry any social prestige; it is experienced as an inevitable social penalty for dropping out. Coupland seems to suggest that the "Basement Person" loses the ability to experience history as a succession of events and replaces those events with a metanarrative about history.

It is important to keep in mind the complicated racial overtones of the adoption of the X as a metaphor for disaffection more generally. The theme of alienation so common to American modernist writing seems to return in a postmodern guise in *Generation X*, but instead of producing better art, disaffection produces better readings. In some ways, Generation X rhetoric reproduces Beat generation clichés about white alienation, but instead of taking the alienated artist as its emblem, Gen X culture focuses on the textual consumer—the alienated critic.[13] From this perspective, Gen X academic critics take what Patricia Hill Collins has called "a curious outsider-within stance" in an academic institution whose paradigms of legitimation alienate teachers and students from a variety of critical perspectives.[14] Although Collins uses this phrase specifically to describe the experience of black female academics, her critique of the way intellectual legitimacy is produced and denied in the academic institution has far-reaching implications for all academics and, indeed, for anyone whose life is touched by the power of the educational institution.[15] Collins's ethical and epistemological questions touch the heart of the problem with school: if work and economic viability are being redefined, we must think seriously about our "personal accountability" in perpetuating socially irresponsible definitions of knowledge and learning, as well as outdated assumptions about the relationship between education and employability (217). As part of an institution that is failing to prepare students for the economic reality of a world without deeply satisfying work, the Generation X academic occupies a peculiar if not impossible position on this social map. Because so much of *Beavis and Butt-head*'s dialogue derives from their relentless resistance to school, their commentaries on music videos serve as metaphors for any kind of outsider knowledge—knowledge that is not institutionally recognized as knowledge.

Despite their lack of institutional legitimacy, Gen X critics produce their outsider knowledge just like academics do, by creatively manipulating other texts. Because the production of outsider knowledge is not accompanied by what Pierre Bourdieu calls *"rituals of social magic"* that underwrite its validity and guarantee its cultural capital, institutions perceive this kind of knowledge only as an object of inquiry or curiosity.[16] *Beavis and Butt-head* uses this kind of critical creativity as a way of combating a sense of powerlessness inculcated by school. Beavis and Butt-head take their status as outsiders, their sense of being both programmed and dismissed by school and advertising, and they make something out of it. Some might argue that what they are making is aesthetically offensive, intellectually worthless, or even politically dangerous. In the process of elaborating *Beavis and Butt-head*'s critical methodology, I address the ways in which these three points of critique are interrelated. But behind these questions about the value of *Beavis and Butt-head* lie some more difficult fundamental questions about academic criticism. How do people outside of institutions theorize the knowledge they produce differently from the way academic theorists do? What kinds of distance and identification determine our intellectual pleasure? What is the relation between internal institutional recognition and our assumptions about the political effects of teaching and scholarship outside the academy?

The pervasive critique of *Beavis and Butt-head* in terms of taste and intellectual unselfconsciousness derives from two unstated assumptions: first, that the production of academic knowledge results in a political efficacy outside of institutions (a trickle-down theory of politics), and second, that narrative qualities of distance and self-consciousness have inherent aesthetic value.[17] The mimesis of academic criticism in *Beavis and Butt-head*, along with its more highbrow equivalent *MST3K*, makes an ironic commentary on the highly politicized academic discourse from the mid-1980s to the early 1990s, which was perhaps optimistic about its power to affect American culture by teaching a set of analytical skills vaguely defined as "critical thinking." The immense popularity of *Beavis and Butt-head* and *MST3K* suggests that rather than trickling down to the culture at large from the vantage point of the university, critical thinking both inside and outside centers of learning derives from a postmodern aesthetic of creative textual consumption. Doubtful about the possibility of a profound political shift, Gen X criticism is nevertheless an attempt to respond to our culture with intelligence, wit, hope, and a sense of fun. Here again we see the failure of schools to help people forge real connections between their knowledge and the world (or their lives, for that matter), between their experience of school and their opportunities to serve people in a way that feels authentic. One of the unintended manifestations of critical thinking is social and emotional paralysis. The translation of critical positioning into entertainment value further distances people from their real experience, so that even critical creativity gets siphoned off into inconsequential activity.

The critics in *Beavis and Butt-head* and *MST3K* occupy opposite ends of a spectrum of self-consciousness, but they draw from critical paradigms that are as coherent as any found in academia. Both shows employ a cogent and tightly organized critical methodology. *MST3K's* precepts and tastes are decidedly highbrow and politically left, incorporating wide-ranging, esoteric textual references in their critiques of gender roles, consumer culture, low-brow movies, and the homoerotics of power. *Beavis and Butt-head,* by contrast, relies on a fairly limited and intensely low-brow, phallocentric set of assumptions: a critical premium falls on videos or dialogue that feature violence, chicks (especially "chicks with big thingies"), loud music, and text that lends itself easily to hypersexualization.[18] Conversely, videos that maintain pretensions to the highbrow, videos that smack of sentimentality, and musicians who unsuccessfully appropriate the codes of heavy metal, grunge, or rap violate Beavis and Butt-head's aesthetic. This critical paradigm, like any other, admits exceptions and allows for some subtlety and self-contradiction; Butt-head astutely points out in the case of one video that features sadly derivative metal and lots of semi-nude women that "just because a video has naked chicks doesn't mean it doesn't suck." Like a reader who has stumbled into a half-awareness of his interpretive theory, Butt-head also points out on another occasion that "sometimes things suck in a different way" than other things that suck.

Not surprisingly, given this set of critical priorities, most attacks on *Beavis and Butt-head* are based on the argument that their remarks are tautological or scatological: Beavis and Butt-head are stupid, the animation is poorly done, and the text is in bad taste. A 1994 article in the *Memphis Commercial Appeal* made a direct connection between Generation X and the style of humor that Judge has developed for *Beavis and Butt-head.* According to the *Commercial Appeal,* "Young adults—the so-called Generation X—say the cartoon show *Beavis and Butt-head* is the TV program they most talk about. A survey of the July 23 issue of TV Guide found 40 percent of older teens and 20-somethings picked the tasteless duo, followed by 21 percent for *Saturday Night Live.*"[19] This characterization of *Beavis and Butt-head's* audience as "the so-called Generation X" not only points to an age gap between the journalist and his subject, but also calls into question the tastes and thus the intellectual legitimacy of Generation X discourse. The description of Beavis and Butt-head as "tasteless" denies their raw aesthetic of violence, heightened physicality, and antiauthoritarianism of any validity or self-consciousness, and it implicitly associates a more restrained, cerebral style with maturity and aesthetic subtlety. Style, taste, and authority are intimately related here; Beavis and Butt-head cannot defend their aesthetics because as producers of outsider knowledge, they do not have an intellectual perch from which to define their critical position. It is interesting to see how often aesthetic and intellectual judgments appear paired together in the assessment of outsider knowledge; a stylistic difference frequently gets apprehended and represented as an intellectual shortcoming or a logical flaw.[20]

The principle of critical distance, a sense of detachment from one's argument in the name of a greater investment in the integrity of intellectual debate, supposedly prevents academics from arguing on the basis of aesthetic preference or simply out of habit. By using *Beavis and Butt-head*'s methodology as a counterexample, however, I hope to show that distance has less to do with any kind of intellectual investment than with the ability to see very clearly the differential between *your own experience* and the assumptions on the part of cultural authorities (parents, teachers, advertisers, politicians, employers, and so on) about *what your experience ought to be*.

In his analysis of social practice, Michel de Certeau offers an explanation of how people who do not typically think of themselves as intellectuals claim critical distance. Such a moment takes place when Beavis and Butt-head actually sit through a video that sucks and enjoy the process of constructing a narrative around it, exercising what Certeau calls "an art of manipulating and enjoying."[21] Certeau maintains that one can view a program, internally acknowledge a kind of irrelevance to one's own aesthetic or intellectual predilections, yet still have a pleasant experience of the distance between what one sees and what one likes. Intellectuals habitually experience this kind of pleasure in the contemplation of kitsch, but we tend to dismiss this process among the uncredentialed on aesthetic grounds. Rather than registering the distance between judgment and pleasure with the intellectual's restrained raised eyebrow, knowing glare, and silent smirk, Beavis and Butt-head are more apt to react to a bad video with wide-eyed amazement and overt verbal criticism ("This sucks," "What is this crap?" "Is this a Clearasil commercial?"), while they continue to watch it. By comparison, this physically demonstrative reaction seems crude, too transparent and predictable to the academic. A distaste for the stylistics of Beavis and Butt-head's reactions derives from the assumption that because they do not respond to kitsch in a properly restrained fashion, they are incapable of understanding and appreciating the contradictory experience offered by kitsch.

It follows from this assumption that Beavis and Butt-head's ability to simultaneously hate and enjoy Judas Priest's "Breakin' the Law" video, for example, has no status as aesthetic or intellectual contemplation. Certeau writes, "the knowledge is not known. In practice, it has a status analogous to that granted fables and myths as the expression of kinds of knowledge that do not know themselves. In both cases it is a knowledge that subjects do not reflect. They bear witness to it without being able to appropriate it. They are in the end renters and not the owners of their know-how" (71). Much to the contrary of most academic characterizations of knowing, Certeau finds a quiet sophistication in common practices of textual consumption, which for him testify both to the pervasiveness of regulatory power and to a resilience that resists it: "These ways of reappropriating the product-system, ways created by consumers, have as their goal a therapeutics for deteriorating social relations and make use of techniques of re-employment in which we can recognize the procedures of everyday practices" (xxiv). The pastiche of film and criticism represented by *MST3K* and *Beavis and Butt-head,* and its attendant poetics of disaffection, constitute a formalized version of the critical folk art that goes on in living rooms all across the United States every night, with the exception that these shows imply the addition of a third layer of narrative: the TV viewers who produce their own narratives about the shows.

From this perspective, Beavis and Butt-head's everyday critical practices question the value of academic criticism and elevate folk criticism to the status of theory; the net effect is a reduction of the amount of cultural capital that separates academics from people who watch TV all day. One might still argue, however, that academic practice does have political implications that are lacking or even countered in *Beavis and Butt-head.* According to Jules Law, the usefulness and integrity of the academic enterprise depends upon protecting the institution as a social space for imagining the politically difficult. Beavis and Butt-head could be seen as very unsophisticated versions of new pragmatists who, in Law's analysis, "have only two psychological categories to classify competing beliefs: what it is easy to imagine, and what it is impossible to imagine," based on the assumptions of their interpretive community.[22] The intermediary category between the easy to imagine and the impossible to imagine, that which is possible but difficult to imagine, constitutes for Law the meaning and legitimacy of criticism: "For those who believe that literary criticism and theory can be something more than a self-confirming cultural reflex, the recognition that ungrounded action does not constitute a monolithic category is a crucial one" (320). It seems that this "self-confirming cultural reflex" continues to reveal itself in the theory of trickle-down politics that I suggested earlier; academics often end up defending the institution itself, and many still have difficulty imagining the implications of knowledge produced outside the university. The exceptions Beavis and Butt-head acknowledge to their critical paradigm suggest that institutions are not necessarily exclusive sites for imagining the difficult. Beavis and Butt-head do allow for what Wittgenstein calls "that which it takes some effort to imagine,"[23] as in the example of the bad video whose value is not redeemed by the presence of "naked chicks." The danger in solidifying the academic's position as a cultural critic lies in our tendency to obscure the material conditions that enable academic production—the command of the resources and leisure time required to imagine the difficult.

One solution to this problem lies in the recognition that Western philosophy has no exclusive claim on the idea of imagining something different even though it is hard to do. In fact, the tendency of Western thought has been to reinforce a kind of rationalist positivism that only distances us further from our emotional, physical, and spiritual experiences that might actually allow us to see something in a new way. Sole reliance upon intellectual contemplation accelerates the economic process bemoaned by Gen Xers: the consolidation of power by corporations who desire to amass money and control the external physical world. The tradition of yoga, which is systematically taught only outside our educational institutions, emphasizes the importance of nongreediness and the necessity of change, a comprehensive, internal change of the whole person: "This change must bring us to a point where we have never been before. That is to say, that which was impossible becomes possible. . . . One of the basic reasons many people take up yoga is to change something about themselves: to be able to think more clearly, to feel better, and to be able to act better today than they did yesterday in all areas of life."[24] Desikachar's elaboration of yoga philosophy implies not only a highly disciplined process of internal development, but a real connection between the ongoing experience of who we are through yoga practice and what changes we want to see in the world, reflected in our everyday behaviors and actions.

Many of the aesthetic objections to *Beavis and Butt-head* arise from a distaste for the kinds of material experience encouraged by yoga practice: unwavering attention to the materiality of the body and to the palpable effects of our everyday actions. An academic paradigm offers the intellectual no way of identifying with the obsessive scatology, repetition, and insistence of *Beavis and Butt-head*'s humor because the intellectual distance seems unbridgeable. Here is the rub in academic politics: how can an elitist form of criticism help anyone form grassroots political connections outside academic institutions? So often, academic pleasure derives from an awareness of belonging to a special class that is uniquely distanced from the culture it analyzes. The drawback to this kind of purported objectivity is that it leads to the belief that we really *are* different from the Beavises and Butt-heads of the world, that it's OK for them to live in bad conditions but we deserve something better because we're so smart. Here the trickle-down theory falls apart, when we have forgotten to acknowledge the essential sameness of spirit, or in yoga philosophy, the atman, that resides in every person. Facilitating such moments of recognition allows us to really see sameness amongst our differences and to learn to work cooperatively. It has become impossible for me to maintain academic distance any longer, but for several years I occupied a position somewhere between Beavis and Butt-head and the institution that produced my identity as an intellectual.

Coupland's novel *Generation X* lies at the other end of the intellectual spectrum in Gen X culture. Insofar as it strives to redefine the value of living at an historical moment that he perceives as a crucial cultural and economic turning point, Coupland's emphasis on emotional sincerity provides an interesting foil for the cynicism of programs like *Beavis and Butt-head*. Despite chapter titles like "Shopping is Not Creating" and "I Am Not a Target Market," Coupland's novel makes it clear that much of Generation X's consciousness has been shaped by advertising and a generational economic resentment he calls "Boomer Envy."[25] The conflict between a desire to jettison all aspects of the consumer culture that continually reminds Gen X of its economic powerlessness and a desire to take pleasure in commodities is bridged by an aesthetics of cool that allows one simultaneously to articulate and disavow that desire. Coupland's account of his characters' aesthetics of "cool" overlaps with and helps account for the Butt-headian binary "cool/sucks." Again we see the tendency to distance oneself from experience, this time emotional experience. Originally adopted from cool jazz players at the turn of the 1950s whose stage presence and performance style sought to enact a kind of distance from the audience in a "low-key, undramatic manner," *cool* has historically served to define a generational aesthetic shift.[26]

The combination of education, a lack of opportunity, and emotional cool results in the production of critical narrative as capital in *Generation X*. Despite Coupland's reinstatement of distance as a critical value for Generation X, his narrator suggests that the abandon and nihilism of Gen X cool also mask a poignant nostalgia for optimism and immediate emotional expression: "The first chink of sun rises over the lavender mountain of Joshua, but three of us are just a bit too cool for our own good; we can't just let the moment happen."[27] Coupland deftly encapsulates the problem of our generation, which is continually gaining momentum: we are unable just to have our experience and be in the moment, to take joy in small moments. Unable to experience the moment without a verbal record of its intensity, one character asks the others to tell impromptu stories about the sun. But even this narrative surface is punctured by another self-referential contact: "The carapace of coolness is too much for Claire, also. She breaks the silence by saying that it's not healthy to live life as a succession of isolated little cool moments. 'Either our lives become stories, or there's just no way to get through them'" (8). In Coupland's universe, group production of narrative and adoption of the cool stance become inadequate compensations for economic disenfranchisement. The third option, not mentioned by Claire, is to really dig into the experience of your life, whether or not it is painful, and to watch how your attentiveness alters your perception, opens you up to new possibilities besides obsessive narrative on the situation and reliance upon peer validation.

Significantly, the process of critical production in both *Beavis and Butt-head* and *MST3K* is also highly interactive. These shows also suggest that cultural criticism is not most accurately represented by an isolated critic surveying the cultural landscape, but by a group of outsiders or prisoners making something out of a culture that has alienated or entrapped them. Hodgson's spaceship-prison and Judge's living room couch become the Palm Springs desert in *Generation X*. Palm Springs, in Coupland's novel, represents a culture that has little to offer outside of material for narrative; there is no outside to the "land so empty that all objects placed on its breathing, hot skin become objects of irony" (8). Coupland's criticism relies upon a self-irony no longer concerned with its connection to cultural capital, but self-irony is required to make the circumstances of its production tolerable. Coupland's novel helps clarify the aesthetics of *Beavis and Butt-head* and *MST3K* by showing how Generation X aesthetics derive from Gen Xers' perception of their economic conditions—both financially and artistically, Gen Xers are trying to make something out of nothing, something out of what they can get for free, or something out of someone else's stuff.

A difference between Coupland's aesthetics and those of *Beavis and Butt-head* and *MST3K* does arise, however, in his use of affect. Coupland's indulgence in innocent sentimentality is countered by cynicism and brutality in *Beavis and Butt-head* and an odd mixture of paranoia, irony, and *joie de vivre* in *MST3K*. Outside the shadow of Coupland's pervasive fear of the future as what hurts and his proactive narratives of self-protection, Beavis and Butt-head may paradoxically look more sophisticated because they don't take themselves quite so seriously, or don't seem equipped to; they have distance from their emotions. Their habit of addressing each other with terms of insult ("dumb-ass," "dillweed," "fart-knocker") and vague threats ("I'm gonna kick your ass, Beavis") suggests that affectively, if not stylistically, Beavis and Butt-head share with academics a suspicion of sincerity and an ethic of highly ritualized humiliation. Whereas academic critics convert their fear of humiliation into cultural capital and intellectual prestige, Beavis and Butt-head translate it into a poetics for judging videos and a somewhat sadistic style of humor. In a similar manner, Mike (formerly Joel), Tom Servo, and Crow on *MST3K* convert their fear of an invasive, Foucauldian power into a less violent kind of humor, as the prisoners live in fear of being forced to watch bad films so that the two lover/observer/scientist-captors can monitor and analyze their responses. The fear works in two directions in this case, however, as *MST3K* also occasionally provides glimpses into the subterfuge of homoerotic power: Mike and the robots' fear is reciprocated by their observers' fear of being exposed as lovers. Beavis and Butt-head interweave both homoerotic and homophobic discursive moments in a more cavalier fashion; the episode entitled "Canoe Trip" most suggestively illustrates Beavis and Butt-head's homophobic contempt for their hippie teacher's attempts to male bond with them by singing "Men Have Feelings, Too" in front of the campfire. Although Beavis and Butt-head's gender politics are consistently disappointing, in this episode Judge also seems to be poking fun at both the men's movement and the teacher's assumptions about the ease with which he can earn his students' trust. While Judge does critique Beavis and Butt-head's sexism and homophobia with strong female characters like Daria, he keeps his main focus on Beavis and Butt-head's indictment of the educational system.

In different ways, both *Beavis and Butt-head* and *MST3K* critique the role of educational institutions in our current postmodern version of alienation; each show emphasizes cynicism as a rational response to the ideological force of schooling and learning. *Beavis and Butt-head* focuses on the manner in which many people are simply discarded by the educational system at a very young age, while *MST3K* makes a more subtle, but perhaps a more disheartening suggestion: the power/knowledge nexus, represented by captor-observers, exists primarily to perpetuate itself and intelligent, creative, energetic people like Joel and Mike are being placed in positions where they are expected to function like Tom Servo and Crow. Subject to a shadowy and anonymous authority, they are expected to behave like robots and fulfill their duties unquestioningly. Their response is to try to wrest some fun out of their existence as prisoners subjected to constant observation by producing subversive countertexts to the films they watch.

Rolling Stone's framing of Charles Young's interview with Beavis and Butt-head misses or perhaps intentionally obscures the show's critique of education during the period of intensified corporate consolidation that spawned the attitudes of Gen X. Echoing the Pepsi ad campaign, "The choice of a new generation," Young's title, "The Voice of a New Generation," firmly places *Beavis and Butt-head* in a tradition of unconscious consumerism. Young's misunderstanding or misrepresentation of Beavis and Butt-head's relation to capital is mirrored in his attitude of condescending distance enabled by educational experience. The only legitimacy Young grants to Beavis and Butt-head is borrowed from a fellow journalist who sees them as "the wonder drug to dissolve the great clot of semiotic theory clogging contemporary rock criticism, as capturing the true essence of rock: 'volume, abandon, radicalism.'"[28]

This statement objectifies Beavis and Butt-head as virile cultural plumbers performing for the pure amusement of their observers. As the interview progresses, however, Beavis and Butt-head's disruption of interview protocol suggests Judge's refusal to relegate their remarks to mere entertainment value.

Beavis and Butt-head consistently subvert the interview format by literalizing Young's utterances and giving other contexts to his questions through malapropism and hypersexualization. Whenever Young makes reference to the reality outside their show, Beavis and Butt-head pull him back inside the discourse of the show and expose his complicity with what they consider to be a completely corrupt educational apparatus. For example, when they are questioned about the disclaimer that MTV runs before their show ("Those words MTV runs before the show warning people about you"), Beavis counters with "Words suck," in effect, sabotaging the interview process (45). Butt-head pushes the critique of self-referentiality further by establishing his absolute disidentification with education: "Yeah. If I wanted to read, I'd go to school" (45). The subtext of *Beavis and Butt-head*, which is only obliquely mentioned in the introductory generalization that "teachers expect nothing" from "the stupid and ugly," is that our educational system alienates, ignores, and labels as stupid those students who detect and resist its role of ideological indoctrination.[29] The conspicuous absence of the family as an ideological state apparatus in *Beavis and Butt-head*, though alluded to in episodes that feature Stuart's parents, suggests the thoroughness of the school's power to act, in Althusser's terms, as an ideological " 'shield' provided by the repressive State Apparatus" that guards against political resistance.[30]

Interrogated on the "circular logic" of his aesthetics, Butt-head indicts the interviewer with the response, "Uh, did you, like, go to college?" charging him with an ideological complicity in perpetuating the questionable power of schools.[31] With his choice of words the interviewer exposes his uncritical assumption of a universal investment in the process of education. Beavis and Butt-head associate his identification with education with a scandalous proliferation of aesthetic offense: "BUTT-HEAD: Then why does so much stuff suck? BEAVIS: Yeah. College boy!" (45). Returning to his assumed regard for the value of education, this time voicing a concern, similar to Coupland's, about the historical awareness of youth culture, Young asks Beavis and Butt-head to choose a formative historical event for their generation that compares with the importance of Vietnam in the production of his generation's consciousness (48). But Beavis and Butt-head find no equivalent defining moment, and at the suggestion that they provide some advice for American youth, they immediately return to their critique of the educational system and its ancillary ideologies: professionalism and the capitalist work ethic. Butt-head offers the observation, "Uh . . . I got one. Like if you go to school and, like, study and stuff? And grow up and get a job at a company and, like, get promoted? You have to go there and do stuff that sucks for the rest of your life" (50). The more attractive contrasting option Beavis perceptively offers is that "if you act like us and just do stuff that's cool? Like sit around and watch TV and burn stuff? . . . Then, ROLLING STONE magazine will come and kiss your butt!" (50). While Beavis and Butt-head's attitude might at first glance seem to value the most irredeemable qualities of a viciously arbitrary capitalist economy, the accompanying article on Mike Judge complicates charges that *Beavis and Butt-head* simply celebrates the workings of the market. Although wealth is cool to Beavis and Butt-head, they are not driven by a desire to accumulate it precisely because its distribution seems so arbitrary to them. On the rare occasions that they do stumble upon money (through cash machine malfunction or a lottery), they are either incarcerated or they use the money in a way that seems wasteful to a capitalist sensibility. In the "Lottery" episode, for example, they spend their money on a riding mower, which they use to mow an anarchy symbol into the school's football field. This symbolic action points to a political impulse behind Beavis and Butt-head's aesthetics, which is borne out in *Rolling Stone*'s accompanying story on Mike Judge. The attitudes of Judge's characters reflect his own sense that even if one follows the rules of the academic game and proves to be an expert player, the best one can hope for is "slow, mindless work," or the worst, to end up at Burger World anyway.

Despite the courageous acts of creativity performed in these Gen X texts, the residual sense of cynical resentment is troubling to me, as is the sense that a great deal of energy is being wasted on these textual games, energy that could and should be directed toward helping someone (even yourself) live better or feel better. This does not necessarily have anything to do with raising material "standards of living." It may start with just learning to experience your experience for what it is. I know how many unhappy, disaffected academics there are out there, whether they are Gen Xers or not. My hope is that we can all learn to feel a little happier, or even a lot happier, by being more honest in and about our work, by taking risks that might make learning institutions more responsive to the entire range of human needs, and by staying open to the possibilities of renewal held out by alternative institutions and independent inquiry.

Notes

1. Charles M. Young, "The Voice of a New Generation," *Rolling Stone* 19 August 1993, 43–50, 50.

2. Greider, William, "The Temporary Miracle," *Rolling Stone,* 19 August 1993.

3. My use of schizophrenia as a metaphor for Gen X academic identity, and my epigraph's reference to Freud as an image of the institutional agency that produces or denies legitimacy are intended as images of dislocation and discomfort imposed on the subject by the academic institution as a "desiring-machine" of capitalism. See Gilles Deleuze and Félix Guattari, *Anti-Oedipus,* trans. Robert Hurley, Mark Seem, and Helen R. Lane (Minneapolis: University of Minnesota Press, 1983), 16. The "strange subject" of capitalism (or schizophrenia), as Deleuze and Guatarri describe it, is "being defined by the share of the product it takes for itself, garnering here, there, and everywhere a reward in the form of a becoming or an avatar, being born of the states that it consumes and being reborn with each new state" (16). Pierre Bourdieu makes a remarkably similar assessment of the existential value of institutions in *Language and Symbolic Power:* "Could rites of institution . . . exercise their power . . . if they were not capable of giving at least the appearance of a meaning, a purpose, to those beings without a purpose who constitute humanity, of giving them the feeling of having a role or, quite simply, some importance, and thus tearing from the clutches of insignificance? . . . The rise of the distinguished class to Being has, as an inevitable counterpart, the slide of the complementary class into Nothingness or the lowest Being" (*Language and Symbolic Power,* trans. Gino Raymond and Matthew Adamson [Cambridge, Mass.: Harvard University Press, 1991], 126). My own critical position here attempts to bridge the distance between the distinguished and the insignificant.

4. See Douglas Coupland, *Generation X: Tales for an Accelerated Culture* (New York: St. Martin's Press, 1991); *Beavis and Butt-head,* MTV, created by Mike Judge; *Mystery Science Theater 3000,* Comedy Central, created by Joel Hodgson. Cited as *MST3K.*

5. John Taylor Gotto, "The Public School Nightmare: Why Fix a System Designed to Destroy Individual Thought?" http://www.talkcity.com/LibraryDr/patt/homeschl.htm

6. Despite the fact that thousands of young people participated in several types of activist work in the 1980s and 1990s—opposition to apartheid, United States involvement in Central America and the Gulf War, and support for abortion rights and gay/lesbian/ bisexual rights—Generation X is continually characterized as an apolitical antigeneration because it has had no spectacular activist "moment" granted the same media attention as Vietnam protest.

7. See Fredric Jameson, *The Political Unconscious: Narrative as a Socially Symbolic Act* (Ithaca: Cornell University Press, 1981), 102; Coupland, *Generation X*, 17.

8. Raymond Williams, *Keywords: A Vocabulary of Culture and Society* (New York: Oxford University Press, 1983), 141.

9. Stories on this phenomenon abound in the popular press. Jeremy Rifkin's article "After Work" offers two competing visions of a future without work; either the disappearance of work will cause a sharp increase in crime as "a growing number of unemployed and unemployable Americans will find ways to take by force what is being denied them by the forces of the marketplace," (Jeremy Rifkin, "After Work," *Utne Reader*, May/June 1995, 56) or the impending crisis will result in "a shortening of the workweek in countries around the world and a concerted effort by central governments to provide alternative employment for workers whose labor is no longer required in the marketplace" (58).

10. Robin Kelley shows how the deindustrialization of Los Angeles, for example, produced a music that emphasizes verbal ability as symbolic economic, sexual, and political power. Grunge reveals a very different response on the part of youth culture (*Race Rebels: Culture, Politics, and the Black Working Class* [New York: Free Press, 1994]). Consider, for example, the indulgence of abjection and victimization fantasies in lyrics by the Offspring ("I'm just a sucker with no self esteem"); Nirvana ("I feel stupid and contagious," "I'm ugly but that's ok so are you"); Soul Asylum ("I want somebody to shove me"); and, I think most markedly, by Hole ("Go on take everything / Take everything / I want you to"). Courtney Love also attempts, with mixed results, to appropriate a wide range of abject identities and turn them into threatening images with her stage persona of bitch-victim. A March 1995 performance included a paradigmatic instance of Love's interaction with her audiences: "Did somebody call me a bitch? 'Cause I am. I'm also a nigger and a whore and a cunt. And a faggot."

11. Macolm X, *The Autobiography of Malcolm X* (New York: Ballantine, 1965), 199.

12. See Ralph Ellison, *Invisible Man* (New York: Vintage, 1972); Coupland, *Generation X*, 26.

13. I do not mean to suggest a strict separation between white Beat poets and black nationalists like Amiri Baraka, who incorporated elements of Beat poetry into his own style. Despite these similarities and the veneration of white Beats by such African American writers as Eldridge Cleaver, the appropriation of racial alienation as a model for general malaise remains a highly charged political problematic in both Beat and Gen X cultural interchanges.

14. Patricia Hill Collins, *Black Feminist Thought: Knowledge, Consciousness, and the Politics of Empowerment* (New York: Routledge, 1990), 11.

15. I am particularly interested in the parallels between my argument here and Collins's challenge to academic epistemological paradigms. As Collins argues, "Reclaiming the Black women's intellectual tradition involves examining the everyday ideas of Black women not previously considered intellectuals" (*Black Feminist Thought*, 15). This work of theorizing knowledge "in alternative institutional locations" and among those "who are not commonly perceived as intellectuals" has far-reaching implications within and beyond the field of African American studies (14).

16. Pierre Bourdieu, *Language and Symbolic Power*, 111. With this observation Bourdieu shows how the production of knowledge in an institution relies upon a fundamental tautology: people inside the institution can produce the truth because people outside the institution believe that those institutions exist to produce truth. "The symbolic efficacy of words is exercised only in so far as the person subjected to it recognizes

the person who exercises it as authorized to do so, or, what amounts to the same thing, only in so far as he fails to realize that, in submitting to it, he himself has contributed, through his recognition, to its establishment" (116). The key here is the "only in so far"—the tautology only works as long as the power of the institution is misrecognized as an objective state. This understanding of tautology becomes more important when we look at the terms on which Beavis and Butt-head are critiqued.

17. Pierre Bourdieu's *Distinction* establishes the economic base of the value placed on self-distancing: "The detachment of the pure gaze cannot be separated from a general disposition towards the 'gratuitous' and the 'disinterested,' the paradoxical product of a negative economic conditioning which, through facility and freedom, engenders distance vis-à-vis necessity" (*Distinction: A Social Critique of the Judgement of Taste,* trans. Richard Nice [Cambridge: Harvard University Press, 1984], 55). One can only sustain a fiction of disinterestedness from a position of economic and/or cultural privilege; remarkably, though, this orientation produces its own version of "gratuitousness" analogous to the gratuitous violence and scatology of Beavis and Butt-head's discourse.

18. Charles M. Young, "Meet the Beavis! The Last Word from America's Phenomenal Pop Combo," *Rolling Stone,* 24 March 1994, 39.

19. *Memphis Commercial Appeal,* 18 July 1994, sec. A, p. 2.

20. I am also exploring more fully the status of Afrocentric academic production as outsider knowledge in a paper in progress entitled "Conjuring Power in African-American Literary Theory." Using Bourdieu's *Language and Symbolic Power* as a model for talking about the structural tautology inherent in academic production (and in all productions of institutional knowledge), I am examining the ways in which academics habitually misrecognize and misrepresent a basic difference in style or taste an intellectual flaw, most notably as circularity.

21. Michel de Certeau, *The Practice of Everyday Life,* trans. Steven Rendall (Berkeley: University of California Press, 1984), xxii.

22. Jules Law, "Uncertain Grounds: Wittgenstein's *On Certainty* and the New Literary Pragmatism," *New Literary History* 19 (1987–88): 320.

23. Quoted in Law, "Uncertain Grounds," 320.

24. T. K. V. Desikachar, *The Heart of Yoga: Developing a Personal Practice* (Rochester, Vt.: Inner Traditions International, 1995), 79.

25. Coupland, *Generation X,* 21.

26. James Lincoln Collier, *The Making of Jazz* (New York: Dell, 1978), 416.

27. Coupland, *Generation X,* 7.

28. Charles M. Young, "The Voice of a New Generation," *Rolling Stone,* 19 August 1993, 43.

29. Ibid. More specifically, the ISA of the school encourages for each social division the absorption of an "ideology which suits the role it has to fulfill in class society" (Louis Althusser, *Lenin and Philosophy* [New York: Monthly Review Press, 1971], 155).

30. Ibid., 150.

31. Young, "Voice," 45.

Bibliography

Althusser, Louis. *Lenin and Philosophy.* Translated by Ben Brewster. New York: Monthly Review Press, 1971.
Beavis and Butt-head. Created by Mike Judge. MTV. 1993–1997.

Bourdieu, Pierre. *Distinction: A Social Critique of the Judgement of Taste.* Translated by Richard Nice. Cambridge: Harvard University Press, 1984.

———. *Language and Symbolic Power.* Translated by Gino Raymond and Matthew Adamson. Cambridge: Harvard University Press, 1991.

Carroll, Traci. "Conjuring Power in African-American Literary Theory." Work in progress.

Certeau, Michel de. *The Practice of Everyday Life.* Translated by Steven Rendall. Berkeley: University of California Press, 1984.

Collier, James Lincoln. *The Making of Jazz.* New York: Dell, 1978.

Collins, Patricia Hill. *Black Feminist Thought: Knowledge, Consciousness, and the Politics of Empowerment.* New York: Routledge, 1990.

Commercial Appeal, 18 July 1994, sec. A, p. 2.

Coupland, Douglas. *Generation X: Tales for an Accelerated Culture.* New York: St. Martin's Press, 1991.

Deleuze, Gilles and Félix Guattari. *Anti-Oedipus: Capitalism and Schizophrenia.* Translated by Robert Hurley, Mark Seem, and Helen R. Lane. Minneapolis: University of Minnesota Press, 1983.

Desikachar, T. K. V. *The Heart of Yoga: Developing a Personal Practice.* Rochester, Vt.: Inner Traditions International, 1995.

Ellison, Ralph. *Invisible Man.* New York: Vintage, 1972.

Gotto, John Taylor. "The Public School Nightmare: Why Fix a System Designed to Destroy Individual Thought?" http://talkcity.com/LibraryDr/patt/homeschl.htm

Greider, William. "The Temporary Miracle." *Rolling Stone,* 19 August 1993, 32–33, 87.

Griggs, Sutton. *Imperium in Imperio.* Miami: Mnemosyne, 1969.

Jameson, Frederic. *The Political Unconscious: Narrative as a Socially Symbolic Act.* Ithaca: Cornell University Press, 1981.

Kelley, Robin. *Race Rebels: Culture, Politics, and the Black Working Class.* New York: Free Press, 1994.

Law, Jules. "Uncertain Grounds: Wittgenstein's *On Certainty* and the New Literary Pragmatism." *New Literary History* 19 (1987–88): 319–336.

Malcolm X. *The Autobiography of Malcolm X.* New York: Ballantine, 1965.

Mystery Science Theater 3000. Comedy Central. Created by Joel Hodgson. Cited as *MST3K.*

Rifkin, Jeremy. "After Work." *Utne Reader.* May/June 1995, 52–63.

Williams, Raymond. *Keywords: A Vocabulary of Culture and Society.* New York: Oxford University Press, 1983.

Young, Charles M. "The Voice of a New Generation." *Rolling Stone,* 19 August 1993, 43–50, 87.

———. "Meet the Beavis! The Last Word from America's Phenomenal Pop Combo." *Rolling Stone,* 24 March 1994, 38–39, 42.

"Await Lightning"
How Generation X Remaps the Road Story

Katie Mills

What are you searching for? They asked me. I answered that I was
waiting for God to show his face.

Jack Kerouac, "Lamb, No Lion"

Each generation writes "road stories," tales about going on the road to
seek freedom and find transformation. Young adults usually narrate
these stories, using them as a forum for negotiating their idealism within
society's inevitable constraints. The Beat writer Jack Kerouac elevated
the road story to a genre of youthful rebellion in postwar America when
he published *On the Road* in 1957. His character Sal Paradise wanted
to find answers to the mysteries of life: "I was half-way across America,
at the dividing line between the East of my youth and the West of my
future."[1] Halfway into the twentieth century, suburbs and interstate
freeways were first being built, and rebels like the Beats still believed
they could escape from the conventionality of the middle class by
avoiding its trappings—especially jobs, wives, and televisions.[2] Kerouac
suspected that television created conformity: "Real hip swinging cats . . .
vanished mightily . . . maybe it was the result of the universalization of
Television and nothing else."[3] Despite the eventual triumph of televisions, suburbs, and turnpikes, the rebel potential of the road story per-
sisted for children born in the mid-1960s and mid-1970s, although the

221

nature of protest certainly changed. By attending to the significance of "the road" in its historical context, we can see how Generation X remaps the road story first developed by other postwar youth.

Generation X learned as children that chanting "I want my MTV" was rebellion, a rejection of monolithic network television in favor of the upstart cable alternative called music television. Consequently, writers weaned on MTV tend to use the road story as a way of thinking about how to incorporate technology, particularly the mass media, in young peoples' universal desire to rebel. For instance, Sonic Youth musician Lee Ranaldo writes in a 1994 poem: "Things are moving / past the window / in a way more / exquisite / than any movie / could ever be."[4] He concludes, "we don't belong" (65), reviving the oppositional stance of the Beats by disengaging from today's mainstream citizens, who now live in hateful condos. Despite rejecting commodity culture, Ranaldo calls his volume of poems *Road Movies* (1994), which highlights the paradoxical presence of mass media technology in road stories written by Generation X. His poems suggest that rather than condemn media, as Kerouac did in decrying television's "universalization," Generation X brings media tropes to bear on its understanding of life, as when Ranaldo adds, "This is life, cut one frame at a time from an endless spool" (73). Even when Gen X feels indelibly marked by television, when it believes there is no escape from commodity status or communication systems, the road story still resurfaces, revealing changing details of narratives of escape, but confirming the desire for it.

The landmark 1991 novel that popularized this generation's name, Douglas Coupland's *Generation X,* remapped the age-old dream of the road as the place of transformation. Yet MTV also profoundly shaped the road genre during the 1990s, turning the Beatnik landscape of the road into the cartoon-like netscape of television, especially since 1995 when it began airing its ongoing "docu-adventure" road story *Road Rules,* and through its production of feature films like *Beavis and Butt-head Do America* in 1996. Nor are Beavis and Butt-head the only cartoon characters to hit the road; Marvel Comics' "Generation X" of mutant teenagers now adds to the subgenre of stories about young adults traveling across the United States in a Winnebago, thanks to J. Stephen York's 1997 novel *Crossroads (Generation X).* Despite the diversity of road stories written in the 1990s, the fantasies of escape and phoenix-like self-transformation link Generation X firmly to other postwar generations.

Beginnings of the Xer Road Story: Coupland's *Generation X*

Generation X alters the road genre by uniting the Beats' romantic urge to escape with its own postmodern romanticism, turned sentimental under the influence of *The Brady Bunch* and ironic thanks to MTV. Underneath its mocking voice, innovative hypertext in the margins, and metaphors drawn from television, *Generation X* is a novel about escape and redemption.[5] In the penultimate chapter, "Await Lightning," the narrator Andy describes his drive to Mexico. The focus of this chapter is not the road trip, but the idea Andy once had for a story, "The Young Man Who Desperately Wanted to Be Hit By Lightning." Andy's unwritten fiction featured a protagonist who took a road trip after quitting a boring job and leaving his fiancée. This young man drove a Pontiac (no doubt a Firebird) through the American prairies, searching unsuccessfully for a storm in which he would be struck by lightning. Next, Andy admits to his personal fantasy that a bird would wound him and thereby create in him a feeling of love and acceptance. This is, in fact, how the novel closes in the last chapter, when Andy drives once again to Mexico and, at the border, is first wounded by a bird, then enveloped in loving embraces by witnesses of the miraculous encounter. The bird flies through a fire, suggesting the bolt of lightning sought by the imaginary young man as well as the transformative bird desired by Andy for himself.

The search in American fiction for adventure and salvation almost always takes place on a road, if not on a road to Mexico, when narrated by a rebel of any postwar generation. Moreover, this rebel, even today, is frequently imagined as a "young man" with the socioeconomic resources to own a car. He will inevitably be white, but he may have deep friendships with people of color, women, or mutants, as we shall see. Coupland's novel is an accomplishment because he remapped such generic desires with a sensibility so uniquely evocative to his generation that the novel's title soon came to characterize all adults born in the twenty-year period after the postwar "baby boom."

Coupland clearly understands that the appeal of autonomy and mobility predates his characters, for he borrowed the designation X from Paul Fussell's *Class: A Guide through the American Status System.*[6] Fussell described people who separate from the mainstream and try to leave behind the restraints of socioeconomic class: "What class are we in, and what do we think about our *entrapment* there? . . . In discovering that you can become an X person you find the only escape from class" (179, emphasis added). Entrapment is a feeling as old as rebellion, of course, and escape by taking to the road is a literary and filmic trope with a long tradition. Consciously or not, Coupland relies upon this tradition in ending his novel with two road trips to Mexico and one imagined road story (even though the novel itself is not focused on the road). Fussell states, "Impelled by insolence, intelligence, irony, and spirit, X people have escaped out the back doors of those theaters of class which enclose others" (186). In this remark, we recognize the basic story line of Coupland's characters, who all live in postmodern Palm Springs. Fussell adds, "Of course X people shun turnpikes and freeways, those tedious, characterless conduits for the middle class, preferring instead slowpoke back roads because of their 'charm'" (182). This describes Andy's imagined but yet-unwritten young man in "Await Lightning," who sneaks out the "back doors" of class by driving away from a job and a woman.

Every road story written in the past forty-five years is compared to Kerouac's *On the Road,* yet there are compelling reasons to compare the Beat urtext to Coupland's *Generation X* because they both portray the road as the source of magic and long-sought love. Both novels approach their finale with a chapter about a road trip to Mexico. In 1991, Andy seeks something quite similar to what Sal awaited in 1957—magic. As Kerouac said, "Behind us lay the whole of America and everything Dean and I had previously known about life, and life on the road. We had finally found the magic land at the end of the road and we never dreamed the extent of the magic."[7] Each novel also finishes with the narrator's transformation, as when Sal is back home in New York and finds, at last, his version of the longed-for bolt of lightning: "the girl with the pure and innocent dear eyes that I had always searched for and for so long" (306). In Andy's case, he is surrounded by a group of teenagers whose "crush of love was unlike anything I had ever known."[8] In both novels, the road is the place for transformation by love and magic, and young adulthood is the time for seeking it.

For this reason, these two watershed novels of post–World War II fiction share with ancient stories the trope of the road as the space where social distances collapse and random encounters become fateful. In theorizing this characteristic of ancient stories, Mikhail Bakhtin calls the road an important "chronotope," that is, a narrative device offering a privileged space (from the Latin word topos) that is inseparable from a special time (in Latin, chronos). Hence, "chronotope" literally means the "time space" that organizes a novel's narrative events, making time material within a well-delineated space. The road represents a place where the hero gains distance and perspective on everyday private life, where "space is filled with real, living meaning, and forms a crucial relationship with the hero and his fate"; the road chronotope is simultaneously "a time of exceptional and unusual events, events determined by chance."[9] Similarly, in her memoir *Dharma Girl* (1996), twentysomething Chelsea Cain recounts an ironic exchange between her traveling companion, her mother, and a Mexican guide after they had taken a road trip to Mexico: "Our Mayan guide: 'What brought you here?' My mother (after deep consideration): 'Destiny.' Our Mayan guide: 'No. I mean did you take a bus?' "[10] Like the Beats' "dharma bums," Coupland's characters and Cain's "dharma girl" transcend the mundane and transform magically while driving to Mexico.

Xers associate this type of yearning with the Beats; as Douglas Rushkoff, editor of *The GenX Reader* notes, "After reading *Catcher in the Rye,* most GenXers turned to *On the Road* for the real scoop on how to conduct one's rite of passage in the coolest manner possible."[11] While the rite of passage may persist, the road upon which it occurs is viewed with the changing sensibilities of "coolness." The Beats hoped that spontaneous art and joyous sex would radically change the world; now, however, Xers realize that avant-garde experiments yielded fewer substantial changes than those offered by technology—including television, which was just the first wave of electronic technologies like home computers, video cameras, Sega and Nintendo, faxes, and now the Internet. The Beats waited for the face of God and tried to avoid television as part of their strategy, whereas Xers use electrons to entertain themselves while awaiting whatever magic they hope will materialize. The Beats had drugs and alcohol, not to mention sex without the fear of AIDS, to embolden them on their dharma. But alcohol killed Kerouac, and now jacking into technology is the transformative path for Generation X, no matter how old fashioned their yearnings may be. Authors self-identified with Generation X use the road story to frame their desire for lightning rather than en-lightening, the state of being once sought by Beats and hippies, but which is now acquired too slowly for the accelerated culture of Gen X.

The Brady Bunch and the Beats

Whereas Gen Xers define themselves through tropes evolving from television, the Beats were the last demographic group to grow up without television. Consequently, television represented to the Beats the triumph of capitalism's mass brainwashing by "entertainment factories," as John Clellon Holmes called them, over the vision and voice of the individual.[12] In 1961, Allen Ginsberg composed his long poem, "Television was a Baby Crawling Toward That Deathchamber." In it, Ginsberg criticizes the "Idiot soap opera horror show we broadcast by Mistake— full of communists and frankenstein cops and mature capitalists running the State Department."[13] Ginsberg's poem speaks of the spiritual search for holy transmission of faith and hope to break through the broadcast technology. Whereas the Beats once feared that "remote control" was something orchestrated by Big Brother at the CIA, Generation X simply sees it as a handheld device that empowers young people to surf through crowded airwaves, a prosthesis for organizing the "ecstasy" of communication.

For if television was indeed a baby crawling through the late fifties, then the television set became a baby sitter for the next generations of American infants—everyone from hippies to yuppies to Xers. The first generations of television babies, including the children of the Beats, experienced television as a new phenomenon, which broadcast unprecedented media events. Although vast in scope, such history-making coverage included Nixon's "Checkers Speech," the Nixon-Kennedy debates, Kennedy's funeral, the March on Washington, the Vietnam War, and the Watergate hearings. Such events seemed to confirm television's ability to universalize attitudes because, for the first time, a national medium was giving the population the same words and images at the same time. Radio had had a similar effect, although television's images made a more visceral impact. As Americans became fluent in television communications throughout the 1960s and 1970s, the novelty of the event televised became less important than the innovation of the representation (except for horrible crises like the Challenger explosion, the Oklahoma City bombing, the Columbine High School shootings, or the attack on the World Trade Center). With growing comfort with the role of television as baby sitter, television networks began targeting children born in the 1960s with shows like PBS's *Sesame Street* (1969–present) and ABC's *The Brady Bunch* (1969–1974). Thanks to electronic input such as this, Gen X grew up "tele-parabalizing," one of Coupland's many portmanteaus, this one referring to "Morals used in everyday life that derive from TV sitcom plots."[14]

The single most important force shaping what would come to be called Generation X was MTV, which began broadcasting in August 1981 with the rise of cable.[15] Of course, affluent children were raised with television enhancements like HBO (which started in 1972), Showtime (1976), Nickelodeon (1979), CNN (1980), and Cinemax (1980). Thus, Gen X differs from previous generations in that it grew up when television options proliferated, when MTV commodified the music and graphics that galvanized its audience. With the rise of cable came tabloid and reality shows, like *Hard Copy* in 1989, which were less expensive to produce. To kids raised in this era, all of life seemed to be one long tabloid documentary, and fantasies looked curiously similar to music videos.

For Generation X, today's mass media no longer seem as univocal as television did to the Beats in the 1950s. Even when one conglomerate, like Viacom, owns several networks—CBS, MTV, VH-1, Nickelodeon, TNN, CMT, UPN, and Showtime—the multiplicity of markets fosters a range of tastes. Not TV, but MTV, has defined and shaped the X generation, speaking to these rebels so well in their own aesthetics that teens used MTV and Nickelodeon to escape from the family without ever leaving home. For instance, Courtney Love described Kurt Cobain in television terms: "There is this sweet Jimmy Stewart, Mayberry, RFD, side of him. His favorite TV shows are *Dragnet* and *Mayberry, RFD*, and *Leave it to Beaver*. To him they represent his lost boyhood."[16] What is on the tube is often more significant to Generation Xers than what is on the road because television gives a much-needed forum to their collective identity, a vehicle for shared culture in a postmodern world no longer universalized by media, but fragmented by the vast choices of technological innovation.

Some Xers regularly use television shows to describe inner states, the way the Beats might have used Buddhist terms forty years ago. For instance, Coupland describes culture consumption in these words: "It makes you sort of like those doors at the beginning of *Get Smart* that open sideways and upside down, and there are just more doors to the core inside of you. You tend to buffer yourself more and protect what you know in yourself because you know how easily it can be trivialized or Hard Copy'd."[17] Just as jazz once framed the expressions of the Beats, now television's continuous flow of recycled images structures Gen X with a self-conscious irony, what Generation X spokesperson Douglas Rushkoff calls "the ability to step back from direct experience and watch oneself experiencing life" (10). Rushkoff also characterizes his generation's media affair this way: "We get criticized for loving the Bradyesque imagery of our childhood, criticized again for exposing it as a naive boomer fantasy, and criticized yet again for reveling in postmodern deconstructional analysis of these images" (56). Despite the Xers' complaint that they are condemned for their "telephilia," most claim it as a signifier of their demographic sensibility, their cable-fed difference from boomer parents. For instance, author David Foster Wallace describes how television inspires many writers his age: "One might trace some of the techniques favored by many young writers to their roots in our experience as consummate watchers. E.g., events often refracted through the sensibilities of more than one character; short, dense paragraphs in which coherence is often sacrificed for straight evocation; abrupt transitions in scene, setting, point of view, temporal and causal orders; a surfacy, objective, 'cinematic' third-person narrative eye. Above all, though, a comparative indifference to the imperative of mimesis, combined with an absolute passion for narrative choices that conduce what might be called 'mood.' "[18] The Beats' search for New Vision has been inherited by the Xers, but colored by television, which the Beats hated. While there are obviously many additional factors that pinpoint how the world has changed in the past forty to fifty years, television remains the central daily difference in defining what Cecelia Tichi calls "the representations of the cognitive and perceptual acts that define a generation."[19] Television's flow has normalized the fragments of time and narrative. As each subsequent postwar generation immerses more deeply in media's many layers, it also becomes more inclined to enjoy the contradictions just below the surface created by the cathode ray.

No doubt, the desire to escape is itself a defining moment in any generation's self-identity, as is the cognitive task of mapping out the difference between the current rebellion and those that preceded it.[20] For instance, Coupland argues that what stands out about X compared to "the 20s expats in Paris, the 50s Beats, 60s Hippies, 70s Punks" is that although each fringe movement "got marketed in the end . . . X got hypermarketed right from the start, which was harsh."[21] But because the crass values of Madison Avenue have always cast a shadow on American road stories, scholars should ask if Gen X has really been hypermarketed any more harshly than any other generation. Back in 1965, for instance, John Clellon Holmes also complained about the rapid commodification of Beat rebellion: "[Beatnik] was immediately adopted by the mass media as a handy caricature for everyone associated with Beatness. . . . If you can't understand them, brand them."[22] Yet, Coupland's disclaimers against hypermarketing recall Kerouac's plaints against the universalization of television, suggesting that both spokesmen share a deep regret for losing control of the representation of their generations to the media. Because they each articulated the longing of so-called X people to escape the constraints of class, they paradoxically found themselves thrust into the role of a "lightning rod" for their generations. The writers had wanted to be bodhisattvas of the adventurous path, but once the media appropriated their images or their words, they lost control. No matter how media savvy the generation, communication networks seem to proliferate faster than the prophets do. Learning to surf the accelerated culture has thus become any postwar generation's first line of defense.

Metonymies of the Road: *Beverly Hills, 90210* Remaps Route 66

To shake off the antagonism between counterculture and mainstream culture, Xers purposefully swoosh in their Nikes through the imaginary doors of *Get Smart*—no longer trying to escape any segment of culture, but simply trying to recombine it all according to their sensibility. If life is like a movie, these young adults want to pick their own soundtracks and locations. In her memoir of driving back to the now-defunct commune on which she had been born, Chelsea Cain bridges temporal and emotional gaps through media: "I pop in the Bob Dylan tape because Dylan is who I had always imagined playing as I drove into Iowa City."[23] Generation X has thus embraced what Coupland termed the "accelerated culture" of the 1990s instead of rejecting it, like the hippies once did in moving "back to the earth" on communes.

If adolescents during the 1990s were more inclined than any previous group to stay home to watch television, they had an unusually large number of road stories to watch. These Xer road narratives contain more happy endings than those written by any other generation. Frequently, these stories purposefully remap the hippie generation's angst in a wicked conspirator's wink toward the tidy closure of television. The film about Gen X gay hookers *My Own Private Idaho*, for instance, frequently compares the road to a "fucked-up happy face."[24] In another example, one January 1995 episode of *Beverly Hills, 90210* specifically reflects upon the chronotope of the road inherited by Generation X from the hippie generation.[25] This episode depicts the now college-aged Dylan and Brandon hitting the road on motorcycles. Gushing excitedly to his anxious parents about the upcoming adventure, Brandon explains, "It's an American tradition, two old buds hitting the road. It's *Easy Rider*."[26] His businessman father looks at him quizzically and patiently replies, "Brandon, that movie ended with both riders being blown to bits." Brandon retorts with Xer attitude: "Guess that means it didn't have a happy ending, huh?" Needless to say, with Xers' ironic but utopian longings and television's narrative formulae, Brandon and Dylan end their road trip happily, after the obligatory arc of conflict and the brief rebellions against authority.

Quoting Kerouac as he tries to pick up a waitress in a roadside diner, Dylan knows his act is hype, but he sports it like a vintage shirt. (In *Generation X*, Coupland calls this type of phenomenon "O'Propriation": "The inclusion of advertising, packaging, and entertainment jargon from earlier eras in everyday speech for ironic and or comic effect.")[27] Even while knowing he can never escape representation, Brandon picks and chooses among images, symbols, texts, and sound bites in order to try to generate the desired road trip experience of transformation. Dylan retains an independent and paradoxical perch by aggressively declaring, "I read *On the Road*—I hated it. I read *The Dharma Bums;* I hated that too." Why, then, does he go on the road? To get out of the *90210* universe, to put home and friendship into perspective by distancing himself, quite literally, from the older generation (which this television show keeps in the script). In this way, Kerouac, *Easy Rider*, and the road remain important symbols of Gen X's atavistic desires, an example of "decade blending" between the now-prevailing irony and the older generations' hope for revolutionary social change.[28] In *90210,* Brandon and Dylan use information for transformation and experiment with the nostalgic notion that alienation still takes someone somewhere.

The Beat generation expressed itself metaphorically and used tropes of automobility, the heroic quest, and the search for meaning. In contrast, Generation X uses metonymy—contiguity and recontextualization—by sampling image or sound bites from the past, then remixing them into a new irreverent pastiche, united by the tape-looped beat of a drum machine. Contrast even the names of television shows like the 1960s-era road story *Route 66* and the 1990s *Beverly Hills, 90210:* the former functions as television's metaphor for traversing the nation without ties or obligations, away from the past of World War II and into the future of the New Frontier, while the latter is a metonymy signaling one affluent neighborhood in Southern California.[29] Further, "90210" mirrors the zip code-sorting technique of mass marketing. Being on the road is too slow for Xers, who rely upon the instantaneous sorting of databases instead of the time-consuming transformations created by driving from state to state.

Furthermore, so many young people have access to image-producing technology that life becomes so many frames or files of raw material that can be recombined into new forms of text, music, and image. As Sonic Youth's Ranaldo says in another poem: "all history to me / the jigsaw images / the feeling of free."[30] Hence, contemporary narratives adopt Beat or road symbols without concern for their historical context. This explains why, for instance, Brandon in *90210* doesn't care about the ending of *Easy Rider* and why Dylan quotes Kerouac without having enjoyed reading him. The message is the symbol, not its original meaning. For this newest generation of storytellers, who now download MP3 files, burn CDs, and IM their friends across the globe, a Quest or an Odyssey represent the ironic names of minivans driven by soccer moms.

Documentaries That Map the Real for Their Generation

After [driving across country,] spending thousands of hours with hundreds of people in their twenties, I am quite hopeful about this twenty-something generation. . . . The people I met seem to be waiting—not

for a hero, but also for a mission. . . . [They] see the challenges, but
they do not have a clear vision of how to overcome them.

Michael Lee Cohen, *The Twentysomething American Dream:
A Cross Country Quest for a Generation*

We were voyaging, passaging and pilgrimaging. I was bound to find
something.

Chelsea Cain, *Dharma Girl*

Even before it was so easy to own culture-making technology like MP3
and PhotoShop, plenty of Xers in the early 1990s rebelled against television network facileness and sought from television something more significant than *Beverly Hills, 90210*. Video cameras afforded Generation
X one means of image production, so PBS and then-underdog channel
MTV sometimes helped put video equipment into the hands of teens.
In particular, PBS relied upon the content provider Independent Television Service (ITVS), which had a project for young adults called "Generations," spearheaded by Lynn Kirby.

ITVS's "Generations" helped launch *The Ride*, an eight-part Gen X
documentary that takes place on the road, which debuted on PBS in
October 1994.[31] *The Ride* proclaimed itself as "anything but packaged."[32]
Produced by thirty-year-old Shauna Garr, who had worked at MTV before going independent, this vérité series was an early intervention in
the changing relationship between television, the road, and the search
for "real" experience among the younger generation. *The Ride*'s goal to
portray teenagers in a less cynical fashion than did commercial networks
resulted in the producers handing the cameras over to the teens. They
traveled by van during one summer vacation, becoming "participant observers," armed with the creative authority to shape their vérité shoot-
ing. Even before MTV had introduced *Road Rules*, this series promised
that its six teen documentarians would discover the "real 'real world' "[33]
While executive producer Garr choose the locations and had authority
over the final edit on footage, she gave the crew sweeping expressive
freedom: "I wanted something not made by and not manipulated by
adults, but *real* teen videos that adults may not even want to watch."[34]

Aged between seventeen and nineteen, the travelers—as *The Ride*'s
teens were called—interview "guides," who are teens living in the eight
cities visited: Denver, Chicago, Dayton, Philadelphia, Dallas, New Or-
leans, Albuquerque, and an Indian reservation in South Dakota. In each

location, half the travelers join up with one guide, who speaks openly to the camera about her or his life, hopes, fears, and dreams. The other half of the crew goes with another local guide, who also hosts a confessional tour of the same city, usually with a contrasting viewpoint on race, class, gender, or sexual identity. Consequently, the two stories interweave in each of the eight, half-hour segments. Guides spice up the series' spontaneous narrative by frankly contending with bulimia, homosexuality, promiscuity, arrest records, gangs, drugs, violence, and other problems that can plague young adults. In the early days of the "reality genre," these were not the types of problems shown on television, at least not with quite this much candor and this little exploitation. The complexity that results from the two contrasting guides in each segment, and the chatty comments and temperate relationships among the traveler-filmmakers, make this documentary worth watching.

Consequently, with *The Ride*, the road is reborn on television for Gen Xers as a hopeful chronotope of identity and transformation, in large part because the young filmmakers have some control over the representations. The third episode is about a fourteen-year-old guide named Maria who flirts with joining a gang in Chicago to earn money by selling drugs. In one segment, the two travelers Paula Patton and Romona Catalanello, who had been taping Maria, discuss the aesthetic and political aspects of their work. Romona says, "I'll have to say, Maria's like one of the realest people. I mean, she doesn't seem like she's putting on airs, or like putting on a show or anything." Paula responds: "I'm so glad we came here 'cause when they talk about cinéma vérité, now I know what they're talking about." The filmmaker's observations point out the preoccupation with reality that colors the rhetoric and values generated by this show, which implicitly positions itself in a more serious pedagogical and aesthetic category than either *The Real World* or *Beverly Hills, 90210*, two series also airing in 1994. Paula's pleasure at transforming the textbook formalism of cinéma vérité into lived experience draws in viewers, who learn from both travelers and guides the benefit of being on the road and interacting with strangers. As witnesses, the travelers demonstrate the construction of social meaning by ordinary people made powerful by holding television cameras. *The Ride* uses television to emphasize process rather than quick narrative closure, valuing each step of questioning, exploration, and creation, for the travelers' mistakes are not edited out of the final product. *The Ride* solicits viewer involvement and investment, not by showing people living in the fish-bowl, talk-show environment, but by encouraging self-reflection and an articulate discussion of representational choices. Consequently, the show won two awards from the National Educational Media Network in 1995, among other awards. In *The Ride,* the road trip is form and content, the space between youth and adulthood, the genre of explora-tion and self-transformation.

ITVS embraced the road metaphor as a path of life for Xers, as dem-onstrated by this passage from promotional materials for *The Ride:* "Drugs, gangs, AIDS, and economic uncertainty are just a few of the obstacles one might encounter on today's journey into adult life. *The Ride* is a series that follows some young people negotiating these roads, making choices, living up to their responsibilities and learning about their cultures, their communities and their families."[35] In contrast, the road trope in *90210* alludes to the real without demanding that anyone abandon her or his protective irony toward mass representation. *90210* makes the road the metonymy of rebellion or a symbol of nostalgic long-ing for the naïve belief in authenticity that Beats once sought. What unites these disparate shows, in other words, is that Gen X maintains its canny awareness that all experience is inexorably mediated, but *90210* does so cynically and *The Ride* does so optimistically.

Additional ITVS documentaries in the mid-1990s also targeted Gen X viewers. In 1996, ITVS distributed a four-part documentary on poetry and spoken word that used the road trip as its formal structure. Aired by PBS in February 1996, *The United States of Poetry* was made by cocreators Joshua Blum and Bob Holman, artistic director for Nuyori-can Poets Café in New York, and directed by Mark Pellington, a music video director who had also worked at MTV.[36] The crew traveled for three months, driving as a caravan across thirty-six states to film eighty-two poets.[37] Not only did ITVS reach out to Gen X audiences, but it offered an expressive outlet to former MTV producers like *The Ride's* Garr and *The United States of Poetry's* Pellington for representing the culture of youth.

Other documentary texts seeking to map the contours of Generation X in the early 1990s also used the road trip as a means of ethnography, no doubt because road travel was cost effective for young writers. For instance, Michael Lee Cohen's *The Twentysomething American Dream,* subtitled "Cross-Country Quest for a Generation," offers Cohen's analysis based on his cross-country drive. He concludes, "This nation needs the dissenters and doubters. The tension they create forces us to continually redefine the American Dream, and to reconsider the horizon toward which we are traveling."[38] Like a phoenix arising from the flames of the past, each generation goes on the road, believing it is searching for something unique.

From the Real to the Rules: Rebels without a Clue

No scripts, no rehearsals.
>   from *The Ride*'s internet promotional materials

You've been picked for the road trip you'll never forget. Survive the adventures planned for you and you will be rewarded handsomely. So empty your pockets and we'll take care of the rest. Throw out your rules; these are Road Rules.

>   *Road Rules*

The Ride's promotional materials make much the same claim—"no scripts, no rehearsals"—that producers Mary-Ellis Bunim and Jonathan Murray were simultaneously emphasizing in their popular "real life soap opera," *The Real World,* shown on MTV. Since 1992, *The Real World* was the first of the new "reality genre" television shows aimed at Gen Xers, with seven young adults selected to live in lavish pads in New York, Los Angeles, and San Francisco. In July 1995, Bunim and Murray merged their "docu-drama" format with the road story when they introduced *Road Rules,* inventing what press releases called "MTV's first docu-adventure series."[39] Murray noted, "MTV came to us and asked for a spin-off of *The Real World.* . . . We had some experience doing a show on the road during *The Real World, LA,* when we followed Tami, Dominic, and Jon across the country in a Winnebago. . . . [We added the missions to] assure us a beginning, middle, and end to each episode as well as give us something on which to hang the inevitable personal drama."[40] Bunim and Murray already had files of applicants, people rejected for *The Real World* but appropriate for *Road Rules,* from which they could cull in order to expedite their search for five cast members.

The difference between the passengers of the Winnebago on *The Ride* and those in *Road Rules* lies in who is permitted to be proactive and who is reduced to reactive roles. All the participants on Bunim and Murray's projects are referred to as "cast" and treated as talent, in contrast to the crew status of the travelers in *The Ride*. Not surprisingly, the difference between these two television road stories is as distinct as that between an educational, college-sponsored internship and a wild spring break. In 1995, Gen X became represented by large media corporations rather than Xers themselves.

At this point in Gen X representations, until 1995 when *Road Rules* was introduced, documentary was still a genre that promised to represent something real; it was a genre that was still desirable. *The Real World* was new enough as a format that it promised to be a bold evolution of vérité rather than the highly manipulative genre it has turned out to be, spawning contemporary television's *Big Brother* and *Survivor* series in 2000 and the films providing metacommentary on the genre, such as *The Truman Show* (1998) and *EdTV* (1999).[41] But by taking the cameras from the stationary living quarters of *The Real World* and putting them into the tight corners of a Winnebago, the "real" turned into an entertaining series of "reality checks," consisting of stumbling blocks (like visiting a nudist camp or jumping from an airplane) and aphrodisiacs (like drinking or driving in close quarters with flirting peers). With *Road Rules*, the road story changed, becoming dominated by MTV's "rules" rather than the idealistic "real" of the ITVS documentaries.

In his 1983 essay "The Ecstasy of Communication," which remained an influential treatise throughout the early 1990s, Jean Baudrillard called television "the ultimate and perfect object of this new era" of the simulacra.[42] Baudrillard was theorizing for older generations the phenomenon that Gen Xers also experienced, but felt no need to name. He argues that communication has transformed the world from a system of objects to one of networks consisting of feedbacks and interfaces. Decrying or resisting this fact only perpetuates the myth that there is no simulacrum, Baudrillard asserts, so it is better to celebrate the eclipse of the real than to protest against it. If the hyperreal is indeed "the map that precedes the territory," it makes sense that *90210*'s Brandon quotes *Easy Rider* without even caring about the content or that Road Rulers can't help but feed to the cameras the clichéd dramas of young adulthood.[43] Since 1995, the Gen X road genre ceased to be about the road and the epiphany experienced by a teen traveling through time as well as space, but has become focused on reworking the simulacrum of past searches, a rite rather than a passage. This simulacrum is part of every television generation, shaping the young adults' search for what was never really there except in a pixilated form. *The Brady Bunch* and *Leave it to Beaver* have stimulated Gen Xers to marvelous and witty expressions, but as simulacra, they have also changed what young adults seek when they imagine transformation.

Once a privileged location of the "real," the road in the MTV series quickly became an arena for pranks, affairs, and clues mandated by road rules. Unlike *The Ride*, the producers of *Road Rules* intervened to create tension or camaraderie between cast members by forcing them to perform for money and prizes. Whereas *The Ride* empowered teens, the Xers in the *Road Rules* Winnebago were purposely given inadequate food allowances, which encouraged them to act out for the cameras in crazy stunts, made up by producers, which would earn them enough money to eat. All the contradictions in the name "Road Rules"—the double entendre of the verb/noun "rules"—work in this play-filled manipulation of young adults' weaknesses and strengths, as Bunim and Murray create a dysfunctional "family" in which the "parents" punish and reward a cast weaned on television's simulacrum of family.

Furthermore, as is true with almost all MTV shows, producers manipulate sexual tension to create the impression that *Road Rules* cast members really are breaking away from family and becoming adults. In the first season of *Road Rules*, Allison made television history by spending the night with the mayor of Nogales, while Kit and Mark finally consummated their flirtations and started sharing the same bunk in the Winnie. No longer were young adults leaving home to escape rules but eagerly following silly requirements and outrageous demands because the "rules" sanctioned id-like exhibitionism. In "mission nine" of the first season of *Road Rules*, cast members felt invincible in performing an illegal con, spending the night in an Illinois hotel without paying for it, simply because they were being followed by a camera crew. The cast members were performers, not people who were really committing misdemeanor crimes on national television, and as expected, the camera crew bailed them out when they were caught the next day.[44]

But even in the first year of this unprecedented series, there was still room for contemplation, for this first "generation" of *Road Rules* participants was establishing the tropes that subsequent casts would inherit. Unfortunately, the format of Bunim and Murray's shows fosters stereotypes about Gen X, as when Allison of *Road Rules* says, "Our generation, Generation X as they call it, has been stereotyped as kind of lazy, unmotivated, lost. . . . Previously, people have been motivated by things more like money and success and a good career, but we're motivated by happiness. We want to find out what we're really meant to do, what's going to make us feel complete. And once we find that we can move on, and we can do more with our lives. But right now, it's not that we're lost, it's just that we're kind of searching . . . searching for what we're really all about and what life's really all about" (65). The searching of young folks is a constant, as is the need to distinguish their quest from those of their antecedents, but the ways the search is described vary considerably. Only one year earlier, *The Ride* had revered the vérité tradition and encouraged teens to think about how they represented others in their generation. In contrast, the format of *Road Rules,* which gives voice to any teen's natural solipsism and ahistoricism, doesn't support any real analysis in its preference for "docu-adventure." Like Coupland's complaint that his generation was the only one hypermarketed from the start, Allison's observation is based on feeling, not fact. Consequently, it appears clueless.

Since 1995, the sense of what's real has changed, now that reality itself has become a hypermarketed "docu-adventure" that audiences crave. The "docu-adventure" genre now has a life of its own, with *Road Rules* having just completed its ninth season, and the genre's latest incarnation, *Survivor,* delighting viewers when (older) cast members can out-manipulate the producers.

Hence we need to look, whenever possible, at the road stories controlled by Gen Xers rather than big corporations in order to see the range of concerns, quests, and questions pursued by a widely diverse group of young adults. One alternative is the memoir *Dharma Girl: A Road Trip across the American Generations,* in which Chelsea Cain seeks to situate herself with respect to older generations, rather than to break away from them altogether. Cain travels with her mother, recently diagnosed with melanoma, and immortalizes their journey taken at this turning point in their individual lives. Cain had recently graduated from the University of California at Irvine when she decided to follow her dharma—"the path to knowledge or something. It's Buddhist"—back to her childhood home in Iowa.[45] Similar to the protagonists in other Xer road stories, Cain searches and waits, but she finds what she wants without much angst, which sets her apart from both the young man desperately seeking lightning, and from the casts of *Road Rules* who want to ignite their sexuality.

By traveling with her mother, Cain finds the boundary between mother and daughter, which is tough to negotiate because her mother is dying. Cain recounts her mom driving interminably along "dark country roads with numbers instead of names" and her thirteen-year-old self whining that she wanted to go home: "And then, suddenly, she pointed off toward the horizon. Rising above a dark field, as if she conjured it, was this huge moon—a great, orange heavenly body. . . . There we were, my mother and me, out in the middle of nowhere, watching this natural phenomenon. . . . Because we had gone looking for it. Because we had driven into the dark, trusting in the experience. Because she kept driving. . . . I feel I am moving forward. I am learning" (170). By switching among remembrances of her childhood in Iowa, the road trip with her mother, and her retrospective moment of writing, Cain weaves together various chronologies with the topos of the road, thereby remapping the ancient chronotope of transformation with the gender difference of Xer women—that "can do" attitude that some young women equate with "third wave feminism," a name that distresses some older feminists.

Cain's successful journey represents a new, commonsense trajectory of Gen X women who go on the road, reminiscent of the older stories from other subcultures, like African Americans, that take place on the road.[46] August Wilson's play *Joe Turner's Come and Gone* is set at the turn of the century and features men and women who travel on the road by foot.[47] Not only do Wilson's female characters ramble as frequently as the males, but the trickster character Bynum seeks magic on the road by searching for his "shiny man." The Gen X road film *Smoke Signals* portrays the search for magic on the road as an American Indian tradition, although the magic belongs equally to the road genre, as we saw with Kerouac's Mexico.[48] Magic comes when a traveler leaves behind the known, be it the geography of home or the familiarity of ethnic sameness. However, stories that emphasize gender without romantic entailment usually narrate transformation without waiting for lightning to strike.

Andy's fantasy in *Generation X*, "The Young Man Who Desperately Sought Lightning," is retrograde in its unconscious gender politics, for it implies that liberation depends upon leaving behind not only a dead-end job but a loving woman. Xer road stories, like those of previous generations, feature male protagonists far more often than not, with notable exceptions. Lisa Krueger's first feature film, *Manny and Lo*, is about two sisters who run away from foster care.[49] They go on the road in their dead mother's station wagon while they ponder the role of mothers and children. Furthermore, gays also hit the highway more than previously, not only in *My Own Private Idaho*. For instance, director Gregg Araki has created dark, fairy tale films about gay Xers who go on the road in a search for love or lust, as in his *The Living End* and *The Doom Generation*.[50] For many road stories aimed at Generation X, however, gender is as carefully balanced as other references to identity, like race, so that viewers do not need to be diverted by the worn-out dichotomies created by previous generations. For instance, Neal Stephenson's novel *Snow Crash* envisions street traffic in a cybernetic future, and pairs the male hero, aptly named Hiro Protagonist, with a female heroine, Y.T., whose name is misinterpreted as "Whitey," thereby poking fun at the problems of race, gender, and identity all at once.[51] The politically correct balance in many Gen X road stories is refreshing compared to stories of white men searching for their dharma in cars with magical names. Gen Xers avoid old-fashioned antagonisms by creating "happy face" formulae.

The Mutations of Generation X Continue

"We'll be purchasing a pair of recreational vehicles and making the rest of the trip home by highway."
　　Jubilee perked up. "Road trip?"
　　Paige smiled broadly. "Road trip!"
　　It wasn't clear who started it, but they began to chant softly, "Road trip, road trip, road trip."

J. Steven York, *Crossroads (Generation X)*

Both music and technology changed when Kurt Cobain committed suicide in 1994 and the internet became an industry in 1995. Between 1991, when *Generation X* was published, and 1995, when *Road Rules* was introduced, the term "Generation X" became a buzzword in American media (making the cover story of *Newsweek* on June 6, 1994). Coupland asked Xers to refuse the label and instead become "monsters": "I'm thinking of millions of monster eggs out there sometime in the future, all hatching small, slimy, horned babies crawling toward some form of truth, tirelessly, en masse, waging war against the forces of dumbness."[52] But like earlier generations that caught unwanted media attention, Xers could no longer control the term nor stop it from being circulated in the vast ecstasy of networks.

The Gen X road story succeeds in the second half of the decade by using "monsters" to comment on television's power. Believe it or not, *Beavis and Butt-head Do America,* MTV's second feature film, is the intelligent offspring of the post-*Road Rules* genre.[53] Unlike the docudrama format of *Road Rules,* which confirms what Baudrillard called the simulacrum of television's "feedbacks and networks," the stupid and horny boys Beavis and Butt-head constantly comment on culture (sparing us their vapid emotions, unlike the protagonists of *Road Rules*). By the time they go on the road in 1996, they had already been seen in their regular MTV series since 1992. (The series ended in 1997.) Xers loved the series' subversive refusal to be bossed around by elders when in the early 1990s, parents became outraged about the television show's refusal to accommodate their demands that the show be less crude. By deconstructing their culture, these two dummies carve their own place in it. Like *The Ride,* Beavis and Butt-head tell the story of youngsters who have some power over their representations, no matter how stupid they are. It is worth wondering whether or not Beavis and Butt-head are the satiric Xer version of *On the Road*'s Sal and Dean, for these MTV antiheroes occupied an outlaw position in the early 1990s. By speaking back to television, they turn this path of electrons into a two-way road, the space of negotiation and—yes, even for Beavis and Butt-head—transformation, as evidenced when they "do" America.

This encroachment of "unreal" or "monstrous" comic characters in the once-"real" space of the road is the newest twist in road stories by Gen X. In addition to the cartoons produced by MTV, the road story in the late 1990s encompasses even superhero characters created by Stan Lee and Marvel Comics in the series about teenaged mutants called "Generation X," the younger generation of Marvel's grown "X-Men." As teen mutants who are nothing like youngsters in the mainstream, they live as societal outcasts at Xavier's School for Gifted Youngsters, rejected by society as being "monsters." Marvel has trademarked the name "Generation X" and all prominent characters in the series, embracing the term but mutating it to symbolize that awkward phase in the road to adulthood when teens cannot yet control and utilize their power. The first Generation X novels with the comic book X characters came out in 1997, then branched out in subsequent years with other titles, including *Crossroads* (1998) by J. Steven York. The back cover of *Crossroads* states, "The young mutants of Generation X have rented a pair of Winnebagos, and are driving across the country on their first-ever road trip. But there's more than sightseeing on their agenda, as between trips to Devil's Tower and Mt. Rushmore, they find themselves caught up in a popular antimutant radio talk show—and shadowed by a vicious terrorist with a vendetta against all mutants."[54] The Winnebago is the only common thread between Marvel's *Generation X* characters and the cast members of *Road Rules,* for even the mutants never use their super powers to perform stunts, only to help out people in trouble. One of the struggles in *Crossroads* is over the power of self-representation, as Paige (who is Husk when in fighting mode) calls in to the syndicated radio talk show that foments hate crimes against mutants. Her difficulties while on the air are due less to the fact that she is a mutant than that she is a teenager, who does not normally have enough power in society to voice her views in a public forum like Walt Norman's daily talk show. Until she learns to deal with Norman's media manipulations, Paige inadvertently becomes the hapless teen who raises his ratings. Nevertheless, she does learn to take power, even when adults manipulate her, and Marvel's *Generation X* heroes end their road trip well.

Yes, Generation X has mutated out of the control of the very people who named it, described it, and shaped it, as has been true with the creation of each generation once hypermarketers smell profit. But rather than decry this fact, rather than argue against the simulacrum, we need to see what road these representations have taken. Use any Internet search engine and see how resilient the term "Generation X" has been, especially outside the United States. One major offshoot of the Generation X movement has been heralded by the Christian youth ministry, which has a high visibility and thoughtful presence on the Web. But European young adults have built electronic shrines to Gen X with web sites that suggest Xers can find power in this label, especially when they are the ones controlling their own representations, as they can on the Internet.

Happy Endings

Who knows, my God, but that the universe is not one vast sea of com-
passion actually, the veritable holy honey, beneath all this show of personality and cruelty.

   Jack Kerouac, "Beatific: The Origins of the Beat Generation"

Coupland's final chapter is titled "Jan. 01, 2000," suggesting a link between his 1991 novel and the new millennium, our present moment in
history. Now Gen Xers have mortgages, kids, and pets, similar to the
boomers, and a new generation is rising from the flames of X culture
and being targeted by films like *Road Trip* (2000). If Generation X
needed tales for an accelerated culture, then what can we expect from
today's young generation: namely, kids who have grown up with the
Internet? Coupland's novel occupies a fascinating moment in history,
for its ironic references to American pop culture are aimed at a post-
Vietnam television generation rather than an Internet generation. In
many instances of the novel's protohypertext—its sibebar definitions
and quoted statistics—television looms large, but computers are not important. In contrast to television, MP3 or RealVideo provide the raw
material for stories created by the new millennium's cohort of young
people. This new generation will create a new breed of road stories.

   That the road remains such a powerful trope in post–World War II
narratives for young generations could not have been predicted.
Changes in concepts of identity, media technology, and storytelling alter
the nature of escape and, thus, could still mutate the road genre beyond
recognition. Under the influence of the X Generation, the road genre
travels the gamut in the 1990s from the Beat countercultural values of
the 1950s to a rejection of *Easy Rider*'s boomer angst of the 1960s to
immersion in the "ecstasy" of communication and acceleration. These
relays and references unexpectedly rely, even in the electronic age of
MTV, on the ancient chronotope of the road. What Gen X did in the
early 1990s was remap that road in the metaphors of television, cutting
and pasting the symbols of youth and reality as if they were just so much
raw material. Coupland replaced the narrative evocations of a word like
"Beat" with the more cryptic, quasi-digital *X*, a perfunctory name that
belies the profound dream of magic and happy endings. In older stories, protagonists spend considerable time on the road; in Gen X stories,
the road is more often a Winnebago "wormhole" to another galaxy, a

shortcut through time and dimension to something long sought but always misunderstood by older generations. Today, the road is the chronotope for the one bright flash of lightning, the ultimate launch pad for megatons of electronic yearnings that we experience in increasingly disembodied ways, now that cell phones, PDAs, and iMacs have created a nation of digital nomads.

In youth, we all await lightning. As we get older, we invariably find it, but we do not always recognize it, for it rarely looks like what we were expecting. Since this hope for lightning or en-lightening is constant in youth, distinguishing between the road stories of different generations becomes significant, because each remaps the road story so powerfully that the road genre seems to be born anew to each generation. In 1995, decrying the exploitation of the concept of "Generation X," Coupland advised, "Refuse to participate in all generational debates." However, he was wrong, and the road story suggests why we should not attempt the impossible dream of eschewing generational difference. For it is the form of waiting and the type of lightning we hope for that distinguishes each generation.

Notes

1. Jack Kerouac, *On the Road* (New York: Penguin, 1976), 17.

2. The Beats considered television antithetical to the road, rejecting it as a symbol of marriage, job stability, and all the constraints of class that self-respecting bohemians ran from. (See Katie Mills, "Route 66: Interstate Between the Beatnik's Road and TV's 'Waste Land,'" *Spectator: Popular Geographies: Theorizing Space, Place and the Media Landscape* 15, no. 2 [1996]).

3. Kerouac, "Lamb, No Lion," 560.

4. Lee Ranaldo, *Road Movies*, Soft Skull Press, no. 7, (Brooklyn: Soft Skull Press, December 1994), 64.

5. Douglas Coupland, *Generation X: Tales for an Accelerated Culture* (New York: St. Martin's, 1991).

6. Paul Fussell, *Class: A Guide through the American Status System* (New York: Summit Books, 1983).

7. Kerouac, *On the Road*, 276.

8. Coupland, *Generation X*, 179.

9. M. M. Bakhtin, *The Dialogic Imagination*, ed. Michael Holquist, trans. Caryl Emerson and Michael Holquist (Austin: University of Texas Press, 1981), 120, 116.

10. Chelsea Cain, *Dharma Girl: A Road Trip across the American Generations* (Seattle: Seal Press, 1996), 167.

11. Douglass Rushkoff, ed., *The GenX Reader* (New York: Ballantine Books, 1994), 120. The descriptions of home in Bruce Craven's road novel *Fast Sofa* (1993) sound like Kerouac's in *The Dharma Bums:* "The hot stomach grid with its square lawns, white

sidewalks, freeway greenbelts. . . . Algebraic apartment complexes, stairwells stacked up around fat jungle plants. The movie studios. The TV studios. The shiny corporate aeries" (Bruce Craven, *Fast Sofa* [New York: Quill, 1993], 121).

12. John Clellon Holmes, "The Game of the Name," in *The Portable Beat Reader,* ed. Ann Charters (New York: Penguin, 1992), 620.

13. Allen Ginsberg, "Television was a Baby Crawling Toward That Deathchamber," *Selected Poems: 1947–1995* (New York: Harper, 1996), 281.

14. Coupland, *Generation X,* 120.

15. Alex McNeil, *Total Television* (New York: Penguin, 1996).

16. John Balzar, "Grunge Rock's Kurt Cobain Dies in Apparent Suicide," *Los Angeles Times,* 9 April 1994, A24.

17. Quoted in Rushkoff, *The GenX Reader,* 14.

18. David Foster Wallace, "Fictional Futures and the Conspicuously Young," *Review of Contemporary Fiction* 8 (Fall 1988): 41.

19. Cecelia Tichi, *Electronic Hearth: Creating an American Television Culture* (New York: Oxford University Press, 1991), 9.

20. As Jack Kerouac observed, "The Lost Generation of the 20s . . . forms the corpus of our authority today, and is looking with disfavor upon us, under beetling brows, at us who want to swing—in life, in art, in everything. . . . The Lost Generation put it down; the Beat Generation is picking it all up again" ("Lamb, no Lion," 563).

21. Douglas Coupland, "Eulogy: Generation X'd," *Details,* June 1995, 72.

22. Holmes, "The Game of the Name," 616.

23. Cain, *Dharma Girl,* 123.

24. *My Own Private Idaho,* directed by Gus Van Sant, 1991.

25. *Beverly Hills, 90210,* "Road Episode," directed by Jason Priestly, Fox Television, 11 Jan. 1995.

26. *Easy Rider,* directed by Dennis Hopper, 1969.

27. Coupland, *Generation X,* 107.

28. In *Generation X,* Coupland defines "decade blending": "In clothing: the indiscriminate combination of two or more items from various decades to create a personal mood" (*Generation X,* 15).

29. *Route 66* was reintroduced by NBC in 1993 as a road trip conducted by two Gen X men, one of whom was the son of the original main character Buz, but the series failed after just a few episodes (*Route 66,* NBC, 1993).

30. Ranaldo, *Road Movies,* 68.

31. *The Ride,* executive producer Shauna Garr, Independent Television Service, 1994.

32. Today, the series lives on in cyberspace, on the ITVS Web site (www.itvs.org), and copies of the video can still be purchased from Select Media in New York.

33. *The Ride,* Independent Television Service, www.itvs.org/external/The Ride.

34. Howard Rosenberg, "To Learn About Teens, Go Along for 'The Ride'," *Los Angeles Times,* 1 November 1994, F9; emphasis added.

35. *The Ride.*

36. Like *The Ride,* this documentary lives on, thanks to the Internet, with a page accessible from the ITVS web site (www.itvs.org) that lists a firm still distributing video tapes.

37. Howard Rosenberg, "Poetry Carries a Big Shtick as PBS Seeks Pulse of America," *Los Angeles Times,* 12 February 1996, F1.

38. Cohen, *Twentysomething,* 307.

39. MTV press release, "MTV and Cox Communications Hit the Road This Summer with the Ultimate Road Rules Promotion," San Francisco, 17 July 1995.

40. Genevieve Field, *Road Rules* (New York: Pocket Books, 1996), 66.

41. *Big Brother,* CBS, Summer 2000; *Survivor,* CBS, Summer 2000; *The Truman Show,* directed by Peter Weir, 1998; *EdTV,* directed by Ron Howard, 1999.

42. Jean Baudrillard, "The Ecstasy of Communication," in *The Anti-Aesthetic,* ed. Hal Foster (Seattle: Bay Press, 1983), 127.

43. Jean Baudrillard, "The Precession of Simulacra," *Art After Modernism: Rethinking Representation,* ed. Brian Walis (Boston: David R. Godine for the New Museum of Contemporary Art, New York, 1984), 253.

44. Field, *Road Rules,* 56.

45. Cain, *Dharma Girl,* 19.

46. See, for instance, Zora Neale Hurston's *Their Eyes Were Watching God* (1937), about a woman who seeks the horizon (in *Novels and Stories/Zora Neale Hurston,* ed. Cheryl A. Wall [New York: Library of America, 1995], 173–333). Hurston stressed the same practical attitude about women's travels while also signifying on a famous passage by Frederick Douglass, when she wrote: "Ships at a distance have every man's wish on board. For some they come in with the tide. For others they sail forever on the horizon, never out of sight, never landing until the Watcher turns his eyes away in resignation, his dreams mocked to death by Time. That is the life of men. Now, women forget all those things they don't want to remember, and remember everything they don't want to forget. The dream is the truth. Then they act and do things accordingly" (175).

47. August Wilson, *Joe Turner's Come and Gone* (New York: New American Library, 1988).

48. *Smoke Signals,* directed by Chris Eyre, 1999.

49. *Manny and Lo,* directed by Lisa Kreuger, 1996.

50. *The Living End,* directed by Gregg Araki, 1992; *The Doom Generation,* directed by Gregg Araki, 1995.

51. Neal Stephenson, *Snow Crash* (New York: Ballantine Books, 1992).

52. Coupland, "Eulogy," 72.

53. *Beavis and Butt-head Do America,* directed by Mike Judge, 1996.

54. York, *Crossroads,* back cover.

Bibliography

Bakhtin, M. M. *The Dialogic Imagination.* Edited by Michael Holquist. Translated by Caryl Emerson and Michael Holquist. Austin: University of Texas Press, 1981.

Balzar, John. "Grunge Rock's Kurt Cobain Dies in Apparent Suicide." *Los Angeles Times,* 9 April 1994, A1.

Baudrillard, Jean. "The Ecstasy of Communication." In *The Anti-Aesthetic,* ed. Hal Foster. Seattle: Bay Press, 1983. 126–134.

———. "The Precession of Simulacra." In *Art After Modernism: Rethinking Representation,* ed. Brian Wallis. Boston: David R. Godine for the New Museum of Contemporary Art, New York, 1984. 253–82.

Beavis and Butt-head Do America. Directed by Mike Judge. MTV. 1996.

Beverly Hills, 90210. "Road Episode." Directed by Jason Priestly. Fox Television. 11 Jan 1995.

Big Brother. CBS. Summer 2000.

Cain, Chelsea. *Dharma Girl: A Road Trip across the American Generations.* Seattle: Seal Press, 1996.

Charters, Ann, ed. *The Portable Beat Reader.* New York: Penguin Books. 1992.

––––––. *The Portable Jack Kerouac.* New York: Viking, 1995.

Cohen, Michael Lee. *The Twentysomething American Dream: A Cross-Country Quest for a Generation.* New York: Dutton, 1993.

Coupland, Douglas. "Eulogy: Generation X'd." *Details,* June 1995, 72.

––––––. *Generation X: Tales for an Accelerated Culture.* New York: St. Martin's, 1991.

Craven, Bruce. *Fast Sofa.* New York: Quill, 1993.

The Doom Generation. Directed by Gregg Araki. 1995.

Easy Rider. Directed by Dennis Hopper. 1969.

EdTV. Directed by Ron Howard. 1999.

Field, Genevieve. *Road Rules.* Produced by Melcher Media. New York: Pocket Books, 1996.

Fussell, Paul. *Class: A Guide through the American Status System.* New York: Summit Books, 1983.

Ginsberg, Allen. "Television was a Baby Crawling Toward That Deathchamber." In *Selected Poems: 1947–1995.* New York: Harper, 1996.

Holmes, John Clellon. "The Game of the Name." In *The Portable Beat Reader,* ed. Ann Charters, 615–22. New York: Penguin Books. 1992.

Hurston, Zora Neale. *Their Eyes Were Watching God.* 1937. In *Novels and Stories/Zora Neale Hurston,* ed. Cheryl A. Wall, 173–333. New York: Library of America, 1995.

Independent Television Service. www.itvs.org.

Kerouac, Jack. "*Beatific:* The Origins of the Beat Generation." 1958. In *The Portable Jack Kerouac,* ed. Ann Charters, 565–73. New York: Penguin Books, 1992.

––––––. "Lamb, No Lion." 1958. In *The Portable Jack Kerouac,* ed. Ann Charters, 562–65. New York: Penguin Books, 1992.

––––––. *On the Road.* 1957. New York: Penguin Books, 1976.

The Living End. Directed by Gregg Araki. 1992.

Manny and Lo. Directed by Lisa Kreuger. 1996.

McNeil, Alex. *Total Television.* Fourth edition. New York: Penguin, 1996.

Mills, Katie. "*Route 66:* Interstate Between the Beatnik's Road and TV's 'Waste Land.'" *Spectator: Popular Geographies: Theorizing Space, Place and the Media Landscape* 15, no. 2 (1996): 23–33.

MTV press release. "MTV and Cox Communications Hit the Road this Summer with the Ultimate *Road Rules* Promotion." San Francisco: 17 July 1995.

My Own Private Idaho. Directed by Gus Van Sant. 1991.

Ranaldo, Lee. *Road Movies.* Second edition. Soft Skull Press, no. 7. Brooklyn: Soft Skull Press: December 1994.

The Ride. Executive producer Shauna Garr. Independent Television Service. 1994. www.itvs.org/external/The_Ride.

Road Rules. Executive Producers Mary-Ellen Bunim and Jonathan Murray. MTV Television. 1995.

Road Trip. Directed by Todd Philips. 2000.

Rosenberg, Howard. "To Learn About Teens, Go Along for 'The Ride.'" *Los Angeles Times,* 1 November 1994, F1.

––––––. "Poetry Carries a Big Shtick as PBS Seeks Pulse of America." *Los Angeles Times,* 12 February 1996, F1.

Route 66. CBS. 1960–64.

Route 66. NBC. 1993.

Rushkoff, Douglas, ed. *The GenX Reader.* New York: Ballantine Books, 1994.

Smoke Signals. Directed by Chris Eyre. 1999.

Stephenson, Neal. *Snow Crash.* New York: Bantam, 1992.

Survivor. CBS. Summer 2000.

Tichi, Cecelia. *Electronic Hearth: Creating an American Television Culture.* New York: Oxford University Press, 1991.

The Truman Show. Directed by Peter Weir. 1998.

Wallace, David Foster. "Fictional Futures and the Conspicuously Young." *Review of Contemporary Fiction* 8 (Fall 1988): 36–49.

Wilson, August. *Joe Turner's Come and Gone: A Play in Two Acts.* New York: New American Library, 1988.

York, Steven J. *Generation X: Crossroads.* New York: Berkley Boulevard Books, 1998.

The Apocalypse Will Be Televised

Electronic Media and the Last Generation

Andrew Klobucar

For the founders of Lead . . . or Leave, an organization formed within the younger American middle classes in response to a growing sense of their own social and economic displacement, current threats to existing levels of social security in the United States demand an equally current agenda of reform. Relegating the more explicit methods of political demonstration associated with the radicalism of the 1960s to historical obsolescence, these activists note, "a generation that reads *Details* and *Spin*, watches *Melrose Place, Seinfeld,* and *The Simpsons,* and waits in line for the StairMaster after work is probably not going to be taking to the streets with guns or Molotov cocktails anytime soon."[1] This is not to suggest that contemporary protesters have simply become politically ambivalent, for as one writer is quick to point out, "just because we're not prepared to die to eliminate the national debt or wipe out poverty doesn't mean we can't get involved in changing the country and protecting our future."[2] Lead . . . or Leave has not been active since 1996— its demise at the beginning of Clinton's second term simultaneously signaled the success of their calls for deficit reduction and their subsequent obsolescence as Generation X's voice of neoliberal social critique. By 1996, the Democrats had, in fact, slashed the deficit by 50 percent just as Lead . . . or Leave had previously challenged them to do. Basing their activism in specific issues of reform without wider ideological analysis, the group remained particularly vulnerable to the ever shifting winds of political attention. Currently, one of Lead . . . or Leave's founders, Jon Cowan, has found new success in attracting media attention with more topical issues like gun safety, albeit while still declaring national debt "an affront to family values."[3]

To instill upon their generation a better, more active engagement with the various political and historical forces currently shaping the American social order, the Lead . . . or Leave activists realize, above all, the importance of outlining a practical agenda of social reform, one that responds directly and logically to the contemporary political environment. Specifically, these writers tend to emphasize a more indirect, private approach to protest, encouraging "personal choices as well as group actions." As one writer declares, the decision "to use a 10-year light bulb . . . to reduce energy consumption" can be considered just as politically significant as a civil rights protest given the proper context.[4]

The basis for what appears to be a set of reduced political aims for social renewal compares well to increases in the degree of social consensus operating throughout the United States. When the Lead . . . or Leave activists critique the American status quo for not adequately addressing the national economic interests of an entire generation, few wider ideological issues enter into the discussions. Conveying primarily a concern for improved political representation, the Lead . . . or Leave movement is not interested in defining a new project or even legitimating a new perspective on power. Rather, contemporary conflicts push toward integration, calling for more central authority and social sharing. This interest in participation stands in marked contrast to many earlier movements of social protest. Past activisms focused attention on the explicit construction of a new order.

Demonstrations in the 1960s for progressive, democratic reform, such as the Berkeley Free Speech movement or the many nationwide protests against the Vietnam War envisioned a wider, more socially connected agenda for political reform. These earlier struggles saw themselves as expressions of a larger force of class and labor suffrage seeking to liberate itself from the rigid territorializing regimes of antidemocratic oppression around the world. When Leftists, student activists, and malcontents alike critiqued political repression and subjugation, their efforts accentuated a deterritorialized process of social liberation, one that threw open the doors of history with its broad claims of agency and revision. Contemporary activisms offer radically different conditions of liberation.

From behind the barricades of "Revolution X," protests against social inequity remain focused on specific fiscal policies, not wider political trends. Even the terms "Republican" and "Democrat," for this reason, are usually absent from the arguments of Lead . . . or Leave. Participants in such social demonstrations are asked to disregard party or ideological affiliation for a more localized concentration on the issues at hand. For the members of "Revolution X," social reform is no longer dependent upon the full participation of a new political subject, but rather the concentrated efforts of different, specialized representatives. All over, the terms of revolution have become decidedly less seditious.

Popular U.S. commentators, both liberal and conservative, continue to paint the last decade in American history as a particularly positive one, emphasizing not only the collapse of the cold war and end of Soviet totalitarianism, but the resurgence of the U.S. economy in general. Since 1995, the United States has been ranked by the Geneva-based World Economic Forum as the world's most competitive state. This distinction, however, comes with several other related qualities of a more questionable nature. By the end of the 1990s, the United States could boast of being first in the widening income gap between rich and poor.

Despite what many would label a clear demise in labor conditions across the country, the United States still popularly typifies the most progressive, flourishing economy in the world. Consistent increases in its GDP (Gross Domestic Product) have continued to signify to policymakers, economists, international agencies and the media robust economic health and well-being. Since 1973, the GDP has risen almost 60 percent. Again, though, such statistics tell only half the story. Not only does a rising GDP say little about actual income distribution, it ignores the social problems of being too dependent upon foreign assets, while treating both the depletion of national income and increases in environmental pollution as gains.

A picture of pure growth remains the primary image behind the GDP, inspiring, in turn, a generally positive view of U.S. society. Across the country, the media present a very unified sense of social consensus, a representation that has also had a profound effect on most forms of social activism over the same period. The intense ideological effort to maintain such consensus is perhaps more evident today after the

economic and political correction of the so-called new digital technol-
ogy-based economy in the spring of 2001. The very subject of labor and
revolt has changed profoundly. With the industrial working class facing
smaller, less prominent roles in most contemporary economic analyses
and political movements, traditional views of industrial labor struggles
have all but disappeared from the public mind. Consequently, activists
no longer seem to possess the same transnational, ideological concerns
that dominated social movements less than forty years ago. Protests such
as the May 1992 revolt in Los Angeles and the 1994 uprising in Chiapas
remain based on immediate regional concerns, rather than on any wider,
globally translatable labor or class struggle. The efforts uniting these
different disputes, if they can be considered at all related, are those of
social exclusion and lack of political representation. Hence, their overall
objectives may draw inspiration from historical movements in suffrage,
yet their immediate aims are fairly limited in political and economic
scope.

Similarly those working with Lead . . . or Leave continue to emphasize a pragmatic perspective in their agenda, expressing a will to negotiate with the state rather than transform it. Again, the emphasis in their
critique is on social inclusion and not wide-scale reformation. Repudiat-
ing both in theory and practice all extreme forms of social activism, Lead
. . . or Leave "accepts the basic political and historical precepts behind
the development of the postwar state. Regardless of what side of the
ideological spectrum they lean toward, most theorists and participants
in the movement accept the general aims and objectives of liberal capitalism, viewing them as the best schema for social freedom. Indeed,
previous subideological differences between the right and left wing
branches of bourgeois thought have all but eroded, revealing a new post-
partisan relationship between the governing and governed classes. As
with most revolts of the last decade, few of the political aims of "Revolution X" extend beyond the limited local concerns of their immediate
sociocultural interests. Further, such consensus prevents these movements from seriously disrupting the ongoing expansion of the postwar
order.

The growth of social consensus within the liberal capitalist state has
provoked many social theorists to reconsider the complex relationship
between modern Western cultural identities and sensibilities and the
global advance of capitalism. Throughout the twentieth century, revi-

sionist studies in Marxism, socialist theory, and even anarchist thought revealed the profound connection between the evolution of Western social consensus and consumer capitalism. The Italian Marxist philosopher Antonio Gramsci argued within the interwar period that the development of bourgeois liberalism yielded a new form of political hegemony, one that functioned at an almost transideological level within society. For Gramsci, the maturation of capital relations involved its steady transformation from a market framework to a more complete, socially comprehensive system of beliefs. As these relations grew beyond nation-state structures and institutions, Gramsci argued, a new cultural ethos based upon precision, routine, specialization, conformity, and discipline emerged.[5] Further, the evolution of such relations would continue to limit the possibility of informed social reflection, marginalizing all intellectual critique and opposition. Characterizations of this type of consensus continue to dominate revisionist Marxist critique as it has through most of the century. Juridical idealism and natural right theories, formalism and systematism can each describe some aspects of it. For example, natural right theories can highlight values of peace and political compromise, while systematization emphasizes the totalizing character of the social process. These are thus the qualities of hegemony and modern authority that form the crux of later Marxist critiques of the Western state where more emphasis upon immaterial critique than social protest is quickly apparent. In Herbert Marcuse's *One Dimensional Man,* for example, modern human relations are resituated with respect to a complex "technological rationality," in which capitalist ideology becomes infused with historical and social content.[6] The impact of this rationality, according to Marcuse, seriously undermines oppositional thought and action, blocking any potential for fundamental social change, while diminishing the role of intellectuals.[7]

Louis Althusser offers a similarly intricate view of ideology and its traditional limits as a model for political authority in the advanced industrialized capitalism of the contemporary West. The question he addresses moves a step ahead of the classical Marxist interest in the relations of production in order to address what he calls the "reproduction of the conditions of production." Every social formation, Althusser writes, must, in order to exist—in order to continue to exist—"reproduce the conditions of its production at the same time as it produces, and in order to be able to produce. It must therefore reproduce: (1) The productive forces; (2) The existing relations."[8] This is guaranteed, he continues, "by giving labor power the material means with which to reproduce itself: by wages—that is, in fact, how it 'works.' "[9] In other words, the industrialization of production means the reproduction of the submission of labor power, a factor that guarantees new forms of ideological subjection within the state itself.

One of the most powerful forms of subjection, Althusser notes, is through ethical persuasion, where the necessary motivations and social values for production are replicated in tandem or even prior to the labor conditions themselves. The growing moral dimension of liberal capitalism appears clearly in many Marxist studies of contemporary Western political economies. As well, most liberal theorists of economic and ideological changes in the West appreciate the strong ethical nature of modern social development, as can be seen in James Livingston's analysis of American consumer culture and its economic origins in the industrial revolutions of the late nineteenth century, *Pragmatism and the Political Economy of Cultural Revolution.*[10]

Like most revisionary Marxists, Livingston, too, holds that the industrialization in America between 1850 and 1940 produced a corresponding transformation in social relations, specifically in the development of a cultural logic based almost exclusively in the mass consumption of industrial goods. Livingston's study continues to investigate this sensibility, theoretically associating it with the simultaneous emergence of intellectual pragmatism as well as contemporary liberal thought.

In his description of the postindustrial consumer society, Livingston manages to isolate several important aspects of the new cultural relations exemplified by Generation X. In many ways, Livingston's notion of pragmatism parallels the diminished terms of intellectual opposition described by critics like Althusser and Gramsci. Most specifically, when Livingston qualifies the relationship between consumer culture and industrial production as an unprecedented social ordering, distinguished primarily by its strong social consensus, many of his points are relevant to the new moderate reformism expressed by groups like Revolution X. In both cultural developments, a strong subjectivism, that is the subjection of the individual to social forces, dominates one's vision of social agency. Coupled with this subjectivism is a corresponding emphasis on issues of social exclusion and regional suffrage. When "Revolution X" organizes social action, it is careful to follow conventional political mechanisms and procedures, rather than waging forms of radical transgression. Such respect for political protocol, according to Livingston, has practically defined American labor relations since the industrial movements of the late nineteenth century. The establishment of a "consumerist ethos," he writes, enabled the United States to avoid some of the more politically extreme movements of social unrest experience by European nation-states at this time: "Modern Industry reduces the labor-time required for the production of finished consumer goods by installing complex machines where simple tools and craft traditions had sufficed; but it expands output and continues to develop only by enlarging that proportion of the labor force which is engaged in the production of those machines and their inputs in the form of raw materials (e.g., coal, iron ore), intermediate goods (e.g., rolled steel), and services (e.g., railroad transportation). So conceived, industrialization is a social process that implicates greater amounts and kinds of labor in production that is preparation for production. . . . It enforces a mechanization of production that enlarges the domain of socially necessary labor even though it reduces the labor-time necessary to produce a given quantity of finished consumer goods."[11] As industrialization began to affect social relations by redefining them as potential sources of labor, Livingston reasons, not only was the corporate sector able to expand exponentially, but a more stable political economy quickly emerged with fewer labor disputes and hence, lower labor costs.

Although not Marxist in any sense of the word, Livingston's study of consumer capitalism emphasizes the predominant tendency in corporate industry to affect an ever wider and more diverse proportion of society. Further, his understanding that labor unions help stabilize and thus promote capitalism's growth resonates with Gramsci's earlier analysis of Fordism and its response to collectivism within labor. As Livingston points out, advanced capitalism exchanges a process based entirely upon production and distribution with one that is primarily organizational in its social function.[12] One witnesses here, in a manner reminiscent of Foucault, the significant emergence of the industrial corporation as a primary model of social control. Livingston summarizes, "the corporation was a means to the ends of reinstating the cultural salience and enlarging the social significance of relations of production."[13] From within these relations there emerges a new culture of consumption, an actual "sensibility" derived, in part, from the social values and morality associated with industrial progress and technological advance. For Livingston, this type of corporate-based order represents an entirely new basis of human relations, one centered in the articulation and satisfaction of material desire.

Livingston describes how corporate capitalism has also affected the development of American subjectivity in the last century. Again, the confluence of capitalism, western ideologies, and the evolution of subjectivity is an important point of study throughout revisionary Marxism. Both Althusser and Gramsci take steps toward formulating a radical sociology of the subject in their analysis of capital. In particular, Althusser understands the evolution of subjectivity within the modern state as part of a larger social formation in which, not just the conditions of production, but also the "reproduction of the conditions of production" continue to inform all industrial labor relations.

Livingston, too, offers a sociological view of industrialization that stresses its development as a cultural sensibility or logic over its economic functions. He considers how technological and industrial characteristics such as efficiency, control, and material satisfaction can end up as human norms, distributed across nearly every mode of human interaction within the modern state.

As discussed earlier, Althusser provides some valuable insights into these processes, specifically in his studies of ideology and the formation of ideological state apparatuses. Yet Livingston, avoiding a strictly Marxist sociology, is not interested in critiquing subjectivity as a social function of the relations of production. Rather, he considers capitalist ideologies as just one aspect of a wider, more general rationality or sense of logical coherence and legitimacy. Subsequently, the shift in cultural orientation described in his reading of corporate capitalism contains few explicit ideological elements. In Livingston's study, cultural relations and the constant evolution of Western subjectivity stand out as parallel formations to industrial production. Hence, when Livingston speaks of "cultural" or "literary" events, he describes them structurally as discourses, operating in an analogous manner to each other as well as to most economic formations, yet not as specific attributes of any one social configuration. Implied in his view of culture, therefore, is a vision of human society that appears inherently systematic or rational even prior to the development of corporate capitalism.

Much of Livingston's sociology is clearly neostructuralist in view of its systematic aspects. A more Marxist examination of his perspective, however, would likely interpret it as strong evidence of the corporate rationalization of American intellectual work in general. Here, too, Althusser's work on ideology and Gramsci's critique of hegemony is very useful in tracing historical changes in cultural relations without referencing any form of larger, structural, yet immaterial rationalism. Seeking to "rediscover" the inherent social value of past "cultural events" without reference to the ideological forces informing their historical context, Livingston runs the critical risk of unconsciously reinscribing the industrial organization of modern society within some sort of moral or idealistic schema. Livingston's history is certainly rationalized. His defense of liberal capitalism's continued expansion is that it offers a nonaggressive schema of social organization, especially when compared to the many totalitarian movements of the twentieth century. The cultural logic of liberal capitalism prioritizes cooperation over antagonism and negotiation over antipathy. If there are examples of difference or variance to be found within the cultural movements Livingston traces in his study, they are not sources of conflict, but rather points of exclusion or improper representation. Cultural struggle, he suggests, is not a part of liberal discourse. In other words, not only is it unacceptable, it is barely comprehensible.

Paralleling the logic behind social activisms such as "Revolution X," what Livingston outlines in his criticism is not the appearance of a new form of sociocultural struggle, but the emergence of a different quality of social movement altogether. In Livingston, one sees the fundamentally new characteristics of most contemporary social discourses, whether actively reformist or not, present. No longer relevant is the past revolutionary tradition of the nineteenth and early twentieth centuries, which overtly sought to blast and disrupt the "weakest link" of imperial oppression. The postrevolutionary world and its social relations display, instead, only a superficial inclusiveness, and in fact, remain drastically disconnected and decentered, offering few clear links or points of disorder. Hence, today's struggles provide neither a clear revolutionary tactic, nor even seem able to conceptualize these types of strategies.

Livingston's analysis of liberal capitalist relations is important as it describes carefully how American culture has developed a unique capacity to influence social conduct and behavior with less and less recourse to specific legislative functions. The beginnings of this shift in culture stand out especially in his readings of American naturalism. Looking at Theodore Dreiser's novel, *Sister Carrie*, for example, he stresses how its ethical deliberations are delivered independent of any type of moral fable or parable. Such implicit social commentary, he notes, has always appeared in the more progressive narratives of contemporary popular culture, including even certain television sitcoms like *Seinfeld* or *Murphy Brown*. Neither program offers strong moral content, yet the social values conveyed are commonly seen as forward thinking and just. What possible social worth does a program like *Seinfeld* have to offer contemporary audiences, especially when even the show's creator, Jerry Seinfeld, accepts that its content and themes are literally "about nothing"? Apparently much, if one follows Livingston's study of naturalism and accepts that viewers from a variety of backgrounds and classes do not need explicit moral codes in order to strongly identify with the characters and subjects appearing within it.

Althusser's study of ideology also emphasizes its advanced capacity to structure all types of social or historical content and even influence the political construction of language as an important device of legitimation within the modern state. In any class society, he argues, "ideology is a representation of the real, but [is] necessarily distorted . . . biased and tendentious—tendentious because its aim is not to provide men with *objective knowledge* of the social system in which they live but, on the contrary, to give them a mystified representation of this social system in order to keep them in their 'place' in the system of class exploitation."[14] Here, Althusser differs in his conception of ideology from classical Marxist thought; he concludes that all ideology is illusion, not just the ideology of the bourgeois classes. As a system of representation, ideology's purpose is to guarantee, in every type of society, the relation of individuals to whatever tasks their social totality may define and promote. It is not, therefore, a system of knowledge, though it may appear as one. As well, ideology does not necessarily provide explicit moral instruction as classical Marxism usually maintained.

The attempt by earlier twentieth-century Marxist movements to replace the dominant (capitalist) ideology with a proletarian one may have provided, Althusser argues, oppressed classes with a stronger political consciousness of their own positions within society, yet such struggles, though often morally based, did not guarantee an objective social or economic theory. Certainly, the domination of bourgeois ideology can be challenged—even successfully—by proletarian ideology. It would be a mistake, however, to view these challenges as deriving from scientific or knowledge-based enlightenment. Shifts in ideology, Althusser believes, constituted primarily an exchange of social illusions, that is, one system of representation and its corresponding set of social relations for another.

What is interesting about Althusser's approach to ideology (as well as other revisionary Marxist approaches) is the obviously expanded conception of social structure and control that emerges. Althusser's correlates representation, illusion, and social power to reconfigure traditional moral positionings within culture. These positionings then become a type of class phenomenon comparable to all other symbolic indications of social value. As such, the representation of cultural legitimacy within society can take on a variety of forms, many of them echoing Livingston's own sense of American naturalism. Naturalist narratives, for Livingston, are supposedly more legitimate than explicit moral instruction, presenting an advanced, liberated mode of social subjectivity. Again, though, Livingston's view of this shift in American subjectivity as a revolutionary change in society from a unified, ultimately confining epistemic position to a progressively democratic, decentered one does not certify, for Althusser, an objective social evaluation.

A profound modification in class struggle and social advancement has occurred throughout the West, according to Althusser, but the setting of these changes has remained confined to the structure of ideology. Transformations in industrial technologies and the liberal capitalist economy have effected profound alterations in the social representation of class structure, though not necessarily in the relations themselves. This is how desires for social change and uprisings can occur within contemporary political states independent of the language necessary to strategize and express such struggles. The symbolic mystification of social relations within contemporary liberal capitalism simply does not allow it. The more explicit revolutionary struggles begun through past ideological movements appear, at least at the level of representation, increasingly irrelevant, often even inexplicable.

The most obvious and recent changes in ideological sensibility—and thus in the social representation of class structure—derive from developments in digital technology and the corresponding emergence of a new information-based economy. Few analysts disagree that the evolution of digital media and high tech industries represents a pattern of labor and economic restructuring on par with the emergence of liberal consumer-based capitalism over a century ago. The widespread effect of digital processing on almost all areas of production can scarcely be overlooked as an important phase of industrialization. Again, it is in the area of ideology and cultural relations that such economic changes appear most evident. Comparable to Livingston's reading of American naturalism, the cultural rationale that has developed around and through this information-based economy has fashioned a highly integrated, rationalized approach to language and social conduct.

As Livingston's study shows, contemporary cultural models of interaction based upon values of compromise, negotiation, and organic legitimacy appear earliest in the naturalist movement within American art and writing. A similarly rationalized sense of communication and social exchange is even more evident in the aesthetics of digital production—a form of "cybernetic naturalism" in which culture appears as an ordered system, accessible to all of society, and hence, a culture to which all language use must inevitably conform.

Perhaps the most prominent example of the technical application of communication systems can be found in the construction of hypertext media. As defined by Ted Nelson in the 1960s, hypertext functions as a nonsequential writing composed of autonomous graphic nodes, each one containing some amount of text or other information.[15] The nodes are connected by predirected links, which in turn are singularly attached to some specific part of the node called an anchor. Although ultimately an elaborate system of information storage, many hypertext aficionados and theorists alike remain convinced that such technology provides the most accurate reproduction of human conversation sequences ever conceived. According to Susan H. Gray, the notion of language presented in hypertext models is consistent with most linguistic studies made in modern psychology.[16] The fact that the paradigm of language common to basic cognitive science perspectives appears reproducible within a certain branch of information technology suggests to Gray that modern engineering has successfully reconstructed a "natural" linguistic process in human conversation. For example, the cognitive science model of language use known as "spreading activation" presents the linguistic functions of the brain as a "spider-web" of interconnected data points. Communication occurs, according to this model, when a series of pre-linked points on this web are concurrently activated. Such a paradigm, this study maintains, explains why certain images or words are consistently grouped together by various subjects in the course of everyday speech. Because a hypertext appears to function similarly, that is, as a network of linked points of information, a sense of cognitive realism or naturalism becomes quickly attributed to this new technology. Gray notes that though the linguistic frameworks provided by cognitive science can often appear too positivist in their methodology, they strongly emphasize the underlying social elements affecting all language use. Central to these models, Gray maintains is an understanding of "text as a social construct, hypertext being both a mechanism and a model for alternate social constructions of meaning or texts. This is the essence of nonlinearity as applied to online systems. Without the ability to socially construct the text, the actor becomes too constrained to perform as anything other than an automaton."[17] Gray uses the terms "web" and textual "navigation" metaphorically in order to affirm a certain orderliness in all human relations, while simultaneously avoiding the constricting abstractions that permeated earlier social schemas. Hypertext models of language present contemporary sociolinguists like Gray with a new paradigm of social coherence, one that stresses a less mechanistic, more viscous interpretation of human interaction.

Similar to Livingston's study of liberal capitalism and its effect upon subjectivity, the hypertext "revolution" in information systems ostensibly articulates further changes in America's and the West's cultural sensibility. Gray clearly associates the hypertext system with a very organic, naturalist approach to knowledge, contrasting it with other, more abstract concepts.[18] Within a naturalist framework, the production of information, she writes, retains its status as an interactive, communicative act and not as some type of unified, fixed system. Gray is not alone in believing that such structures mimic actual social relations, which follow, in general, a less linear or uniform coherence. An authentic representation of social behavior and conduct appears to be functioning for many sociolinguists within hypertext frameworks.

George P. Landow qualifies hypertext technology as a more organic writing system, devoid of the restrictions of past cultural hierarchies and hegemonic canons. Landow declares, "in this ideal text, the networks are many and interact without any one of them being able to surpass the rest; this text is a galaxy of signifiers, not a structure of signifiers; it has no beginning; it is reversible; we gain access to it by several entrances, none of which can be authoritatively declared to be the main one; the codes it mobilizes extend as far as the eye can reach, they are indeterminable."[19] For Landow, the newer electronic methods of organizing texts and text linkages appear as more than just another technological novelty: they constitute an entirely reformed basis of knowledge, one that better approximates, in his words, a "freer, richer form of text . . . truer to our potential experience."[20]

Like Gray, Landow also notes the significant social connections between techno-industrial developments and the specific social relations and behaviors informing such production. His work on hypertext explicitly locates a close and remarkably visible relationship between certain modes of cultural production and the manner of subjectivity engaging with these modes. Here, too, there is a naturalism at work. As in Livingston's work, cultural production displays a formal correspondence between a society's institutions and its subjective experience of them. To this end, both authors qualify this correspondence with reference to its legitimacy, where certain schemas for organizing knowledge are accepted as more naturalistic or organic than others. In describing the hypertext format, Landow consistently draws the reader's attention to its nonlinear, artless qualities. Contrasting electronic texts to books and other analogue forms of information storage, Landow suggests that the new media can even be qualified as a type of "non-system" due to its unique feature of "constant inter-reference."[21] Hence, not only does the development of hypertext technology represent an entirely new paradigm of writing, its seamless, nonsystemic features suggest a more legitimate relationship to actual social relations and forms of subjectivity.

The resulting information networks and changes in cultural production are not without their political components; they evoke a much less hierarchical, more loosely structured social order. For Landow as well as Livingston, such changes reflect a more progressive shift in contemporary liberalism. For others, like sociologist Richard Merelman, the "loosening" of American relations, results primarily in widespread social disruption and a profound "weakening" of past American "cultural codes."[22] Contrasting the current decentered social order with traditional American liberalism, Merelman notes, "Loose-boundedness turns individualism into a consumption-oriented, morally flexible, uncertain cultural course, whereas liberalism makes of individualism a highly efficient, rigid, productive, purposeful force."[23]

In effect, Merelman affirms Livingston's own reading of the changing terms of American liberalism, describing contemporary social frameworks as less ideologically and politically conscious. It is clear, however, from Merelman's conception that the shift in individualism "from the realms of politics and the economy to the realms of the social and the personal" entails a corresponding decrease in social authority.[24] Without the ideological identities of left or right, political agency is rendered ineffectual at best.

In Landow's vision, the widespread liberal rejection of past ideological structures for a more fluid sense of epistemology and social position implies in all a superior form of individualism. Landow writes, "all hypertext systems permit the individual reader to choose his or her own center of investigation and experience. What this principle means in practice is that the reader is not locked into any kind of particular organization or hierarchy."[25] Missing in Landow's critique of hierarchy, however, is a more refined understanding of ideology as a mode of representation, rather than as an explicit intimation of political and economic struggle. To compare, as Althusser does, notions of legitimacy with ideological authority is to recognize within liberal capitalism the specific forms of symbolic domination necessary to ensure "class oppression and guarantee . . . the conditions of exploitation and its reproduction."[26] There is little that is natural with respect to legitimacy and its measure within society. Its function is to help guide subjectivity into accepting and following prescribed social roles. Any naturalism associated with such arrangements remains, thus, an effect of their ongoing reproduction throughout the state via media that is both technically possible and available. Clearly, technological advancements in these modes of reproduction can help further naturalism's effect, especially since it is so strongly dependent on them. For Althusser, the Web and hypertext in general would have represented liberal capitalism's most efficient mode of reproduction yet devised. Landow's own perspectives on the technical and social capabilities of this new medium provide some of the grounds behind this observation: "As readers move through a web or network of texts, they continually shift the center—and hence the focus or organizing principle—of their investigation and experience. Hypertext, in other words, provides an infinitely re-centerable system whose provisional point of focus depends upon the reader, who becomes a truly active reader in yet another sense. One of the fundamental characteristics of hypertext is that it is composed of bodies of linked texts that have no primary axis of organization. In other words, the metatext or document set . . . has no center."[27] The hypertext reader or "surfer" as subject has no notion whatsoever of his or her class position, save for the knowledge that they have the immediate capital necessary to engage with the technology at hand. The illusion of dialogue is innate to the medium itself, evoking the widespread existence of an unseen, yet powerful network of ongoing production. Despite the omnipresent quality of this network however, the possibility of symbolic confrontation has been effectively nullified, given each user's respective distance and de-centered location from any specific point of reference, cultural, political, or otherwise. The operating system itself is interpreted as a neutral medium of assemblage with little inherent value, save for providing a new framework for self-expression.

For Landow, such a relationship between system and user, between writer and reader, represents a climactic moment in the development of a truly democratic social order. Literary critic J. Hillis Miller argues similarly that Internet "technologies are inherently democratic and transnational . . . help[ing] to create new and hitherto unimagined forms of democracy, political involvement, obligation, and power.[28] Bereft of the authorizing influence of a single "metatext" or explicit legislative code, the responsibility of conscious intention shifts entirely to each individual reader. Little can be evaluated or judged as unacceptable since the medium or network, itself, remains hardly coherent enough to provide a reliable platform from which to establish any serious social position. Even the most ideologically violent movements on the Web, such as white supremacy or neo-Nazism, appear within an online context as mere blocks of information to be dealt with as individual readers may wish, however few of them there are. Much like the Los Angeles riots of 1992, social conflicts within Internet communities remain easily localized and contained, allowing all other unaffected networks of exchange, even those sympathetic to the conflict, to continue without disruption.

For this reason, the most serious threats to the sociocultural institutions and networks of the Internet are neither ideological nor even moral critiques of content, but rather the disruption of online service itself, as exemplified by the menaces of hacking or electronic viral infection.

Similar to the manner in which the Taylorist division of labor and Fordist automation effectively broke down worker solidarity a century ago, online information networks appropriate intellectual workforces and reform what technological capacity and scientific literacy they possess to further the aims of liberal capitalism. In a classic instance of what Paul Virilio terms "endocolonisation," the security network apparatuses, nominally facing outward to defeat external foes, is turned against the "enemy within."[29] Throughout the last quarter century, both the corporate sector and the apparatuses of government increasingly adopted technologies previously nurtured by the military in its quest of battlefield control—microelectronics, computer-mediated communications, video recording, expert systems, artificial intelligence, robotics—now adapted and diffused to provide a similar scope of overview and precision intervention in the workplace and civil society.

Thus the neoliberal sensibility operating throughout the contemporary industrialized West is supported by a whole new level of intensity and sophistication in the governmental use of information technologies. In this new and social framework, capital supports not just production, nor even the reproduction of labor, but the entire form of life. To be socialized is to be made productive, and to become a subject is to be made a subject of value—not only as an employee, but also as a parent, shopper, student, and home worker, in short, as an audience in communicative networks. The demarcation between the production, circulation, and reproduction of capital is dissolved in a network of various, highly differentiated, yet confluent mechanisms "that mixes in new and indefinite labor all that is potentially productive" so "the whole of society is placed at the disposal of profit.[30]

In one of the more influential works on postwar media developments, Marshall McLuhan notes that old "forms of being" tend to become newly visible "just as [they] reach their peak performance, much like the way sound waves become visible on the wings of the plane . . . just before [it] breaks the sound barrier."[31] Revealed, then, by the fragmented, decentered networks of contemporary liberal society, both online and off, are perhaps the last traces of civic agency just prior its apocalyptic redundancy within the new naturalism of global culture.

Notes

1. Rob Nelson and Jon Cowan, *Revolution X: A Survival Guide for Our Generation* (Toronto: Penguin Books Canada, 1994), 8.

2. Ibid.

3. Douglas Pike, "Going into the Red Again: Our Rising National Deficit is a Dirty Trick on Our Children," *Philadelphia Inquirer,* 4 June 2002.

4. Ibid., 10.

5. Antonio Gramsci, *Selections from the Prison Notebooks,* ed. and trans. Quintin Hoare and Geoffrey Nowell Smith (New York: International Publishers, 1971), 291.

6. Herbert Marcuse, *One-Dimensional Man* (1964; reprint, Boston: Beacon Press, 1991), 146.

7. Ibid., 151.

8. Louis Althusser, "Ideology and Ideological State Apparatuses," in *Lenin and Philosophy and Other Essays* (London: New Left Books, 1971), 161.

9. Ibid.

10. James Livingston, *Pragmatism and the Political Economy of Cultural Revolution, 1850–1940* (Chapel Hill: University of North Carolina Press, 1994).

11. Ibid., 101–2.

12. Ibid., 102.

13. Ibid., 97.

14. Louis Althusser, "Theory, Theoretical Practice and Theoretical Formation: Ideology and Ideological Struggle," in *Philosophy and the Spontaneous Philosophy of the Scientists,* ed. G. Elliott (London: Verso, 1990), 62.

15. Ted Nelson, *Literary Machines* (Swarthmore, Pa.: self-published, 1981), 49.

16. Susan H. Gray, *Hypertext and the Technology of Conversation* (Westport, Conn.: Greenwood Press, 1993), 5.

17. Ibid.

18. Ibid., 6.

19. George P. Landow, *Hypertext: The Critical Convergence of Contemporary Critical Theory and Technology* (Baltimore: John Hopkins Press, 1992), 3.

20. Ibid., 6.

21. Ibid.

22. Richard M. Merelman, *Making Something of Ourselves* (Berkeley: University of California Press, 1984), 25.

23. Ibid., 33.

24. Ibid., 33–34.

25. Landow, 13.

26. Althusser, "Ideology," 171.

27. Landow, 11–12.

28. J. Hillis Miller, "Literary Theory, Telecommunications, and the Making of History," *Conference Papers from the International Conference of Scholarship and Technol-*

ogy in the Humanities, sponsored by the British Library, the British Academy, and the American Council of Learned Societies (Elvetham Hall, England, May 1990), 20.

29. Paul Virilio, *The Vision Machine* (London: British Film Institute, 1994), 43.

30. Ibid., 44.

31. Marshall McLuhan, *Understanding Media: The Extensions of Man* (Toronto: New American Library of Canada, 1964), 12.

Bibliography

Althusser, Louis. "Ideology and Ideological State Apparatuses." In *Lenin and Philosophy and Other Essays.* London: New Left Books, 1971.

————. "Theory, Theoretical Practice and Theoretical Formation: Ideology and Ideological Struggle." In *Philosophy and the Spontaneous Philosophy of the Scientists,* ed. G. Elliott. London: Verso, 1990.

Boggs, Carl. *Intellectuals and the Crisis of Modernity.* Albany: SUNY Press, 1993.

Gramsci, Antonio. *Selections from the Prison Notebooks.* Edited and translated by Quintin Hoare and Geoffrey Nowell Smith. New York: International Publishers, 1971.

Gray, Susan H. *Hypertext and the Technology of Conversation.* Westport, Conn.: Greenwood Press, 1993.

Landow, George P. *Hypertext: The Critical Convergence of Contemporary Critical Theory and Technology.* Baltimore: John Hopkins Press, 1992.

Livingston, James. *Pragmatism and the Political Economy of Cultural Revolution, 1850–1940.* Chapel Hill: University of North Carolina Press, 1994.

Marcuse, Herbert. *One-Dimensional Man.* 1964. Reprint, Boston: Beacon Press, 1991.

McLuhan, Marshall. *Understanding Media: The Extensions of Man.* Toronto: New American Library of Canada, 1964.

Merelman, Richard M. *Making Something of Ourselves.* Berkeley: University of California Press, 1984.

Miller, J. Hillis. "Literary Theory, Telecommunications, and the Making of History." *Conference Papers from the International Conference of Scholarship and Technology in the Humanities.* Sponsored by the British Library, the British Academy, and the American Council of Learned Societies. Elvetham Hall, England, May 1990.

Nelson, Rob and Jon Cowan. *Revolution X: A Survival Guide for Our Generation.* Toronto: Penguin Books Canada, 1994.

Nelson, Ted. *Literary Machines.* Swarthmore, Pa.: self-published, 1981.

Pike, Douglas. "Going into the Red Again: Our Rising National Deficit is a Dirty Trick on Our Children." *Philadelphia Inquirer,* 4 June 2002.

Virilio, Paul. *The Vision Machine.* London: British Film Institute, 1994.

Conclusion

Generation X X

The Identity Politics of Generation X

Andrea L. Harris

Culture is what we make it Yes it is
Now is the time
To invent
   Sleater-Kinney, "#1 Must-Have"

The attention paid to Generation X in the mass media in the 1990s puts
a new spin on the much-debated topic of identity politics. Generations
now appear to be the privileged way to categorize and define identity.
But much of this generational debate looks at age to the exclusion of
other cultural characteristics that mark people and that have become
increasingly important as categories of analysis in the wake of feminism
and critical race studies. This blindness to cultural difference is especially problematic with regard to Generation X, since this is the most
racially and ethnically diverse generation to date, as well as the first
generation to grow up in the light of the civil rights, women's, and gay
and lesbian liberation movements. This blindness is also problematic
given that much of Generation X culture, particularly music, also goes
by the label of "alternative," and yet this music is produced and con-
sumed by predominantly white, male, heterosexual, middle-class youth.
Indeed, the very term " 'alternative' youth (sub)culture," as in the title
of this volume, more or less signifies white male youth, a group that
seems more mainstream than alternative when compared to the women
of this generation.

In this essay, I shall discuss the identity of Generation X with regard to two factors ignored in most of the discourse surrounding this term so far—gender and sexuality—as a way to open up the question of the identity of Generation X in the broadest sense (that is, beyond those factors that may indeed affect an entire generation such as economics and social upheavals). If we fail to look at Generation X from this wider perspective, we will homogenize a very heterogeneous group. While some of the articles in this volume address issues of gender and sexuality (primarily the essays by Neil Nehring, Catherine Creswell, and Jim Finnegan), these terms of analysis are not the central focus of any of the essays. Although second wave feminism introduced gender into mainstream cultural discussions, it seems that thirty years later women are still a separate issue that must be addressed as such and that Generation X discourse replicates the by now familiar marginalization of women in American culture. Quite a few volumes have been published since 1994 on third wave feminism, however, and I will turn to several of these as well as to mid-to-late 1990s music by young women in order to suggest why the term Generation X fails to designate the more feminist women of this generation.[1] Rose Glickman's ethnographic study *Daughters of Feminists* and Barbara Findlen's *Listen Up: Voices from the Next Feminist Generation* present the views of feminist young women on everyday life in the 1990s, while the women writing in Eric Liu's *Next: Young American Writers on the New Generation* approach issues from a more conservative standpoint.[2] Leslie Heywood and Jennifer Drake's *Third Wave Agenda: Being Feminist, Doing Feminism* brings together academic and personal writing on a range of issues.[3] Robin Stevens's *Girlfriend Number One: Lesbian Life in the 90s* is a lighthearted collection of performance pieces from a lesbian-owned performance space.[4] The music of Hole from the mid-1990s and of Sleater-Kinney from the late 1990s and early 2000s provides an interesting counterpoint to the nonfiction texts. Much of this work by women is explicitly marked by gender and sexuality, particularly through the use of strategies of feminist critique and resistance. Hole's music, for example, revolves around themes of alienation and violence, especially violence against women, and the prevailing tone of these songs is one of explosive rage. While such subjects and moods also mark the music of Nirvana, for example, there is a profound difference in the two bands' focus on such subjects: the negativity of Hole's music is very much a product of gender oppression, not economic misfortune or self-willed marginalization. Generation X women's music employs several strategies of resistance that mark it as unique: Courtney Love's performance of femininity is highly ironic, and Sleater-Kinney combines razor-sharp feminist critique with explicit resistance strategies. Finally, the work of Generation X women as a whole is political in a way that male-authored Generation X work is not. That is, these Generation X women delineate a political critique of and resistance to the consumerist, misogynist American culture that typifies the end of the last century.

In examining 1990s youth culture from the perspective of the politics of gender and sexuality, I argue that we need to rethink our use of the concept of the alternative, which implies choice, and replace it with the concept of the marginal, which implies exclusion against one's will. Further, the so-called alternative position of 1990s white male youth culture is in fact a position appropriated from the truly alternative or marginalized of American culture—women, African Americans, lesbians and gays, and the poor. From this position—the culturally marked position of the marginal—a more authentic and radical questioning of dominant culture is already being made.

The Third Wave and Generation X

Just as there was a publishing boom in Generation X anthologies in the mid-1990s, so there was a similar boom in third wave feminist anthologies at the same time.[5] In examining the divergence between Generation X and third wave feminism, or the marginalization of women in Generation X discourse, the study *Daughters of Feminists: Young Women with Feminist Mothers Talk about Their Lives* (1993) by Rose Glickman is useful, since it involves interviews with Generation X women themselves. Of the texts I'll discuss here, Glickman's work presents one of the more mainstream portraits of this generation. The back cover blurb suggests that the book counters Generation X discourse: "[The book] vividly demonstrates the inadequacy of facile media oversimiplifications about the women of Generation X."[6] The author interviewed fifty women from four geographical areas in the United States whose mothers self-identified as feminist throughout their daughters' childhoods. The author herself is a second wave feminist mother of a Generation X daughter. Although Glickman attempts to present a wide-ranging and diverse sample of women, these differences get lost in the shuffle and the picture we're left with is primarily white, heterosexual, and middle-class. The book uses ethnography to examine the impact of feminism on young women's lives when it comes from a seemingly direct source—one's mother, and in some cases, one's father. Among these women, feminism is alive and well, but it's a very different kind of feminism than that of the second wave. And yet, the younger women take feminism for granted in a way that their mothers and many women before them could not. This tendency to take the political struggles of the past for granted sounds a lot like apathy, which is a frequent criticism of Generation X youth.

First, some examples from Glickman's book. When a young woman named Nina is asked by her mother why she and other members of her generation are letting the women's movement drop, Nina answers, "Complacency," and this same reason is offered by a number of daughters. Some of the daughters point the finger at other women (160). Yet others attribute this complacency to contemporary attitudes, and here some generational thinking comes into play. Rita explains, "The advances for women made a huge leap when my mother and the women of her generation were fighting for them, like in the awareness of sexist laws . . . it's not that way now, and it is totally depressing. It's not that women are apathetic or that they have slacked off. It's that society's mind-set has changed" (161). Several of the third wave women also refer to socioeconomic factors when explaining their disinterest in feminist activism and the women's movement. Given the tight economy and the increasing difficulty of finding and keeping well-paying jobs, many things have to go and activism is one of them. A woman named Ingrid defends herself in this way: "Group work takes a lot of time and energy. . . . It's hard to get from one week to another. If it wasn't such a struggle to make a living and get through life day by day, we might all have more energy for the overall ideals" (162). While it's easy to empathize with this position, it's also easy to be reminded of slacker apathy here. One of the daughters seems to anticipate this response when she says women have not "slacked off"; rather, the times have created such widespread apathy.

The rhetoric of individualism also plays a large role in how these women formulate their views of feminism. The women share the idea that one's sphere of influence is narrow and that it's best to stay firmly within that sphere. Not surprisingly, it's the private sphere—always marked feminine—that is being invoked here. The daughters speak of changing their boyfriends, not sex roles; their bosses, not the workplace; their own behavior, not the behavior of others. One woman, Adrienne, gives the following advice: "You do it from the ground up. . . . From inside your own little family—like with the one man whose mind you can change—or the company you work for, changing the minds of the people around you" (182). Glickman seems as distressed by this attitude as I am. Here, she discusses the women's responses to pornography: "The daughters opt for the long, slow haul, for the private rather than the public approach. Get your own relationships in shape! Educate your own boyfriends! And they have another word for women as well: get your own act together" (179). That is to say, if you're a sex worker, stop being one; if you're in an oppressive relationship (battering as such is not mentioned), get out of it (154).

When the rhetoric of individual choice is put in the service of such glib dismissals of the very real, very material oppression of women, it is time to question this rhetoric seriously. Of course, individualism has its roots in American culture long before the women's movement of the 1970s. I'm far too familiar with this line of thinking because it is a common thread that unites so many of my students, despite their various backgrounds and political affiliations. But should we attribute this emphasis on individual choice (and thus, individual responsibility) to adolescent invincibility, Generation X apathy, or the American way? While it is difficult to sort out these causes, sorting out the results proves to be easier. Claiming that the individual is entirely responsible for the condition of her life makes it very easy to blame the victim of sexual harassment in the workplace rather than her boss, the perpetrator ("Get a new job!" I imagine these third wavers saying) or to blame the working mother who comes home to the second shift of housework ("Get a nicer husband who'll babysit!" I imagine these women saying). To what extent is feminism responsible for this tendency to blame the victim? If these daughters were all "raised feminist" to some degree, isn't feminism part of the mix? Where does it fit in? I think some of this emphasis on individual choice comes from the feminist rhetoric of empowerment, which the daughters frequently invoke (often lamenting that they missed out on the collective empowerment that benefited their mothers greatly). The daughters of feminists, and to some extent, most young women today, grew up with a different sense of possibilities than their mothers did. I'm constantly reminded of this by my students. Part of this is the sense of their own capability: as Glickman summarizes, "When I ask the daughters whether there is anything they cannot do because they are women, the answer is a resounding no" (67). This kind of optimism is heartening but also disheartening because it omits a large part of the picture—the material realities of women's lives. We only need look at the daily paper to see that women's so-called choices are still severely limited by tenacious traditional sex-roles, legal barriers, and institutionalized misogyny. In some cases, a woman can only achieve certain things, such as be awarded tenure, work in a harassment-free environment, and so on by suing for gender discrimination.

What creates this sense among women of the third wave that women's possibilities are absolutely unlimited? As Glickman notes, and as many other writers have, "The women's movement triumphantly elevated female 'personal' experience from the unworthy and the trivial to a high level of importance in the culture. The issues may often be distorted, co-opted, and reviled, but they are discussed on talk shows and on the editorial pages of large and small newspapers. . . . Women's issues have become part of the public discourse in our time" (188). Indeed they have, but being part of public discourse does not guarantee change. Race relations have been part of public discourse in the United States for hundreds of years, and yet racism surrounds us still. Now that sexism is also part of everyone's vocabulary, how much better off are we? These days, much lip service is paid to the need to avoid sexist language and behavior, but it seems to me, as it does to many of the women Glickman interviewed, that sexism operates in much more subtle forms now; it has simply gone underground, where it may be harder to detect, much less to root out. One of the daughters calls this "insidious fake feminism"—a useful phrase—and cites TV sitcoms and advertising that "convey the message that 'it's kind of OK for women to have careers and families as long as they're still 'feminine' and don't threaten men'" (163). Being the daughter of a feminist has helped this woman to spot sexism when she sees it. The mainstreaming of feminism and women's issues has gotten us very far, but it's also a stumbling block if it blinds women of the third wave to the ongoing oppression in many women's lives.

Despite my frustration with Glickman's subjects' views of feminism, these women are at least aware of their position in society on some level, which is not the case with the Generation X women whose work appears in *Next: Young American Writers on the New Generation.* Most of the selections by women in this gender-integrated volume are distressingly conservative, and as a result, this volume for me represents Generation X women's discourse at its most mainstream. For example, this volume includes an argument that it's the job of feminists to make feminism palatable for young women (Paula Kamen, "My Bourgeois Brand of Feminism"); a celebration of the return to 1950s style dress and court-ship rituals that comes down squarely on the side of individualism (Karen Lehrman, "Flirting with Courtship"); and an attack on so-called victim feminism that seems strongly influenced by Katie Roiphe's book *The Morning After* (Cathy Young, "Keeping Women Weak"). Consider the following passage from "My Bourgeois Brand of Feminism," the essay on mainstreaming feminism for the consumption of the young. Kamen laments the fact that the word "feminist" has such negative con-notations that many young women refuse to identify themselves as femi-nist despite their support of equality for women (the "I'm not a feminist, but . . ." problem).[7] Kamen recounts the responses she received when interviewing young women about their associations with the word "femi-nist": "I imagine: bra-burning, hairy-legged, amazon, castrating . . . bunch a lesbians . . . man-haters, man-bashers" (84). The list goes on for ten or so lines, and Kamen sums it up by saying, "I guess you get the picture." The picture she wants us to get is that we'd all want to avoid the label feminist since it calls up such dreadful associations. Instead of the familiar feminist gesture of reading the misogynist implications behind such stereotypes, Kamen, like the Generation X women she in-terviews, buys into the backlash that is fueled by such stereotypes. In other words, she advocates the cleaning up of feminism, not a critique of and resistance to a dominant culture that continues to portray femi-nism as deviant. This passage exemplifies a disturbing inversion of con-cepts and strategies that were generated by feminists of the second wave.

The anthology *Listen Up: Voices from the Next Feminist Generation,* edited by Barbara Findlen, former managing editor of *Ms.* magazine, by contrast, has an unquestionably feminist outlook. The collection pre-sents a serious assessment of feminism from a new standpoint, for a new era. The range and quality of the writing in the volume is impressive. In an interesting parallel to the Glickman book, one author, Ellen Neuborne, the self-described "child of professional feminists," describes her increasing awareness of "sexist programming," even in herself.[8] She cautions that "it is a dangerous thing to assume that just because we were raised in a feminist era, we are safe. We are not. They are still after us" (31). She is able to critique the second wave but does not dismiss it, as do the conservative women writing in *Next*. Nor does she become mystified by the notion of empowerment as in *Daughters of Feminists*. Neuborne critiques the cerebral, abstract quality of so much second wave thinking on equality and calls for more concrete, action-oriented feminism. She sees this as especially necessary given the relative mainstreaming of feminism of which all third wavers seem quite aware. The writers' overall sense of material reality is much stronger in *Listen Up*, and a greater emphasis is placed on concrete resistance strategies and activism. White women explore body image in essays on bulimia, fat oppression, and feminist aerobics teaching; a Korean American woman analyzes the women's movement's continuing failure to adequately deal with difference; and women speak out on experiences of disability, racism, the effects of rape, and what it means to live with AIDS.

Unlike the women discussed in Glickman's book, the women whose essays are included in *Listen Up* do represent a very broad spectrum of backgrounds and cultures. Findlen addresses these differences specifically in her introduction, in which she links the feminist recognition of difference to the disunity attributed to Generation X.

Generation X, 13th generation, twentysomething—whatever package you buy this age group in—one of the characteristics we're known for is our disunity. . . . Even in eras that offer unifying forces more momentous than *The Brady Bunch*, each individual's personal experiences define the time for her. Women's experiences of sexism are far from universal; they have always been affected by race, class, geographic location, disability, sexual identity, religion and just plain luck. How patriarchy crosses our paths and how we deal with that can also be determined by our families, school systems, the degree and type of violence in our communities and myriad other factors. So what may appear to be a splintering in this generation often comes from an honest assessment of our differences as each of us defines her place and role in feminism. (xiii)

For me, this passage indicates that second wave feminist thinking is still relevant and still influences young women today. Findlen's gesture of recognizing and celebrating difference owes itself to years of feminist work on precisely this issue. While the failures of feminism in this area are notorious, here is a sign of some success: perhaps the third wave not only exists, despite media accounts that feminism is dead, but is actively working to achieve the most important goals of feminism, such as the recognition of differences of all kinds.

Leslie Heywood and Jennifer Drake position their essay collection *Third Wave Agenda: Being Feminist, Doing Feminism* as picking up where Rebecca Walker's *To Be Real* and Findlen's *Listen Up* left off, and this seems to be a fair assessment. One focus of the volume is the media's preoccupation with conservative feminists such as Katie Roiphe, Naomi Wolf, and Camille Paglia, who are frequently consulted as the only true spokespeople for feminists.[9] Carolyn Sorisio's "A Tale of Two Feminisms" deals critically with these media darlings, as do the two pieces by the editors ("Introduction" and "We Learn America like a Script"). A major contribution of this collection is the attention paid to terminology: what exactly is the third wave beyond a generational designation for feminists born from the early 1960s to the early 1980s? Here are some of their answers: "we define feminism's third wave as a movement that contains elements of second wave critique of beauty culture, sexual abuse, and power structures while it also makes use of the pleasure, danger, and defining power of those structures."[10] Heywood and Drake go on to write, "In the current historical moment, then, third wave feminists often take cultural production and sexual politics as key sites of struggle, seeking to use desire and pleasure as well as anger to fuel struggles for justice" (4). The editors repeatedly acknowledge debts to the second wave and negotiate many of the same issues. They also write with a genuine awareness of multiculturalism in the discussion of culture at large as well as in feminist culture in particular. Although United States feminism has been divisive to its own detriment, particularly in reference to race and sexuality, the editors describe women of the third wave as working to create a feminism that "strategically combines elements" of such disparate bodies of thought as equity feminism, women-of-color feminism, and pro-sex feminism (3). The result of this return to feminisms of the past is the "development of modes of thinking that can come to terms with the multiple, constantly shifting bases of oppression in relation to the multiple, interpenetrating axes of identity, and the creation of a coalition politics based on these understandings" (3). While the essays in this volume take on key issues of mainstream Generation X discourse, such as the poor economy and male popular culture figures such as Henry Rollins, the editors' pieces are quite critical of what passes for an inclusive Generation X discourse (47–48). In particular, they critique "the Gen-X portrait of the artist as a bored young man" (48), an important yet frequently overlooked feature of this discourse. In the face of the bleakness of contemporary American life, the editors and contributors do not recommend mute acceptance, or a detached, ironic stance, as is so often the case in Generation X writing. Rather, they speak of the ongoing and diverse political work undertaken by women of this generation: "Many young cultural workers from a wide variety of communities are making these connections, building coalitions, and positioning themselves as participants in the ongoing history of radical thought and action. Refusing to panic about the complexity of public life and public dialogue in the contemporary United States, these third wave activists approach American culture as multiculture; hybrid, creole, made and remade in dialogue and conflict" (51). Finally, in this distinct emphasis on political activism and resistance to the dominant culture, *Third Wave Agenda* is a welcome addition to the literature by Generation X women.

Although *Listen Up* and other books on the third wave attempt to include writing by lesbians and bisexual women, the focus is typically on heterosexual women. Happily, the mid-1990s also saw the publication of a lesbian Generation X anthology entitled *Girlfriend Number One: Lesbian Life in the 90s,* edited by Robin Stevens and published by a small women's press, Cleis Press of Pittsburgh. The essays originated as performances at Red Dora's Bearded Lady, a "dyke-owned and run café and performance space" in San Francisco.[11] Like many of this generation, the writers define themselves against previous generations, in this case, against 1970s lesbian feminists. Many of these comparisons are implied: in one case, the editor points out that the focus of the performances wasn't coming out, but "How do we cope?" (9). Despite the volume's grounding in 1990s lesbian culture, Stevens claims kin with Generation X at large, writing "we are the lesbians of *Generation X,* continuing defiantly to celebrate our lives in a pessimistic age" (9, emphasis in original). Stevens also describes the film *Slacker,* directed by Richard Linklater, as a prototype of Generation X in general and lesbian Generation X in particular: *Slacker* "captured the anti-mood of our age. . . . It is Linklater's landscape, infused with popular culture, conspiracy theories, and information overload, that the lesbians of Generation X inhabit" (9). In another parallel with mainstream Generation X culture, the text does not have the average size and shape of a paperback, much like Douglass Coupland's 1991 novel *Generation X,* as pointed out by G. P. Lainsbury in his essay in this volume. Like that novel, *Girlfriend Number One* includes plenty of visuals: pages are adorned with graphics from comics, flyers advertising lesbian bars (21), and buttons from activist groups like the Lesbian Avengers (130). The essays in the volume are all explicitly lesbian, and are largely concerned with relationships, particularly break-ups. The tone of individual pieces ranges from the romantic (Achy Obejas's "Wrecks") to the comic (Penny D. Perkins's "What is a Lesbian Date?" and the parodic (Martha Baer's "Theories of Lesbianism: From Freud to Moi"). Lesbianism is decidedly a way of life rather than an issue for these writers, hence the 1990s focus on "how to cope?" as opposed to the 1970s focus on coming out as mentioned above. The book is a fun read. It emerges from a hip, urban, educated lesbian world, and assumes a lesbian audience that comes from that same world.

Feminism on Stage: Hole and Sleater-Kinney

Although Courtney Love's persona has undergone a major overhaul in the past five years, her mid-1990s Hole persona was so powerful that it still lingers in the imagination, at least the imagination of this fan. Love is now a full-blown sell-out, but she characteristically anticipated and troped this selling out in her most recent album, *Celebrity Skin.*[12] Courtney Love's position as the Generation X poster girl seems fitting since her husband, Kurt Cobain, has been designated the prophet of his generation, particularly after his 1994 suicide. Love's music employs various strategies of resistance that mark it as unique: first, her performance of femininity is highly ambiguous and ironic; her hyperbolic expression of anger is used in a transformative way; and, at the same time, understatement serves to underscore the acuteness of women's despair in other songs.[13]

In addition to her music and lyrics, Love's self-presentation requires commentary. Love's "kinder-whore look" received a good deal of press: even if you don't know Hole's music, you may very well know that Love's uniform in the mid-1990s consisted of pastel baby doll dresses, black lacy slips, deep red lipstick, bleach-blond hair, and high-heeled Mary Janes. This mixture of children's attire, punk style, coy femininity, and brazenly sexual femininity revolves around hyperbole and paradox. Love's aesthetic was a punk aesthetic with a feminine spin, which provides an interesting contrast to the so-called grunge look of certain male Generation X musicians. The latter was a very masculine uniform, although this gender coding was rarely noted: the flannel shirt, ripped jeans, cardigan sweaters, and general scruffy naturalness of Cobain could not have been more different from the highly stylized, made-up artifice of Love.

Love's feminine exterior appears to be a deliberate strategy. In an interview in *Rolling Stone,* Love explains how her baby doll look began and how it was appropriated by young women in a way that she finds disturbing: "When I see the look used to make one more appealing . . . it pisses me off. When I started, it was a Whatever Happened to Baby Jane thing. My angle was irony."[14] As Love points out earlier in this interview, irony and sarcasm are her standard modes of expression, yet she is always read literally: "The fact that people don't realize I'm sarcastic—*yet.* I'm still insanely amazed by this" (66, emphasis in original). The very hyperbole of her gestures, her appearance, her lyrics, and her stage presence does indeed seem enough to alert her audience to the fact that she's being ironic, but the public has a persistent blind spot about this. While Love's feminine good looks mask her explosive style, her blunt lyrics, and her rage, none of these seem to go unnoticed, whether she looks good or not. In fact, it seems that her exceedingly feminine persona with its odd combination of sexuality and innocence is more confrontational than anything, and as such, it attracts a good deal of attention. Love's appearance is as discordant as the contradictory remarks she makes about it, and the same discord exists between her good, ultrafeminine looks and her rage. A further discordant note emerges in the responses to her appearance in the music press and by fans: she is reviled for being ugly as much as she is lusted after for being beautiful, which is a common dilemma for women.

Love's femininity is a double-edged sword. Her simultaneous invocation and critique of our standard notions of womanhood resembles the strategic move of the masquerade as analyzed by feminist theorists from Joan Riviere to Luce Irigaray and Judith Butler.[15] Masquerade involves a self-conscious putting on of feminine traits, which draws attention to the unnaturalness of femininity—the fact that it is constructed and artificial, not natural. Love's use of femininity as masquerade is evident in a bit of cover art and text that appears on the "Doll Parts" single. The text consists of an obsessively detailed description of a woman's negligee: "dreamy peignoir set in cloud soft blue nylon and snowy white lace, pale blue ribbon tie holds the peignoir at Empire waist, pretty pink bedroom scuffs knocked against the plumbing below the sink as he held her up and the only sound was Niagara Falls, later she dreamed of the apocalypse on a pale satin pillow with lace edging."[16] This passage, which is nearly free of punctuation, zeroes in on a woman's attire during a scene of lovemaking (or rape) that takes place, perhaps, on the woman's honeymoon ("the only sound was Niagara Falls"). The "dreamy," soft, pastel, pretty image is tainted by the description of her shoes knocking against the pipes in unison with the man's movements against her. The woman's state of mind afterwards is also "dreamy" in a sense, but what she dreams of is "the apocalypse." As is typical of Love's writing and self-presentation, there is a jarring contrast here between the emotions evoked. Most importantly, the woman's femininity seems somehow bound up with her violation.

Love explores the same terrain through her lyrics as she does through her appearance—the dilemmas of femininity in a culture that denigrates the feminine. Again, Love's strategy is not to reject or move beyond gendered norms but to multiply and proliferate signs and emblems of femininity. Her lyrics are a compendium of references to the female body, female desire, and female identity and are filled with female rage, anger, and critique. Two songs that exemplify Hole's feminism are "Violet" and "Doll Parts" from the 1994 release *Live Through This*.[17]

The lyrics to "Violet" are allusive, not explicit. The speaker of the song refers in various ways to being stripped of her possessions, or perhaps her soul, through the unspecified actions of another, a generic "they." In the chorus, Love sings, "they get what they want, and they never want it again." Someone, presumably a man or men, takes something valuable from the woman, but once he has this thing, its value diminishes. This is hardly startling. Love describes a familiar heterosexist scenario in which women and their bodies are traded like objects, but presenting it from the women's perspective as a violation or robbery makes it powerful. After it is taken, the speaker/owner more or less gives up her ownership: "Go on, take everything, take everything, I want you to." The lack of direct referents in the lyrics to this song lends it power while leaving nothing unclear: it is easy to infer that the woman is "taken" sexually, which amounts to a loss of power and a loss of self. The video depicts a gendered scenario, as is always the case with Love. We see female performance of various kinds: shifting scenes of women as ballerinas, artists' models, strippers, and lastly as rock stars being passed through the crowd at a show. In other shots, men are positioned as spectators who watch, or peep, as well as controlling the lights and the camera (the old bearded man who appears a few times seems to be running the camera in a cinema or peep show).

A superficial reading of "Violet" might say that it glorifies stripping or the objectification of the female body, but such a reading is only possible if we entirely overlook the last few shots where Love, in close-up, lashes out at her own body in frustration and anger while singing the final chorus and if we overlook the lyrics' expression of anger and futility. Again, Love's mode is feminist critique—she indicts a culture that not only supports an incredibly lucrative pornography and prostitution industry, but also uses images from these industries in advertising, primetime television and film. Her indictment is a very material critique of the degradation suffered by women who strip for a living, as Love herself once did.

The song "Doll Parts" also raises the issue of the degradation of women. Love as a musician and as a person is obsessed with dolls: Love's dress is called the "tarnished baby doll" look; her early bands were named Sugar Baby Doll and Sugar Babylon; Love also collects dolls and doll accessories. During Hole's *MTV Unplugged* appearance in 1994, the stage was strewn with many old and tattered baby dolls. What is behind this fascination? Certainly, dolls are symbols of femininity as well as being the exclusive domain of young girls according to dominant cultural values. But Love takes this connection between women and dolls and pushes it as far as it can go: dolls are not women; rather, women are dolls. In the video (shot in sepia tones like parts of "Violet"), the camera cuts back and forth between two scenarios: Love in a baby doll dress, looking demure while playing guitar on a bed and Love walking in a bleak backyard and passing a children's table set for a tea party. The camera rests on various old, decrepit dolls that lie about. The song begins, "I am doll eyes / Doll mouth, doll legs," which calls to mind the image of a woman who is beautiful, small, and artificial like a doll. This allusion, which may be appealing or repulsive depending on your perspective, is then magnified in the next line, which is gruesome: "I am doll arms, big veins, dog bait." Later in the song, this gruesomeness escalates even further: "I am doll parts / Bad skin, doll heart." The monosyllabic words delivered slowly in this dirge-like song drive home the bluntness of the metaphor—women are dolls. The woman's exterior surface is a mere collection of dismembered plastic parts but her heart is that of a doll's as well, meaning of course, that her heart is gone, for we all know that dolls are hollow on the inside. Similarly, "Violet" focuses on being robbed of one's identity and soul (one line reads "And I'm the one with no soul") by being appropriated as a spectacle for the male gaze. Being not simply a doll but the dismembered parts of a doll, the epitome of the objectified female body, has a dramatic effect on the woman in the song: she cries out her pain. The chorus, with which the song closes, seems to me to be the crux of the song: "I fake it so real I am beyond fake / And someday, you will ache like I ache / Someday, you will ache like I ache." Here, Love herself hints at her strategy of critiquing feminine cultural norms through masquerade. She plays the part of doll, of woman, so well that she is "beyond fake," that is, she becomes real. But there's a high price to this expertise at female impersonation—pain. Who is being addressed in the line, "someday you will ache like I ache"? We could read the "you" as other women, women who perhaps see a distance between themselves and Love's doll-woman. It's as if she's saying once women become aware of the gender politics of our culture, we can't help but feel pain, or we can't help but ache, for ourselves as well as for other women. Yet, if we read the "you" as men, just as the nonspecific "they" of "Violet" refers to men, then it seems that Love is gendering pain as well. That is to say, if women ache now due to a misogynist culture that glorifies the violation of women, Love imagines a future in which men will feel similar pain. While our culture denigrates women and thus brings women together as a class, it does not do this to men, for of course, it is men who are primarily behind this mass denigration of women.[18]

Although "Violet" and "Doll Parts" position women as a class, several of Hole's songs depict the divisions among women. In Love's world, the female subject simply has nowhere to turn. The song "Softer, Softest" from *Live Through This* is also about suffering, and the speaker suffers at the hands of other women, particularly mother figures. The speaker of the song is the "pee-girl"—the girl who smells and who is hated by everyone in school. (On *MTV Unplugged,* Love identified herself as the pee-girl.) This girl is powerless and beholden to her mother or a mother stand-in, who is identified as a witch. The mother's milk, instead of being nourishing and consolatory, is sickening. The "dyed" milk is unnatural, as well as sexual and sexually ambiguous, for it has a "dick." One of the more frightening lines of the song appears toward the end: "your milk turns to mine"—the girl who is punished and tormented now becomes one with her punisher and tormentor. Annihilation is alluded to, as is frequently the case in Hole songs: "The abyss opens up / It steals everything from me." The abyss is mirrored by the hole inside, the hole alluded to in the name of Love's band. Love claims her inspiration for the name comes from Euripides's Medea: "There's a hole pierces my soul."[19] "Softer, Softest" speaks of an even more profound pain and longing than the other songs discussed here. This pain is marked by gender: the girl's femininity—her marginalization—is what causes her suffering. For what often drives women apart, as is the case with the young girl and the older woman-mother depicted here, is the fact that they are pitted against one another by a culture that relegates them to the margins and then makes them compete with each other for acceptance into that culture by men.

Hole's 1998 recording *Celebrity Skin* appeared during the height of Love's glam phase. In the late 1990s, Love was a fixture at Hollywood awards ceremonies and she appeared in haute couture on the cover of the September 1997 issue of *Harper's Bazaar.* She is sometimes so glitzy and glamorous as to be unrecognizable, in fact.[20] Despite these apparent changes in her persona, the lyrics to most tracks on this CD are rather similar to her mid-1990s lyrics in their focus on women's marginalization and alienation. The music, however, is much more slick and pop-influenced than was the case on earlier Hole releases. One song that has that familiar disturbing quality of vintage Hole, is "Awful" with the lines "Swing low sweet cherry / Make it awful / It's your life, it's your party, it's so awful . . . They know how to break all the girls like you / And they rob the souls of the girls like you / And they break the hearts of the girls." The music to this song, however, is very benign, compared to the lyrics. Gone are Love's screeches and groans and gone as well are the band's discordant notes. Similarly, the lyrics to "He Hit So Hard" address a pressing issue—a woman is being battered by a man—but the music is anodyne with its smooth, lilting melodies: "He hit so hard / I saw stars / He hit so hard / I saw God . . . He's so candy my downfall / Melts in my mouth, 'til he's nothing at all / This keeps me, I can't sleep." The track "Dying" is a dirge, essentially, with Love nearly whispering lyrics over what sounds like a respirator: "I am so dumb / Just beam me up / I've had it all forever / I've had enough." Love clearly hasn't abandoned her focus on women's suffering. The disappointing turnaround in Love's self-presentation is recuperated in part by her words in the title track "Celebrity Skin," the first cut on the CD. This song ironically addresses Love's new star image, over which she most likely has lost her share of fans: "Oh make me over / I'm all I want to be / A walking study / In demonology . . . Oh, look at my face / My name is might have been / My name is never was / My name's forgotten." Not only does Love put a spin on her new image and some media accounts of her as Kurt Cobain's neglectful and domineering spouse with the reference to "demonology," but she also alludes to one source of her power and artistry—women's infinite capacity for using femininity as a tool—the masquerade.

While Love's feminism may be hard to detect on the surface, the feminism of riot grrrl and bands like Sleater-Kinney that have roots in riot grrrl is blatant and unmistakable. Sleater-Kinney is a Portland, Oregon-based three-woman band whose fifth album, *All Hands on the Bad One*, has been described by Michael Goldberg as "an all-points bulletin, a rock state-of-the-union address."[21] Ray Rogers calls them "a powerhouse band" and describes *Call the Doctor* as "raw and fresh, dissecting fear, alienation, and sickness with candor, vulnerability, and brute force."[22] Sleater-Kinney consciously defy mainstreaming: they record with an independent label, Kill Rock Stars (early in their career, they recorded with Chainsaw, a woman-owned independent label); they manage themselves financially; and they drive their own van on tours. Their songs cover a wide range of topics, but they frequently address decidedly feminist issues. It is difficult to understand Sleater-Kinney and their politics without knowing a bit about the history of riot grrrl.[23] An essay by Melissa Klein in *Third Wave Agenda* traces one branch of riot grrrl (which for the most part grew out of Olympia, Washington) to the mid-to-late 1980s Washington, D.C., punk scene. This scene, undoubtedly like many others in punk, was a thoroughly masculine one, where young women occupied only marginal roles. Klein and others began to question their place in the scene and realized "they felt disenfranchised within their own supposedly 'alternative' community."[24] As a result, they and other women formed riot grrrl, which had its first convention in D.C. in 1991. Riot grrrl used many of the techniques of second wave feminism but fine-tuned them to the needs of young women in punk. Thus, women created their own "safe space" in the mosh pit and demanded "equal access" to the stage by forming their own bands rather than occupying positions on the sidelines as support for boys' bands (215). As for the music itself, Klein writes that contradiction was inherent in riot grrrl: "Stage presence often reflected duality as well, for example, contrasting a physical emphasis on overt sexuality with lyrics about sexual abuse. Vocals swung back and forth between harsh, wrenching screams, sweet soulful siren intonations, and childish singsong" (216). Despite the great divide between Hole and riot grrrl (although both are Northwestern in their roots), this type of contradiction marks both.[25]

In an interview, Corin Tucker, singer, songwriter, and guitarist of Sleater-Kinney, explains that she found her initial inspiration to become a musician when she first saw Bikini Kill, the premier riot grrrl band, in 1991. She was so moved by the feminism in action on stage that she decided then and there to be in a band: " 'It was the first time I'd seen feminism translated into an emotional language. . . . That I saw those kinds of thoughts and ideas put into your own personal life, that's not in a textbook or an academic discussion. For young women to be doing that, basically teenagers on a stage, to be taking that kind of stance, that kind of power, was blowing people's minds. And it totally blew my mind. I was like,' Ms. Tucker said with happy determination, 'O.K., that's it. That's it for me—I'm going in a band, right now. You had the feeling they had started the band the week before: you can do it too.' "[26] It was clearly the political gesture and the political content of riot grrrl that drew Tucker into music. But it was these very politics that also drew critics. Now, Sleater-Kinney also draws criticism for their political content. Carrie Brownstein, guitarist, singer, songwriter, comments: "I think a lot of the way we've been treated is like, politics is something you grow out of. . . . We felt like in the past we were being labeled as having arisen from the riot grrrl ghetto, or out of this political yet immature sort of hub of politics that didn't make any sense."[27] Of course, when your politics are feminist, it's not a surprise to be labeled immature. Sleater-Kinney has not buckled under the pressure, however.

As female rock musicians, they're forced to be conscious about their gender, and their feminism brings it to the forefront. In short, rock has long been a male domain, as all the fuss in the media over "women in rock" makes clear. Sleater-Kinney talks about the position of the female rock musician in several songs, notably "Male Model" from *All Hands on the Bad One*.[28] "Male Model" vents a female musician's anger at male rock stars being held up for constant comparison: "You always measure me by him . . . We're here to join the conversation / and we're here to raise the stakes . . . It's time for a new rock 'n' roll age / History will have to find a different face." The song begins with sing-song, light-hearted melodic lines that alternate between Corin Tucker and Carrie Brownstein. After a set of these lines, the mood turns and Tucker takes over with her vibrant, blunt delivery. The band proclaims nothing less than the end of male domination in rock: the "different face" is clearly a feminine one. For such a young group—all in their late 20s or early 30s—they already have a clear sense of their own place in rock history. In a 2002 interview about their newest release, *One Beat,* Brownstein addresses the position of women with respect to rock music: "A lot of our songs have been about stepping into the shoes of these rock musicians or commenting on rock and I think that can be liberating and righteous but it can also be futile. Because women are never going to save rock, you know . . . It's like the only thing you can do is invent your own language, and I think that's what we try to do . . . It sometimes just feels like a dead end to try to emulate rock 'n' roll. No matter how hard you try, it seems like people just want the same thing from rock music and that's just always a man."[29] Brownstein's point here is also captured in the epigraph to this essay, lines from the song "#1 Must-Have." Not using the master's tools to dismantle the master's house, to borrow from Audre Lorde, the members of Sleater-Kinney are building their own house with their own tools in a different neighborhood.

The band also brings gender into the spotlight by articulating clearly and repeatedly their dissatisfaction with the status quo for young women. When asked by interviewer Michael Goldberg what they're "laying out there" on *All Hands on the Bad One,* Tucker replies that various events in 1999 led directly to songs on the album: "there were some things that happened last year that really made me feel a sense of urgency about making music and writing. . . . Nineteen-ninety-nine was a really nasty year and a lot of really sexist things happened in rock and that's the area where we work. The most popular bands have really misogynistic lyrics and a lot of women were raped at the Woodstock concerts. So, to me, it was a reminder that . . . even if we're older and we're successful and we've made this niche for ourselves as musicians, we can't give up. We can't say there's not these really sexist things happening because they are affecting women, young women."[30] Sleater-Kinney is willing to stick its neck out and cling to a political vision despite the flak the members have been given for it. As Tucker sings on *All Hands on the Bad One*, "the Number One Must-Have is that we are safe." You can't get more feminist or more political than that.

The powerful song "#1 Must-Have" is not just about women's safety from violence, but also about the pressure on women to sell out not just as musicians, but as women. As Brownstein's comment about the pressure to give up your politics makes clear, these are related issues. Over a leisurely paced opening of moody, distorted guitars, Tucker sings, "Bearer of the flag from the beginning / Now who would have believed this riot grrrl's a cynic / But they took our ideas to their marketing stars / And now I'm spending all my days at girlpower.com / Trying to buy back a little piece of me."[31] This riot grrrl has not sold out willingly—she's been sold out despite herself but has consequently become complacent and complicit with the mainstream. Nevertheless, a part of her is missing and she wants to retrieve it. The chorus contains more self-critical lyrics in which the speaker questions her own superficiality while the band takes the volume and energy up a notch: "And I think that I sometimes might have wished / For something more than to be a size six / But now my inspiration rests / In-between my beauty magazines and my credit card bills." Sleater-Kinney critiques here our culture's obsession with consumption and the way that women in particular are pressured to consume in order to adorn themselves and thus become more enticing objects of male consumption.[32] The song continues with more critique and then ends with nothing less than a triumphant rallying cry:

And will there always be concerts where women are raped
Watch me make up my mind instead of my face

The Number One Must Have is that we are safe . . .
And for all the ladies out there I wish
We could write more than the next marketing bid
Culture is what we make it Yes it is
Now is the time
To invent.

With insistent, driving guitars backing her up, Tucker belts out these
lyrics in her full-throttled soprano. The feminism of these lines could
not be more direct: the song urges women to stop consuming and to
stop focusing on the superficial and instead to create culture of their
own, in the do-it-yourself spirit of riot grrrl and punk before it. The lyrics
suggest that even after being co-opted by the mainstream, it's possible to
bounce back and "invent," or create one's own genuinely alternative
culture.

    The song "#1 Must-Have" alludes to the history of riot grrrl's relation
to mainstream media, which raises the familiar question of "selling out."
After being taken up with a frenzy by the mainstream press, the women
of riot grrrl called a media ban and refused all interviews and coverage.[33]
The women of Sleater-Kinney, at least two of whom were in riot grrrl
bands earlier in their careers, also discuss the media ban in interviews.
Sleater-Kinney itself was very reserved during interviews with the press
early in their career. Janet Weiss, drummer, notes that when they were
"guarded with the media," they were assumed to be "selling out," in an
ironic twist.[34] In a 1996 interview, Tucker discusses the band's concerns
with the attention of the mainstream—the fear of selling out or being
co-opted: "If a band who are all women, who have queer musicians in
it, and who are musicians before anything else . . . if we can sell more
than 5,000 records and there's more people with access to our music,
will that change things? Or will it just be totally co-opted?"[35] Various
essays in this volume address this question of the position of the "alternative" with relation to the mainstream, but none address women's alternative, or I would argue, marginal, culture. For example, Leslie Haynsworth argues that the band Green Day has not been appropriated by
the mainstream; rather, it has in a sense infiltrated it. Although Green
Day has lost its "purely" oppositional stance, it has brought its values
into the mainstream and made it a more alternative place. It would be

difficult to argue the same for riot grrrl bands. As Sleater-Kinney sings in "#1 Must-Have," riot grrrl did get co-opted to some degree, despite all the best efforts of the women involved. The co-optation of riot grrrl happened not because all forms of cultural rebellion are impossible in the postmodern age (what Neil Nehring in this volume critiques as the "incorporation thesis"), but because the media reduced riot grrrl to its lowest, most marketable aspects and then flooded the stores with it. Whether it's "girlpower.com," as Sleater-Kinney sings, or shirts sporting "Girls Rule" slogans purchased at the mall, riot grrrl was hauled unwillingly into the marketplace, and this transfer of milieu alters its message, which is a crucial one. By resisting this co-optation, however, the women of riot grrrl managed to preserve much of its (and their) integrity and revolutionary spirit.

What I hope to have shown here is that when women do present a portrait of their generation, as we find in most of the books discussed here as well as the music, they specifically address women's place in contemporary American culture at large, often from a distinctly feminist perspective. While reading and listening to the work of third wave women, I'm repeatedly struck by the connections between their issues and those of second wave women. The style is worlds apart, but the substance is quite similar. This continuity with the previous generation is not typically found in Generation X cultural production by men, who mostly distance themselves from the baby boomers, although not perhaps from the Beats.[36] What links women of the second and third waves is women's continued oppression and marginalization in American culture as well as active resistance to that status. Generation X women grew up, as their mothers did, in a culture that trades in feminine objectification. Young women today still face a set of social ills that either do not affect their male peers at all, or do not affect them to nearly the same degree: workplace discrimination, sexual harassment, rape, domestic violence, and limitations on reproductive choice. Without specifically attending to these material realities of women's lives in the 1990s, and what women of this generation are saying and doing about them, we cannot produce a politically informed and inclusive picture of Generation X. By looking at the margins, we'll find critique, resistance, and, as Sleater-Kinney sings, the invention of new cultural forms that offer genuine alternatives to mainstream culture.

Notes

1. In writing this essay, I benefited from audience feedback to earlier versions at Mansfield University (1995); Southern Connecticut State University's Fifth Annual Women's Studies Conference (1995); and the Northeast Modern Language Association Convention in Montreal, Canada (1996).

"Third wave" is the accepted term for the generation of young feminists active in the 1990s to the present, and it corresponds well with Generation X. Second wave feminism refers to what many call "the women's movement": feminist activism of the 1960s and 1970s. The 1980s are widely referred to as the backlash against feminism, following Susan Faludi's book of the same name (Susan Faludi, *Backlash: The Undeclared War Against American Women* [New York: Anchor Books, 1991]). I would like to note where I fit in to this generational picture: born in 1962, I'm able to squeeze (just barely) into Generation X and feel much closer to that generation than I do to the baby boom. However, I find myself caught between the second wave and the third wave, since I came of age, both literally and as a feminist, in the 1980s. I feel many connections with both the second wave and third wave, and as a women's studies professor, I try to bridge the gap between these two feminist generations since I was educated by second wave women and teach third wave women.

2. Rose L. Glickman, *Daughters of Feminists* (New York: St. Martin's, 1993); Barbara Findlen, ed., *Listen Up: Voices from the Next Feminist Generation* (Seattle: Seal Press, 1995); Eric Liu, ed., *Next: Young American Writers on the New Generation* (New York: Norton, 1994).

3. Leslie Heywood and Jennifer Drake, eds., *Third Wave Agenda: Being Feminist, Doing Feminism* (Minneapolis: University of Minnesota Press, 1997).

4. Robin Stevens, ed., *Girlfriend Number One: Lesbian Life in the 90s* (Pittsburgh: Cleis Press, 1994).

5. For other prominent texts from the mid-1990s to the present on and by third wave women, see the following: Hillary Carlip, *Girl Power: Young Women Speak Out* (New York: Warner Books, 1995); Rebecca Walker, ed., *To Be Real: Telling the Truth and Changing the Face of Feminism* (New York: Anchor Books, 1995); Tristan Taormina and Karen Green, eds., *A Girl's Guide to Taking Over the World: Writings from the Girl Zine Revolution* (New York: St. Martin's, 1997); Marcelle Karp and Debbie Stoller, *The Bust Guide to the New World Order* (New York: Penguin, 1999); Ophira Edut, ed., *Body Outlaws: Young Women Write about Body Image and Identity* (Seattle: Seal Press, 2000).

6. Glickman, *Daughters,* back cover. The blurb is from *Booklist.*

7. Paula Kamen, "My Bourgeois Brand of Feminism," in *Next: Young American Writers on the New Generation,* ed. Liu, 81–94.

8. Ellen Neuborne, "Imagine My Surprise," in *Listen Up,* ed. Findlen, 29.

9. Heywood and Drake, *Third Wave Agenda,* 1.

10. While I'm concerned about what the authors mean by the "pleasure" and "defining power" of sexual abuse, since they do not clarify, I'm pleased to see an acknowledgment of the second wave by the third wave.

11. Stevens, *Girlfriend Number One,* 8.

12. Hole, *Celebrity Skin,* Geffen Records, DGCD 25164, 1998. Jennifer Baumgardner and Amy Richards in *Manifesta* make brief mention of Love's dual personality, referencing Hole's double guises in a list of third wave figures: "Courtney Love as the slatternly, snarly singer, Courtney Love as the creamy Versace model" (*Manifesta:*

Young Women, Feminism, and the Future [New York: Farrar, Strauss, Giroux, 2000], 135).

13. Karina Eileraas situates Hole in the context of "girl bands" rather than the context of Generation X as in the present essay. Eileraas's focus is performance while mine is lyrics, music, and a more static notion of self-presentation. Her analysis of the deliberate use of ugliness and of the meaning of terms like "witch" and "bitch" is a convincing one. I tend to read Hole's depiction of female suffering and degradation in a more literal way than Eileraas. For example, she writes, "Hole's lyrics, then, can be read as ambivalent traces of—and playful challenges to—women's sexual degradation." I argue that Hole quite deliberately reinscribes women's sexual degradation in order to draw our attention to women's suffering in this misogynist culture. Further, their lyrics perform feminist readings of such degradation and suffering. See Karina Eileraas, "Witches, Bitches and Fluids: Girl Bands Performing Ugliness as Resistance," *Drama Review* 41, 3 (Fall 1997): 129. My thanks to Christine E. Atkins for sharing this citation with me.

14. David Fricke, "Life After Death," *Rolling Stone,* 15 December 1994, 67.

15. See Luce Irigaray, *This Sex Which Is Not One,* trans. Catherine Porter (Ithaca: Cornell University Press, 1985), 76–78; Joan Riviere, "Womanliness as a Masquerade," in *Psychoanalysis and Female Sexuality,* ed. Hendrik M. Ruitenbeek (New Haven: College and University Press, 1966), 209–20; and Judith Butler *Gender Trouble: Feminism and the Subversion of Identity* (New York: Routledge, 1990), 47–53. Irigaray uses the related term "mimesis" to describe a "playful repetition" that brings to light "the cover-up of a possible operation of the feminine in language" (76). For further discussion of masquerade and mimesis, see Mary Ann Doane, "Film and the Masquerade: Theorising the Female Spectator," *Screen* 23 no. 3–4 (1982): 74–87.

16. Hole, *Doll Parts,* Geffen Records, 1994.

17. Hole, *Live Through This,* Geffen Records, DGCD 24631, 1994.

18. Heywood and Drake convincingly gloss several lines from "Doll Parts" in reference to second wave and third wave feminism. They see Love combining "second wave critique" with "third wave postmodern individualism facilitated by the third wave." Finally, for them, "Someday, you will ache like I ache" expresses "the lived cost of female ambition" (*Third Wave Agenda,* 5).

19. Love has discussed this in interviews, stating for example, that *Medea,* and, by extension, her music, are "about the abyss that's inside" (Lucy O'Brien, *She Bop* [New York: Penguin, 1995], 165.

20. Phillip Weiss describes Love in harsh terms during this period in her career: "Once an icon of uncompromising female rage, she now seemed grasping and shallow, hungering for fame and acceptance as a movie star, putting on designer gowns to attend the Academy Awards and posing for Richard Avedon ads for Versace. Was she anything more than just desperately ambitious?" ("The Love Issue," *Spin,* October 1998, 94). While I tend to agree to a certain extent with his assessment, I would also note that Love is a lightning rod for Weiss's misogyny (as well as the misogyny of so many other critics): after all, what is worse than a "desperately ambitious" woman? Needless to say, when describing a man, most do not attach "desperately" to "ambitious" and the designation itself is one of praise not opprobrium.

21. Michael Goldberg, "Return of Riot Grrrl Rock: The Sleater-Kinney Interview," Addicted to Noise. http://www.addict.com/issues/6.05/html/hifi/Cover_Story/Selater-Kinney/index.html

22. Ray Rogers, "Sleater-Kinney: The Powerhouse Trio Face Their Fear, and Their Success," *Out Magazine,* November 1996.

23. For a discussion of the power of anger in riot grrrl music, and the way this counters common arguments in the music press that see all countercultural expression as co-opted by the mainstream, see Neil Nehring's essay in this volume. For a discussion of the function of zines in the riot grrrl community, see Stephen Duncombe, "Let's All Be Alienated Together: Zines and the Making of Underground Community," in *Generations of Youth: Cultures and History in Twentieth-Century America,* eds. Joe Austin and Michael Nevin Willard (New York: New York University Press, 1998), 440–46.

24. Melissa Klein, "Duality and Redefinition: Young Feminism and the Alternative Music Community," in Heywood and Drake, *Third Wave Agenda,* 211.

25. Evidently, Courtney Love is no fan of riot grrrl. On *Live Through This,* the song "Rock Star" is a send-up of riot grrrl with lines like the following: "When I went to school in Olympia / Everyone's the same / What do you do with a revolution / . . . We look the same / We talk the same." Olympia, Washington is the home of Evergreen State College, from which many riot grrrl bands emerged. Carrie Brownstein of Sleater-Kinney lived until recently in Olympia.

26. Greil Marcus, "Raising the Stakes in Punk Rock," *New York Times,* 18 June 2000.

27. Goldberg, "Return of Riot Grrrl Rock."

28. "Words and Guitar" from *Dig Me Out* is a celebration of the power and transformative energy of rock music. The lyrics express the sheer thrill of belting out high-powered rock ("words + guitar / i got it words + guitar / i like it / way way too loud / c'mon and turn turn it up / i wanna turn turn you on / i play it all"). These lines practice what they preach. The chorus then describes in sing-song the female singer's contrasting notion of "pretty song" ("i dream of quiet songs / i hear the silky sounds"). The chorus calls to mind mainstream women's music that is very palatable and apolitical, unlike the music of Hole, Sleater-Kinney, and much of the music by women's bands today.

29. Margaret Wappler, "The Beat Goes On," *Venus Envy* 13 (Summer 2002): 44.

30. Goldberg, "Return of Riot Grrrl Rock."

31. Sleater-Kinney, *All Hands on The Bad One,* Kill Rock Starts, KRS 360, 2000.

32. As Tucker says in an interview, "I think it's a really honest song about feeling so apathetic and numb. And I think that it's easy to do, as you get older, to sort of internalize the stuff that society puts out there. Especially with the commercialization and consumerism that's put out there. It so targets the 30-year old white woman. . . . There are more important things than just spending all your time on outward appearance" (Goldberg, "Return of Riot Grrrl Rock").

33. Evelyn McDonnell, "Riot Grrrl Returns, With a Slightly Softer Roar," *New York Times,* 2 June 1996.

34. Goldberg, "Return of Riot Grrrl Rock."

35. Rogers, "Sleater-Kinney: The Powerhouse Trio Face Their Fear, and Their Success."

36. See the essay by Katie Mills in this volume.

Bibliography

Baumgardner, Jennifer, and Amy Richards. *Manifesta: Young Women, Feminism, and the Future.* New York: Farrar, Strauss, Giroux, 2000.

Butler, Judith. *Gender Trouble: Feminism and the Subversion of Identity.* New York: Routledge, 1990

Carlip, Hillary. *Girl Power: Young Women Speak Out.* New York: Warner Books, 1995.

Doane, Mary Ann. "Film and the Masquerade: Theorising the Female Spectator." *Screen* 23, 3–4 (1982): 74–87.

Duncombe, Stephen. "Let's All Be Alienated Together: Zines and the Making of Underground Community." In *Generations of Youth: Youth Cultures and History in Twentieth-Century America,* edited by Joe Austin and Michael Nevin Willard. New York: New York University Press, 1998, 427–51.

Edut, Ophira, ed. *Body Outlaws: Young Women Write About Body Image and Identity.* Seattle: Seal Press, 2000.

Eileraas, Karina. "Witches, Bitches, and Fluids: Girl Bands Performing Ugliness as Resistance." *The Drama Review* 41, 3 (Fall 1997): 122–39.

Faludi, Susan. *Backlash: The Undeclared War Against American Women.* New York: Anchor Books, 1991.

Findlen, Barbara, ed. *Listen Up: Voices from the Next Feminist Generation.* Seattle: Seal Press, 1995.

Fricke, David. "Life After Death." *Rolling Stone,* 15 December 1994, 59.

Glickman, Rose L. *Daughters of Feminists: Young Women with Feminist Mothers Talk about Their Lives.* New York: St. Martin's, 1993.

Goldberg, Michael. "Return of Riot Grrrl Rock: The Sleater-Kinney Interview." *Addicted to Noise,* 28 December 2000.

Heywood, Leslie and Jennifer Drake, eds. *Third Wave Agenda: Being Feminist, Doing Feminism.* Minneapolis: University of Minnesota Press, 1997.

Hole. *Celebrity Skin.* Geffen Records, DGCD 25164, 1998.

———. *Doll Parts.* Geffen Records, 1994.

———. *Live Through This.* Geffen Records, DGCD 24631, 1994.

Irigaray, Luce. *This Sex Which Is Not One.* Translated by Catherine Porter. Ithaca: Cornell University Press, 1985.

Kamen, Paula. "My 'Bourgeois' Brand of Feminism." In *Next: Young American Writers on the New Generation,* ed. Eric Liu. New York: Norton, 1994, 81–94.

Karp, Marcelle and Debbie Stoller. *The Bust Guide to the New World Order.* New York: Penguin, 1999.

Liu, Eric, ed. *Next: Young American Writers on the New Generation.* New York: Norton, 1994.

Marcus, Greil. "Raising the Stakes in Punk Rock." *New York Times,* 18 June 2000.

McDonnell, Evelyn. "Riot Grrrl Returns, With a Slightly Softer Roar." *New York Times* 2 June 1996.

Neuborne, Ellen. "Imagine My Surprise." In *Listen Up: Voices from the Next Feminist Generation,* ed. Barbara Findlen. Seattle: Seal Press, 1995, 29–35.

O'Brien, Lucy. *She Bop.* New York: Penguin, 1995.

Riviere, Joan. "Womanliness as a Masquerade." In *Psychoanalysis and Female Sexuality,* ed. by Hendrik M. Ruitenbeek. New Haven: College and University, 1966, 209–20.

Rogers, Ray. "Sleater-Kinney: The Powerhouse Trio Face Their Fear, and Their Success," *Out Magazine.* November 1996.

Sleater-Kinney. *All Hands on the Bad One.* Kill Rock Stars, KRS 360, 2000.

———. *Dig Me Out.* Kill Rock Stars, KRS 279, 1997.

———. *One Beat.* Kill Rock Stars, KRS 387, 2002.

Stevens, Robin. *Girlfriend Number One: Lesbian Life in the 90s.* Pittsburgh: Cleis Press, 1994.

Taormino, Tristan and Karen Green, eds. *A Girl's Guide to Taking Over the World: Writings from the Girl Zine Revolution*. New York: St. Martin's, 1997.

Walker, Rebecca, ed. *To Be Real: Telling the Truth and Changing the Face of Feminism*. New York: Anchor Books, 1995.

Wappler, Margaret. "The Beat Goes On." *Venus Envy* 13 (Summer 2002): 40–45.

Weiss, Phillip. "The Love Issue." *Spin*, October 1998, 90–100.

Contributors

Index

Contributors

TRACI CARROLL received her Ph.D. in English from Northwestern University in 1992. Formerly assistant professor of English at Rhodes College, she is currently working on a book about play. She lives with her two children in Johnson City, Tennessee, where she writes, plays, and teaches yoga.

CATHERINE CRESWELL received her Ph.D. in English from the State University of New York at Buffalo. She currently lives in Minneapolis and works as a managing editor of an online magazine.

KIRK CURNUTT is professor of English at Troy State University Montgomery in Montgomery, Alabama, where he serves as department chair. He is the author of *Wise Economies: Brevity and Storytelling in the American Short Story* (1997), *The Critical Response to Gertrude Stein* (2000), *Ernest Hemingway and the Expatriate Modernist Movement* (2000), *Alienated Youth Fiction* (2001), *An Historical Guide to F. Scott Fitzgerald* (2003), as well as a book of short stories, *Baby, Let's Make a Baby* (2003).

JIM FINNEGAN teaches academic writing and American literature as a lecturer at the University of Illinois at Urbana-Champaign, where he also received his Ph.D. He is completing a book entitled *Writing to Shake the World*, a cultural studies analysis of John Reed.

ANDREA L. HARRIS is associate professor of English at Mansfield University of Pennsylvania, where she also teaches women's studies. She is the author of *Other Sexes: Rewriting Difference from Woolf to Winterson* (2000).

LESLIE HAYNSWORTH is assistant professor of English at Columbia College, Columbia, South Carolina and coauthor of *Amelia Earhart's Daughters: The*

297

Wild and Glorious Story of American Women Aviators from World War II to the Dawn of the Space Age (2000).

ANDREW KLOBUCAR received his Ph.D. from the University of British Columbia, in Vancouver, British Columbia and currently works in digital sound and media art. He is the author of articles and reviews on experimental poetry, sound art, and literary theory, which have appeared mostly in small presses. His most recent book is an anthology on radical Vancouver poetry in the 1980s and 1990s, entitled *Writing Class* (1999).

G. P. LAINSBURY teaches writing and literature at Northern Lights College in Fort St. John, British Columbia. "Generation X and the End of History" first appeared in *Essays on Canadian Writing* (1996).

DANIEL W. LEHMAN was a reporter for fifteen years and is currently professor of English at Ashland University in Ohio, where he directs the program in American Studies. He is the author of *Matters of Fact: Reading Nonfiction Over the Edge* (1998) and *John Reed and the Writing of Revolution* (2002). Lehman is coeditor of *River Teeth: A Journal of Nonfiction Narrative.*

KATIE MILLS received her Ph.D. from the University of Southern California, where she currently teaches in the writing program. She has contributed to *The Road Movie Book* (1997) and to "Hollywood Star Cars," an exhibition and film festival at the Petersen Automotive Museum in Los Angeles. She is currently completing a book, *Remapping the Road Story: A Postwar History of Old Stories, New Media, and Emerging Rebels.*

NEIL NEHRING is associate professor of English at the University of Texas at Austin and the author of two books: *Popular Music, Gender, and Postmodernism: Anger Is an Energy* (1997) and *Flowers in the Dustbin: Culture, Anarchy, and Postwar England* (1993).

JOHN M. ULRICH is associate professor of English at Mansfield University of Pennsylvania. He is the author of *Signs of Their Times: History, Labor, and the Body in Cobbett, Carlyle, and Disraeli* (2002).

Index

Aaron, Charles, 148
Abrams, Alexander, 116; *Late Bloomers*, 116
academia: and Beat Generation, 22; and cultural studies, 123–24, 126, 155–56; and feminism, 157n. 6; and Generation X (demographic group), 28, 200, 205–6, 208–9, 211; and Generation X (term and concept), 28, 67–68, 126–27, 130–31, 155–56, 157n. 6; and music journalism, 59–61, 70, 72–73; politics of, 23; and postmodernism, 26, 59–61, 63–64, 66–68, 70, 72–74, 133; and riot grrrl, 143–46; and *Spin* magazine, 158n. 11; and subcultures, 155–56
"accelerated culture," and Generation X, 10–11, 25
ACT UP, 124, 137–38, 149–52, 159n. 33; and postmodernism, 151
Adorno, Theodor, 53–54, 64; *Dialectic of Enlightenment*, 53
Advertising Age, 116, 118
The Advocate, 95, 159n. 33
AIDS, 79–80, 86, 138; coverage of in *Spin* magazine, 135–37, 159n. 33; and cultural studies, 136–37; as metaphor for contagion, 99n. 30
AIDS demo graphics (Crimp), 148, 151
All Hands on the Bad One (Sleater-Kinney), 284, 286
alternative, concept of, 268, 270, 289
alternative music, 25–26, 41–57; anger and emotion as empowering force in, 71–75; authenticity of, 55–56; commercialization of, 42–45, 55–56; and gender, 100n. 61; and Generation X, 41–45, 57; iconoclasm of, 54–55; and irony, 83, 91, 94, 96–97; popular success of, 45–51; subversive potential of, 42–45, 51–52, 54–57

Althusser, Louis, 29, 215, 219n. 29, 253–54, 256–59
Anderson, Laurie, 68
anger, 279–81, 292n. 23; as empowering force in alternative music, 71–75
anti-corporate activism, and Generation X, 24–25
apocalypse, 188
Appignanesi, Richard, 154
Araki, Gregg, 240
Arm, Mark, 85–86
Armstrong, Billie Joe, 47, 51, 56
Armstrong, Tim, 46–48, 55
"Awful" (Hole), 283
Azerrad, Michael, 50, 56

Baby Boomers, vs. Generation X, 27, 105–9, 116, 118–19, 129–30, 132
Bad Company, 158n. 19
Bad Religion, 46
Bakhtin, Mikhail, 73–75, 225; *Rabelais and His World*, 73–74
Bangs, Lester, 13, 33n. 20
Barris, Chuck, 112–13
Baudrillard, Jean, 14–16, 236, 241
Bauhaus, 48
Baumgarner, Jennifer, *Manifesta*, 290n. 12
Beat Generation, 231; and academia, 22; commodification of, 229; and Generation X, 20–23, 28, 205; and Lost Generation, 245n. 20; and race, 218n. 3; and television, 225, 228, 244n. 2.
Beavis and Butt-head, 28, 113, 205–10, 214–16; *Beavis and Butt-head Do America*, 241; critique of, 206; and self-consciousness, 202

299